Complex Tools + Clear Teaching = Powerful Results ™

LEAN SIX SIGMA THE STATSTUFF WAY

A Practical Reference Guide for Lean Six Sigma

Thanks for using StatStuff!

MATT HANSEN

Essentials
Publishing™

Essentials Publishing ™

To order additional copies, please visit http://StatStuff.com. For bulk orders, please send an email to orders@statstuff.com.

Published by Essentials Publishing.
Printed in the United States of America.

ISBN-13 978-0-9888376-0-7

Acknowledgements

To my wife and kids,
for enduring my many late nights
and loving me anyway.

~M@ & D+

Table of Contents

Unit 6: Six Sigma Analyze Phase　　199

Unit 7: Six Sigma Improve Phase   297

Unit 8: Six Sigma Control Phase   323

Endorsements

The training videos from StatStuff have helped so many people. Below are a few examples of the comments some people were kind enough to share.

"StatStuff provides a wealth of information that is extremely helpful. I will definitely share it with my colleagues."
R.W., Infrastructure Operations Analyst, PepsiCo

"I was extremely impressed that this resource is available. I plan to share this within the BPI organization at our company. Thanks for putting this together!"
D.M., Master Black Belt, The Nielsen Company

"I truly enjoyed the videos. I love the way you explain some of these concepts."
W.D., Operational Excellence Director, eBay

"I am really impressed. The content is very clear to understand, there's a logical flow through the different tools and techniques, the examples are easy to relate to and you try to interact with the audience."
J.F., Process Design Specialist, BP

"Absolutely great videos. I have been teaching Six Sigma and Lean for 5 years and feel that your approach is very easy to follow and right on with the content. Your real world examples make the lessons clear, contributing to understanding at a deeper, more practical way. Thank you for making this available to the world. Many will benefit."
R.A., Dir of Continuous Improvement, Staples Inc.

"I viewed your videos. Really good stuff."
M.C., Global Program Leader, DuPont

"Thanks so much for sharing with us these training videos."
T.L., Order Management, Apple Inc.

"Excellent content that's easy to understand with practical applications to make each concept real and relevant. I wish I had this content when I was preparing for my certifications but it's great info to refer back to for reinforcement and reference."
J.G., SVP, Bank of America

"I've been checking out some of the videos and am impressed with the quality and thoroughness!"
J.S., Sr. Business Development Rep, Minitab Inc.

"First I am overwhelmed with the generosity of Matt's offering so much free. Rather than using a few of them as free teasers to entice us to purchase more of what he has available, when the previews are so good. They are all so good. Second, I know a lot of what Matt is teaching in his videos, I just can't say it as clearly he can. So I'm watching them to get the same amazing clarity of communication. Third I simply feel gifted by all that Matt offers, and want to be able to as clearly gift to others what I know. Thank You Matt!"
B.B., Senior Systems Engineer – Control Systems, UOP, A Honeywell Company

"I am sharing your website with my peers at my company. Love your videos on the site."
K.W., VP HR Business Partner, SunTrust Banks, Inc.

"Your videos are bang on. StatStuff.com is a commendable initiative and after watching your videos I feel mastered in Lean and Six Sigma concepts. StatStuff.com makes me feel rich in knowledge today and saved me at least $5000 I would have otherwise spent at a school to understand Six Sigma. The quality of information and the way each video is organized and concepts illustrated are the best I have ever seen for a training video."

> S.K., Project Manager, Wells Fargo

"StatStuff is Great Stuff!"

> V.M., Head - Business Development & Migration,
> Six Sigma Process Solutions (SSPS)

"I'm such a fan of your work and your StatStuff site. I follow your video lessons and appreciate your clear no nonsense approach to Six Sigma."

> J.J., SVP Ops Managed Care, AEMERUS Consulting

"A great way to present & teach Lean Six Sigma. All should find time to go through the videos."

> A.C., CEO, Bissoft Technologies

"The videos are great, easy to understand and watch. They have been extremely helpful."

> T.S., Reg. Dir. of Process Improvement, Cox Ent.

"StatStuff offers high quality video lectures with user friendly interface. It is a great compilation of free videos that simplifies the industry specific benchmarking tools and concepts to the global audience. StatStuff videos enable us to judge the usefulness of these tools and ensures we keep on creating value."

> A.R., Process Coordinator, M&R Consultants Corp.

"The videos are great! Excellent content and very well done. I have enjoyed watching the videos and will continue doing so."

> C.C., Lean Six Sigma Black Belt, Genesis Energy

"Thanks a lot Matt. You made such a great effort on those videos. They are just amazing. You are really serving humanity."

> R.G., Six Sigma Instructor, ITI

"I've seen StatStuff.com and think it's great. I'd like to start suggesting to my clients that they view your website too."

> D.H., Director, Orbital Training and Consulting

"Your videos are technically solid, understandable, and high quality. You are a gifted communicator."

> J.J., Sr. Manager of Operations, NP Photonics

"StatStuff is full of rich info that will add value to anyone's learning - new or experienced. I've been using it for weeks now. Matt is a great teacher and excellent presenter. He should be charging for those videos. Matt, thanks for putting this out there. I will recommend your site to anyone."

> E.E., President & CEO, Eliason Consulting Group,

"The Lean Six Sigma stuff in StatStuff is simply awesome & the best thing is it's FREE, which makes it a winner hands down any time!"

> V.M., Senior Consultant, enRICH

"I use your videos all the time to help explain the concepts of Lean Six Sigma to Green belts. Your explanations are easy to understand with great visual support on each topic. Outstanding job!!!"

> M.W., Lean Six Sigma Black Belt, Molex Inc.

"StatStuff is a fantastic resource."

> L.R., Ops Foreman at Wisconsin Water Utility

"I used your videos to prepare for both my Lean and Six Sigma Black Belt certifications. The lessons and structure were easy to follow, clear and broken into digestible sections. They were a great help and I continue to reference them and refer them to others. I really appreciate the level of effort and time spent on putting this material together for use. Many thanks."

> E.H., Dir of Op. Excellence, Cross Match Tech.

"StatStuff has to be one of, if not the best free resource of its kind on the internet."

> A.S., Logistics Manager,
> Premier InfoAssists Pvt Ltd for Gemini Corp.

"StatStuff is my new favorite site! Everything that I have learned, should have learned and will review all in one place! Love it."

> C.C., Director of Change Management,
> Chambers Business Consultant

"Great website and content! I'm really impressed with the quality and volume of your material. Thanks for making this available."

> R.F., Information Systems Support Engineer,
> University of Illinois at Chicago

Preface

What is Lean Six Sigma?

It seems rather ironic how something like Lean Six Sigma, which is built on a premise of reducing waste and variation, can cause so much wasted time among many experts who have a high variation in how they define it. I don't pretend to have the only definitive answer, but here's how I would simplify the definitions:

- **Lean** - A philosophy (i.e., not a methodology, but more of a belief or way of thinking) focused on improving efficiency (e.g., cost, flow, timeliness) in a process. For more details, see page 49.
- **Six Sigma** - There are actually two separate ways to define this:
  - As a measurement, Six Sigma refers to the number of standard deviations between the mean and an observation (e.g., a customer's lower or upper specification limit). By squeezing six standard deviations between these data points generally means the process is so precise (little variation) that it yields only about 3.4 defects per one million opportunities. For more details, see page 87.
  - As a methodology, Six Sigma is most commonly executed using the DMAIC methodology which is an acronym representing 5 different phases typically focused on improving the effectiveness (e.g., quality, accuracy) of an output from a process. For more details, see page 81.
- **Lean Six Sigma** - The term reflects the blending of the tools and concepts of both the Lean philosophy and Six Sigma methodology in order to yield a more holistic approach to process improvement.

The ultimate purpose of Lean Six Sigma is NOT to reduce waste or variation

Many people (including experts) will state that the purpose of Lean is to reduce waste and the purpose of Six Sigma is to reduce variation. But I think that's like saying the purpose of a hammer is to hit a nail. While that is technically true, the real purpose of the hammer is to accomplish the purpose of the carpenter, which could be to build a house. I think this confuses the "what" with the "why" where the "what" is hitting the nail, which in and of itself is meaningless without the "why", i.e., building the house.

In the same way, reducing waste for Lean and variation for Six Sigma are merely the "what". They define the technical purpose without correlating them to the ideal purpose of the one using them. They are merely tools which, like a hammer to a skilled carpenter, are only as effective as the one using those tools. Until we make that clear distinction, we'll never fully succeed in accomplishing the "why".

What is the "why" for Lean Six Sigma?

The ultimate purpose for Lean Six Sigma is to make the business successful primarily by improving its financial performance. Yes, it primarily comes down to *money*. Every organization, including non-profit organizations, must have money to survive. It doesn't matter how altruistic an organization's products, services or goals are, how satisfied their customers are, nor how beloved they are in the marketplace (all other Level 1 CTQs in the CTQ Drilldown as reviewed on page 10) - without a positive financial value (e.g., cash, assets, etc.) the organization will not be able to survive very long.

So how does the "what" of Lean Six Sigma fit into this? By reducing waste in a process, Lean can help a business be more efficient which is typically measured by improved flow and productivity (for people, machines, or equipment). This kind of improvement can often be realized through reduced payroll which helps to improve the financial performance of the business.

Likewise, by reducing variation in the output from a process, Six Sigma can help a business be more effective which is typically measured by improved quality and accuracy to meet a customer's requirements and less product scrap or waste. These kinds of improvements can be realized through more revenue, less returns, and reduced cost from scrapped materials which help to improve the financial performance of the business.

Lean Six Sigma will fail if we don't focus on the "why"

I believe every Lean Six Sigma effort must be focused on improving the Level 1 CTQs of the business, especially financial performance. If you cannot tie a Lean Six Sigma project to a financial improvement in the business (as defined on page 16), then I believe that project is a failure.

That's right. It's a failure. Otherwise why would we spend our own time and resources to work a project that doesn't yield any measurable improvement back to the organization? Was it just for fun? Was it just for trying to grow the personal or political control for ourselves or our business leaders? If so, then please do the rest of us a favor and don't apply the "Lean Six Sigma" label to it; it's counter-productive to it's true intent and only gives a bad name to it and those who practice it as such.

What about Lean Six Sigma certifications?

Those who know me well know I have strong opinions about certifications. I address some details about certifications on page 25, but there are a few comments I'd like to add here.

What many folks don't realize is that there is no central governing organization that grants certifications for Lean, Six Sigma, Lean Six Sigma, or any of the variety of similar types of certifications promoted in the marketplace. Because of this, any organization can define its own requirements for certifying people. Despite the flexibility this offers, it unfortunately means there are many organizations who dilute the requirements by certifying people who can't truly demonstrate any form of Lean Six Sigma expertise.

Certifications can get you the interview, but proven experience will get you the job

With such a disparity in certification requirements, is it worth getting one? Yes! A certification can certainly open doors for career opportunities and in many cases can help someone command a higher salary. However, a certification is meaningless if the person being certified doesn't have the skills to back it up.

Instead, focus on learning to successfully apply the Lean Six Sigma tools and concepts in order to build your expertise. Then the certification will simply validate what skills and expertise you can demonstrate. And it's in the demonstration of those skills you can accelerate in your career.

Where should you pursue certification?

An airline pilot may have obtained his flight training from an unknown flight school, but if he has a lot of experience where he can demonstrate his command and control of the plane, then that's all that matters. In the same way, there are many great choices for where you can get certified, but in my experience, where you get certified isn't as critical as how you can demonstrate the skills for which you're certified.

Generally, I recommend avoiding any training organization that has low certification requirements making it too easy to get certified. I most strongly recommend finding someone who can mentor you through it. But regardless of where you go, you can always supplement your training using the resources from StatStuff.

~M@

How To Use This Guide

What does this guide contain?

StatStuff has produced many videos that simplify the Lean Six Sigma tools and concepts. Since each video contains a lot of information, this guide compiles the written text and illustrations (not the commentary) used in those videos in order to help the viewer save time from taking notes and referencing the content.

Just as in each training video, each lesson in this guide identifies if there is a pre-requisite lesson that may be helpful to review prior to reviewing the content for that current lesson. In addition, each lesson ends with a "Practical Application" section instructing the user on effective ways to apply the respective tool or concept.

What does this guide not contain?

This guide isn't intended to be an exhaustive resource on either Lean Six Sigma or on statistics. For example, many tools don't include a comprehensive review to explain every nuance of how each tool works or how it can be applied. There may even be some Statisticians who disagree with some unconventional ways the statistics are interpreted or applied. From a classical approach to applying statistics, they may be justified. But an expert in Lean Six Sigma doesn't necessarily have to be an expert statistician; what's more important is that they know how to expertly adapt their statistical analysis in a practical way that benefits the business.

The training video resources from StatStuff are designed to address the most critical tools and concepts that help the user quickly learn and apply those tools and concepts most effectively. To that end, there may be some statistical shortcuts used in this guide. Therefore this guide should not be used as a defense against any contradictions to the classical approach to statistics. Despite that, it's always best to consult with an expert (like a Master Black Belt) who can advise how to apply the tools to your unique situation.

How can I make the most of learning Lean Six Sigma using this guide?

The StatStuff lessons are ordered in such a way that the information builds on itself. Generally, if you're new to Lean Six Sigma, then it may be best to start with the Introduction set of videos and continue in order through all the remaining videos. But if you're more seasoned in Lean Six Sigma, then you may prefer to deviate from the order of the lessons and go directly to a particular tool or concept that interests you.

The best way to learn the Lean Six Sigma tools and concepts is to apply them in a real-world circumstance. To be most effective you should follow the instructions in each lesson's "Practical Application" section and try to apply them using current or historical data or experiences. If possible, it's recommended that you find a Lean Six Sigma Black Belt or Master Black Belt who can mentor you through the tools and concepts and review the results of each practical application you follow.

If you're a Lean Six Sigma trainer, this guide can make you more efficient

If you do any form of training on Lean Six Sigma as a trainer, mentor or consultant, then the StatStuff resources can help you be more efficient. For example, if you're leading a training class where you may spend 90 minutes covering a particular Lean Six Sigma tool, then you can assign your students in advance to watch the free StatStuff video about the tool so that by the time you start the training class, they should already have a solid understanding about it. Then you can either reduce your training time (since you don't need to review the tool yourself) or you can enhance the training time by spending more time on practical examples that can help reinforce the application of the tool.

Unit 1: Introduction

A general overview of Lean and Six Sigma concepts including some generic tools that can be used for finding, prioritizing, and managing Lean and Six Sigma projects and initiatives.

Introduction – Lesson 1: StatStuff Orientation

An opening orientation to the resources available on the StatStuff.com website.
Pre-Requisite Lessons:
   o None

<u>Orientation Video Transcript</u>

Hi, I'm Matt Hansen, and thanks for checking out StatStuff.com. We have a bunch of videos that teach the fundamentals of Lean and Six Sigma and how to apply them to our work. There are a lot of other great resources available that teach Lean and Six Sigma, so what makes StatStuff so different? Well our videos are all free, they're available online 24/7, and rather than bundling several tools and concepts into each session like a typical classroom environment, each of our videos cover just one topic at a time so you can quickly and easily jump to the tool or concept you want to learn.

If you're not sure where to start, just follow the full list of videos in order from the top all the way to the bottom. We start with some introductory tools and concepts, then touch on a variety of Lean tools and concepts, then we spend the rest of the time of time swimming in the deep waters of Six Sigma through the DMAIC methodology.

Before you begin, you may be wondering why do we even need Lean and Six Sigma. Well honestly, we don't! There are many people throughout history who have been extremely successful in business long before the Lean and Six Sigma methods were developed. So does that mean they don't add value? Of course not! I think of Lean and Six Sigma like putting a scope on a rifle - sure, a skilled marksman can hit the target without a scope, but for the rest of us who aren't skilled in marksmanship, a scope can help us more confidently aim at and hit our target.

In the same way, the Lean and Six Sigma methods use statistical analysis on data to help us be more confident that we're aiming at and hitting the right target, or solution to the problem we're trying to solve. Now, don't let the term "statistical analysis" scare you off. I don't consider myself to be a mathematician or statistician by any means, but I know and can teach you enough of the fundamentals to help you apply these analytical concepts in practical and relevant ways to help make you successful.

And finally, some people believe that Lean and Six Sigma can only be applied to manufacturing environments. But I strongly disagree. It's true that these methods were primarily born out of and are generally easier to apply to a manufacturing environment. But I've been very successful at applying these same tools and concepts across several non-manufacturing industries too. Every company is built on a variety of processes; as long as we're willing to believe that those processes aren't necessarily "perfect", there should always be opportunities to improve those processes that could help improve the company's bottom-line. Lean and Six Sigma can be very effective methods for finding and improving those opportunities.

So please feel free to check out all our free resources here at StatStuff.com. I'm Matt Hansen. Thanks for watching.

Introduction – Lesson 2: Introduction to Lean and Six Sigma

An introduction to the fundamental concepts of the Lean and Six Sigma methodologies using the IPO model.

Pre-Requisite Lessons:
- None

What are Lean and Six Sigma?
- Lean and Six Sigma are methods that help improve business processes & performance.
  - Despite many similarities, they have different tools that focus on different areas of the IPO flow.
- Input > Process > Output (IPO) flow model.
  - Below is a brief example of IPO and how Lean and Six Sigma are applied:

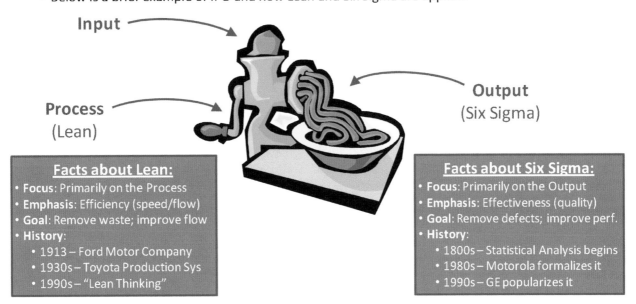

Facts about Lean:
- **Focus**: Primarily on the Process
- **Emphasis**: Efficiency (speed/flow)
- **Goal**: Remove waste; improve flow
- **History**:
  - 1913 – Ford Motor Company
  - 1930s – Toyota Production Sys
  - 1990s – "Lean Thinking"

Facts about Six Sigma:
- **Focus**: Primarily on the Output
- **Emphasis**: Effectiveness (quality)
- **Goal**: Remove defects; improve perf.
- **History**:
  - 1800s – Statistical Analysis begins
  - 1980s – Motorola formalizes it
  - 1990s – GE popularizes it

Efficiency vs. Effectiveness
- Improvement projects primarily focus on improving Efficiency and/or Effectiveness.

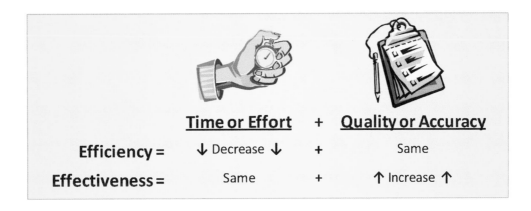

	Time or Effort	+	Quality or Accuracy
Efficiency =	↓ Decrease ↓	+	Same
Effectiveness =	Same	+	↑ Increase ↑

- What is Efficiency?
  - Achieve same level of effectiveness (quality/accuracy) in less time or with less effort.
- What is Effectiveness?
  - Achieve same level of efficiency (time/effort) with less error or higher quality/accuracy.
- Despite this difference, they are not mutually exclusive.
  - Though a project may target efficiency or effectiveness, they generally end up improving both.

Balancing Efficiency and Effectiveness

- o Which is more important between efficiency & effectiveness?
  - Neither! It depends on your goal.
  - For example, suppose you had a car and a truck. Which vehicle is "better"? It depends on your purpose for each.
    - ▪ Purpose A: Transport a couple people across town.
      - – *Both vehicles are equally effective, but the car is more efficient (consumes less fuel to achieve same purpose).*
    - ▪ Purpose B: Haul a large quantity of furniture and appliances across town.
      - – *Only the truck would be effective.*

Car: 30 MPG   **Truck:** 15 MPG

- o How does this compare to Lean and Six Sigma?
  - Effectiveness (i.e., quality or accuracy) should always be considered first.
    - ▪ For example, who cares how efficient the car is if it's incapable of achieving Purpose B? Most of the Six Sigma tools are designed to improve effectiveness.

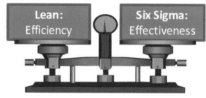

- Efficiency can improve time/cost, but shouldn't compromise effectiveness.
    - ▪ When targeting efficiency, the output should always be measured to ensure quality isn't compromised. Lean tools are designed to improve process efficiency.
- o Can Lean and Six Sigma apply to non-manufacturing environments?
  - Absolutely! Intangibles (like transactions) can be more challenging to measure and improve.
  - Regardless, the Lean and Six Sigma tools can apply to any process fitting the IPO model.

Practical Application

- o Identify at least 3 different functions in your work that fit the IPO model.
  - What are the inputs going into each?
  - What are some of the general processes being performed in each?
  - What are the outputs coming out from each?
- o Identify the efficiency and effectiveness metrics for each function.
  - How is effectiveness (e.g., quality or accuracy) being measured in each?
  - How is efficiency (e.g., timeliness) being measured in each?

Introduction – Lesson 3: Lean and Six Sigma Project Methodologies

An introduction to five project methodologies (Lean, DMAIC, DMADV, DFSS & PMI) and when to use each.

Pre-Requisite Lessons:
- Intro #02 – Introduction to Lean and Six Sigma

IPO Flow and Efficiency vs. Effectiveness

- Remember, nearly all we do can be modeled in the IPO flow.
- Comparing Efficiency vs. Effectiveness.
  - Efficiency focuses on improving the process by asking...
    - Can we produce the output in faster time or with less effort/cost at the same level of quality or accuracy?
  - Effectiveness focuses on improving the output by asking ...
    - Can we produce the output at a higher level of quality or accuracy within the same time or level of effort/cost?
- These distinctions will help us understand the different project methodologies.

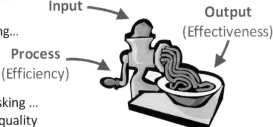

Project Methodologies Decision Tree

- Use the following decision tree to help determine which project methodology to use:

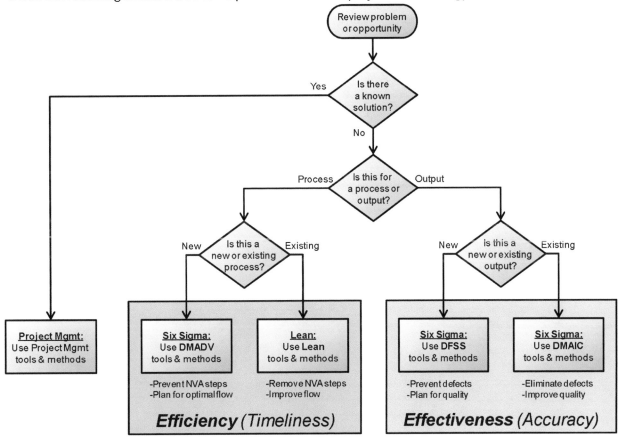

Which project method do I use?

- There are 5 general types of project methods:
  - Project Management (PMI)
  - Six Sigma – DMADV (create new process)
  - Lean (fix existing process)
  - Six Sigma – DFSS (create new output)
  - Six Sigma – DMAIC (fix existing output)

- o Not every project requires Lean or Six Sigma.
  - • Many of the same PMI, Lean & Six Sigma tools overlap the different project methodologies.
  - • It's not uncommon to start with one project method and change midstream to another.
- o The ideal project method to use depends on 2 critical factors:
  - • Root Cause: Is the root cause (and solution) already known?
    - ▪ Yes? Use project management (PMI) tools & methods.
    - ▪ No? Use Lean or Six Sigma tools & methods.
  - • Process vs. Output: Is the problem efficiency in the process or effectiveness of the output?
    - ▪ Process? Use Lean or Six Sigma tools & methods that identify & fix the root cause in the process.
    - ▪ Output? Use Six Sigma tools & methods that identify & fix the root cause of the output.
- o Most projects target opportunities for existing processes or outputs.
  - • Therefore, most projects where the root cause is unknown will use Lean and/or DMAIC.

Practical Application
- o Identify at least 3 prior projects that were worked in your area.
  - • Of the 5 methodologies listed, which one was applied for each?
  - • Based on the decision tree, was the correct methodology applied to each?
    - ▪ If not, then which method was used and why?
    - ▪ Was the outcome of the project affected by the methodology that was applied?
- o Identify one or more potential future project opportunities.
  - • For each opportunity, which of the 5 methodologies should be applied and why?

Introduction – Lesson 4: Corporate CTQ Drilldown

A review of how to align a project opportunity to the overall business strategy and needs by understanding the business CTQs in a CTQ Drilldown.

Pre-Requisite Lessons:
- None

Aligning to the Business Strategy and Needs
- Why do we need to align our project to the business strategy and needs?
  - In general, everyone wants to do work that's meaningful and makes a positive contribution.
  - What if we don't see the value or positive results of our work?
    - It could negatively influence how we see ourselves: "If my work isn't adding value, then I'm not of value".
    - It could negatively influence how leadership views us and put our job at risk.
  - If we want to know if our work adds value, then we must understand what the business values.
    - Just as a small gear can indirectly affect the movement of larger gears, we need to understand how our work (no matter how small) affects the strategy and needs of the business at the top.
- How can we understand what the business values?
  - The values of the business are also described as that which is Critical to Quality (CTQ).
  - A CTQ is a measurable characteristic of what the customer requires, expects, or considers a priority.
- What are the CTQs of the business?
  - To learn the CTQs, you have to answer the following:
    - Who is the ultimate customer?
    - What does that customer want/expect?
  - The CTQ Drilldown helps answer these questions (see the example on page 13).
    - The CTQs are typically drilled down 3 levels and can be generally applied to most corporations.
    - The CTQ Drilldown includes some common measurements in many companies:

CTQ Drilldown: From the Top
- Who is the company's ultimate customer?
  - Hint: It's NOT the person buying the company's product or service.
    - Yes, they are the primary revenue source, but a company's value is based on net worth (equity).
    - If the company mismanaged its funds, then revenue won't help – it only prolongs the inevitable.
  - The ultimate customer is the Shareholder.
    - The shareholder is the true owner of the company as represented by the Board. The CEO is the primary steward of the company who is ultimately accountable to the shareholder.
    - The satisfaction of the Shareholder can be measured by the company's stock price.
- What does the Shareholder want or expect?
  - The Shareholder's CTQs are for the company to perform well (improve stock price) in two ways:
    - Marketplace Performance (e.g., generally measured by various Analyst Ratings)
      - *The CEO and executive staff have only indirect influence over the company's performance in the marketplace.*
    - Corporate Performance (e.g., generally measured by Earnings per Share or EPS)
      - *The CEO and executives have direct control over the company's corporate performance.*

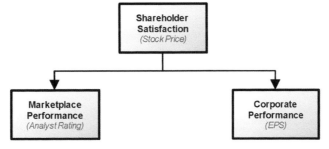

CTQ Drilldown: Level 1

- o What is the CTQ for the Marketplace?
  - Corporate Brand (e.g., corporate image, integrity, speculation of performance, etc.)
    - This doesn't mean the Marketplace doesn't care about corporate performance, but that the Marketplace represents the public perception of the company.
- o What are the CTQs for Corporate Performance?
  - Employee Satisfaction (e.g., % turnover, # of grievances/lawsuits, employee sat. surveys, etc.)
  - Customer Satisfaction (e.g., % turnover (a.k.a., churn), customers sat. surveys, etc.)
  - Financial Performance (e.g., EPS, Economic Value Added or OIBDA, Net Equity, etc.)

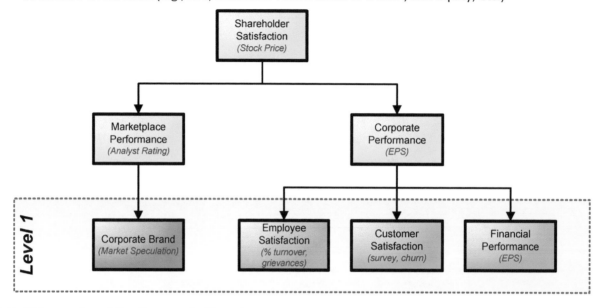

CTQ Drilldown: Level 2 – Corporate Brand

- o The CTQs for the Corporate Brand can be categorized by the following:
  - Uncontrollable –areas the company can't control
    - Examples include the economy, government regulations, weather/disasters, etc.
  - Controllable –areas the company can control or influence
    - Examples include audits, advertising, government compliance, safety, environment, etc.

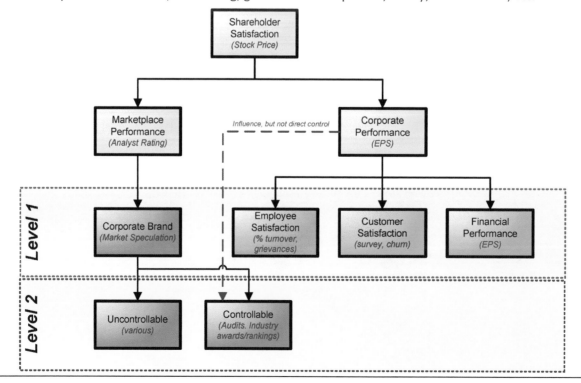

CTQ Drilldown: Level 2 – Employee Satisfaction

- o The CTQs for Employee Satisfaction can be categorized by the following:
  - Opportunities/Environment
    - E.g., advancement potential, improving skillsets/retention, working conditions, safety, etc.
  - Compensation
    - E.g., competitive wages, insurance benefits, time off, bonuses, discounted services, etc.

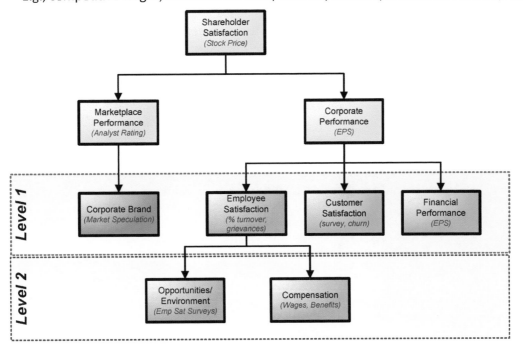

CTQ Drilldown: Level 2 – Customer Satisfaction

- o The CTQs for Customer Satisfaction can be categorized by the following:
  - Product/Service – WHAT products/services we offer
    - Do we offer the products/services that meet the needs, wants and price-point for customers?
  - Quality – HOW effective are the products/services we offer
    - Are our products/services meeting needs or wants to give the customer a perceived value?

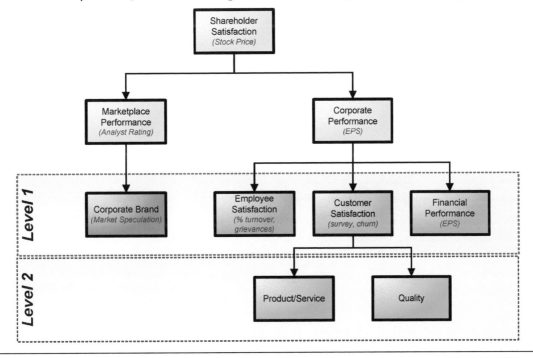

CTQ Drilldown: Level 2 – Financial Performance

- o The CTQs for Financial Performance can be categorized by the following:
  - Manage Assets (part of the corporate Balance Sheet)
    - Examples include how fast we collect cash (A/R), controlling asset purchases, capital investments, etc.
  - Manage Liabilities (part of the corporate Balance Sheet)
    - Examples include how fast we pay off debt, how slow we pay expenses (A/P), managing debt ratio, etc.
  - Operating Revenue, Operating Expenses & Non-Operating Expenses (part of Income Statement)
    - Examples include increasing revenue, decreasing bad debts, reducing payroll, efficient operations, etc.

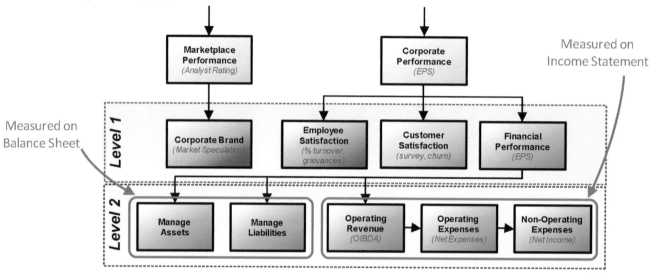

CTQ Drilldown: Level 3

- o What are the Level 3 CTQs?
  - Level 3 CTQs drill down to key metrics and initiatives from their respective Level 2 CTQ.
    - Level 3 is generally the lowest and most detailed level necessary.
    - They are generally at the department-level and will vary across the organization.
    - They are more likely to change over time compared to Level 1 and Level 2 CTQs.
- o How can you know what are the right Level 3 CTQs?
  - Level 3 CTQs are often outlined in any vision or strategy from departmental leadership.
    - Any key metrics, projects or goals for the department are likely candidates for Level 3 CTQs.
    - For these candidate CTQs, use your judgment as to which Level 2 CTQ they should be aligned.
    - Some Level 3 CTQs may align to more than one Level 2 CTQ.
  - If possible, validate the Level 3 CTQs with your leadership to ensure they're correctly aligned.
- o How do your projects and initiatives align with the Level 3 CTQs?
  - You should be able to easily see where your functional work aligns to at least one Level 3 CTQ.
  - Any work that does not align to a Level 3 CTQ should be re-evaluated with leadership.
    - In these cases, consider eliminating that work or researching it more in case a Level 3 CTQ is missing.
- o Which Level 3 CTQs are ideal for me to target for projects?
  - From a Lean Six Sigma perspective, target any CTQ that is measurable and critical to your area.
  - If you have the option, always select projects that affect Financial Performance.
    - Projects improving Financial Performance are generally more measurable and have more "Wow" factor.

Corporate CTQ Drilldown

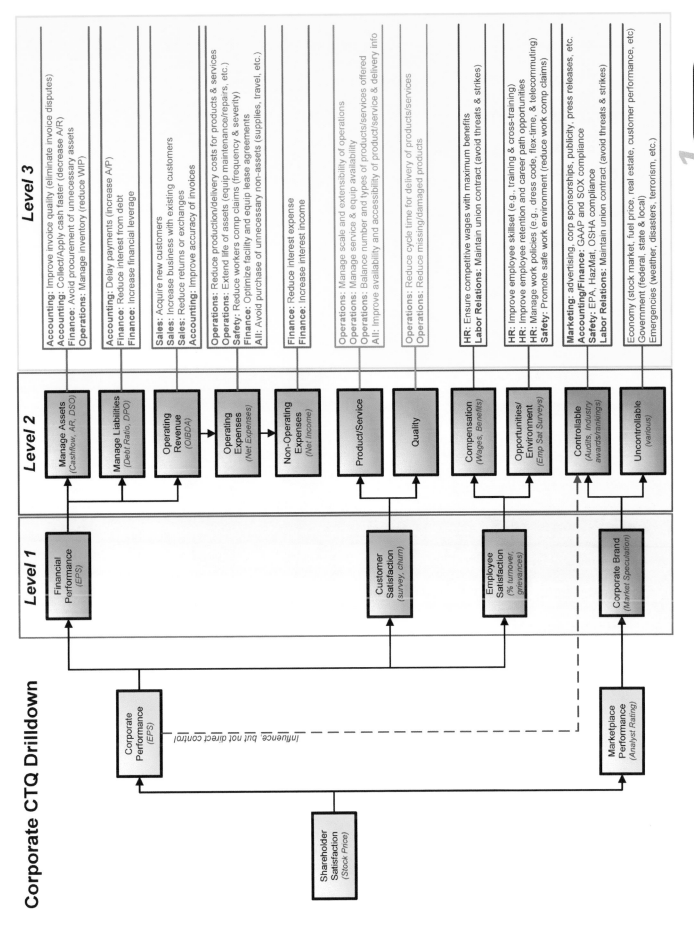

Practical Application

- What do you think are the level 3 CTQs in your department or functional area?
  - What level 1 & 2 CTQs do these align to?
  - What critical metrics from your functional area can't be aligned to the CTQ drilldown?
- Compare these level 3 CTQs to your normal and ad-hoc job functions.
  - Which of these functions can't be aligned to the CTQ drilldown?
    - If these don't align to the CTQ drilldown, then why do them?
  - For the functions that align to the CTQ drilldown, how does their alignment affect their priority?

Introduction – Lesson 5: Project Financial Savings

A review of how to identify and categorize financial benefits from a project.

Pre-Requisite Lessons:
- Intro #04 – Corporate CTQ Drilldown

Introduction to Financial Savings

- Financial Savings Must Be Reported Accurately.
  - It's a measurement of success for…
    - Our projects or business areas we support.
    - Our contribution to the company's profitability (Financial Performance).
  - It's a decision tool to determine:
    - Prognosis and risk for "failing" projects (e.g., Are the potential savings worth the continuing effort?).
    - Prioritization of opportunities or projects within the business.
  - It's a gauge for Sponsors and Champions to…
    - Enforce accountability to their budget and resources.
    - Brag to their executive leadership about achieving their goals.
- Financial Savings Must Be Reported Consistently.
  - Adds credibility to your time and effort in successfully leading a project.
  - Helps build a common language for how we communicate savings.

Return on Investment (ROI)

- It's all about Return on Investment (ROI).
  - Every Project Has a Financial Cost ("Investment").
    - Be aware of direct and indirect costs (e.g., costs for training, costs to implement safety/policies, etc.).
  - Every Successful Project Has Savings ("Return").
    - Savings may not be financially measurable (negative ROI).
  - It's critical to estimate potential ROI as early as possible in the project.
- There are two primary goals when working with ROI:

Goal #1: Calculate the ROI	Goal #2: Communicate the ROI
• Determine what's important to the business. What CTQs does the Sponsor use to measure success? • Measure the return on the potential or actual project improvements. • Measure the investment on the required costs for implementing the improvements.	• Use financial terms that the business understands; speak their language. • Use visual displays to communicate complex logic/concepts. • As needed, ensure a Finance SME validates the financial benefits.

Formal Validation Process

- o Below is an example of a formal process for validating savings with Finance.
  - • This example process is mostly ideal for a Lean Six Sigma program following execution of DMAIC.

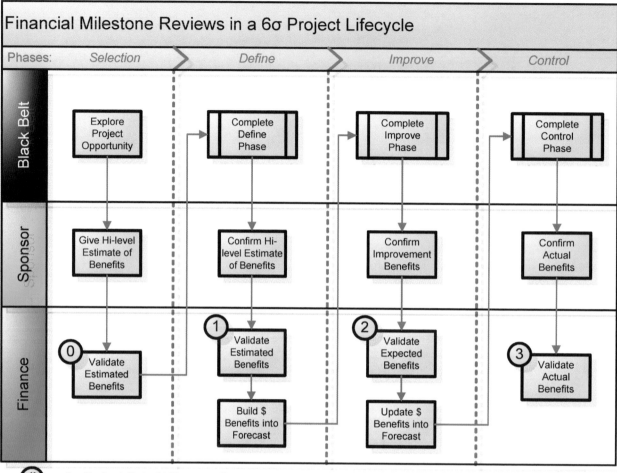

Financial Milestone Reviews in a 6σ Project Lifecycle

(#) = 6σ Project Gate / Milestone Reviews

Savings Categories

- o Project Savings Categories & Definitions
  1. **Direct Tangible**
     - ▪ Actual dollars that impact cash flow.
  2. **Indirect Tangible**
     - ▪ Measurable but no impact to cash flow.
  3. **Direct Intangible**
     - ▪ Actual dollars that could have impacted cash flow.
  4. **Indirect Intangible**
     - ▪ Not quantifiable in dollars, but adds value to the business.

		Impact to Cash	
		Direct	**Indirect**
Impact to Business	**Tangible**	Increase revenue Reduce existing costs Reduce headcount/OT (1)	Shift (not reduce) headcount Accelerate existing cash flow (2)
	Intangible	Avoid lost revenue Avoid additional costs (3)	Compliance Issues Customer satisfaction Employee satisfaction (4)

- o How to Determine the Savings Category
  1. Does the project affect cash flow (increasing revenue or decreasing costs)?
     - ▪ Yes = Direct Savings; No = Indirect Savings
  2. Does the project have a financially measurable improvement to the business?
     - ▪ Yes = Tangible Savings; No = Intangible Savings

Finding Savings
- How do you find potential financial savings for a project?
  - Convert the project Y (measureable output or primary CTQ) to cash.
    - How does the Y affect cash (increase revenue or decrease costs)?
    - What other measurements can be used to determine if improvements affect cash?
    - Explore how the Y will benefit your upstream and downstream stakeholders.
  - Define the equation for converting the Y to cash.
    - Map out the logical flow for any complex equations.
    - If using labor hours to calculate costs, include a fringe benefits factor as approved by Finance.
    - Remember, savings for salary employees are less likely to affect cash unless through headcount reduction.
    - Savings from reserves (like write-offs or worker's comp) are not directly affecting cash flow.
  - Calculate the savings using the equation.
    - Normalize each factor in the equation.
      - *For example, if a project is trying to reduce past due revenue, then any decline in past due revenue doesn't necessarily mean the project was successful – it may be due to revenue declining. Normalize it by dividing it into total revenue.*
    - Annualize the predicted savings (as a default).
      - *Drill down potential savings to the lowest level in time (hours, days, etc.) and multiply it over a year.*
      - *If the cash savings is known to be less than a year (e.g., a 6 month labor contract), then don't annualize the savings, but calculate it only for that remaining time when the cash is actually saved.*
      - *If the cash savings are known to be fully realized or even grow over the next few years, then use the annual average by calculating the total expected savings over that time and divide it by those number of years.*
  - Validate with the Team and Finance if the equation used and the savings calculated are practical.

Example 1 – Write-Offs
- Project Goal:
  - Streamline a Collections Team's 18K hrs/yr manual process of reviewing past-due bills to write off.
- Project Results:
  - Below is how the savings can be communicated visually using the As-Is and To-Be process maps:

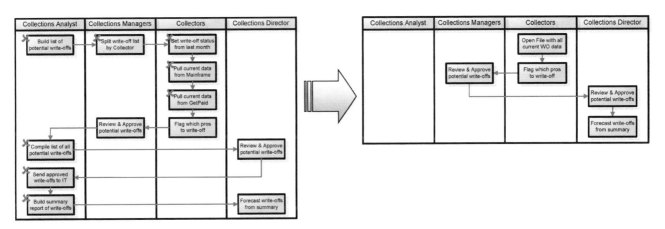

- The savings equation:
  - (Bill Vol/mo) x (Employee time/bill) x (Labor Cost) x (12 mos.)
  - Actual savings calculation is shown at right.
- The summarized savings:
  - There was no headcount reduction, so they had $258K/yr indirect tangible (category 2) savings.

	Collector	Coll Mgrs	Total
# of Write-offs (Avg Jan/Feb '08)	14,235	n/a	
Avg Minutes to work	6	n/a	
Total Minutes to work/mo	87,186	n/a	
Total hours to work/mo	1,453	n/a	
Estimated time saved	50%	n/a	
Total hours saved/mo	727	27	754
Estimated hourly labor*	$ 19	$ 38	
Estimated labor fringe benefits*	46%	30%	
Total estimated hourly labor	$ 27.74	$ 48.91	
Estimated labor cost saved/mo	$ 20,155	$ 1,320	$ 21,475
Estimated labor cost saved/yr	**$ 241,855**	**$ 15,846**	**$ 257,700**

Example 2 – Invoice Time
- Project Goal:
  - In order to help reduce Days Sales Outstanding (DSO), optimize for 4 different operating companies how soon an invoice can be sent while ensuring it's as accurate as possible.
- Project Results:
  - Here's how the savings were communicated visually using an As-Is and To-Be timeline:

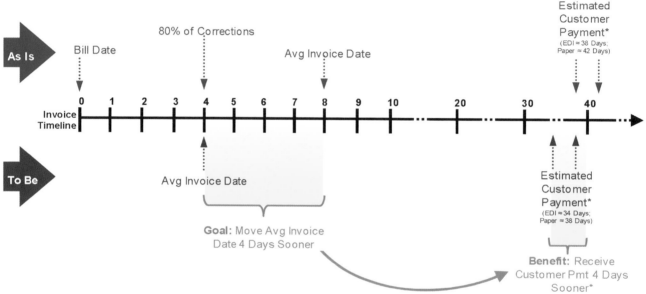

- The savings equation was very complex:
  - Filter only to revenue impacted by invoice timeliness (since not all revenue is affected).
  - Drilldown each invoice process (e.g., paper, EDI, etc.) and determine the invoice cycle time reduced for each.
  - Calculate the impact each cycle time reduction has on revenue, DSO and debt/capital savings.
- The summarized savings:
  - Cash was accelerated by $37.3M/yr in indirect tangible (Category 2) savings which saved $3.73M/yr in cost of capital, a direct tangible (Category 1) savings. This resulted in a reduction 1.56 days DSO.

Practical Application
- How does this categorization of financial savings differ from your typical approach?
  - What are the advantages and disadvantages of the method described in this module?
- Identify 3 to 5 projects in your area that had reported some financial savings.
  - What were the financial savings reported for those projects?
  - How were those financial savings treated by the company (e.g., did they reduce the budget)?
  - How would you categorize the savings from those projects based on the method in this module?
  - For any that you noted as not direct tangible (category 1) savings, if you had done this savings categorization upfront, how would it have affected each project's outcome (if at all)?

Introduction – Lesson 6: Project Prioritization Using a QFD

A review of how a Quality Functional Deployment (QFD) tool can be used to prioritize items, such as project opportunities.

Pre-Requisite Lessons:
- None

QFD Definition
- What is a "Quality Functional Deployment" Tool (QFD)?
  - A QFD (a.k.a., "House of Quality") is a tool that helps objectively prioritize subjective items.
  - A QFD helps a team of people prioritize items across their most critical prioritization factors.
    - Though a QFD can get very complex, we'll focus on its most simple and common application.
  - A QFD helps unify the team by resolving potential conflicts over competing initiatives.
  - A QFD for prioritizing projects can be built by a team of experts during a meeting (2 to 4 hours).
- What are the key elements for a QFD?
  - List of Parameters (What items need to be prioritized?)
    - Projects, customer requirements, opportunities, tasks, etc.
  - Prioritization Factors (How do we determine the priority?)
    - The factors or measurements that are most critical for the group that owns the above parameters.
      - *Examples include revenue/cost impact, improving customer satisfaction, level of risk, timeliness, etc.*
  - Impact Scores (How do we rank each parameter by each priority?)
    - The level of high/medium/low impact the team believes each factor has on each parameter.
- What does the overall process look like for building this QFD?

The QFD Process
- INPUT to Meeting
  - #1 - Define List of Parameters
    - The items to be prioritized should be informally collected prior to the meeting.
    - Every team member should be allowed to contribute an item to the list.
      - *A definition of each item should be included.*
      - *Items should not be removed from the list nor discussed once they're added to the list.*
    - The meeting should be scheduled and include all team members (ideally not more than 10 people).
      - *The meeting may take 2 to 4 hours depending on the number of parameters defined (ideally not more than 25).*
- PROCESS During Meeting
  - Meeting Kick-Off (~20 min)
    - The Sponsor/Champion should kick off the meeting and return at the end to review the results.
    - The list of parameters should be agreed upon by the team; allow for some clarification as needed.
  - #2 – Define Prioritization Factors (~30 min)
    - The factors should represent what's critical to that team (ideally only 3 to 5 factors).
    - Thresholds for determining High, Medium, and Low should be defined.

- Example prioritization factors and thresholds:

Prioritization Factor	Low	Medium	High
Financial Impact *(e.g., Revenue, Expenses, etc.)*	$0 - $100K/yr	$100K - $1M/yr	Over $1M/yr
Customer Satisfaction *(Internal & External)*	No Impact	Impacts either internal or external customers	Impacts both internal and external customers
Project Timeliness	Over 6 months	3 to 6 months	Less than 3 months
Probability of Success	Less than 50%	50% to 75%	Over 75%

- #3 – Rank Prioritization Factors (~10 – 20 min)
    - The prioritization factors themselves must be ranked in order of priority (highest priority should get highest numerical rank; i.e., something ranked as 1 is actually the lowest ranking).
    - If one or more factors are significantly more important than others, then it may be necessary to weigh the ranking even higher.
        - *For example, if there are 5 factors, they could be easily ranked from 5 to 1. However, if the #5 ranking is significantly more important than the other remaining factors, it could be given a higher rank like 7 or 10.*
        - *The scale for ranking (i.e., using 5 to 1, or 100 to 1, or 1000 to 1, etc.) is not as important as getting them in the proper order and assigning appropriate weighting to each factor.*
- Below is an example of the "QFD 1 Definition" tab where these items are entered...

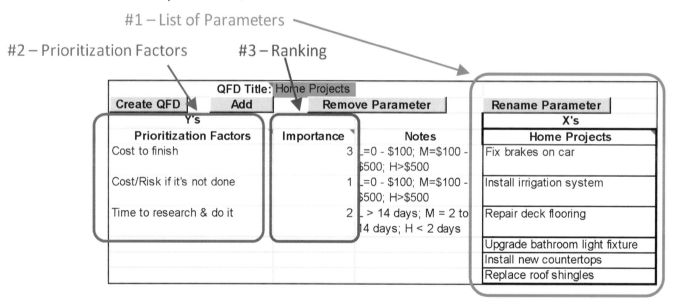

- #4 – Score Each Parameter per Factor (~30 – 60 min)
    - Click the "Create QFD" button on the "QFD 1 Definition" tab and a new worksheet is created (named after the "QFD Title" in cell B1). All items on the QFD (except for the scores) are automatically entered.
    - It's generally easiest to take one parameter column at a time and ask the team to assess the High, Medium or Low impact they believe that parameter has on each prioritization factor.
    - This scoring process should be VERY quick; allow only 10 to 30 seconds to score each item.
        - *The items to score is equal to the # of parameters multiplied by the # of factors. So if you have 10 parameters and 5 factors, that's 50 items to score. If the team spends 2 minutes of discussion for each, that can drag out to 100 minutes!*
        - *To help it move quickly, tell the team that anyone can shout out the score and then immediately enter their answer and move to the next item. You can allow an extra minute or two to review the answers before going to the next parameter.*

- Below is the QFD tab example for scoring these items...

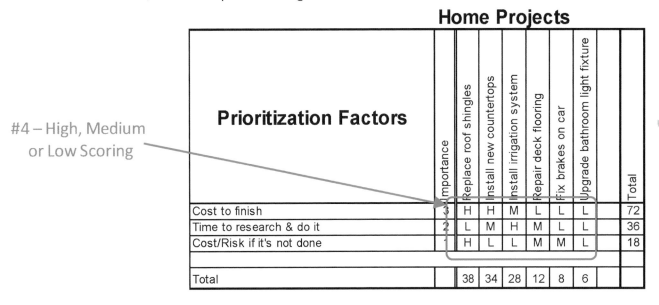

Home Projects

#4 – High, Medium or Low Scoring

Prioritization Factors	Importance	Replace roof shingles	Install new countertops	Install irrigation system	Repair deck flooring	Fix brakes on car	Upgrade bathroom light fixture		Total
Cost to finish	3	H	H	M	L	L	L		72
Time to research & do it	2	L	M	H	M	L	L		36
Cost/Risk if it's not done	1	H	L	L	M	M	L		18
Total		38	34	28	12	8	6		

- o OUTPUT From Meeting
  - #5 – Calculate & Sort Parameters by Score (~10 – 20 min)
    - Once all scoring is done, click the "Sort QFD" button and all parameters will sort automatically with those having the highest scores on the left and those having the lowest score on the right.
    - How are these scores calculated?
      - *Hidden in the QFD are assigned values for your High, Medium & Low scores. H (or High) = 9, M (or Medium) = 3, and L (or Low) = 1. The respective H, M, or L value is multiplied by the weighted rank (importance) for each factor.*
    - Review the results to see if the prioritized order makes sense to everyone.
      - *It's OK if the team wants to change some scores – as long as the entire team agrees with the change.*
      - *If scoring changes are made, click the "Sort QFD" button again to re-sort the parameters.*
  - Review this prioritized list with the Sponsor/Champion to get their agreement.
- o Now What?
  - Here are a few options for what to do next with the prioritized list:
    - If it's a small list (5 to 10) items, each item can be assigned to a team member to lead.
    - If it's a large list (Over 10 items), then review the total score assigned to each parameter in the list. If there are logical breaks or gaps in the scores, then only target items with higher scores.
      - *If these are project opportunities, then consider selecting the top 3 or 5 from the list, assign a person or small team to investigate each opportunity to help define and size (in scope & benefits) each one.*
      - *Items to the far right of any logical breaks or gaps should probably not be considered at all (the reason is because once all the other ones are complete, new items may fill the pipeline that will require this QFD exercise to be run again).*
  - This QFD may need to be built periodically depending on how often the parameters change.

Practical Application

- o What competing projects, initiatives, or opportunities exist in your functional area?
  - How are these usually prioritized?
  - How would you prioritize them? Would other people in your area agree with you?
  - Do these items need formal prioritization (like using a QFD tool)?
    - If so, then follow the steps for building a QFD for all these items.

Introduction – Lesson 7: Project Pre-Assessment using a Min/Max Analysis

A review of why it's important to do a project pre-assessment and how to do it using a Min/Max Analysis.

Pre-Requisite Lessons:
- Intro #04 – Corporate CTQ Drilldown
- Intro #05 – Project Financial Savings
- Intro #06 – Project Prioritization using a QFD Tool

Introduction to Pre-Assessment

- What is a project pre-assessment?
  - Helps validate the potential problem, scope, & benefits of the project.
  - Ensures there is adequate agreement on the need and expected value of the project.
- Why do we need a project pre-assessment now?
  - It fits in the logical order of how we have so far identified & prioritized project opportunities:
    - QFD – Helped prioritize various project opportunities to find which ones are most critical.
    - CTQ Drilldown – Helped ensure project opportunities align to the corporate needs & strategy.
    - Pre-Assessment – Will help validate if projects are critical and aligned to the business strategy.
- Is a project pre-assessment required?
  - No, but what's the risk if we don't do a pre-assessment? What if we find out…
    - …the scope is too large requiring more time, cost & resources?
    - …the opportunity doesn't align to the corporate CTQs?
    - …the Sponsor isn't bought-in as expected?
    - …the benefits aren't as large as expected?
  - A pre-assessment won't eliminate all these risks, but it can help us address these concerns at the start of the project to help mitigate them and ensure we achieve a reasonable ROI.

How do you do a Pre-Assessment?

- A pre-assessment is like a checklist that generally includes answering the following:

☑ **Understand the problem** *(part of Define phase in DMAIC)*

    ☑ What is the background for this opportunity? (E.g., Background Statement)
    ☑ What is the measurable pain being felt in the business by this problem? (E.g., Problem Statement)
    ☑ What is in and out of scope?

☑ **Project Support**

    ☑ Who would be the Sponsor & Champion and do they agree to fully support/resource this project?
    ☑ Who else would be considered a critical stakeholder for this project opportunity?
    ☑ How does this project opportunity align with the corporate CTQs? (E.g., CTQ levels 1 to 3)
    ☑ Are data readily available to measure and analyze the problem?

☑ **Expected Benefits**

    ☑ What are the minimum and/or maximum benefits expected? (E.g., Min/Max Analysis)
    ☑ What are the type and amount of financial savings expected?

- How do you get this pre-assessment information?
  - Contact the person(s) from whom you originally learned of the project opportunity.
    - While in pursuit of answers to the above questions, you may quickly learn how viable the opportunity is.
    - Our later training of the Define phase tools may help you in researching these answers.
    - Next, we'll review the Min/Max Analysis that may help to quickly size this opportunity.

- What do you do with this pre-assessment information?
  - Compile your answers and review them with your primary contact (Sponsor, Champion, etc.).
    - If the opportunity is viable, then these answers can be embedded as part of your normal project.
    - If it's not viable, then ensure the Sponsor agrees with your findings and is willing to close it down.

Min/Max Analysis
- What is a Min/Max Analysis?
  - A quick calculation that asks "What's the minimum or maximum benefits we can expect?"
    - If the minimum (worst case) benefits are substantial, then it's could be a worthwhile opportunity.
    - If the maximum (best case) benefits are not substantial, then it's probably not a worthwhile opportunity.
    - If the opportunity "feels" small, then calculate the minimum; otherwise, calculate the maximum.
- Example: Issue Resolution (IR) project
  - Problem: A call center has 6% of customers answer "I Don't Know" (IDK) when surveyed if their issue was resolved. It's assumed these customers will be easier to convert to "Yes" than those answering "No" and could significantly improve the Issue Resolution (IR) metrics.
  - Min/Max Analysis: What's the maximum IR benefit we can expect by converting an IDK to Yes?

1. Impact to IR Rate

	As Is	To Be	Diff
# of Surveys	100	100	0
Answer YES	80	86	6
Answer NO	14	14	0
Answer IDK	6	0	-6
IR (Yes/(Yes+No))	85%	86%	1%

Max Benefit: IR would improve only 1% point

2. Impact to Call Volume

Calls/Mo		11,000,000	
Answer IDK		6%	
Total IDK Calls			660,000
Callback Diff	Y = 11%; IDK=12%		1%
Fewer Callbacks		Per Month	6,600
Fewer Callbacks		Per Year	79,200
Callback Savings		$3/call	$237,600

Max Benefit: Call Vol would decline 79K calls/yr

- Conclusion: Cancel project since the maximum (unrealistic) benefit is smaller than expected.

Practical Application
- What previous projects or analyses have you worked where you wish you had performed a pre-assessment?
  - How would a pre-assessment have made a difference?
  - If you had done a pre-assessment, would your leadership have agreed to cancel it or change the direction or scope of the project?
    - If not, then what additional information would have influenced them to agree with the pre-assessment?
- What projects or analyses are you working now that should have a pre-assessment?
  - If a pre-assessment revealed the opportunity is not worthwhile, would that make a difference?

Introduction – Lesson 8: Key Roles in a Lean Six Sigma Project

A review of the project and functional roles in Lean Six Sigma projects.

Pre-Requisite Lessons:

  o None

Project Leadership

  o A Six Sigma project is usually led by a collaborative team of internal & external experts...

Characteristics	External Resources	Internal Resources
Lean Six Sigma Expertise =	Strong	Not Required
Functional Expertise =	Not Required	Strong
Roles =	Green Belt, Black Belt, Master Black Belt	Sponsor, Champion, Process Owner, SMEs

Lean Six Sigma Resources

  o The Six Sigma external resources fall into these three general roles:

Characteristics	Green Belt (GB)	Black Belt (BB)	Master Black Belt (MBB)
Expertise of Tools/Concepts	Moderate	Strong	Very Strong
Dedication to projects	Part-Time	Full-Time	Full-Time
Project Benefits	Generally small (< $250K/yr)	Generally large (> $250K/yr)	Manage multiple projects (> $1M/yr)
Project Timeframe	Generally shorter (1 to 3 months)	Generally longer (3 to 6 months)	Generally longer (3 to 6 months)
Project Scope	Generally limited to functional area	Often extends across multiple functional areas	Manage BB Training and/or Team of BBs
Typical Certification Req'ts	GB Test & 2 GB projects	BB Test & 2 BB projects	Varies (Sponsorship)

  o A project can have one or more of any of these roles assigned (depending on scope).
  - In many ways, these resources serve as consultants or "Change Leaders" for the business.
  o The definition & certification of these roles vary by organization/company.
  - Some organizations create other roles like "White Belt", "Yellow Belt", etc. These are less common and generally less stringent in qualifications.

Functional Resources

o The internal resources of the functional area fall into these four general roles:

Characteristics	Sponsor	Champion	Process Owner	SMEs
Leadership Position	Executive (VP or Director)	Mid-Level (Director or Mgr)	Lower-Level (Mgr, Sup, or Lead)	Not typically in leadership
Communication Frequency	Infrequent (2 to 5 times during project)	Frequent (Every 2 wks or so)	Very Frequent (1 to 2 times/wk)	Varies (as needed)
Process Ownership	Ultimately owns process and effects across departments	Controls process and effects within department	Direct ownership of process and its effects	Support role; no direct ownership
Project Involvement	Final decision maker for getting resources & removing roadblocks	Strong decision maker for getting resources and removing roadblocks	Drives coordination for resources and elevating roadblocks to Champion	As needed support related to expertise

o Projects usually have multiple SMEs, but only one of each of the other roles.
o The definition of these roles don't vary much by organization/company.
   • Some organizations have formally certified the Sponsor and Champion roles, but that's rare.

Practical Application

o Think of a few previous projects you worked on:
   • If they were Lean Six Sigma projects, who filled the Lean Six Sigma roles on each project?
   • Who filled the functional roles for each project?
   • Was there any project that didn't have any of these roles identified?
      ▪ If so, then how did the lack of that role affect the progress or results of the project?

Introduction – Lesson 9: Project Strategy Using the IPO-FAT Tool

A review of how to build a strategy for a project and how the IPO-FAT tool can be used for developing that strategy.

Pre-Requisite Lessons:
- o Intro #02 – Introduction to Lean and Six Sigma

Project Strategy: Introduction
- o What does it mean to have a project strategy?
  - The project strategy outlines the "plan of attack" for the specific problem of the project.
    - The DMAIC methodology is a general guideline that should influence how you attack the project.
    - The project strategy consists of the process steps to specifically and logically attack the project's problem.
- o Example 1: Repeat Caller Alert (RCA) Analysis
  - Problem: A call center uses the RCA in the system to detect when a customer recently called so the agent can know if they're calling for a recurring issue. Does this improve issue resolution (IR)?
  - Strategy: Acquire customer satisfaction survey data and answer the following questions:
    - 1. How often is the RCA "On" (indicating the customer recently called in)?
    - 2. Is the RCA effective at finding repeat calls? (i.e., Did the customer's survey confirm it's a repeat call?)
    - 3. Is the RCA process effective at improving IR as expected for these verified repeat calls?
- o Example 2: Improve Repeat Contact Prevention (RCP) at a Call Center
  - Problem: RCP for the call center is 10% pts lower than Enterprise RCP.
  - Strategy: Build an equation to find what factors (inputs) are causing the RCP performance gap:

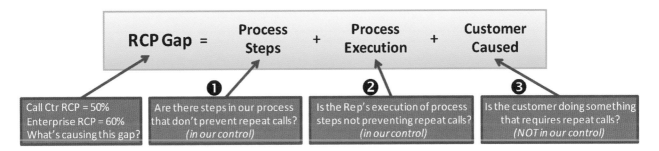

IPO-FAT Tool: Introduction
- o What is the IPO-FAT tool?
  - It's a method of evaluating a business area to identify & prioritize potential opportunities.
  - As opposed to a QFD that prioritizes existing, known opportunities, the IPO-FAT method can help a team identify new/different opportunities that haven't necessarily been considered.
- o When is the IPO-FAT tool used?
  - It's most effective when a business area has several problems with potentially inter-related root causes and it's not immediately known what order to target the root causes and problems.
  - It can be an effective method for building and communicating the project strategy.
- o What is the premise behind the IPO-FAT tool?
  - As previously discussed, virtually every area of the business has an INPUT that goes through a PROESS to create an OUTPUT (a.k.a., "IPO").

- Each IPO stage is viewed across 3 "FAT" perspectives:
  - Flow – How items pass through each IPO stage.
  - Accuracy – Effectiveness of each IPO stage.
  - Timeliness – Efficiency of each IPO stage.
- The IPO-FAT tool also identifies the priority for each opportunity and the Lean and/or Six Sigma methodology to use.

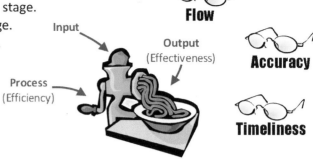

IPO-FAT Tool
- Below is the IPO-FAT tool:

	Input →	Process →	Output
Flow	❶ **Incoming Volume** *(What opportunities are there to reduce the incoming volume from the prior output?)*	❷ **Workflow Rhythm** *(How can throughput (takt time) be optimized by evaluating FIFO, batch processing or schedule balancing?)*	**Production Rate or RTY** *(What does takt time or rolled throughput yield (RTY) reveal about what processes need improving?)*
Accuracy	❹ **Readiness** *(How complete or accurate are the inputs before the process?)*	❸ **Quality/Value-Add** *(What process steps don't add value, aren't required or don't meet policy/specs?)*	**Defects (DPMO)** *(What is the rate of defects, scraps or First-time-yield (FTY)?)*
Timeliness	❺ **Arrival/Setup Time** *(How much delay between prior output and current input? How much setup or lead time is required before process?)*	❻ **Handle Time** *(How much time to perform value-added steps in process?)*	**Turnaround Time (TAT)** *(How much time from current input to current output?)*

❶ to ❻ = Potentially the fastest & easiest path for finding biggest opporutnities

Preferred Methodology:
- = 6 Sigma (Effectiveness)
- = Lean (Efficiency)
- = Lean &/or 6 Sigma

- What does the suggested priority (1 to 6) mean?
  - The priority suggests what could be the fastest & easiest path for finding & fixing potential opportunities.
  - For example, why improve the handle time for items being processed (#6) if you can eliminate some of them from the incoming volume in the first place (#1)? Doing #1 first will save time when doing #6 later.
- How do you use the tool?
  - Review the tool with the team and brainstorm potential opportunities for each cell.
  - Validate with the team if the suggested priority (1 to 6) is recommended for their opportunities.

IPO-FAT Tool Example

- o Below is an example of how the IPO-FAT tool was used for a project.
  - Problem: A back office team was failing in some of its performance goals, yet the team didn't know what opportunities to target.
  - Strategy: The team's strategy was as follows:
    1. Identify & explore opportunities using the IPO-FAT tool. (example below)
    2. Pilot and implement improvements to the back office.
    3. Build controls to measure and sustain the improvements.

	Input	Process	Output
Flow	❶ **Incoming Volume** ✓ 1. Pending Adj Approvals ✓ 2. Change of Ownership X 3. Invalid Transfers of Disputes	❷ **Workflow Rhythm** X 4. Staffing Levels	**Production Rate or RTY** N/A
Accuracy	❹ **Readiness** X 5. Fraud (Lost/Stolen)	❸ **Quality/Value-Add** N/A	**Defects (DPMO)** N/A
Timeliness	❺ **Arrival/Setup Time** ✓ 6. System Import Delays	❻ **Handle Time** N/A	**Turnaround Time (TAT)** N/A

❶ to ❻ = Potentially the fastest & easiest path for finding biggest opporutnities

Preferred Methodology:
- = 6 Sigma (Effectiveness)
- = Lean (Efficiency)
- = Lean &/or 6 Sigma

Practical Application

- o Think of a few previous projects you worked on:
  - Was a project strategy developed for each one? If so, what was it?
    - If any project didn't have a strategy developed, would it have helped if you had one? If so, how?
- o Review those previous projects in light of the 6 prioritized areas of the IPO-FAT tool?
  - Were any of those 6 prioritized areas not considered in the project?
    - If not, would it have made a difference in the results of the project?
  - Did any of the projects follow a different priority than the 6 proposed in the IPO-FAT tool?
    - If so, would it have made a difference if the priority posed in the IPO-FAT tool were followed?

Introduction – Lesson 10: Project Storyboard

A review with examples of how to effectively communicate the progress of a project using a project storyboard.

Pre-Requisite Lessons:
- o None

Project Storyboard: Introduction
- o What is the project storyboard?
  - It's a document (typically a set of PowerPoint slides) that "tells the story" of the project.
    - It generally summarizes the premise, analysis, & results of the project.
    - It can be used during the project (for getting team/stakeholder buy-in) or as a post-project reference.
  - It often changes throughout the duration of the project.
    - Don't be afraid to add, delete, or modify parts of the storyboard if it enhances the overall project story.
- o What method or style should be used for the storyboard?
  - There is no official or formal storyboard style.
    - Some Lean Six Sigma organizations require a standard storyboard layout.
    - If a formal storyboard layout isn't required, then use what is easiest for you to communicate the story.
  - Use the KISS method (Keep It Simple, Stupid).
    - Target the language & concepts of the storyboard to a 6th grade level.
    - Explain any unique business concepts, terms & acronyms along the way.
      - *It may be helpful to add a glossary of operational definitions as an appendix to the storyboard.*
    - Use pictures or charts to help explain key or complex concepts.
      - *Only use clipart if it's relevant; if complex statistical tools are necessary, simplify them and use call outs to explain them.*
  - Use the KILL method (Keep it Logical, Loser).
    - The flow of the story should be logical and consistent; if any part doesn't make sense, then exclude it.
- o Storyboard Tips:
  - Keep your main points of the story at the front of the storyboard; use the appendix for details.
  - Try using a Question: Answer format; this lets the audience know what you're trying to answer.
  - Add an executive summary to front of the storyboard and add a "Takeaway" to each page.

Project Storyboard: Example 1

○ Project Example 1: Back Office Processes
  • This project had 6 different opportunities that were explored based on using the IPO-FAT tool.

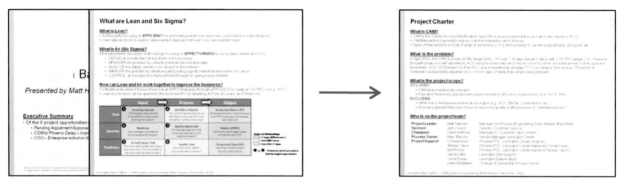

Pg 1 (Cover) included an Exec Summary and pg 2 had a brief summary about Lean 6Sigma (to introduce the methodology).

Pg 3 summarizes the Project Charter (problem statement, scope, and team members).

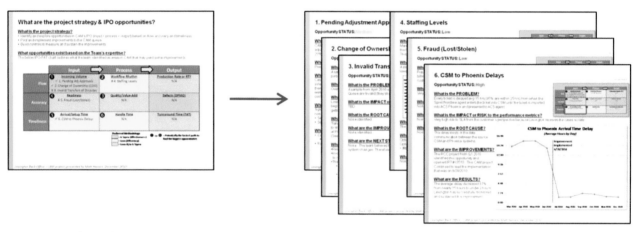

Pg 4 uses the IPO-FAT as a project strategy with each cell noting potential opportunities.

Pg 5 – 10 each summarize one opportunity (problem, root cause, improvement & results). Each page references the IPO-FAT from pg 4 to help the reader follow the project story.

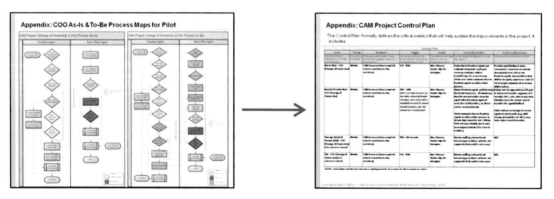

Pg 11 compares an As-Is & To-Be process map that supports opportunity #2 (pg 6); it's helpful but not critical to the story ,so it's in the appendix.

Pg 12 is a Control Plan that covers some of the project opportunities. It's critical to the project but not the story so it's added to the appendix.

Project Storyboard: Example 2

o Project Example 2: Call Reduction Project

- This project started as a pilot to find ways to significantly reduce call volume at a call center.

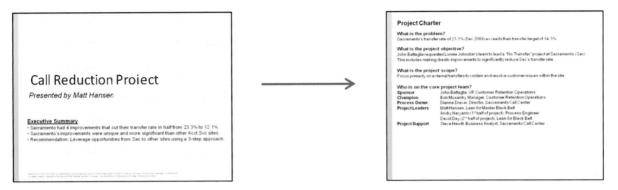

Pg 1 (Cover) included an Exec Summary.

Pg 2 summarizes the Project Charter (problem statement, scope, and team members).

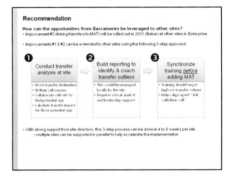

Pg 3 - 4 explain the implemented improvements, their results, and answers other potential questions the audience may have. The analysis to find the improvements weren't critical to the story.

Pg 5 summarizes the team's recommendations by laying them out visually as 3 simple steps.

Project Storyboard: Example 3

- o Project Example 3: Repeat Caller Alert (RCA) Analysis
  - Though this was more of an analysis than a DMAIC project, a storyboard was used to explain it.

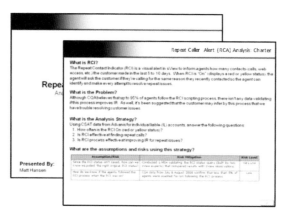

Pg 1 (Cover) didn't have an Exec Summary; Pg 2 described the problem and explained the analysis strategy as answering 3 simple questions.

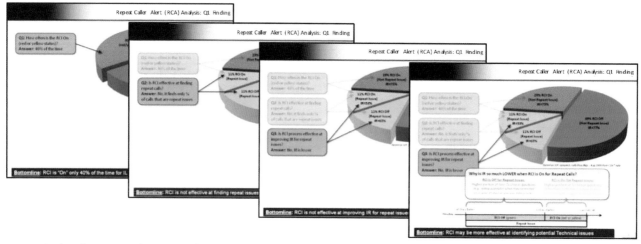

Pg 3 – 6 answer the 3 simple questions in the strategy. They're depicted visually using the same pie chart and then layering the subsequent question/answer on top of each other. This method adds consistency to the story for the audience.

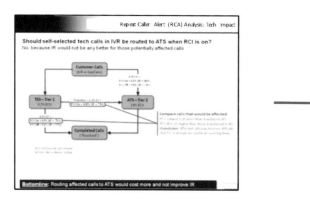

Based on the results from the analysis, pg 7 does a Min/Max analysis to find the opportunity isn't worth it (low ROI).

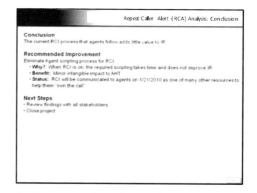

Pg 8 summarizes the analysis conclusions &recommended next steps.

Project Storyboard: Example 4

o Project Example 4: Road Empty Miles Project
- This project reflects a more formal and comprehensive storyboard layout.

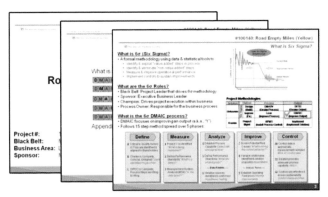

Pg 1 is the cover page, pg 2 is a table of contents (since the storyboard was long), and pg 3 gave a brief summary about Lean Six Sigma.

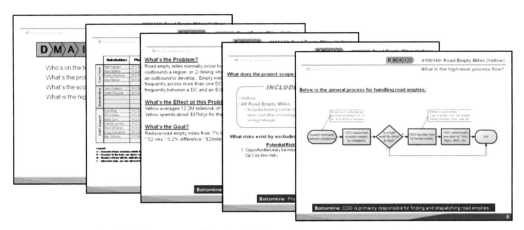

Pg 4 – 8 included content for the Define phase such as a stakeholder analysis, project charter, scope definition and high-level process map.

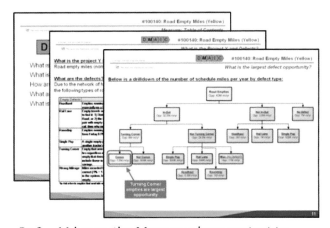

Pg 9 – 11 began the Measure phase content to explain how a defect was defined and to size up the potential opportunity.

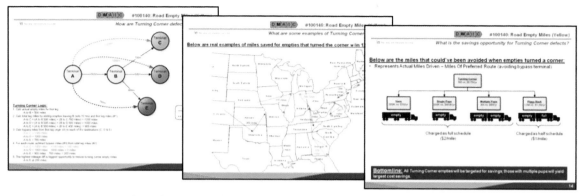

Pg 12 – 14 explain the method used for finding defects, real examples across the U.S. of where these defects exist, and a more detailed sizing of potential benefits. The rest of the project slides are omitted from this example.

Practical Application

- o What are some examples of project storyboards that you or others have created?
  - In what ways were they effective?
  - In what ways were they not effective?
  - Did the audience respond to the storyboard message as was intended?
    - If not, then how could the storyboard have been more effective in communicating to the audience?
- o What storyboard tips & techniques would help for your future storyboards?

Introduction – Lesson 11: Analysis of Behavior & Cognition (ABC) Model

A review of the ABC model that explores how we think so we can understand the risks and evidence behind our decisions and how to influence others.

Pre-Requisite Lessons:
  o None

ABC Model: Introduction
  o What is the Analysis of Behavior & Cognition (ABC) model?
    • The ABC model explores the phrase "ideas have consequences" in order to understand how we think (absorb & assess information internally) and how it influences our external behavior.
    • It helps us understand our assumptions that could significantly affect how we do data analysis.
  o Overview of the ABC model:
    • It can be said that 3 Internal layers...
      ▪ **Arguments >> Beliefs >> Conclusions**
    • ...may lead to 3 External layers...
      ▪ **Actions >> Behaviors >> Consequences**
    • "Internal" reflects the thought processes not visible by others.
    • "External" reflects the outward actions visible by others.
    • These layers illustrate a natural order:
      ▪ Each layer is dependent on the previous layer.
      ▪ Each layer won't necessarily trigger the next layer.
    • A person's actions may indicate their beliefs and the arguments that influence those beliefs.

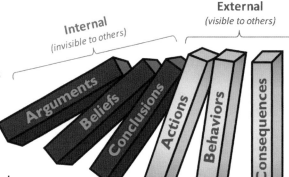

Overview of the ABC Model
  o The ABC model is shown on page 41.

Illustrating the ABC model
  o The ABC model can be illustrated as a construction project for a 3-story building:

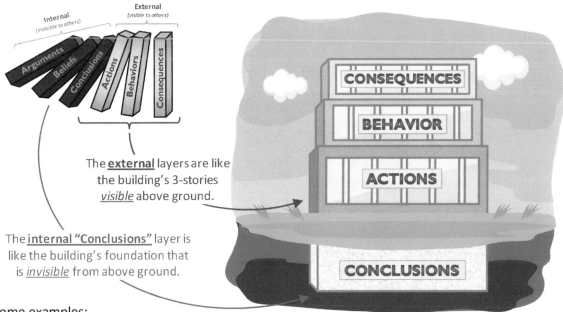

The **external** layers are like the building's 3-stories *visible* above ground.

The **internal "Conclusions"** layer is like the building's foundation that is *invisible* from above ground.

  o Some examples:
    • Consequence: A thief is caught robbing a jewelry store; what may have been their conclusions?
    • Consequence: Someone wins a $10 Million lottery; what may have been their conclusions?
    • CAUTION: Don't let your guess of a person's internal conclusions lead to prejudice.

Conclusions are based on beliefs

o The conclusions or decisions we make are formed from our beliefs...

What materials (beliefs) are we using
to build our foundation (conclusions)?

o Our beliefs can be like concrete that's formed by a mixture of materials.
   • The mixture of materials (beliefs) can either strengthen or weaken our foundation.
   • If we don't examine/test our beliefs that form our foundation (conclusions), it could compromise the structural integrity of our building (actions and behaviors).

How beliefs are formed

o Beliefs account for uncertainties in life.
   • Since no one knows the future with full certainty, our beliefs are formed by balancing what we _do know_ and what we _don't know_ so we can make reasonable conclusions.
   • In this way, beliefs are a balance of how we evaluate risks vs. rewards.
o Below is an illustration of how we may evaluate risks/rewards to influence our beliefs:

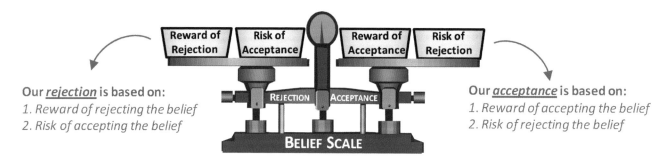

Our _rejection_ is based on:
1. _Reward of rejecting the belief_
2. _Risk of accepting the belief_

Our _acceptance_ is based on:
1. _Reward of accepting the belief_
2. _Risk of rejecting the belief_

o What are the potential risks and rewards for each proposed statement?

Proposed Statement	Reward of Rejection	Risk of Acceptance	Reward of Acceptance	Risk of Rejection
I can win the lottery	Save lottery ticket money	Waste time & money	Improve chance to win	Miss chance of winning
I can text and drive	Ensure safety in driving	May cause an accident	Undisrupted comm.	Miss out on fast comm.

Beliefs are based on arguments

- Each risk & reward is like an argument we use as evidence to accept or reject a belief.
  - **Problem**: Not all arguments are created equal. How can they be properly compared?
    - Each argument should be weighed for their significance (of reward) or severity (of risk).
    - For example, compare two types of arguments (Ignorance vs. Facts) having different weights:

Ignorance:
Light-weight argument; something with no tangible or repeatable evidence

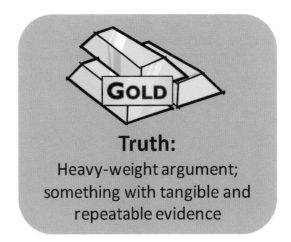

Truth:
Heavy-weight argument; something with tangible and repeatable evidence

- Beliefs don't need indisputable facts, but only more heavily weighted arguments.
  - Risk is normal and should be expected.
    - Virtually every decision we make accounts for some level of risk.
    - The plot of the comedy "What About Bob?" was based on a man who was considered mentally unstable because he wouldn't accept any risk.
  - Risk helps "fill the gaps" of evidence toward shaping our beliefs.
    - We only need enough heavily-weighted arguments (like facts) to _reasonably_ out-weigh the opposing arguments.

Courtesy Touchstone Pictures

Weighing the types of arguments

- How do we determine the weight for each argument of evidence?
  - One method is to categorize the arguments in 5 groups (ITEST) from light to heavy as illustrated below (Note: These groups are intended to describe a general order and are not mutually exclusive):

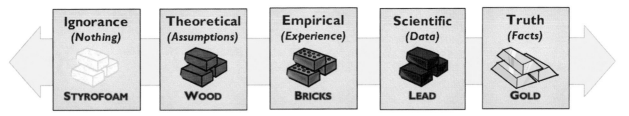

Ignorance (Nothing)	Theoretical (Assumptions)	Empirical (Experience)	Scientific (Data)	Truth (Facts)
STYROFOAM	WOOD	BRICKS	LEAD	GOLD

Lighter Weight   **Heavier Weight**

Intangible	← - - - - →	Tangible
Not Repeatable	← - - - - →	Repeatable
Limited Application	← - - - - →	Universal Application
Limited Accessibility	← - - - - →	Universal Accessibility
More Emotions	← - - - - →	Less Emotions
Less Confidence	← - - - - →	More Confidence

- Ideally, we want to answer the following:
  - What are the types (weights) of my current arguments?
  - How can I make them heavier?

Testing and balancing arguments

- o Each argument can be independently examined (or weighed) to assess the following:
  - Is the argument an absolute truth based on indisputable facts?
    - Is the argument verifiable with our human senses (tangible)?
    - Is the argument repeatable with consistent results?
    - Is the argument universally applicable to and universally accessible by anyone?
    - Any "No" may indicate the argument is not an indisputable fact or absolute truth.
  - Is the argument based on scientific or statistical data that's been tested?
  - Is the argument based on real-life (though unscientifically tested) experience?
  - Is the argument based on logical (though not yet experienced) assumptions ?
- o The weighted arguments can be applied to the respective risk or reward.
  - The collection of weighted arguments is what influences what beliefs we accept or reject.

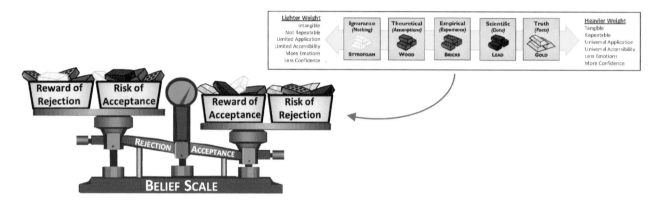

Sources for our arguments

- o Let's stretch this construction example a little bit further…
- o What are the sources for our arguments? Where are we getting our information?
  - Truth (like indisputable facts) can come from almost any source – even unreliable sources.
    - If we consider a source to be unreliable, do we automatically disregard their information, even if it's fact?
  - Can we objectively separate the information from the source to discern its proper weight?
  - Why do some people accept all information from any source?
    - Skepticism is like adding a counterbalance to the information until we can adequately process or weigh it.

Putting the ABC Model all together

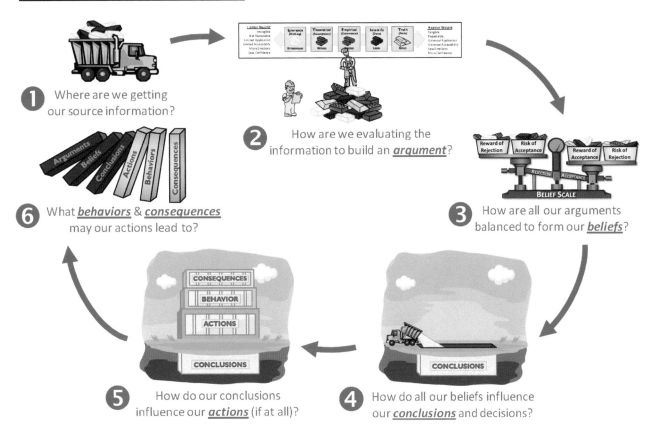

① Where are we getting our source information?

② How are we evaluating the information to build an **_argument_**?

③ How are all our arguments balanced to form our **_beliefs_**?

④ How do all our beliefs influence our **_conclusions_** and decisions?

⑤ How do our conclusions influence our **_actions_** (if at all)?

⑥ What **_behaviors_** & **_consequences_** may our actions lead to?

Applying the ABC Model to a Historical Example

○ An example in history: A battle over the Geocentric and Heliocentric models.

- It is widely accepted today that the earth and planets revolve around the sun (heliocentric model) instead of the sun and planets revolving around the earth (geocentric model).
    - The heliocentric model (discovered by Copernicus and strongly defended by Galileo) defied the geocentric model supported by Aristotle & Ptolemy and widely accepted for over two millennia.

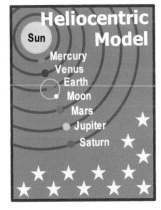

- What are the arguments used by each side?
    - Geocentric supporters appear to have more fact-based evidence:
        - *Movement of the sun & planets appear tangible (visually confirmed).*
        - *The movement is also repeatable and universally applicable & accessible.*
    - Heliocentric supporters have more logical/mathematical evidence (lighter weight than facts).
- Though the geocentric model appears to be factual, in reality neither model is factual.
    - To observe either model, you would have to remain in a fixed point in space for a long time.
    - What appears to be tangible evidence for the geocentric model is probably more experiential.
    - The heliocentric model has more mathematical and logical evidence outweighing the geocentric model.
- Does that mean the heliocentric model may be wrong?
    - No, though we don't have tangible, fact-based evidence, the evidence we do have is reasonable enough.

A Practical Application of the ABC Model

o How can we practically apply the ABC model on the job? Below are four ways:

1
Evaluate adverse consequences (e.g., a pilot)
Adverse consequences may come from not identifying risks or having too much light-weight arguments.

Example – Finding unexpected results or more defects after piloting improvements to a process:
• What risks were not considered or properly evaluated that could've prevented the consequence?
• What assumptions were used for finding the root cause and improving the process?

2
Evaluate the weight of our own arguments
What weight do we apply to our arguments or what risks haven't been considered in our assessment?

Example – Doing root cause analysis in the Analyze & Improve phases:
• Are there other statistical tests that can further prove or disprove our conclusions?
• Do we need more data samples to become more confident in the test results?

3
Build arguments to influence your audience
If you know your audience is improperly weighting their arguments, then you can either challenge their weighting or add arguments they haven't considered.

Example – An executive is ready to eliminate a department because their performance is low:
• How is the executive measuring performance?
• How are the metric targets being set?
• Are there assumptions the executive is making about the process when benchmarking to similar processes?

4
Build a case to challenge/disarm an opponent
Look for emotions that may be disguising light-weight arguments as heavy-weight arguments.

Example - If an opponent states a "fact", challenge it by identifying the right type (weight) of their argument.
Example – If your argument isn't a fact, then don't treat it like one so your opponent can't easily challenge you.
• Keep your own emotions at bay and be sure to communicate potential risks.
• It disarms your opponent and raises your credibility.

Practical Application

o Think of a few previous projects you worked on:
• What were some of the challenges or obstacles in getting buy-in from key stakeholders?
▪ What were some of the arguments they used to challenge your position?
▪ How would you "weigh" their arguments on the Scale of Evidence?
▪ How would you "weigh" your own arguments in comparison? Did you present them fairly?
▪ How could their arguments have been peacefully challenged to persuade them to change?

Introduction – Lesson 12: Change Acceleration Process (CAP) Model

A review of the CAP model that outlines a change mgmt method and set of tools for getting buy-in and ensuring successful implementation of the change.

Pre-Requisite Lessons:
- o Intro #04 – Corporate CTQ Drilldown
- o Intro #11 – ABC Model

Change Effectiveness Equation

- o GE wanted to find out what makes a project successful (yielded the expected benefits).
  - They studied hundreds of projects and business initiatives. Here were their findings:
    - 100% of successful projects had a good technical solution or strategy.
    - 98% of unsuccessful projects also had a good technical solution or strategy.
  - They concluded that a good technical solution is not enough to make a project successful.
    - What makes a project successful? Acceptance (or buy-in) of the change.
- o GE created the following Change Effectiveness Equation to describe this phenomena:

$$Q \: x \: A \: = \: E$$
Quality   Acceptance   Effectiveness

  - This equation can be described as:
    - The EFFECTIVENESS (E) of any initiative is equal to the product of the QUALITY (Q) of a strategy and the ACCEPTANCE (A) of that strategy.
    - A multiplicative relationship is used because if the Acceptance is zero, then the total Effectiveness will be zero regardless of the Quality of the strategy. Likewise, if Quality is zero, then it will not be effective.
- o Since Acceptance is so critical, GE developed the Change Acceleration Process (CAP).
  - CAP Tools were developed to teach how to get the buy-in to successfully implement change.
  - The ABC Model can play a significant role in how we acquire that buy-in:
    - It helps us understand the level of evidence our audience may use for decision-making.
    - The more our strategy's level of evidence meets/exceeds the audiences', the more likely they'll accept it.

Overview of the CAP Model

- o The Change Acceleration Process (CAP) can be adapted to manage any major change.
  - This module will define how the CAP Model and Tools can be adapted for Lean Six Sigma projects.
    - Many of the CAP tools are the same as other Lean Six Sigma tools so they will not be addressed in detail here, but will be covered more in-depth later in training.

- Below is an illustration of the CAP model:

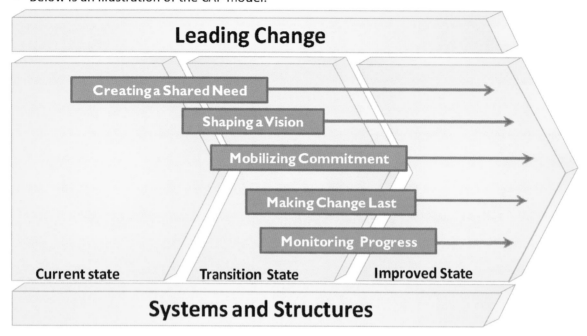

Leading Change
- o What is "Leading Change"?
  - In a word, "Sponsorship".
    - No project can be successful at implementing change without committed leadership throughout the duration of the project.
  - Leadership support should be visible and active.
    - A Sponsor should be fully engaged in supporting the project by being aware of the need and providing the necessary resources.
    - A Sponsor may not need frequent communication or updates, but they ensure full support.
- o What if the sponsorship wanes or changes?
  - A significant change in sponsorship support can be a serious risk of failure to the project.
    - If the Sponsor is not fully supportive (changes direction, withdraws resources, isn't fully engaged, etc.), then stop the project and make every attempt possible to meet with the Sponsor to assess their support.
    - If the Sponsor changes roles, the stop the project (if possible) and make every attempt to acquire the support of the new Sponsor. If possible, include the former Sponsor in a meeting with the new Sponsor.

Creating a Shared Need
- o What is "Creating a Shared Need"?
  - The reason or need for the change.
    - The need for change must exceed any resistance or inertia in the organization to maintain the status quo.
    - Change can be driven by threat or opportunity.
    - The reasons for change must be compelling not just for leadership but any stakeholder affected by the change.
- o How do you communicate the need?
  - The need can be identified and aligned with the corporate CTQ Drilldown.
    - The CTQ drilldown aligns low level initiatives to the corporate need of satisfying shareholders.
  - The need can also be communicated by using the 3 D's:
    - **Data** = The degree internal/external data sources show the need for change (benchmarking).

- **Demonstration** = The degree that best practices or piloted projects show the need for change.
- **Demand** = The degree which executive leadership simply demand the change to occur.
  - *Depending on the degree of change, "demand" should be used as a last resort due to potential stakeholder resistance.*
- How do you handle opposition or disagreement of the need?
  - "Data" and "Demonstration" are only effective if the arguments are heavily weighted.
  - Use the ABC model to answer the below questions for persuading the opposition:
    - What are the opposing arguments? How does the weight of their arguments compare to yours?
    - What other arguments (e.g., "rewards of acceptance" or "risks of rejection") can be explored?
    - How can your existing arguments be reinforced to give them more evidential weight?

Shaping a Vision
- What is "Shaping a Vision"?
  - Painting the Future or To-Be State after the change.
    - The leadership (especially the Sponsor) must communicate the vision of what the world will be like after the change initiative.
    - Every journey must have a destination or else you risk everyone wandering aimlessly.
  - The vision must be clear, attainable, and widely understood.
    - The end-state should not be described using business results, but behavioral terms, i.e., observable, measurable terms.
    - Define the vision in 1 to 3 sentences; keep it simple and direct (like an elevator speech).
    - The vision should be clearly understood by everyone (avoid having lots of individual visions).
    - Ensure the vision isn't too general or too complex; either can cause confusion.

Mobilizing Commitment
- What is "Mobilizing Commitment"?
  - It's building a strategy to win support from key stakeholders.
    - Springboard off the existing strong sponsorship, the identified need, and the defined vision to rally stakeholder support.
    - The objective is to build momentum so these stakeholders can be the advocate for change that affects their area.
    - If the change hasn't been piloted yet, then identify stakeholders who can be "early adopters" to test the change so you can identify and fix unexpected errors or risks.
- How do you build the strategy to win stakeholder support?
  - First, identify who your key stakeholders are.
    - Use a Stakeholder Analysis to identify all stakeholders and their predicted level of support.
    - For any stakeholder not considered "strongly supportive", identify their source of resistance:
      - *Technical – They fear they lack the skills/resources to support change; it's their nature; fear unknown, etc.*
      - *Political – They fear a loss of power (e.g., influence, resources, authority, etc.); create power struggles, etc.*
      - *Cultural – They fear change ("it's not how we always do things"); old cultural mindset, etc.*
  - Build a plan of what the order will be for communicating the change.
    - Begin with the strongest supporters and target the lowest leadership level before the highest.
      - *Often the highest level of leaders lean on their subordinate leaders input; if you acquire the lower support first, then you can reinforce your message to the higher leaders that the subordinate leaders are already in agreement.*
    - Assign for each stakeholder the team member responsible for communicating the change.
    - Consider exploring why any stakeholders may be against the change.
      - *This may not be necessary, but it can be done using the ABC model to evaluate how you can influence the stakeholders.*

- Validate the strategy with the Sponsor.

Making Change Last

- o What is "Making Change Last"?
  - Integrating the change to the rest of the organization.
    - The prior steps in the CAP model lead up to the change.
    - The remaining steps focus on making the change permanent.
    - This requires transferring knowledge and best practices from the change to other key (and even competing) initiatives.
    - It includes building momentum by celebrating early successes.
  - The change should be "baked in".
    - The change should not be quickly dropped once the organization gets in a pinch.
    - The change should become part of the organization's natural behavior, not a desired behavior.

Monitoring Progress

- o What is "Monitoring Progress"?
  - Measuring the results of the change.
    - "You can't improve what you can't measure."
    - How do you know if the change is successful? Look for clearly defined measurements that reflect the before/after state.
    - The measurements should be real (objective) to ensure the progress is real.
    - Benchmarks and goals should be defined to ensure accountability in measuring the progress.
  - Ensure the measurements have "teeth".
    - It should be a cause for celebration when the measurements reveal the progress is successful.
    - But if the progress lags or declines, then there should be accountability to help turn it around.

Changing Systems and Structures

- o What is "Changing Systems and Structures"?
  - Embedding the change into the organizational structure.
    - The current systems & structure of an organization was designed for the "As-Is" state prior to the change.
    - If these systems & structures aren't included in the change, then they may undo the change and push everyone backwards.
      - *It will make the change look like the "flavor of the month".*
    - The systems & structures of the organization may include:
      - *Human Resource issues (hiring, staffing, training, etc.)*
      - *Management Issues (performance management, rewards/incentives, etc.)*
      - *Communication and Documentation*
      - *Organizational Design*
      - *Information Technology Architecture (security, access, system design, integration, etc.)*
  - Identify how these systems & structures influence the changed behavior.
    - Use a systematic approach to evaluate each system & structure that may directly or indirectly influence the change.
    - Modify all systems & structures that pose as a risk or resistance to the change.
      - *They should be modified to complement and reinforce the change.*

Practical Application

- o Think of a few previous projects you worked on:
  - How much of the "acceptance" piece of Q x A = E contributed to each project's success or failure?
  - In what way could more or better "acceptance" have made the project more successful?
  - What were some of the buy-in obstacles or challenges that were encountered in each project?
    - What could you do differently to prevent or overcome similar challenges in future projects?

Unit 2: Lean

A mix of the most common Lean tools and concepts that are more specifically applied for improving the efficiency of a process.

Lean – Lesson 1: Introduction to Lean

An introduction to Lean including a brief history, the philosophy of Lean, and a summary of some common Lean tools and concepts.

Pre-Requisite Lessons:
- o Intro #02 – Introduction to Lean and Six Sigma

A Brief History of Lean
- o The principles of Lean are themselves a "continuous improvement" throughout history:
    - The modern concepts of Lean can be traced back to Benjamin Franklin's writings about waste, efficiency, and cost savings.
    - Henry Ford credited Ben Franklin as a major influence in his business practices and is credited himself for early adoption of lean principles and proving their value in the manufacturing assembly line.
    - Toyota Production System (TPS) extended the concepts of Lean by drawing more attention to the flow or smoothness of work.
- o Though its principles were used for many decades, the term "Lean" wasn't coined until 1988.
    - It was first used by a MIT student in a Master's thesis which influenced the production of the book *The Machine That Changed The World* (by Jim Womack, Daniel Jones, and Daniel Roos).
- o It quickly grew as a business management philosophy that complemented Six Sigma.

The Philosophy of Lean
- o Lean isn't a methodology, it's a philosophy.
    - It's not like Six Sigma, which is a formal methodology that uses tools to resolve problems.
    - Lean is an informal philosophy or mindset that uses tools to resolve problems.
    - What's the difference?

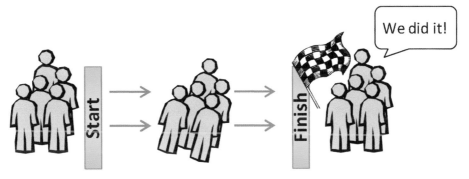

Six Sigma is generally treated as having a definite end where a measureable goal is reached and sustained.

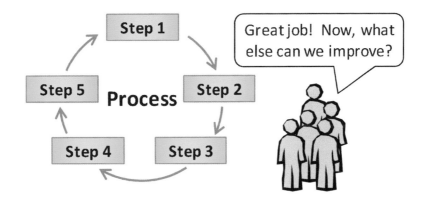

Lean is usually open-ended where each person in a process finds opportunities contributing to *continuous* improvement.

- o Lean primarily focuses on improving a process.
  - What is the purpose of Lean?
    - Improve efficiency/flow in a process.
  - How do we improve the process efficiency/flow?
    - Use tools to identify & eliminate waste.
  - Does this mean Lean won't improve the output?
    - No, the output is dependent on the process, so improving the process may also improve the output.
    - When improving efficiency, the focus is on decreasing time/effort while maintaining the same or better quality/accuracy.

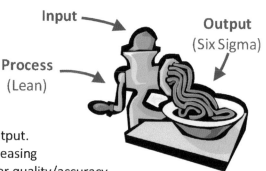

Summary of Lean Concepts & Tools

- o If there's no formal Lean methodology, then how do you find & make improvements?
  - There are many tools & concepts that Lean employs to help improve a process.
  - Below is a list of the most common ones that we'll review in this training:

Lean Concepts	**Lean Tools/Metrics**
•Value-Added vs. Non-Value-Added •One Piece Flow vs. Batch Processing •Kanban or JIT (Pull vs. Push design) •5S Program •7 Deadly Wastes •Poka-yoke	•Spaghetti Diagram •FTY & RTY •Work-in-Process (WIP) •Process Mapping (As Is vs. To Be) •Value Stream Mapping (VSM) •Takt Time

- A broad application of these tools & concepts can be described as:
    - First, the process is evaluated for flow or waste-reduction opportunities using the concepts.
    - Next, the above tools/metrics help measure and implement improvements to that process.
    - A Lean workout (described later) can help sync these tools & concepts into a practical application.
- o Lean tools & concepts work best in a manufacturing environment.
  - Non-manufacturing environments still have processes and can still benefit from Lean.
  - Since manufacturing has tangible products moving along a visible production or assembly line, it's easier to find opportunities for eliminating waste and improving the process flow.

Practical Application

- o Have you already heard of or used some of these Lean tools and concepts?
  - If so, which ones have you had exposure to?
  - What are some positive results or outcomes from that experience?
  - What are some negative results or outcomes from that experience?
  - What could have been done differently (if anything) to have mitigated those negative results?
- o Identify at least 3 different processes that you actively control or participate in.
  - What opportunities for improvement are there in these processes?
    - If you think there are none, then do you believe those processes are "perfect"? If not, then there must be some improvement opportunity, even if it's small. If so, what are some examples?

Lean – Lesson 2: System Flow Methods

An introduction to the Lean concept of system flow methods such as one piece flow, push vs. pull systems, and just-in-time inventory.

Pre-Requisite Lessons:
- None

System Flow Methods
- What is Batch Processing vs. One Piece Flow?
  - Each describes the quantity of product flowing through the production system.
  - Batch Processing occurs when large quantities of products move in unison through a system.
  - One Piece Flow describes a process where each product moves individually through a system.
    - This process helps avoid downstream waste from waiting, overproduction, and excess inventory.
    - One Piece Flow is only effective when the system equipment/operators can sustain the flow.
      - *There is a significant risk of failure when the one-piece flow isn't in balance with the constraint of the equipment or operators involved in the process.*
- What is a push vs. pull system?
  - From the customer or receiver's perspective, it describes how they get the item from upstream.
  - In a push system, the upstream process pushes items downstream w/o balancing to demand.
  - In a pull system, the downstream process pulls items from upstream as they need it.
    - A pull system is more efficient by eliminating overproduction upstream and excess inventory downstream.
- What is JIT (just-in-time inventory)?
  - It's an inventory management method that supports a pull system by filling downstream demand of products just when it's needed.
    - Since it complements a pull system, it helps minimize waste from excess inventory and overproduction.

Practical Application
- What are some examples of batch processing that you work with?
  - How could this batch processing be improved by a one-piece-flow system?
- What are some examples of push systems that you work with?
  - How could these push systems be improved by converting them to a pull system?
  - In what ways could a Just-In-Time inventory system also help improve the flow of these systems?

Lean – Lesson 3: Kanban Systems

An introduction to the Lean concept of improving and monitoring efficiency through visual cues called Kanban systems.

Pre-Requisite Lessons:
  - None

Kanban System

  - What is a kanban system?
    - Japanese term meaning "visual" or "signal".
    - It's a production control system (often used with a JIT system) that uses visual cues to measure, trigger, and control the flow of products at critical junctures within a process.
    - Examples of visual cues that act like a kanban system:
      - Checkout Lanes – Illuminated checkout line numbers are a visual queue to control the flow of the shopping process. They help customers quickly know which line is open and they help managers know when there's a problem (e.g., if the flow has stopped).
      - Barcode Scanning – Most cash registers in checkout lanes are operated by barcode scanners that help control inventory levels and automatic re-ordering of products.
      - Electronic Traffic Signs – In many metropolitan areas, electronic signs are used to post accidents, construction or travel times to help alert drivers and balance the flow of traffic.

Practical Application

  - Identify at least three kanban systems you interact with regularly?
    - Describe the process that is affected by each kanban system.
    - What are the visual cues used in each process?
    - How do these kanban systems make each process more efficient (if at all)?
    - What would be the potential impact or results if each process didn't have those visual cues?

Lean – Lesson 4: Value Added

An introduction to the Lean concept of identifying value-added and non-value-added steps within a process.

Pre-Requisite Lessons:
- None

Value-Added vs. Non-Value-Added

- What does Value Added (VA) vs. Non-Value-Added (NVA) mean?
  - In this context, "value" is defined by that which the customer is willing to pay for.
    - For example, "value" is anything that enhances a product to meet customer requirements.
    - The opposite is "waste" – steps in the process that do not enhance the product to meet customer requirements.
- How can VA & NVA steps be categorized?
  - VA – steps in a process that add value (as defined by customer's requirements).
  - NVA – steps in a process that do not add value.
  - NVA-Required (NVAR) – steps in a process that do not add value to the customer, but are required for the manufacturer. Examples include:
    - Steps that conform to safety or government regulations.
    - Steps that preserve financial integrity (e.g., internal controls, etc.).
    - Steps that prevent future waste (e.g., documentation, audit-trails, etc.).
- What do you do when you find VA steps?
  - Explore opportunities to eliminate waste & defects that touch those VA processes.
    - For example, look for the 7 deadly wastes, add quality & timeliness measurements to the process, etc.
- What do you do when you find NVA steps?
  - For NVAR steps, validate their level of requirement & treat them like VA steps.
  - For NVA steps, eliminate them and plan for how to link the surrounding VA or NVAR steps.
    - Eliminating NVA steps may change the cycle time and takt time; measure the impact and ensure the preceding & subsequent steps can support the change without adding more waste (e.g., WIP or waiting).

Practical Application

- Identify at least three processes you interact with regularly.
  - What are some value-added steps within each process?
    - What criteria did you use to determine which steps are value-added?
  - What are some non-value-added-required steps within each process?
    - What makes these steps required?
    - Is there any opportunity to avoid or streamline this process?
  - What are some non-value-added steps within each process?
    - How should the value-added steps that are before and after the non-valued-steps be properly synced?
    - How would eliminating these non-value-added steps improve the overall process?

Lean – Lesson 5: 7 Deadly Wastes

An introduction to the Lean concept on the 7 deadly forms of waste that can be found within a process.
Pre-Requisite Lessons:
- None

7 Deadly Wastes

- The 7 Deadly Wastes describe the most common types of waste lurking in a process.
  - A good rule of thumb is to start with these potential wastes when looking for opportunities:
    1. TRANSPORTATION
       - Movement of the product to an area that doesn't add value (i.e., enhance it per the customer's requirements) and increases the risk of it being damaged (i.e., a future defect).
    2. INVENTORY
       - Raw materials, work-in-process (WIP) or finished goods that aren't creating income (they represent capital outlay without any immediate return).
    3. MOTION
       - Unnecessary movement of equipment or operator to work on the product (as opposed to Transportation that is movement of the product itself) which increases risk to safety and capital assets.
    4. WAITING
       - Time that the product sits and waits to be processed or transported.
    5. OVER-PRODUCTION (often considered the worst kind of waste)
       - When more product is produced than what the customer requires (often stemming from batch processes). It will usually generate and hide other forms of waste like inventory, waiting, etc.
    6. OVER-PROCESSING
       - Doing more work to a product than is required by the customer. This may also include using complex tools, advanced equipment, or over-experienced operators than what is necessary for the product.
    7. DEFECTS
       - Any product not meeting customer requirements will cause re-work, rescheduling, delays, etc.
- Several other forms of waste have been suggested as the 8th deadly waste.
  - These include unused human talent or having products/services not meeting customer specs.

Practical Application

- Identify at least three processes you interact with regularly.
  - Review each of the 7 deadly wastes in light each of those processes.
    - Which of the 7 deadly wastes do you think may exist in each process?
    - How often do you see each of those deadly wastes occur within each process?
    - What's the potential improvement opportunity if you were to eliminate those deadly wastes?

Lean – Lesson 6: 5S Program

An introduction to the Lean concept of the 5S program and how it can help keep improve and sustain efficiency in a process.

Pre-Requisite Lessons:
- None

5S Program
- What is 5S?
  - They are 5 actions (each beginning with "S") that are used for creating a work environment that exposes waste and errors.
  - The 5S actions are as follows:
    1. SORT (cleaning and organizing a work area)
       - Keep only tools or items that are necessary and in working order (all other items should be removed or stored away).
       - This promotes a safer work environment and eliminates clutter and confusion.
    2. SET in Order (putting everything in their proper place and creating a system to keep it that way)
       - Define and label the location for tools/equipment (e.g., labeling tools, shadows on tool boards, marking shelves, etc.).
       - This promotes efficient and effective retrieval and return of items necessary to get the job done.
    3. SHINE (daily cleaning the work area)
       - Ensure the area remains clean and organized or else it will return to the way it was.
       - While daily cleaning, inspect the tools and equipment to ensure they're in proper working order.
    4. STANDARDIZE (simplify the practices for the new work environment)
       - Define simple, attainable, and consistent instructions to ensure the work area stays in order.
       - This may include "visual management" (e.g., signs, posters, or banners) to remind everyone of the standards.
    5. SUSTAIN (follow-up to ensure sustainability)
       - Use training and visual management to educate about the new work environment standards.
       - Align 5S to the performance measurement for employees to keep them accountable for the new standards.
  - The lack of these 5S actions could be indicative of waste.
  - At a minimum, use 5S to sustain the changes when new/improved processes are implemented.

Practical Application
- Identify at least three processes you interact with regularly.
  - Review each of the 5S actions in light each of those processes.
    - Which of the 5S actions do you think may be missing from each process?
    - What's the potential improvement opportunity if you were to add those 5S actions to each process?

Lean – Lesson 7: Work in Process (WIP)

An introduction to the Lean concept of work in process (WIP) as a form of significant waste within a process.
Pre-Requisite Lessons:
- Lean #05 – 7 Deadly Wastes

Work in Process (WIP)
- What is Work-In-Process (WIP)?
  - A.k.a., work-in-progress, it refers to unfinished items that are still in production.
    - Since they're unfinished, they reflect the least valuable capital because they don't yet meet the customer's requirements (value) and are no longer raw materials (i.e., not re-sellable as raw materials).
    - WIP generally requires additional storage and is often a victim of the 7 deadly wastes (e.g., over-production, waiting, inventory, etc.).
  - WIP should be measured for quality and timeliness.
    - Many production environments add RFID or bar codes to their products to measure & control WIP.
    - For example, shipping tracking numbers are like a way a customer can measure WIP.
      - *For the shipper, it's a way to avoid customer phone calls to inquire about the shipping status or expected delivery date.*

Practical Application
- Identify at least three processes you interact with regularly.
  - What forms of work in process (WIP) exist within the process?
  - How is the WIP measured within each process?
  - What opportunities are there to reduce the WIP?
  - How could the reduction of WIP translate to financial savings?

Lean – Lesson 8: Poka-Yoke

An introduction to the Lean concept of poka-yoke and how it can be used to help sustain process improvements.

Pre-Requisite Lessons:
- None

Poke-Yoke

- What is Poka-yoke?
  - A Japanese term meaning "mistake-proofing".
  - It refers to steps, controls or mechanisms designed to prevent mistakes (potential defects).
    - It implies a method in the process that quickly and easily detects, fixes and prevents errors as they occur.
  - Practical examples of a poka-yoke:
    - Stepping on a vehicle's brake pedal before shifting out of Park (ensures safety).
    - Polarized AC electrical plugs & sockets (the bigger side of a two-prong plug – helps prevent shock hazard).

Practical Application

- Identify at least three processes you interact with regularly.
  - What are some types of poka-yoke that exist in each process?
    - What are the kinds of mistakes or errors that they are trying to prevent?
    - How effective are they at preventing those errors?
  - What other errors in each process could've been prevented if poka-yoke were applied?
    - What measurable impact could be realized if that poka-yoke were implemented?

Lean – Lesson 9: Spaghetti Diagram

An introduction to the Spaghetti Diagram, a Lean tool that helps expose motion and transportation forms of waste.

Pre-Requisite Lessons:
- Lean #05 – 7 Deadly Wastes

Spaghetti Diagram
- What is a Spaghetti Diagram?
  - It visually maps the TRANSPORTATION (path of a product's movement) or MOTION (path of equipment or operator movement) in a process in order to expose potential waste.
    - It is usually used for mapping the paths of movement within a fixed environment like an office floor, a warehouse, between multiple buildings on a campus, etc.
- How do you create a spaghetti diagram?
  - Map the area on a sheet of paper.
    - For example, if it's for a warehouse, be sure to draw (close to scale) any walls, equipment, shelving, etc.
  - Draw the path from beginning to end.
    - Paths must be drawn continuously from the beginning of the flow to its end.
    - Each movement bouncing multiple times between the same location should be individually drawn in order to highlight that overlapping movement.
    - Do not draw through walls, equipment or shelves; draw actual paths taken.
    - Measure time/distance for each path.

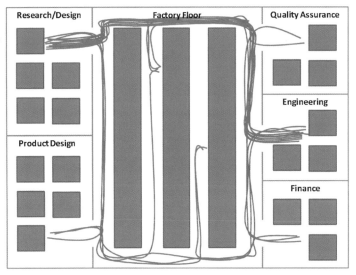

  - Review with your team
    - The team should agree the paths drawn are accurate; any overlapping path is potential waste.
  - Re-draw an ideal state with your team
    - When evaluating an ideal state, compare cost to create that ideal state vs. any efficiency gained from it.

Practical Application
- Identify at least three processes you interact with regularly that may involve motion or transportation types of waste.
  - Draw on a sheet of paper the layout of the areas affected by the process.
    - Follow from beginning to end an item flowing through the process and map out the motion of the people involved in the process.
    - In addition, separately map out the transportation of the item itself through that same process.
  - What areas stand out as having excessive motion or transportation?
    - How can the motion or transportation be minimized in the process?
    - What costs may be involved for streamlining the process?
    - What savings can be expected for streamlining the process?

Lean – Lesson 10: FTY and RTY

An introduction to first time yield (FTY) and rolled throughput yield (RTY) metrics and how they can be used to measure process performance.

Pre-Requisite Lessons:
  - None

FTY and RTY

- What is First Time Yield (FTY)?
    - FTY measures the % of non-defective units successfully output the first time through a process.
        - FTY gap (100% minus FTY) is equal to the potential waste (defects) in the process that can be eliminated.
        - FTY is ideally a measurement of the capability at the sub-process level contributing to the RTY.
        - To adequately measure FTY, the definition of a defect and how to measure it must be predetermined.
- What is Rolled Throughput Yield (RTY)?
    - RTY measures the true yield or capability of a process (generally made up of sub-processes).
    - The RTY calculation is RTY = ($FTY_{ProcessA}$ x $FTY_{ProcessB}$ x $FTY_{ProcessC}$ x $FTY_{ProcessD}$ x etc.)
    - An example of how to calculate RTY:

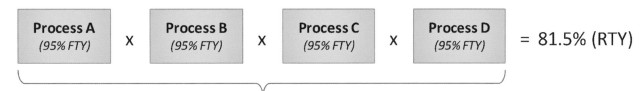

Although the yield for each sub-process is 95% (considered good), the
RTY (reflecting the best possible capability for all sub-processes) is only 81.5%

- RTY can help expose "hidden factories" for processing that could risk defects or delays.
    - The measurement of every sub-process should be rolled up to measure their contribution to the overall process they support.

Practical Application

- Identify at least one process you interact with regularly that has more than one sub-process where each sub-process is being measured.
    - Determine the FTY for each sub-process.
    - Then, calculate the RTY for the entire process.
    - How does this RTY differ from how the entire process was previously measured and evaluated?
    - Which sub-process is making the greatest negative contribution to the RTY?
        - What opportunities are there to improve that particular sub-process?

Lean – Lesson 11: Takt Time

An introduction to the takt time metric and how they can be used to measure process flow.
Pre-Requisite Lessons:
- None

Takt Time

- What is takt time?
  - It's a measurement of the consistent flow required for a process to meet customer demand.
    - "Takt" is the German word for "drum beat"; it implies a consistent flow (or pace) in the process.

$$\text{Takt Time} = \frac{\text{Total available work time per day/shift}}{\text{Total customer demand per day/shift}}$$

  - When calculating takt time, use the lowest reasonable level of units for measuring time (this usually means using a numerator value that exceeds the denominator value).
  - Examples of Takt Time:
    - For a production line that operates 10 hours/day and the customer wants 300 units per day, then takt time would be 2 minutes (10 hrs = 600 min, then 600 min / 300 units = 2 min).
      - *This means each unit should be running through the production line about every 2 minutes (or 240 seconds).*
    - A company that operates 2 production lines 24 hrs/day to meet a customer demand of 5000 units/day, the takt time would be 34.6 seconds (24 hrs x 2 production lines = 48 hrs/day or 2,880 min/day or 172,800 sec/day; divide by 5000 units/day and the takt time is 34.6 seconds).
- What if the customer demand changes?
  - If demand decreases, then takt time will increase (slower process) to meet the demand.
    - It may not be ideal to slow production, so you could also reduce the numerator (staffing or shift hours).
  - If demand increases, then takt time will decrease (faster process) to meet the demand.
    - If the production is maximized to capacity (i.e., can't make it go faster), then look for other potential waste (e.g., setup time) that could help reduce production cycle time or Turnaround Time (TAT).
  - Production load should be balanced by comparing Takt Time to TAT.

Practical Application

- Identify at least one process you interact with regularly is measured in cycle time.
  - Calculate the takt time using the cycle time and volume or customer demand.
  - Now, calculate that same takt time using historical volume or customer demand (e.g., from 3 months ago, 6 months ago or 1 year ago).
  - How has the takt time changed over those time periods?
  - How has the process changed (if at all) to accommodate those changes in takt time?
  - If the takt time has increased (indicating a slower process), how has it affected the production costs impacted by the "slower" process?

Lean – Lesson 12: Value Stream Maps

An introduction to Value Stream Maps, a Lean tool used for tracking various elements within the steps of a process.

Pre-Requisite Lessons:
- Lean #04 – Value Added vs. Non Value Added
- Lean #07 – Work in Process

Value Stream Maps

- What is a value stream map (VSM)?
  - Like a process map, a VSM diagrams the flow of a process.
  - VSMs differ from process maps in these ways:
    - VSMs don't diagram decision points or detailed process steps (which are usually grouped).
    - VSMs focus on the timeliness (efficiency) within the flow of products through the process.
    - They track VA & NVA steps, process cycle times, takt time, inventory, staffing, etc.
    - They generally focus on the overall process (beginning/ending with customer) rather than sub-processes.
  - VSMs are ideal when tracking tangible items through a process.
    - They're ideal for products or transactions, but not variable, intangible items like customer calls.
  - Below is a generic example of a VSM with the various parts identified:

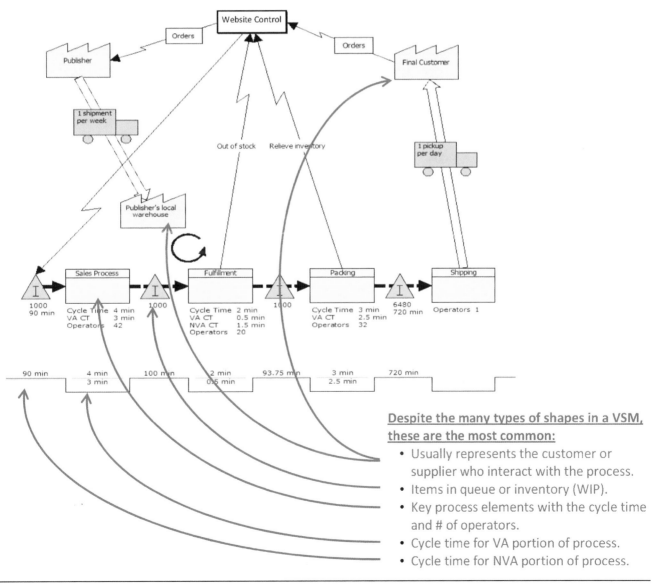

Despite the many types of shapes in a VSM, these are the most common:
- Usually represents the customer or supplier who interact with the process.
- Items in queue or inventory (WIP).
- Key process elements with the cycle time and # of operators.
- Cycle time for VA portion of process.
- Cycle time for NVA portion of process.

Value Stream Maps (Example)

○ Below is an example of a VSM used for processing Travel transactions:

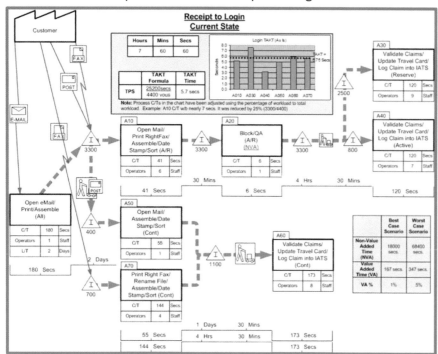

Current (As Is) State Problem:

- Average 4 days to process travel voucher
- 1% of vouchers were misrouted/lost
- 23% of vouchers were duplicates
- 4% of duplicates were paid in error
- Received ~30K calls/mo

VP's Original Solution:

- Add more operators to existing process

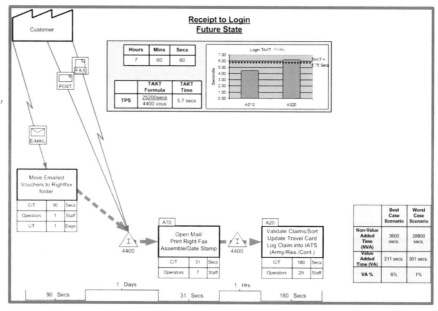

Future (To Be) State Solution:

- Modified process for 13 of the operators
- Significantly reduced wait time, motion, & defects

Results/Benefits:

- Reduced process time from 4 days to 8 hrs
- Reduced wait time from 5+ hrs to less than 1 hr
- Reduced call volume by 25%
- Eliminated duplicate vouchers (via poka-yoke)

Practical Application

○ Identify one process you interact with regularly that has many sub-processes with measurable steps.
- Build a VSM for the process.
    - Track every critical process step and their value-added vs. non-value-added cycle times.
    - Notate any inventory (i.e., WIP) at each process step and the number of operators and the amount of time those operators spend at each process step.
    - Include any additional information that could help in measuring each process step.
- What process steps appear to have the most non-value-added cycle times?
- What process steps appear to have the most inventory or WIP (an indication of a bottle neck)?
- What opportunities are there to streamline the process and how much more efficient could it be?

Lean – Lesson 13: Adapting Lean to Six Sigma DMAIC Flow

A description of how the Lean tools and concepts can be adapted to the Six Sigma DMAIC methodology.

Pre-Requisite Lessons:
- o Six Sigma Overview #01 – Problem Resolution using DMAIC
- o Six Sigma Overview #05 – The DMAIC Roadmap

Adapting Lean to the Six Sigma Methodology

- o Despite the differences between Lean & Six Sigma, Lean can be easily adapted to Six Sigma.
  - Remember, the DMAIC steps in Six Sigma follows the basic 5 steps for problem resolution.
  - Lean also resolves problems and can therefore follow the same 5 steps similar to DMAIC:

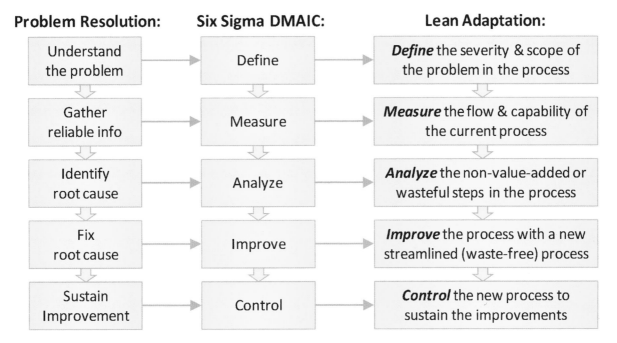

Lean Tools in the DMAIC Method

- o Following are the tools/concepts that may be used at each problem resolution stage:
  - Note: the Define phase is virtually identical to what would be used for a Six Sigma project.

	Question Levels 1 to 2	Tool/Resource
Define	**Do you fully understand the severity and scope of the problem?**	
	Can you clearly define the problem and its potential impact to the organization?	CTQ Drilldown, Problem Statement, Project Scope, Project Financial Savings, Pre-Assessment (Min/Max Analysis)
	Do you have a team that agrees with the project focus?	Stakeholder Analysis (ARMI), Buy-In/Sponsorship (CAP model)
	Do you understand the high-level process related to the problem?	High-level Process Map, SIPOC
	Do you have a method for communicating the project information?	Project Charter, Project Storyboard
	OUTPUTS: Project Storyboard, Charter, CTQ Drilldown, ARMI, SIPOC, High-Level Process Map, and Benefits Pre-Assessment.	

	Question Levels 1 to 2	Tool/Resource
Measure	**Do you understand the flow and capability for the current process?**	
	Do you know what time/cost metric reflects the output described by the problem statement?	Takt Time, First Time Yield (FTY), Rolled Throughput Yield (RTY)
	Have you identified all potential input>process>output opportunities according to the flow, accuracy and timeliness perspectives?	IPO-FAT Model
	Have you mapped out the flow of the As-Is process including sub-processes leading to (inputs) and coming from (outputs) the target process?	Detailed Process Map, Value Stream Map (VSM)
	Do you know if your process maps and collected data are accurate, repeatable and reproducible?	Measurement System Analysis (MSA)
	OUTPUTS: Updated Project Storyboard, As-Is Process Map, As-Is Value Stream Map (VSM).	

Analyze	**Do you know what are the non-value-added or wasteful steps in the process?**	
	Have you reviewed the process map(s) to identify all Non-Value-Added (NVA) & Value-Added (VA) steps?	7 Deadly Wastes, VA & NVA steps, Work-in-Process (WIP), Spaghetti Diagram
	Have you identified any steps in the process where 5S is not used?	5S Program
	Have you identified any push flows or batch processing in the process?	Push vs. Pull, Batch Processing vs. One-Piece Flow
	If enough data is available, have you applied statistical tools to measure the input, flow and output of sub-processes that could reveal additional areas of waste?	Six Sigma Hypothesis Testing
	OUTPUTS: Updated Project Storyboard, identification of all VA and NVA process steps.	

Improve	**Do you have a new streamlined process design that will resolve the process problem?**	
	Have you mapped out the flow of a new To-Be process including sub-processes leading to (inputs) and coming from (outputs) the target process?	Detailed Process Map, Value Stream Map (VSM)
	Do you know the level of rewards (value) and risk expected from the new To-Be process?	Impact Matrix (PICK chart), FMEA
	Did you pilot the new To-Be process and get successful results?	Pilot/Implementation Plan, Pilot Duration, Scorecard, MSA
	OUTPUTS: Updated Project Storyboard, To-Be Process Map or VSM, data/charts (e.g., scorecard) validating success of the pilot.	

Control	**Does the new process resolve the original problem and will it be sustained?**	
	Did you implement the new To-Be process?	FMEA, Pilot/Implementation Plan, Scorecard, MSA
	Did you optimize the new To-Be process with controls and visual queues?	5S Program, Kanban System, Poke-Yoke
	Are the improvements successfully meeting expected results (sustained and in control)?	Control Charts
	Did you fully transfer control and responsibility of the improvements to the process owner?	SOPs, Control Plan
	Does the team (including the Sponsor & Champion) agree the project is complete?	Project Closure, Sponsorship
	OUTPUTS: Updated final project storyboard, control plan, SOP, agreement from entire team that the project is complete.	

Practical Application

- For the processes you interact with regularly, which ones may be ideal for improvement?
  - Try exploring the potential opportunities for each process by reviewing them with the tools and concepts as described in the adaptive DMAIC methodology.

Lean – Lesson 14: Leading a Lean Workout (Kaizen Event)

A review of how to improve a process by leading a Lean workout (a.k.a. Kaizen Event).

Pre-Requisite Lessons:
- Lean #02 – #12 – Multiple lessons on various Lean tools
- Six Sigma Improve #09 – Piloting Solutions: Build the Pilot Plan

Introduction to the Lean Workout
- What is a Lean workout?
  - It is an extended meeting that focuses on improving processes using Lean tools and concepts.
    - The workout can last between 1 to 5 days, depending on the scale and complexity of the process.
  - A workout will allow you to use many of the Lean tools & concepts in one setting.
    - The workout is often referred to as a "Kaizen Event"; "Kaizen" is the Japanese term for "improvement".
      - *Kaizen is usually referred to as the philosophy of continuous improvement. A Kaizen Event is usually a concentrated effort by all process stakeholders to improve a process during a short time (e.g., in one week).*
  - The workout should include all stakeholders who are critical to the process.
  - The goal of the workout is to design an improved process with an implementation plan.
    - The implementation plan details the actions, owners and due dates to implement the improved process.
- What is the overall process for a Lean Workout?
  - Below are the basic steps for a Lean workout outlined using the IPO model:

How to Lead a Lean Workout
- INPUT to Workout
  - #1 - Define Problem & Scope
    - The first step is to build <u>before the workout</u> a project charter that everyone agrees to.
      - *A project charter should include a problem statement, scope, team/stakeholders, and expected benefits.*
      - *The Sponsor/Champion should agree with the project charter and can help identify the stakeholders to include.*
      - *It will help save time in the workout if all the workout participants review and agree to the project charter ahead of time.*
    - The meeting should be scheduled and include all team members (ideally not more than 10).
      - *The meeting duration depends on the complexity and scale of the process being reviewed.*
      - *Simple and small processes may be done in one day; more complex processes with many stakeholders may take 5 days.*
      - *It's always better to over-estimate the workout duration and end it early than vice-versa.*
      - *Be sure the Sponsor/Champion agree to dedicate the stakeholder resources for the duration of the workout.*
- PROCESS During Workout
  - Meeting Kick-Off
    - The Sponsor/Champion should start the meeting and return at the end to review the results.

- The Sponsor/Champion should reinforce the need for the workout and team commitment.
- #2 – Build As-Is Process Map or VSM
  - The As-Is process map is extremely critical to the success of the workout.
    - *The team may be unfamiliar with process mapping; it may help to include an ice-breaker to explain how to build it.*
    - *This may require the longest time during the workout, but it's essential that it be accurate and agreed to by the team.*
  - This As-Is mapping process may require dividing the team to build sub-processes.
    - *For complex processes, try dividing into sub-teams to build the maps for sub-processes and later out-brief to everyone.*
  - Which do you build: Process Map or VSM?
    - *Build a process map if you're trying to improve quality/accuracy in the process including communication & hand-offs.*
    - *Build a VSM if you're trying to improve cycle-times/efficiency in the process or if it involves more tangible items.*
    - *If you're not sure which to use, start with a process map and build a VSM if the need arises.*
- #3 – Identify and Measure Waste
  - Identify VA vs. NVA steps in the As-Is map.
    - *Notate each step as either value-added (VA), non-value-added (NVA) or non-value-added-required (NVAR).*
  - Review the As-Is map with the 7 deadly wastes.
    - *For each type of waste, walk through the entire As-Is map and ask for each process step if that waste exists.*
  - Notate within the process map each type of waste identified.
    - *Use different colored post-its or stickers to flag each type of waste (e.g., all "motion" waste gets a red sticker, etc.).*
    - *If possible, notate the relative ease of measuring each identified waste (e.g., use "H" for wastes with "High" probability of measuring, "M" for medium probability, and "L" for low probability).*
    - *Be sure to add to a "Parking Lot" any potential waste identified that is out of scope for the project.*
  - Try other Lean tools (like a spaghetti diagram) to find more waste.
  - Select the process steps having the greatest potential of waste noted.
    - *For multiple processes having a lot of waste, focus first on those having more "H" probabilities and so on.*
  - Measure the potential wastes identified for each process step.
    - *If focusing on efficiency (timeliness), calculate cycle times, wait time, VA time, NVA time, overall takt time, etc.*
    - *If focusing on effectiveness (accuracy), calculate FTY, overall RTY, WIP, etc.*
  - Eliminate any overlapping measured waste.
    - *If one opportunity causes multiple forms of waste, be sure the measurements of the waste are not duplicated.*
  - Normalize all measured waste.
    - *When calculating waste for each process step, be sure calculation methods and values (e.g., dollars, minutes/seconds, etc.) are consistent across all process steps.*
- #4 – Build To-Be Process Map or VSM
  - With the waste identified and measured in the As-Is map, the To-Be map should be easy to build.

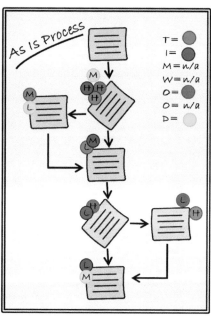

- Begin by preserving the As-Is map and use it as a guide to start building the To-Be map.
  - *The As-Is map should not be modified; take a picture of it or transfer its content online using Visio or PowerPoint.*
  - *Flow through the As-Is map from beginning to end and replicate the process steps for the To-Be map.*
- Eliminate each NVA process step and be sure the preceding & subsequent steps can be linked.
- For each VA process step that has waste identified, discuss how the waste can be removed.
  - *The process step may need to be treated as a sub-process to completely evaluate how the waste can be removed.*
- Once all the steps are rebuilt on the To-Be map, identify any unnecessary cross-functional waste.
  - *This is where swimlanes or a spaghetti diagram may help identify any motion across different areas or operators.*
  - *In such cases, explore the necessity of that motion and new ways to reduce or eliminate it.*
- Apply other Lean tools/concepts to the To-Be map (e.g., 5S, kanban system, poka-yoke, etc.)
- Review the entire flow in the To-Be map to ensure it's logical and still meets the customer's requirements.
  - *Be sure to review the map with any stakeholders who aren't in the workout but may be affected by the new process.*

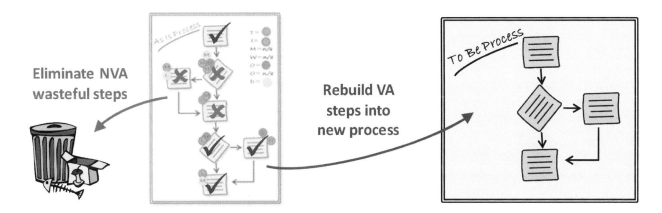

o OUTPUT From Workout
  - #5 – Build Implementation Plan
    - The steps for building an Implementation Plan (or Pilot Plan) are covered in more detail in the Improve lesson #9 on "Piloting Solutions: Build the Pilot Plan".
      - *The steps below briefly outline the critical points necessary for building the implementation plan in a Lean workout.*
    - Compare the As-Is and To-Be maps to each other and identify the critical gaps between the 2 processes.
      - *Notate each gap as an action to be added to the implementation plan.*
      - *It's OK if one major gap needs to be identified as multiple, unique actions.*
    - For each gap/action, identify the sub-actions necessary to make that action occur.
      - *For example, sub-actions may include communication, documentation, system changes, training, visual displays, etc.*
    - For each sub-action, identify any pre-requisite sub-actions, the priority level, action owner & due date.
      - *This is extremely critical to ensure the entire team understands the plan and their responsibility in implementing it.*

- Review the Implementation Plan with the Sponsor/Champion and any other stakeholders of the process.

Improvements noted as actions   **Sub-actions & pre-requisite actions**   **Priority of each sub-action**   **Owners & Due Dates**

		Action Description	Prereq	Priority	Biz Area	Owner	CT	Due
		Action 1: Load flat file into Retail System						
1	A	Determine if rates (calc'd from codes & pricing model) can be loaded into department system from a flat file; may require "lying" to the system to make formulas work	N/A	High	Finance	Jones	N/A	7/18
		Action 2: Get LOE from IT to add values to Corporate System						
2	A	Submit work request & get IT LOE hours needed to update to accommodate new code designations	N/A	High	Pricing	Smith	10d	9/3
	B	Define % thresholds for bucket determination	2A	High	Pricing	Smith	16d	9/3
	C	Update Retail system to accommodate all 11 code designations	2B	High	IT	TBD	350h	TBD
	D	Update Corporate system to accommodate 11 code designations (part of action 5F)	2B	High	IT	TBD	420h	TBD
	E	Determine rates for each bucket	2C, 2D	High	Finance	Jones	25d	9/12
	F	Create flat files to be loaded into each system	2E	High	Pricing	Brooks	10d	10/14
	G	Communicate bucket concept to L&P folks	2F	Medium	Pricing	Brooks	2d	TBD

Practical Application

- For the processes you interact with regularly, which ones are relatively small and in your control and may be ideal for improvement?
  - Try following these Lean workout steps for your own process under your control.
    - This will get you comfortable to the process for the Lean workout to see how it works.
- For other processes that are larger in scale and over which you don't have full control, which ones may be ideal for improvement?
  - Try investigating these further to see if a Lean workout may help in streamlining the process.
    - Who would be the Sponsor for the effort? Will that Sponsor allow you to lead a Lean workout?
    - Talk to the Sponsor about getting his/her support for letting you lead a Lean workout.
    - Then, follow the remaining steps for planning and leading the workout.

Unit 3: Six Sigma Overview

A general overview of tools and concepts that apply to Six Sigma projects, especially those using the DMAIC methodology.

Six Sigma Overview – Lesson 1: Problem Resolution using DMAIC

A review of how the DMAIC methodology follows the typical steps we follow when trying to resolve a problem.

Pre-Requisite Lessons:
- Introductory #02 – Introduction to Lean and Six Sigma
- Introductory #03 – Lean and Six Sigma Project Methodologies

Six Sigma is Problem Resolution

- Six Sigma is best known as a formal methodology for resolving problems.
  - Practically, it's a way we can increase confidence (lower risk) for critical business decisions.
- Six Sigma methodology is built on the 5 basic steps of problem resolution:

- Let's review an example using the problem resolution steps.
  - Scenario: Doctor diagnoses and cures Matt's daughter Hannah.
  - Based on this scenario, let's explore the following:
    - What are the various roles and how do they apply to Six Sigma?
    - How does the problem resolution method apply to the Six Sigma methodology of DMAIC?

Applying the Problem Resolution Method

- Roles in Scenario:
  - Hannah   = The business or process itself
  - Dad/Mom   = Sponsor and/or Champion
  - Doctor   = Six Sigma Black Belt
- Method in Scenario:

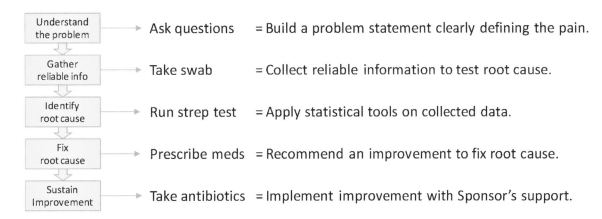

Translating Problem Resolution to Six Sigma

- o How does the problem resolution method compare to Six Sigma?
  - DMAIC is an acronym representing 5 phases for problem resolution using Six Sigma tools.

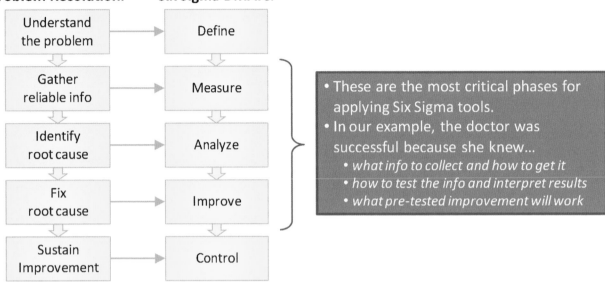

Problem Resolution: → **Six Sigma DMAIC:**

Problem Resolution	Six Sigma DMAIC
Understand the problem	Define
Gather reliable info	Measure
Identify root cause	Analyze
Fix root cause	Improve
Sustain Improvement	Control

- These are the most critical phases for applying Six Sigma tools.
- In our example, the doctor was successful because she knew…
  - *what info to collect and how to get it*
  - *how to test the info and interpret results*
  - *what pre-tested improvement will work*

- o What if the root cause and improvement are unknown?
  - The doctor relied on prior analysis & testing to know the right root cause & improvement.
  - Six Sigma focuses on this analysis & testing when the root cause & improvement are unknown.

Practical Application

- o Think of at least 3 different problems you recently resolved (either at home or work)?
  - For each of those problems, try to answer the following:
    - Define phase (understand the problem):
      - *How would you define the problem?*
      - *What information helped you assess the size and severity of the problem?*
    - Measure phase (gather reliable information):
      - *What information did you collect in order to assess or measure the problem?*
      - *What assumptions did you make about the information you collected?*
      - *What if the information or your assumptions was wrong? How would that have affected the situation?*
    - Analyze phase (identify root cause):
      - *Did you determine what was the root cause?*
      - *How did you differentiate between a possible symptom and the actual root cause?*
      - *What information helped you confirm what was the root cause?*
    - Improve phase (fix root cause):
      - *What improvement did you make to fix the root cause?*
      - *Did you test the improvement to ensure it would truly fix the root cause?*
      - *What would have been the outcome if you implemented the improvement but found it didn't fix the root cause?*
    - Control phase (sustain improvement):
      - *Has the root cause recurred? If so, why?*
      - *What measurements or controls have you put into place to prevent that root cause from recurring?*

Six Sigma Overview – Lesson 2: Risk Analysis – The Reason We Use Statistics

A review of the importance of risk in decision-making and how statistics can be used to measure that risk.

Pre-Requisite Lessons:

- Six Sigma-Overview #01 – Problem Resolution using DMAIC

The Effects of Risk

- Risk affects every decision we make!
    - Would you drive your car if you knew there was a high risk it would break down?
    - Would you eat at a restaurant that you knew had a high risk of food poisoning?
    - Remember Hannah's strep throat? There could have been risks in finding & fixing the root cause.
- Prudent business decisions should assess and measure risk.
    - Let's use an example of a glass of water…

The entire glass represents our available understanding for making decisions

The empty portion (air) represents assumptions (risk)

The filled portion (water) represents data (confidence)

Just as adding water displaces air, adding data displaces our assumptions.

- Risk has an inverse relationship with confidence.
    - Data (i.e., proof, evidence, etc.) builds confidence; the lack of data (i.e., assumptions) creates risk.
- To reduce risk and build confidence, get data!
    - Nearly all statistical tests measure risk (typically reflected as the P value).

Methods for Gathering Data

- The overall goal of statistics is to use a sample to make inferences about a population.

For example, what if I want to know how many red jelly beans there are in a jar?

There are two general methods to answer this….

Method 1:	Method 2:
Empty out all the jelly beans and manually count all the red ones	Take out a small portion of jelly beans, count the red ones and multiply by the proportional volume in the jar
Pro: More *Accurate*	**Pro**: Less *Time*
Con: More *Time*	**Con**: Less *Accurate*

- Method 2 uses the concept of statistics where a small portion (sample) is used to make an estimate (inference) across an entire group (population). But is Method 2 better?

3 SS: Overview

Risks, Rewards and Constraints

- Is Method 2 better? Maybe – it depends on RISK.
- Evaluate the CONS for each method; these represent their risk:
  - Method 1 CON: How much more time will it take to manually count the red jelly beans?
  - Method 2 CON: How accurate do I have to be in my estimate of the red jelly beans?
- Compare the risks and rewards.
  - RISK: Time vs. Accuracy – which is more important?
  - REWARD: Which method would you choose if the prize was...
    - A T-Shirt
    - $100
    - $1,000,000
- Consider the constraints.
  - What if you were only given 1 minute to answer?
  - What if the jar was 10 ft tall?
  - What if you weren't given access to the entire jar?
- How does Six Sigma deal with risk, rewards and constraints?
  - Understanding the VOC helps us understand any constraints and balance risks with rewards.
  - Statistical tools are designed to analyze data and evaluate the levels of risk.
  - The goal is not to eliminate risk; the goal is to answer...

> ## *How can I __minimize risk__ and __maximize rewards__ within the constraints?*

Understanding Our Assumptions

- It's very rare in life to have an opportunity to analyze a population.
  - Measuring data across a population is always ideal, but not always practical.
  - We rely on statistics for elections, market analysis, employee performance, etc.
- Prudent data analysis requires understanding our assumptions.
  - We assume our sample of jelly beans represents the population.
    - What if our sample only includes 10 jelly beans?
    - How big should our sample be to ensure it represents the population?
    - How do we know our method for collecting the sample is correct and random?
  - We assume we know the volume of the jar.
  - We assume the jelly beans in the jar are evenly mixed by color (random).
  - What's the risk if we don't consider these assumptions before we collect our sample?
    - We may be making very wrong conclusions leading to very wrong actions.
- Assumptions are a primary form of risk.
  - When we validate our assumptions, we're reducing risk and increasing our confidence.

Practical Application

- Have you ever said to yourself "If I only knew then what I know now"?
  - This phrase generally infers a previous situation when we made a wrong or uninformed decision.
  - Think of at least 2 situations like that in your personal or work life.
    - For each of those situations, try to answer the following:
      - *What information would've helped me make a different/better decision in that situation?*
      - *How could I have acquired that critical information in that situation, if at all?*
      - *If I were in that similar situation today (with the same limited knowledge), would I do anything differently in my decision process?*
        - *If not, then why not?*
        - *Or if so, then what is different in my decision process?*
    - Based on your answers above, what does this reveal about how you balance risk vs. reward in your decision process? (E.g., are you more prone to make quick, "risky" decisions?)

Six Sigma Overview – Lesson 3: Overview of Statistical Terms and Concepts

A high-level review of the fundamental terms and concepts associated with statistics, such as population vs. sample data, distributions, etc.

Pre-Requisite Lessons:
- None

Population vs. Sample
- What is a population?
  - Represents every possible observation. It is ideal but very rare to get and often unnecessary.
- What is a sample?
  - A subset of the population that is generally a fair representation of the population.
  - An adequate sample can allow someone to make inferences about the population.
  - The difference between the conclusions from the sample vs. reality in the population is _RISK_.

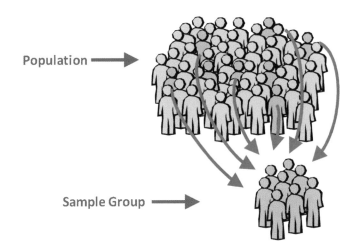

Population

Sample Group

Risk: Does this sample represent the population fairly?

Distributions
- We expect most things in life to be random and have a normal distribution (bell curve).
  - For example, measuring the age of employees or the temperature in different rooms.

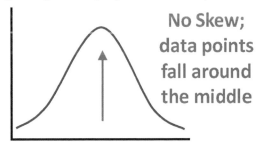

No Skew; data points fall around the middle

- If something is not normally distributed, we tend to think it's skewed (has bias).
  - For example, the age of employees in entry-level positions is probably lower than management positions. Or the temperature in network server rooms may be lower due to high-tech equip.

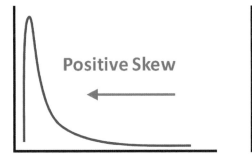

Positive Skew

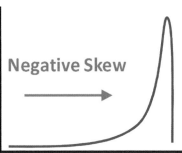

Negative Skew

Central Tendency
- Central tendency explains where on a scale most of the data points are centered.
  - The type of distribution (normal vs. non-normal) affects the central tendency we use.
- For Normal distributions, the AVERAGE (Mean) is the central tendency.
  - Normal distributions don't include outliers that could move the average.
  - For example, what is the age of people in an office building?
    - We assume the people will mostly be employees and/or customers and is therefore a normal distribution.
- For Non-Normal distributions, the MEDIAN (50th percentile) is the central tendency.
  - Non-Normal distributions include outliers which don't affect the percentile.
  - For example, what is the age of people in an office building on "bring your child to work" day?
    - Since children would be included, then it could skew the results and shift the average.
    - How could you reduce the risk of this kind of bias in your data collection?
      - *Use the median or limit your sample to just employees.*

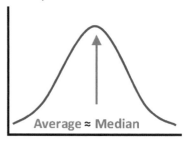
Average ≈ Median

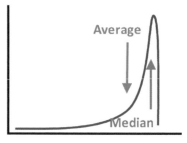
Average
Median

Variation
- Variation measures how data is spread around the central tendency (mean/median).
  - For two processes of throwing darts, which process would you prefer to have?

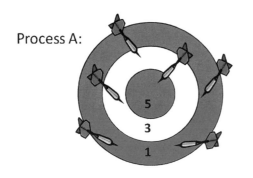
Process A:

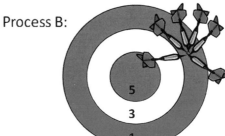
Process B:

  - Process A yields a higher score, but Process B is more consistent & predictable (less variation).
- Variation reflects where we have less control and where we feel the most pain.
  - The degree of variation affects the degree of difficulty to correct/fix.
  - The degree of predictability affects the degree of control and comfort.
    - Thermostat calibration – consistently 3 degrees too low is easier to control than inconsistently high & low.
    - Prices at discount stores – the slogan "Always low prices...Always" implies consistency in low prices.
- Standard Deviation is represented by the Greek lowercase letter σ (sigma).
  - Standard Deviation measures variation around the mean (for normal distributions).
  - Inter-quartile Range (IQR) and Stability Factor measure variation around the median.

Defects and Sigma Levels

- ○ Defects are anything outside the customer's requirements (Voice of Customer or VOC).
  - • Customer requirements are tolerances defined as lower or upper spec limits (LSL or USL).
    - ▪ Anything beyond the LSL or USL (the customer's requirements) is considered a defect.

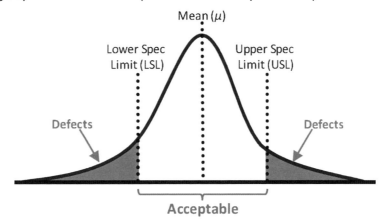

- ○ A sigma level measures the # of standard deviations between the mean and LSL/USL.
  - • Sigma level also measures quality/accuracy as the defects per million opportunities (DPMO).
    - ▪ One Sigma = 690,000 defects per 1 million opportunities (or 31% accurate)
    - ▪ Two Sigma = 308,537 defects per 1 million opportunities (or 69.2% accurate)
    - ▪ Three Sigma = 66,807 defects per 1 million opportunities (or 93.3% accurate)
    - ▪ Four Sigma = 6,210 defects per 1 million opportunities (or 99.38% accurate)
    - ▪ Five Sigma = 233 defects per 1 million opportunities (or 99.98% accurate)
    - ▪ Six Sigma = 3.4 defects per 1 million opportunities (or 99.9997% accurate)

Comparing Sigma Levels

- ○ 3 Sigma at 93.3% may sound good enough, so why bother pushing for Six Sigma?
  - • Remember, it all depends on the amount of RISK the customer is willing to take.

3 Sigma	6 Sigma
20,000 wrong drug prescriptions per year	25 wrong drug prescriptions per year
500 incorrect surgical operations per week	One incorrect surgical operation every 2 weeks

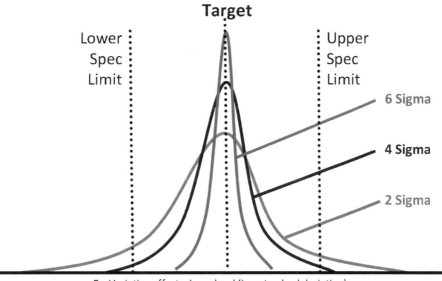

Ex. Variation affects sigma level (i.e., standard deviation)

Practical Application

- What are the most critical metrics used by your organization?
  - Which of those metrics are based on sample data vs. population data?
    - For those based on sample data, how confident are you that the sampled results reflect the population?
    - What are you basing your confidence on? Is there a way to prove it with data?
      - *It's okay if you're not sure how to prove it with data; that's what we'll go over as we learn more about statistical analysis.*
  - Which of those metrics are measures of central tendency?
    - What is the measurement used for central tendency (i.e., mean or median)?
  - Which of those metrics are measures of spread or variation?
    - Very few organizations use variation as a critical metric. If yours doesn't, then what risks could there be by not measuring variation?

Six Sigma Overview – Lesson 4: Transfer Function

A review of the transfer function and the critical part it plays as a fundamental concept in the DMAIC methodology.

Pre-Requisite Lessons:
- o Introduction #01 – Introduction to Lean and Six Sigma

Using Data Analysis to Build a Transfer Function
- o Why do we need data analysis?
  - Remember, the goal of Lean Six Sigma is to improve a process's...
    - Effectiveness (improving the quality or accuracy of the outputs coming from the process)
    - Efficiency (improving time, effort or cost of the process itself)
  - To do that, we must understand what changes will improve the process.
  - To do that, we must understand what controls the process.
    - The control of a process is expressed through a transfer function that we build through data analysis.
- o What is the transfer function?

$$Y = f(X) \quad \text{or} \quad Y = f(X_1, X_2, X_3...)$$

- Depicted as $Y = f(X)$, it's described as "output response Y is a function of one or more input X's".
  - It applies an equation to the IPO flow model by describing the relationship between various independent input factors (X's) and how they influence a dependent output response (Y).

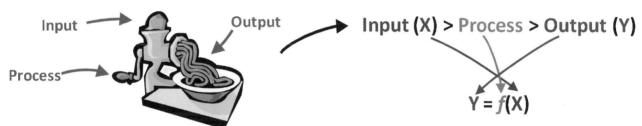

Input Output

Process

Input (X) > Process > Output (Y)

$Y = f(X)$

Importance of Transfer Function
- o Why is the Transfer Function so important?
  - The transfer function is like a control panel for a process: the more you can understand the levers and input controls, the more you can control and improve the output.
    - Think of the picture settings for a TV.
      - *The transfer function would be: TV Display = f(color, brightness, tint)*
    - Another example is a stereo equalizer.
      - *The transfer function would be: Sound Quality = f(bass, mid, treble)*
  - Transfer functions often have coefficients (a multiplier for each factor).
    - For example, in the equation [250 = 4A + 2B + 10], what are the coefficients and how do they relate to each other?
- o The transfer function is a pivotal step in the Six Sigma DMAIC methodology.
  - Once you can build a transfer function, you can more easily identify, fix & control the root causes.
- o Example: Why is our monthly fuel expense going up?
  - Build Transfer Function:
    - Fuel Expense = f(Fuel Price, Engine Size, Vehicle Weight, Driving Speed, Driving Habits, Tire Inflation, etc.)
  - Questions:
    - Which factor has the greatest influence on fuel expense? (large coefficient)
    - Which factor has the least influence on fuel expense? (small coefficient)

- Which factor(s) can you control and how much control do you have over them?
- If one factor changes significantly, how would that affect the other factors? (interdependencies)

Practical Application

o Identify 3 of the top metrics used by your organization and answer the following:
- What are all the potential factors (i.e., inputs or Xs) that influence the metric?
- Which factor do you think has the greatest influence on the metric?
- Which factor do you think has the least influence on the metric?
- Which factor(s) can you control? How much control do you have over them?
- If one factor changes significantly, how would that affect the other factors, if at all?

Six Sigma Overview – Lesson 5: DMAIC Roadmap (Levels 1 & 2)

An introduction to the DMAIC roadmap that identifies critical steps and tools for navigating a project through the DMAIC methodology.

Pre-Requisite Lessons:
- Six Sigma Overview #01 – Problem Resolution using DMAIC

DMAIC Roadmap (Level 1)
- Below is how problem resolution steps apply to the DMAIC project methodology.
  - Each phase of DMAIC has a high-level question that can be answered:

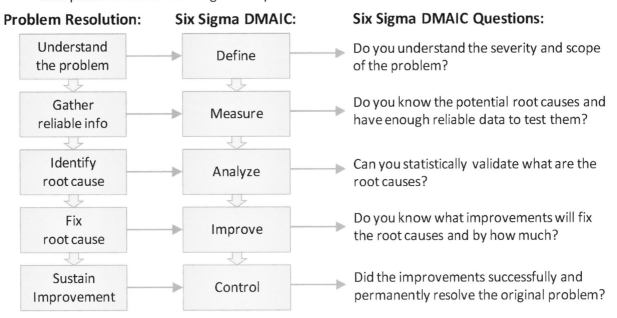

Problem Resolution:	Six Sigma DMAIC:	Six Sigma DMAIC Questions:
Understand the problem	Define	Do you understand the severity and scope of the problem?
Gather reliable info	Measure	Do you know the potential root causes and have enough reliable data to test them?
Identify root cause	Analyze	Can you statistically validate what are the root causes?
Fix root cause	Improve	Do you know what improvements will fix the root causes and by how much?
Sustain Improvement	Control	Did the improvements successfully and permanently resolve the original problem?

DMAIC Roadmap (Level 2)
- The DMAIC roadmap can be followed in detail by asking 3 or 4 questions per phase.
  - The recommended tools/resources are identified that may help answer those questions.

	Question Levels 1 to 2	Tool/Resource
Define	**Do you fully understand the severity and scope of the problem?**	
	Can you clearly define the problem and its potential impact to the organization?	CTQ Drilldown, Problem Statement, Project Scope, Project Financial Savings, Pre-Assessment (Min/Max Analysis)
	Do you have a team that agrees with the project focus?	Stakeholder Analysis (ARMI), Buy-In/Sponsorship (CAP model)
	Do you understand the high-level process related to the problem?	High-level Process Map, SIPOC
	Do you have a method for communicating the project information?	Project Charter, Project Storyboard
	OUTPUTS: Project Storyboard, Charter, CTQ Drilldown, ARMI, SIPOC, High-Level Process Map, and Benefits Pre-Assessment.	

	Question Levels 1 to 2	Tool/Resource
Measure	**Do you know the potential root causes (inputs or Xs) and have enough reliable data to test them?**	
	Do you know what metric reflects the output described by the problem statement?	Project Y (output)
	Do you know how to define defects in the process and/or outputs?	Voice of Customer (VOC), Operational Definitions
	Do you have enough data measuring the Y and potential inputs (Xs)?	C&E Diagram, 5 Whys, C&E Matrix, Data Collection Plan (DCP), Sample Size Calculator, Short/Long Term Data
	Do you know if your collected data is accurate, repeatable and reproducible?	Measurement System Analysis (MSA)
	OUTPUTS: Updated Project Storyboard, Definition of the VOC, Y & Xs, and a reliable and relatively complete dataset.	

	Question Levels 1 to 2	Tool/Resource
Analyze	**Can you statistically validate what are the root causes (inputs or Xs)?**	
	Do you know what the process capability is (a.k.a. Voice of Process or VOP)?	Descriptive Statistics, I-MR chart, Normality Plot (AD test), Process Capability (with six pack)
	Do you know what the target sigma level or performance objectives are for the project?	Performance Objectives
	Have you done hypothesis testing to identify which potential Xs are statistically significant?	Hypothesis Testing
	OUTPUTS: Updated Project Storyboard, key process capability metrics, and hypothesis testing results.	

	Question Levels 1 to 2	Tool/Resource
Improve	**Do you know what improvements will fix the root causes (inputs or Xs) and by how much?**	
	Do you know which potential Xs are independent and statistically significant?	Compiling Statistical Test Results, Transfer Function
	Do you know what improvements can be made to fix the root causes (inputs or Xs)?	Brainstorming Solutions, Impact Matrix (PICK chart), FMEA
	Did you pilot the improvements and get successful results?	Pilot/Implementation Plan, Pilot Duration, Scorecard, MSA
	OUTPUTS: Updated Project Storyboard, list of improvements, data/charts (e.g., scorecard) validating success of the pilot.	

	Question Levels 1 to 2	Tool/Resource
Control	**Did the improvements successfully and permanently resolve the original problem?**	
	Did you implement the improvements?	FMEA, Pilot/Implementation Plan, Scorecard, MSA
	Are the improvements successfully meeting expected results (sustained and in control)?	Control Charts
	Did you fully transfer control and responsibility of the improvements to the process owner?	SOPs, Control Plan
	Does the team (including the Sponsor & Champion) agree the project is complete?	Project Closure, Sponsorship
	OUTPUTS: Updated final project storyboard, control plan, SOP, agreement from entire team that the project is complete.	

Practical Application

- Identify at least 2 projects you led or worked on in the past.
  - For each project, review all the questions in the DMAIC roadmap.
    - What questions and related tools/resources were not addressed in the project?
    - Why were they not addressed?
    - What different outcome or results could've been realized if they were addressed in the project?

Unit 4: Six Sigma Define Phase

The most common tools and concepts that pertain to the Define phase of the DMAIC methodology of Six Sigma which is intended to help us understand the problem we're trying to solve.

Six Sigma-Define – Lesson 1: Define Phase Roadmap (Level 3)

A deeper look into level 3 of the DMAIC roadmap that identifies critical steps and tools for navigating a project through the Define phase.

Pre-Requisite Lessons:

- Six Sigma Overview #05 – DMAIC Roadmap (Levels 1 & 2)

DMAIC Roadmap (Level 1)

- This topic reviewed here was originally covered on page 91.

DMAIC Roadmap (Level 2)

- This topic reviewed here was originally covered on page 91.

Define Phase Roadmap (Level 3)

- The DMAIC roadmap can be drilled down even deeper to a 3rd level for each phase.
  - Level 3 questions can guide someone to the specific tool(s) for navigating a project or initiative.

Phase	Question Levels 1 to 3	Tool/Resource
Define	**Do you fully understand the severity and scope of the problem?**	
	Can you clearly define the problem and its potential impact to the organization?	
	Can you align the problem to a corporate CTQ?	CTQ Drilldown
	Can you clearly & succinctly define the pain point being felt in the organization?	Problem Statement
	Do you have a clear and reasonable scope for focusing the project?	Project Scope
	Do you know what are the potential project benefits for the project?	Project Financial Savings
	Are the minimum (worst case) and/or maximum (best case) potential benefits worth continuing with the project?	Pre-Assessment (e.g. a Min/Max Analysis)
	Do you have a team that agrees with the project focus?	
	Do you know who is on the team and what role they all play?	Stakeholder Analysis (ARMI)
	Does each person on the team agree with the problem definition and scope?	Buy-in/Sponsorship (CAP model)
	Do you understand the high-level process related to the problem?	
	Do you know what the primary steps are within the process and the inputs that feed into it?	High-level Process Map
	Do you know who the suppliers & customers are for the process?	SIPOC
	Do you have a method for communicating the project information?	
	Do you have a project charter?	Project Charter
	Do you have a project storyboard?	Project Storyboard
	OUTPUTS: Project Storyboard, Project Charter, CTQ Drilldown, ARMI, SIPOC, High-Level Process Map, and Project Benefits Pre-Assessment	

Practical Application

- Identify at least 2 projects you led or worked on in the past.
  - For each project, review all the questions in the Define phase level 3 roadmap.
    - What questions and related tools/resources were not addressed in the project?
    - Why were they not addressed?
    - What different outcome or results could've been realized if they were addressed in the project?

Six Sigma-Define – Lesson 2: Building a Problem Statement

A review of what a problem statement and background statement are and the characteristics of an ideal problem statement.

Pre-Requisite Lessons:
- o Introduction #01 – Introduction to Lean and Six Sigma
- o Introduction #04 – Corporate CTQ Drilldown

Problem Statement Defined
- o What is a problem statement?
  - It's a clear and succinct description of the problem being solved by the project.
- o What is the purpose of the problem statement?
  - To briefly define the symptoms behind the critical pain-point in the business.
  - To validate the need of the project (i.e., it answers "why are we working on this project?").
  - To remind and unify the team around why they are part of the project.
- o What should an ideal problem statement include or exclude?

Includes ————————————
- Explain *how* it is a problem *(e.g., use measurements)*
- Explain *why* it is a problem *(e.g., sizing or tie to CTQ)*
- Explain any key assumptions *(e.g., cite previous studies)*
- Include only info/data relevant to the problem

Excludes ————————————
- Defining the root cause
- Planning the project strategy
- Proposing the solution
- Identifying risks

- o A problem statement should only be about 3 sentences or less.
- o If more context is needed, consider adding a Background Statement.
  - Background statements help explain the affected business area (e.g., including magnitude of business area, standard metrics/goals, high-level processes, organizational structure, etc.).
  - Background statements should also be 3 sentences or less.
  - Background statements should only contain contextual information that is relevant to the project.

Building a Problem Statement
- o How do you build an ideal problem statement?
  - Use the following resources when building a problem statement:

Resource	How it can help
CTQ Drilldown	Aligns the "pain-point" to the overall business needs
Reports (metrics & goals)	Identifies performance gaps
Assumptions	Reveals (often unrealistic) performance expectations
Risks	Identifies urgency or uncovers potential benefits
Team	Clarifies all of the above

- o After writing the problem statement, ask yourself the following questions:
  - If you answer "Yes" to any question, then the problem statement should be adjusted accordingly.

Examples of Problem Statements
- o Example 1: Doctor visit
  - What is a typical problem statement you'd give to a doctor?
  - What are the critical elements the doctor wants?
  - Does the doctor want your opinion or your online research findings?
- o Example 2: "Houston, we have a problem statement." (Apollo 13 movie clip)
  - What is their problem statement?

- The Lunar Module doesn't have enough CO_2 filters and the only other filters available are a different shape and won't fit the same hole. As a result, the CO_2 levels are quickly rising to toxic levels.
  - What is their background statement (if any)?
    - Could describe the mission, the problems that caused them to be in the Lunar Module longer than expected, the difference in the filter cartridge shapes, etc.
- Example 3: Customer Satisfaction (CSAT) scores between two sales regions
  - Scenario: Executive asks why one sales region has much worse CSAT scores than a similar region.
  - What questions would you ask to build the problem statement? Some examples include...
    - What are the similarities and differences between the two sales regions?
    - What are the historical CSAT scores and trends for both sales regions?
    - How is the CSAT data collected, scored and calculated?
    - What is the financial impact (if any) for having the lower CSAT score and how is that calculated?

Practical Application
- Identify at least 3 projects or issues you have worked in your organization.
  - What is the problem statement for each? (Create one if one doesn't already exist.)
  - For each problem statement, ask yourself the six questions to test it:
    - Does it include any info not relevant to the problem?
    - Does it propose a solution?
    - Does it include or imply any assumptions?
    - Does it describe the analysis strategy?
    - Does it not fully explain the severity of the symptoms?
    - Does it presume what the root cause is?
  - If you answered "Yes" to any of the above six questions, then how would you change your problem statement?

Six Sigma-Define – Lesson 3: Defining a Project Scope

A review of what a project scope is, the value it adds to a project, and how to define it.

Pre-Requisite Lessons:

  o Six Sigma-Define #02 – Building a Problem Statement

Project Scope Defined

  o What is the project scope?
    • The scope defines the boundaries of the project.
      ▪ It describes what the project *should* focus on (Includes) and *shouldn't* focus on (Excludes).
      ▪ Like on a rifle, the scope helps you aim at the target to ensure you hit it.
  o What is the purpose of the project scope?
    • To remind and unify the team around what specific problem they're trying to fix.
    • To keep the project at a manageable level (not too big or small).
    • To prevent the project from drifting in the wrong direction and focusing on the wrong target.
  o How do you define the scope?
    • Always start with the project Sponsor!
      ▪ When meeting with the Sponsor to define the problem, ask what they want in or out of scope.
    • Verify the scope with rest of the team.
      ▪ The team can probably provide more details as to what's included or excluded from the project.
    • The Scope should complement the Background and Problem Statements.
      ▪ Use the Background and Problem statements to prompt other questions that could help narrow or expand the project scope.
    • Validate the final scope with the Sponsor and the entire team.

Sizing the Project Scope

  o What is the right size for a project scope?
    • The project scope can often influence the duration of the entire project.
      ▪ A scope that is too big can make the project take too long (can easily lose momentum).
      ▪ A scope that is too small can make the project finish too quickly (results may seem irrelevant).
    • Aim for a scope that can get the project done in 3 to 6 months.
      ▪ Be careful; projects often take 50% longer than the original estimate.
      ▪ The findings in the project pre-assessment may reveal an ideal level of scope for the project.
    • Gauge the project scope by the resources needed.
      ▪ If you need many different resources from many different areas, then the scope may be too big.
      ▪ If the you're the only one needed to accomplish the entire project, then the scope may be too small.
    • It's easier to expand the scope than to shrink it.
      ▪ If you're in doubt about the scope, then suggest to the Sponsor about starting small and expand outward, as needed.
    • Look for logical groups or divisions in the business area.
      ▪ A project can be scoped down to certain groups the business already uses for reporting (e.g., locations, customer type, etc.).
  o How do I handle or avoid "scope creep"?
    • Requests for expanding the scope are not uncommon.
      ▪ Use the project charter to remind anyone of the original scope.
    • Remember: Scope Affects Risk!
      ▪ Increasing project scope can increase the risk of project failure.
      ▪ Validate all scope changes with the team (especially the Sponsor).

Don't "boil the ocean"

Practical Application

  o Identify at least 3 projects or issues you have worked in your organization.

- What were the parameters defined for each one?
  - What items (e.g., customer types, regions, locations, timeframes, departments, etc.) were specifically included and excluded for the project?
- Did those parameters (the scope) change before the project ended? If so, then...
  - Why did the scope change?
  - Was it a necessary change? (i.e., was it for the better?)
    - *If not, then who allowed the change and why was it allowed?*
  - What affect did the change have on the overall project? (i.e., did it delay the project, cost more money/resources, increase the risk level, etc.?)
  - What could've been done differently at the beginning of the project to have anticipated the scope change and accounted for it much sooner?

Six Sigma-Define – Lesson 4: Building a Project Team

A review of how to build a project team and stakeholder analysis using the ARMI tool.

Pre-Requisite Lessons:
- Introduction #08 – Key Roles in a Lean Six Sigma Project
- Introduction #12 – CAP Model

Building a Project Team

- How do I build a project team?
  - Begin with a top-down approach.
    - When reviewing the project with each level (from the top-down), be sure to ask who the next layer of team members will be.
  - Talk to each person on the team.
    - Visit with them 1 on 1 to find out:
      - *Do they agree with the problem statement?*
      - *Do they agree with the scope?*
      - *Do they agree with who else is on the team?*
      - *What is their level of experience/expertise with the problem?*
      - *Who are the other potential stakeholders for the project?*
    - Be sure to probe them if they answer "No" to any question.
      - *You may find other team members feel the same way - it may change the entire direction of the project.*
  - Resolve any team conflict immediately.
    - It's not uncommon for a Process Owner or SMEs to have conflicting opinions about the project's direction.
    - If there's disagreement on a major point in the project (e.g., priority of the problem/project, scope, etc.), then get it resolved quickly! Don't ignore it!
      - *Some team members may not tell you about their disagreement or lack of support, but their behavior may indicate it (e.g., won't return calls/emails, late for meetings, many negative comments, indifference, etc.).*
      - *These people are not "bad apples"; they can often become your greatest advocate. Listen to their perspective and consider elevating their concerns to the team (without making them appear like a naysayer).*
- Building a project team takes time, but it's well worth the investment.
  - Having the right team should give you confidence you'll find the right solutions more quickly.
  - If the project is well scoped, the team size should be between 5 to 10 people.

Stakeholder Analysis (ARMI) Defined

- What is a Stakeholder Analysis?
  - It's a tool to help evaluate who the project stakeholders are and their level of support.
- What does ARMI mean?
  - It refers to the 4 different levels assigned to each stakeholder in the analysis. They are...

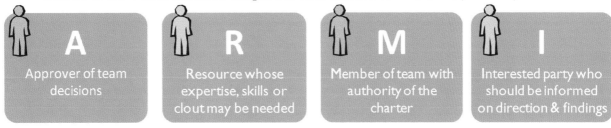

A	R	M	I
Approver of team decisions	Resource whose expertise, skills or clout may be needed	Member of team with authority of the charter	Interested party who should be informed on direction & findings

- What is the purpose of a Stakeholder Analysis?
  - To understand all the different business areas affected by the project.

- To identify potential gaps or conflicts in the level of support by the stakeholders.
- To help plan what stakeholders to talk to and how to talk to them to increase their support.
  o The Stakeholder Analysis (ARMI) helps identify any risk of acceptance.
    - The goal is not to get a perfectly accurate or agreed upon assessment of each person's support.
    - The goal is to identify any perceived or potential gaps in each person's support.
      ▪ Each gap represents a risk of "Acceptance" ($Q \times A = E$).
      ▪ How can we improve the gaps to gain stronger support for the project and help ensure its success?

Stakeholder Analysis (ARMI) Example

  o Below is an example of a Stakeholder Analysis (ARMI):

	Stakeholders	Title/Influence	Project Phase					Stakeholder Analysis
			Define	Measure	Analyze	Improve	Control	
Core Team	Mickey Mouse	Black Belt (Project Leader)	M	M	M	M	M	Strongly Supportive
	Minnie Mouse	Sponsor	A	A	A	A	A	Strongly Supportive
	Goofy	Champion	A	A	A	A	A	Strongly Supportive
	Pluto	Process Owner	M	M	M	M	M	Moderately Supportive
	Daisy Duck	SME 1	M	M	M	M	M	Low Support
	Donald Duck	SME 2	M	M	M	M	M	Moderately Supportive
Stakeholders	Buzz Lightyear	VP, Sales (Stakeholder)	I	I	I	I	I	Moderately Supportive
	Woody	VP, Pricing (Stakeholder)	I	I	I	I	I	Moderately Supportive
	Hamm	VP, Marketing (Stakeholder)	I	I	I	I	I	Low Support
	Rex	VP, Training (Stakeholder)				I	I	Moderately Supportive
	Mr Potato Head	VP, Customer Service (Stakeholder)	I	I	I	I	I	Strongly Supportive
Add'l Support	Mike Wazowski	Director, Business Development			I	R	R	Moderately Supportive
	James P Sullivan	Master Black Belt (Mentor)	I	I	I	I	I	Strongly Supportive
	Mr Waternoose	Manager, Pricing	I	I	I	I	I	Moderately Supportive
	Celia	Director, Sales	I	I	I	I	I	Low Support
	Randall	Manager, Customer Service				R	R	TBD
	Roz	Business Analyst (Reporting)	I	R	R	R	R	Moderately Supportive
	Phlegm Bile	Data Analyst	I	R	R	R	R	TBD

Legend:
A = Approval of team decisions outside their charter
R = Resource to the team; one whose expertise, skills or clout may be needed on an ad hoc basis
M = Member of team with the authority and boundaries of the charter
I = Interested party, one who will need to be kept informed on direction and findings, if later support is needed

Building a Stakeholder Analysis (ARMI)

  o How do you build the Stakeholder Analysis (ARMI)?
    1. Identify all the core team members, outside stakeholders, and any additional support needed.
    2. For each person, identify the type of support each may contribute for each project phase.
    3. Estimate the level of support each person may have toward the entire project.
    4. Review the analysis with the team to get their feedback.
    5. For any stakeholder with less than strong support, discuss with the team how to improve it.
      ▪ Evaluate the level of risk each person may contribute to the project and prioritize them.

Stakeholders	Title/Influence	Define	Measure	Analyze	Improve	Control	Stakeholder Analysis
Core Team							
Mickey Mouse	Black Belt (Project Leader)	M	M	M	M	M	Strongly Supportive
Minnie Mouse	Sponsor	A	A	A	A	A	Strongly Supportive
Goofy	Champion	A	A	A	A	A	Strongly Supportive
Pluto	Process Owner	M	M	M	M	M	Moderately Supportive
Daisy Duck	SME 1	M	M	M	M	M	Low Support
Donald Duck	SME 2	M	M	M	M	M	Moderately Supportive
Stakeholders							
Buzz Lightyear	VP, Sales (Stakeholder)	I	I	I	I	I	Moderately Supportive
Woody	VP, Pricing (Stakeholder)	I	I	I	I	I	Moderately Supportive
Hamm	VP, Marketing (Stakeholder)	I	I	I	I	I	Low Support
Rex	VP, Training (Stakeholder)				I	I	Moderately Supportive
Mr Potato Head	VP, Customer Service (Stakeholder)	I	I	I	I	I	Strongly Supportive
Add'l Support							
Mike Wazowski	Director, Business Development			I	R	R	Moderately Supportive
James P Sullivan	Master Black Belt (Mentor)	I	I	I	I	I	Strongly Supportive
Mr Waternoose	Manager, Pricing	I	I	I	I	I	Moderately Supportive
Celia	Director, Sales	I	I	I	I	I	Low Support
Randall	Manager, Customer Service				R	R	TBD
Roz	Business Analyst (Reporting)	I	R	R	R	R	Moderately Supportive
Phlegm Bile	Data Analyst	I	R	R	R	R	TBD

As core team members, these represent the biggest risk. Start with Daisy, then Donald & Pluto.

As executive stakeholders, these are the next biggest risk. Start with Hamm, then the others.

As additional support, these represent the least risk. Start with Celia; and consider contacting the others as needed.

Practical Application

o Think of 2 project teams you were part of (personally or at work) and answer the following questions:
- Were the roles and expectations clearly defined for each team?
  - If not, then what impact did this cause? (i.e., confusion, political battles, lack of participation, etc.)
- Was there anyone that had low support at the beginning of the project?
  - If so, then how did the project leader (or others) handle this?
  - Did the support from that person improve by the end of the project?
    – If so, then what do you think influenced it the change?
- Was there anyone that started with high support but later decreased to low support?
  - If so, then how did the project leader (or others) handle this?
  - What do you think influenced the change in their level of support?
- What would you do differently in building a team that could prevent some problems that you may have experienced in the other project teams?

SS: Define

Six Sigma-Define – Lesson 5: Building a SIPOC

A review of how to extend the IPO flow model by building a SIPOC.

Pre-Requisite Lessons:

- o Introduction #02 – Introduction to Lean and Six Sigma
- o Six Sigma-Overview #01 – Problem Resolution using DMAIC

IPO, SIPOC & Process Maps

- o Remember, our goal for the Define phase is to understand the problem.
  - This can be done by understanding the business processes where the problem exists.
  - To do that, we can use the IPO, SIPOC and Process Mapping tools:

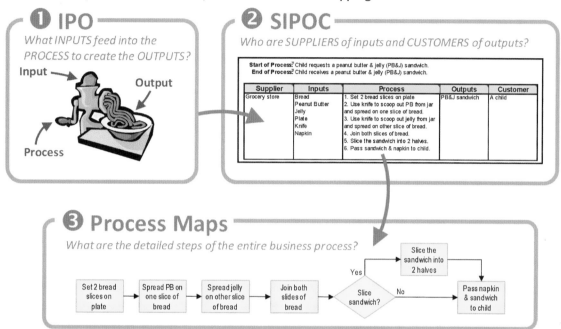

SIPOC Defined

- o What is a SIPOC?
  - A SIPOC extends the Input>Process>Output (IPO) by identifying the Supplier (S) providing the inputs and the Customer (C) receiving the outputs.
- o What is the purpose of a SIPOC?
  - To identify the required inputs and all possible sources providing those inputs.
  - To identify the high-level, critical steps in the business process.
  - To identify the ultimate customer or receiver of the outputs created by the process.
  - To understand the relationship for the entire process from the Supplier to the Customer.
- o Below is an example of a SIPOC:
  - The example below explores the process for building a peanut butter & jelly sandwich:

Start of Process: Child requests a peanut butter & jelly (PB&J) sandwich.
End of Process: Child receives a peanut butter & jelly (PB&J) sandwich.

Supplier	Inputs	Process	Outputs	Customer
Grocery store	Bread Peanut Butter Jelly Plate Knife Napkin	1. Set 2 bread slices on plate 2. Use knife to scoop out PB from jar and spread on one slice of bread. 3. Use knife to scoop out jelly from jar and spread on other slice of bread. 4. Join both slices of bread. 5. Slice the sandwich into 2 halves. 6. Pass sandwich & napkin to child.	PB&J sandwich	A child

Building a SIPOC

o How do you build a SIPOC?
- Gather the team to build it together.
  - The SIPOC should be the collaborative product by the team; it should not be created by just one person.
- Define the start and end of the process.
  - These must be clearly defined first in order to set the boundaries & context for the elements in the SIPOC.
- Fill in each column of the SIPOC by using one of two methods:
  - SIPOC – Begin with the Supplier and continue to the right until you complete the Customer.
  - COPIS – Begin with the Customer and continue to the left until you complete the Supplier.
    - *This reverse method can be very effective when trying to first understand the customer and their output expectations.*
- Identify the requirements for the Inputs and Outputs.
  - Input Requirements – what is the criteria for an acceptable (non-defect) INPUT to feed into the process?
  - Output Requirements – what is the criteria for an acceptable (non-defect) OUTPUT created by the process?

Start of Process: What is the starting point of the process?
End of Process: What is the stopping point of the process?

Supplier	Inputs	Process	Outputs	Customer
Who provides the info, resources or materials used in the process?	What are the info, resources or materials needed for this process? Requirements: What is the criteria for an "acceptable" input?	START... What are the high-level steps that transform the inputs into a desired output? ...STOP	What is the output from the process that the customer is willing to pay for? Requirements: What does the customer expect of the output (Voice of Customer or VOC)?	Who is benefiting from or willing to pay for the output?

Practical Application

o Think of 2 processes (personally or at work) that you deal with regularly:
- For the first process build a SIPOC using the questions below:
  - Start of Process: What is the starting point of the process?
  - End of Process: What is the stopping point of the process?
  - Supplier: Who provides the info, resources, or materials used in the process?
  - Inputs: What are the info, resources, or materials needed for this process?
    - *Input Requirements: What is the criteria for an "acceptable" input?*
  - Process: What are the high-level steps that transform the inputs into a desired output?
  - Outputs: What is the output from the process that the customer is willing to pay for?
    - *Output Requirements: What does the customer expect of the output (Voice of Customer or VOC)?*
  - Customer: Who is benefiting from or willing to pay for the output?
- For the second process build a COPIS (use the above SIPOC questions in reverse order).
- Which method was easier to follow: the SIPOC or COPIS? Why?

Six Sigma-Define – Lesson 6: Building a Process Map

A review of how to extend the IPO flow model and SIPOC by building a process map.

Pre-Requisite Lessons:
  o Six Sigma-Define #05 – Building a SIPOC

IPO, SIPOC & Process Maps
  o This topic reviewed here was originally covered on page 105.

Process Maps Defined
  o What is a process map?
    • It visually diagrams the flow of an entire process across critical steps & decision points.
      ▪ It can be reflected at a high-level or detailed level that should be determined by the team.
      ▪ For the Define phase of DMAIC, a high-level process map is generally all that is needed.
    • They can reflect just one sub-process or can inter-connect multiple sub-processes.
    • Below is an example of a simple, high-level process map for making a sandwich:

  o What are the different parts of a process map?
    • Process maps can either be very simple or extremely complex.
      ▪ This training module will only focus on a few components and a simple format for process maps that are most often used for Lean and Six Sigma initiatives.
    • Below are the most common shapes used in process maps:

•A unique & critical *action*.	•A critical *requirement*.	•Identifies the beginning or end of a process flow.	•Connects shapes to show how the process flows.
•Text begins with a verb.	•Text is a question having only 2 or 3 answers (e.g., Yes/No).	•Only 1 arrow going in (ending) or coming out (beginning).	•Each arrow should only have one head.
•Has 1 arrow going in & coming out from it.	•Has 1 arrow going in & 2 or 3 (1 per answer) coming out.		

Swimlanes Defined
  o What are swimlanes?
    • They display who (in different functional areas) executes the process steps or decisions.
      ▪ The process steps are drawn within the swimlane that performs the process.
      ▪ The arrows that illustrate the flow of the process cross between the swimlanes to reflect hand-offs.
    • They are also known as "functional bands".
      ▪ This is the term used in Microsoft Visio.
    • Swimlanes can be drawn vertically (as columns) or horizontally (as rows).
      ▪ Either format is acceptable; use the format best suited for displaying the process map.
      ▪ For example, if printing the process map on paper, a vertical map maximizes the space on the page. But if displaying in PowerPoint or on the computer, a horizontal map is better at maximizing the space.

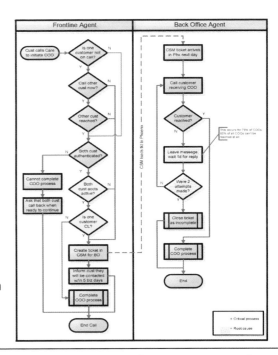

High-Level vs. Detailed Process Maps

- o What is a high-level process map?
  - They generally summarize only the very critical steps in a process.
    - They are not intended to show the intricate details of each process.
  - The process steps are often the same as those in the "process" column of the SIPOC.
    - The process is generally limited to 4 to 10 steps.
    - Very few (if any) decision points are included in a high-level process map.
    - Terminator shapes and swimlanes are not typically used for high-level process maps.
  - Below is an example of a high-level process map.
    - This has a little more detail focusing on the "make sandwich" step in the process map displayed earlier:

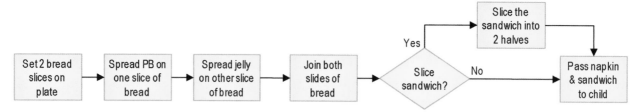

- o How does this differ from a detailed process map?
  - The level of detail in a process map can vary; it should be determined by the team.
    - The level of detail should be based on the presumed level of knowledge/experience of the reader.
    - Most detailed process maps assume the audience has some basic knowledge about the mapped process.
    - When mapping processes for building computer systems, there should be no assumed knowledge – all intricate details of every action and requirement should be clearly defined in the process map.
  - At a minimum, all critical requirements (reflected as decision points) should be included.
    - This can help you evaluate each step to identify any non-value-added steps or requirements.
    - Detailed process maps are often necessary for defining As-Is & To-Be maps in Lean workouts.

Practical Application

- o Refer to the two processes for which you built a SIPOC and COPIS in the prior pre-requisite lesson.
  - For each of those processes, take the steps defined in the "Process" portion and build a process map from them.
    - Be sure to include a starting and ending terminator shape.
    - Integrate the input and output requirements from the SIPOC as decision points in the process map. Be sure that each decision point has at least two labeled arrows exiting from the shape.
    - Be sure that all arrows are correctly flowing through the entire process without any premature stops or unresolved loops.
    - Be sure to separate the process steps into swimlanes, if applicable.
  - Are there any duplicate process steps or loops within the process?
    - If so, try to reorganize the flow of the process to avoid duplication (this is acceptable as long as it still accurately reflects the flow of the process).

Six Sigma-Define – Lesson 7: Compiling Operational Definitions

A review of what operational definitions are and how to compile them for a project.

Pre-Requisite Lessons:
- None

Operational Definitions Defined
- What are operational definitions?
  - A list of definitions for key terms and acronyms used in a particular business area.
- What is the purpose of tracking operational definitions?
  - It unifies the discussion for the team when working through the project.
  - It prevents confusion and reveals potential assumptions about the business area & processes.
  - It helps people who are new or unfamiliar with the business area to be quickly acclimated.
- How do you build a list of operational definitions?
  - Listen for and write down any unique terms, codes or acronyms used by the team.
  - Notate the definitions for each or ask a key SME on the team for their definition.
  - Compile the definitions in a list and send it to the team for their approval.
  - Update the list whenever you encounter new terms throughout the duration of the project.
- Are operational definitions required?
  - No, not if there are very few terms or the scale of the project is small.
  - It's especially helpful if you are new to the business area that's sponsoring the project.
- How do you communicate the operational definitions?
  - They can be included as an appendix to the project storyboard.
  - They can be tracked in a separate file that is sent to and reviewed by the team members.

Practical Application
- Try writing down at least 20 different operational definitions for your organization.
  - Be sure to include all forms of acronyms that may be used to describe metrics, departments, common phrases in your industry, etc.
  - For any metrics, be sure to clearly define the equation and sources of data (if possible) used to calculate those metrics.

SS: Define

Six Sigma-Define – Lesson 8: Setting Project Milestones

A review of how to set milestones for a typical Six Sigma DMAIC project.

Pre-Requisite Lessons:
- None

Setting Project Milestones

- What are the project milestones?
  - They refer to the future dates when each phase of the project is expected to be complete.
- What is the purpose of the project milestones?
  - To give the project Sponsor an expectation of the project's progress and completion.
  - To help the team understand and plan for their expected level of commitment over time.
  - To help maintain a high sense of urgency for all team members.

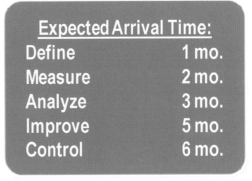

- What milestones should I set for each phase of the project?
  - Since every project is different, every set of milestones may be different.
  - A general guideline is to estimate 1 month for each phase except 2 months for Improve phase.
    - Improve phase is given more time to allow for coordination of piloting and implementing improvements.
    - Be sure to adjust the milestones for holidays and vacation time for key team members.
  - If the project is expected to take longer than 6 months, then consider scoping it down.
    - Likewise, if the Sponsor or team expect it to go much faster, then it may need to be scoped down.
- Be sure the team agrees with the original milestones and any changes.
  - The milestones should be closely managed to ensure the project isn't delayed.
    - If you finish a phase early, don't adjust the milestones; you may need the extra time in a later phase.
    - Don't push out the milestones too often; being late for a milestone may help motivate the team.

Practical Application

- How are milestones usually treated for your organization?
  - Are they strictly enforced for every project, or are they unexpected or loosely followed?
    - How does the leadership in your organization handle situations when milestones are not met?
    - How do they define their own milestones? Do they use "hard", specific dates or only "soft", general dates (e.g., rather than projecting a milestone for an exact day, it's described for a month, quarter, or season)?
- How do you generally handle milestones?
  - Do you set them voluntarily, or only when you're asked or expected to set them?
  - How successful have you been at meeting your milestones?
    - If you're less than 80% successful, then what can you do differently to improve your success?

Six Sigma-Define – Lesson 9: Building a Project Charter

A review of how to compile the various Define Phase tools for building a project charter for a typical Six Sigma DMAIC project.

Pre-Requisite Lessons:
- o Six Sigma-Define #02 – Building a Problem Statement
- o Six Sigma-Define #03 – Defining the Project Scope
- o Six Sigma-Define #04 – Building a Project Team

Project Charter Defined
- o What is a project charter?
    - • It's typically a one-page document summarizing the answers to the Define phase questions.
- o What is the purpose of the project charter?
    - • To validate the need for the project and the team who will be leading it.
    - • To acquire and sustain Sponsor approval for the project .
- o What elements should or shouldn't be in a project charter?

Question Asked	How It's Answered	Include in Charter?
What is the background context for the business area?	Background Statement	As needed
What are the symptoms (pain-points) being felt by the business area?	Problem Statement	Required
What is included or excluded?	Project Scope	Required
What are the potential benefits?	Pre-assessment of savings	As needed
How does the problem align to the business?	CTQ Drilldown	As needed
Who is on the team?	List of core team members	Required
What is the plan for attacking the problem?	Project Strategy	As needed
What is the process for the targeted area?	SIPOC and/or Process Map	No (add to appendix)
What are the key terms used in the business?	Operational Definitions	No (add to appendix)

- • Some organizations require more elements for the project charter (e.g., project Y, Finance Leader, pre-assessment details like DPU or DPMO, etc.). Keep it simple for your audience.

Project Charter Examples
- o Below are some examples of project charters:

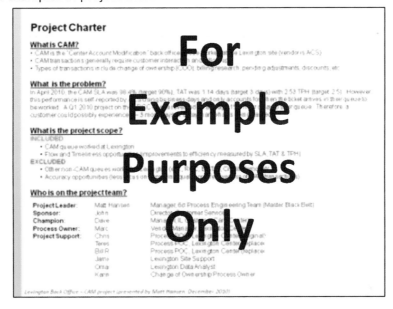

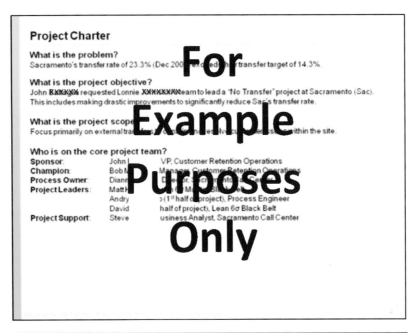

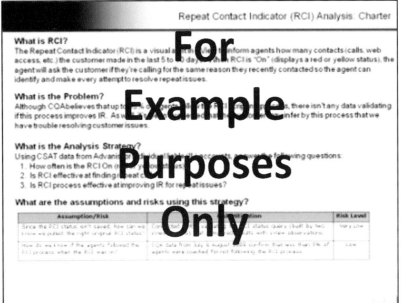

Practical Application

o Identify at least 2 prior projects or issues you've worked in your organization.
  • For each project or issue, build a project charter.
    ▪ Be sure to include the most critical elements such as the problem statement, scope, and team.
    ▪ Consider including a background statement, description of expected financial savings, project strategy, or how the project aligns to the business CTQs (i.e., critical to quality items on the CTQ Drilldown).
  • Review your project charter and eliminate any unnecessary or irrelevant content.
    ▪ If you or your team had a charter like these before beginning the project, how would it have affected the outcome of the project (e.g., faster execution, faster team buy-in, improved communication, etc.)?

Unit 5: Six Sigma Measure Phase

The most common tools and concepts that pertain to the Measure phase of the DMAIC methodology of Six Sigma which is intended to help us ensure we're gathering reliable data for the problem we're trying to solve.

Six Sigma-Measure – Lesson 1: Measure Phase Roadmap (Level 3)

A deeper look into level 3 of the DMAIC roadmap that identifies critical steps and tools for navigating a project through the Measure phase.

Pre-Requisite Lessons:

- Six Sigma Overview #05 – DMAIC Roadmap (Levels 1 & 2)

DMAIC Roadmap (Level 1)

- This topic reviewed here was originally covered on page 91.

DMAIC Roadmap (Level 2)

- This topic reviewed here was originally covered on page 91.

Measure Phase Roadmap (Level 3)

- The DMAIC roadmap can be drilled down even deeper to a 3rd level for each phase.
  - Level 3 questions can guide someone to the specific tool(s) for navigating a project or initiative.

Phase	Question Levels 1 to 3	Tool/Resource
Measure	**Do you know the potential root causes (inputs or Xs) and have enough reliable data to test them?**	
	Do you know what metric reflects the output described by the problem statement?	Project Y (output)
	Do you know how to define defects in the process and/or outputs?	
	Do you know what are the customer's performance standards (LSL & USL)?	Voice of the Customer (VOC)
	Do you have the key operational definitions like defect, defective, unit, opportunity, etc.?	Operational Definitions
	Do you have enough data measuring the Y and potential inputs (Xs)?	
	Do you know what the potential Xs are for the problem? (i.e., Theoretical Significance)	C&E Diagram & 5 Whys
	Do you know which Xs may have the most potential influence? (i.e., Empirical Significance)	C&E Matrix
	Do you know what data is necessary to measure the Y and most influential Xs?	Data Collection Plan (DCP)
	Do you know how much data you need?	Sample Size Calculator
	Do you know what timeframe your data should span?	Short/Long Term Data
	If collecting the data manually (via time studies, observations, etc.), do you have a plan and the support needed to collect it?	Buy-in/Sponsorship (CAP model)
	Do you know if your collected data is accurate, repeatable and reproducible?	Measurement System Analysis (MSA)
	OUTPUTS: Updated Project Storyboard, Definition of the VOC, Y & Xs, and a reliable and relatively complete dataset	

Practical Application

- Identify at least 2 projects you led or worked on in the past.
  - For each project, review all the questions in the Measure phase level 3 roadmap.
    - What questions and related tools/resources were not addressed in the project?
    - Why were they not addressed?
    - What different outcome or results could've been realized if they were addressed in the project?

Six Sigma-Measure – Lesson 2: The Necessity of the Measure Phase

A review of why the Measure phase is so important to the DMAIC process and why it's so often neglected.
Pre-Requisite Lessons:
- o Six Sigma-Overview #01 – Problem Resolution using DMAIC
- o Six Sigma-Overview #02 – Risk Analysis

The Necessity of the Measure Phase
- o Remember, we're solving a problem that requires gathering reliable information.
  - In the Define phase, you should have a clear understanding of the problem's severity & scope.
  - Now in the Measure phase, you need to gather *reliable* information that you can trust.
    - ▪ The analysis and improvements are only as good as the data on which they're based.
- o The Measure phase is probably the most critical and yet most neglected phase.

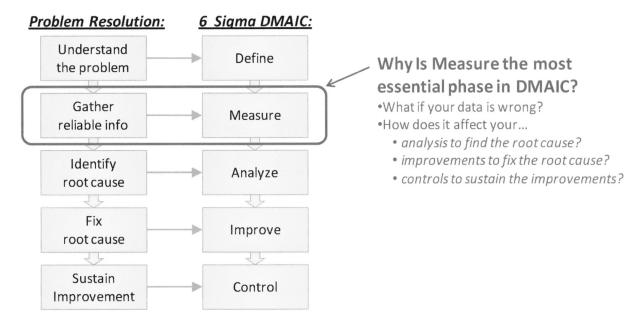

Why Is Measure the most essential phase in DMAIC?
- •What if your data is wrong?
- •How does it affect your…
  - *analysis to find the root cause?*
  - *improvements to fix the root cause?*
  - *controls to sustain the improvements?*

Why is the Measure Phase Often Neglected?
- o Remember the jelly bean example from the lesson on risk analysis?
  - This topic reviewed here was originally covered on page 83.
- o Which method of counting the jelly beans is best?
  - This topic reviewed here was originally covered on page 84.
- o What does this have to do with the Measure phase being often neglected?
  - To validate the data, the Measure phase may require more time that we're not willing to invest.
    - ▪ Do we regard time (speed of resolution) as a higher priority than accuracy (the right solution)?
      - *– How can we appropriately balance speed vs. accuracy in the jelly bean example?*
      - *– What if the analysis was for testing health risks for new medicines? Or testing safety in new cars?*
  - Remember, the goal is *not* to eliminate risk, but to *balance* risk with rewards.
    - ▪ The pre-assessment in the Define phase can help us predict the potential benefits (reward).
      - *– If the benefits are low, then risk is probably low; therefore, the speed of analysis may be more important.*
      - *– If the benefits are high, then risk is probably high; therefore, the accuracy of analysis may be more important.*
    - ▪ Always validate the risks vs. rewards with the Sponsor; this will help in planning your analysis timeline.

Practical Application

- o Think of at least 3 prior situations you've worked that required some data analysis.
  - For each situation, try to answer the following questions:
    - When the situation began, which was more important: getting quick results or getting accurate results?
      - *Who determined that level of importance?*
      - *If it was not you, then do you agree with that level of importance?*
    - How much time was spent collecting the data and validating it before you began analyzing it?
    - After you began to analyze the data, did you find that any of it was wrong or incomplete?
      - *If so, how much extra time was spent re-collecting and validating the data?*
      - *How much time could have been saved if you had more thoroughly collected and validated the data the first time?*
    - After the situation was completed, did the priorities change between quick or accurate results?
      - *If so, why did it change?*
      - *Did the priority really change, or was the risk neither fully understood nor fully communicated from the beginning?*
      - *What would you do differently next time if you suspect the priority between quick or accurate results may change?*

Six Sigma-Measure – Lesson 3: Different Sources of Data

A review and comparison between the different sources of where we generally collect data.

Pre-Requisite Lessons:
- None

What are the paths for data?
- Source Data will either come from one or more systems or manual observations.
  - Data from a system can come from direct queries or system-generated reports.
  - Manual observations are never ideal, but they may be necessary if no source system exists.
- For this training, the destination will be Minitab after first being configured in Excel.
  - Minitab® Statistical Software is one of the most common among many software tools for doing statistical analysis.

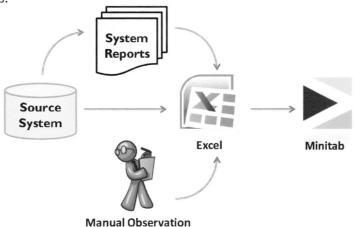

Comparing the Sources of Data
- What are the differences between each type of data source?

General Characteristics	Source System	System Reports	Manual Observation
Can you get the data quickly?	Usually	Yes	No
Is the data detailed?	Yes	No	Yes
Is the data consistent?	Yes	Yes	No
Is historical data available?	Yes	Yes	No
Is the data easy to get (not requiring unique expertise)?	No	Yes	Yes
Is the data customizable?	Maybe	No	Yes
Is the data generally accepted as reliable?	Yes	Yes	No

- Based on these characteristics, the ideal priorities for source data are:
  1. **Source System** – consistent, comprehensive and generally accepted as reliable by SMEs.
  2. **System Reports** – fast and consistent, though they may not have enough detail for analysis.
  3. **Manual Observation** – small samples and inconsistent, but often the only source available.
- The data source should balance with the analysis risks vs. rewards (time vs. accuracy).

Practical Application

o Think of at least 3 prior situations you've worked where you had collected data.

- For each situation, try to answer the following questions:
  - What was the source for the collected data (i.e., source system, system report, or manual observation)?
  - Why was that particular source used for collecting your data?
  - What were some of the disadvantages (if any) by using that particular data source?
  - If time were not a concern, then what would've been the most ideal source of data for the situation?

Six Sigma-Measure – Lesson 4: Data Configuration for Analysis

A review of how to configure data into an ideal format for doing statistical analysis in Minitab.
Pre-Requisite Lessons:
- Six Sigma-Measure #03 – Different Sources of Data

Configuring Data for the Destination

- Since Minitab is the destination, how should the data be configured for Minitab?
  - Each unique record should be setup in rows (not columns).
    - Minitab has a worksheet interface similar to Excel (except it does not allow for functions in the cells).
    - Minitab requires each record to be represented horizontally in each row across multiple columns (fields).
      - *Use the Copy > Paste-Special > Transpose option in Excel to easily change the layout from columns to rows.*
  - The data should be as detailed as possible.
    - System-generated reports often have summary level data; what's the risk of using summarized data?
    - Detailed data allows for more samples (N) in the statistical tests which increases confidence in the results.
      - *Example 1: if you wanted to analyze your weight, how often would you want to measure it?*
      - *Example 2: Compare measuring average revenue per customer by month vs. by day. What's the advantage of each?*
  - Each column (field) of data should be properly formatted.
    - Statistical tests generally require the data to have a consistent format and data type (e.g., numeric, dates).
      - *In a future training session we'll explore this in more detail on the subject of "Data Characterization".*
    - Any column (field) containing the wrong data type, Minitab will generally treat the entire field as text.
    - Dates – These must conform to normal date values like in Excel (typically displayed as M/D/YYYY).
      - *For example, "4-APR-2012" or "April 4, 2012" will be treated by Minitab as text unless they're already identified as a date value in Excel yet having this custom formatting.*
    - Numbers – Minitab requires every cell in the column (except for Nulls) to only have numeric values.
      - *For example, a cell having a textual character (e.g., space, $, etc.) will be treated as text unless it's Excel's formatting.*
    - Text – Minitab allows for text, but the text used for statistical analysis should be unique and consistent.
      - *For example, "Kansas" and "KS" may logically represent the same state, but Minitab will analyze them as different values. If this text is necessary for analysis, then these differences should be corrected so that they're consistent.*
    - Null Values – Minitab can analyze null values, but will generally convert them to an asterisk (*).

Examples of Configuring Data

- Use Excel to properly configure all data before importing it into Minitab.
  - Example 1: Use "*Test 1 – Raw Data.xls*" example to configure data for analysis:
    - *To download this file, go to this respective video on the StatStuff.com website.*
    - Use "*Test 1 – Reformatted Data.xls*" to see an ideal configuration of the data.
      - *To download this file, go to this respective video on the StatStuff.com website.*

- Example 2: Use "*Test 2 – Raw Data.xls*" example to configure data for analysis:
  - *To download this file, go to this respective video on the StatStuff.com website.*

Practical Application
- Open the "*Test 1 – Raw Data.xls*" file referenced in this lesson.
  - Try to configure the data to a format that would be ideal for doing analysis in Minitab.
    - Arrange the data so that each unique record is setup in rows (not columns).
    - Arrange the data so that there are no redundant columns.
      - *For example, rather than having the similar data values spread across multiple columns representing a different month, try re-stacking the data so that there's only one column representing the month.*
    - Ensure the data is as detailed as possible (i.e., no summarized values).
    - Ensure the formatting of the data is correct (i.e., dates are truly date values, numbers are truly numerical values, etc.).
  - Compare your final result with the "*Test 1 – Reformatted Data.xls*" file referenced in this lesson.
    - How many differences do you see between the datasets?
    - How do you think those differences would affect the analysis eventually done in Minitab?

Six Sigma-Measure – Lesson 5: Advanced Excel Features

A review of many features and functions in Excel that are often essential for configuring and analyzing data.

Pre-Requisite Lessons:
- None

Excel Filters
- What does it do?
  - Filters quickly display all unique values within a column or field of data.
  - Filters quickly drilldown the dataset by one or more of the unique values in a column.
- How do I access this feature?
  - The data must be configured where each unique record is setup in rows (not columns).
  - To setup filters, do the following:
    - Click in any cell of the dataset where you want to create the filters.
    - In the Home tab of Excel 2007/2010, click "Sort & Filter" > "Filter"
  - This will add arrows in each cell at the top of each column that is within the dataset.
    - Any non-adjacent column will not add a filter unless you highlight the entire dataset first.
- How can it be used?
  - Quickly sort by any of the values in the selected field.
  - Easily see all the unique values for the field for quickly drilling down.
    - One or more items can be selected for the drilldown.
    - Custom filters can be created when there is a long list of unique values.
  - Quickly identify any errors within the unique values.
    - For example, a filter can show how "New York", "NY", and " NewYork " are treated as 3 unique text values that should represent the same place.
  - See Excel's HELP for a more detailed explanation of filters.

Excel Pivot Tables
- What does it do?
  - Pivot tables can quickly sort, filter & organize large amounts of data into a meaningful format.
  - Pivot tables can easily calculate, summarize and graphically chart data. See examples below...

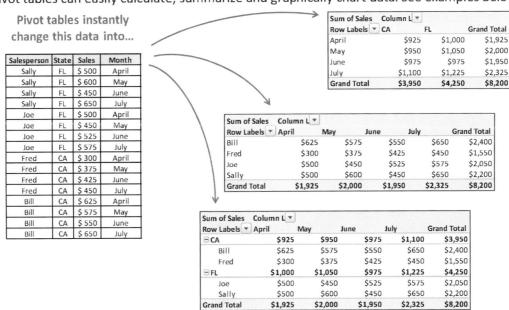

- How do I access this feature?
  - The data must be configured where each unique record is setup in rows (not columns).
  - To setup a pivot table, do the following:
    - Click in any cell of the dataset that will be your pivot table source.
    - In the Insert tab, click "Pivot Table" (see image at right).

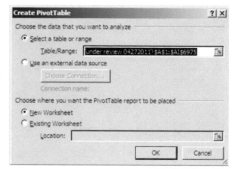

    - Excel tries to automatically select the source data you want included, but you can change it or even get data from another source.
      - *Pivot tables can connect to other Excel files, Access files, or other databases.*
    - A box displays (example at bottom-right) listing all your data columns plus 4 other pivot table fields where you drag/drop your columns:

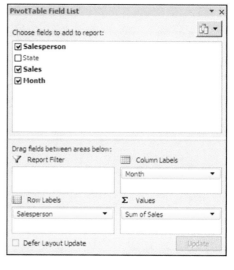

      - *Report Filter – add fields for data you want to filter in the pivot table.*
      - *Column Labels – add fields for values to show horizontally as column headings.*
      - *Row Labels – add fields for values to show vertically as row headings.*
      - *Values – add fields for the data values that you want calculated.*
        - ➢ *These can be calculated as a sum, count, average, % of row, etc.*
    - Pivot tables also allow for a variety of designs & layouts for the data.
- How can it be used?
  - Quickly filter, sort and calculate data.
  - Easily calculate volume proportions (e.g., % of row/column).
  - Instantly create a variety of graphical charts of the pivoted data.
  - Create a pivot table of a pivot table for further analysis.
  - See Excel's HELP for a more detailed explanation of pivot tables.

Helpful Excel Functions
- Text Functions
  - Extracting text from other cells:
    - **LEFT**(cell ref, # of char) – Returns the stated # of characters from the beginning of the cell's contents.
    - **RIGHT**(cell ref, # of char) – Returns the stated # of characters from the end of cell's contents.
    - **MID**(cell ref, start #, # of char) – Returns the stated # of characters beginning at the specified starting #.
  - Other helpful text functions:
    - **CONCATENATE**(cell ref1[, cell ref2, cell ref3...]) – Combines the text from all stated cells in the listed order.
    - **EXACT**(cell ref1, cell ref2) – Returns TRUE if the 2 referenced cells have the same values, otherwise FALSE.
    - **SEARCH**(text to find, cell ref[, start #]) – Returns the character # where "text to find" is found within "cell ref", otherwise it returns an error; use "start #" to begin at any point in "cell ref".
    - **LEN**(cell ref) – Returns the number of characters within the referenced cell.
- Date/Time Functions
  - Standard Date Functions:
    - **DATEVALUE**(date text) – Converts a date that is in text format to a date format.

- **WEEKDAY**(date) – Returns a number representing the day of the week for the stated date.
- **WEEKNUM**(date) – Returns the week # within the year for the stated date.
  - Customized Date Formulas:
    - **CHOOSE**(**WEEKDAY**(date), "Sun", "Mon", "Tue"…) –The CHOOSE function translates the number of the weekday from the WEEKDAY function to a meaningful description.
    - (date cell ref – (**WEEKDAY**(date cell ref))) – Returns the week starting date for the date in "date cell ref".
  - Lookup and Logical Functions
    - **COUNT**(range of values) – Returns the number of cells within the range that contain numeric values.
      - *Use COUNTA(array) to return the number of cells within the array that contain any non-empty value (includes text).*
      - *Use COUNTIF(array, criteria) to return the number of cells in the array that match the specified criteria.*
    - **IF**(test, true condition, false condition) – Logical function that returns the true condition if the test is true or returns the false condition if the test is false.
    - **VLOOKUP**(value to lookup, source dataset, offset #) – Looks in the "source dataset" to find "value to lookup" and returns the value that is "offset #" of cells to the right.
      - *HLOOKUP function is similar except it searches the top row of "source dataset" and then downward "offset #" of cells.*
      - *INDIRECT and MATCH functions can be very helpful for extracting data dynamically in a similar way as VLOOKUP.*
  - Analytical Functions
    - **STDEV**(range of values) – Returns the standard deviation of a range of values.
    - **PERCENTILE**(range of values, Nth %ile) – Returns the specific Nth percentile (stated inclusively from 0.0 to 1.0) within the specified array of data. Or use **MEDIAN** function to get the 50th percentile.
      - *Avg + (2 x StDev) is an empirical rule that represents the 95th percentile; this is helpful as a quick validation if the 95th percentile cannot be calculated. This rule demonstrates the exponential influence of variation on data.*
    - **SLOPE**(known Y's, known X's) – In the linear equation of $y = mx+b$ (where m is the slope and b is the y-intercept), it returns the slope (m). This can be extremely useful for understanding current trends and can be used for predicting by multiplying the slope by the number of periods reflected in the equation.
      - *For example, if a slope over 15 weeks of data is calculated as 0.25%, then you can predict that if it keeps its current trend, it will increase 1% every 4 weeks.*
    - **CORREL**(known Y's, known X's) – Returns the Pearson correlation coefficient for two sets of continuous values to reflect the extent of a linear relationship between the two variables.
      - *The PEARSON function operates the same way. In either case, this doesn't necessarily imply how much X is <u>causing</u> Y.*
      - *RSQ(known Y's, known X's) – Squares the correlation coefficient to show the proportion of the variance in Y explained by X. Generally, the closer the result is to -1.0 or 1.0, the more that a relationship between the 2 factors can be explained.*

Other Excel Features
  - Helpful Features:
    - "Conditional Formatting" (under the Home tab) changes various formatting (e.g., text color, cell color, etc.) based on customizable conditions of a cell's value.
    - "Remove Duplicates" (under the Data tab) can quickly delete any rows of data that meet your customizable conditions defining what is a duplicate.

5

- "Data Validation" (under the Data tab) can control data that's input in a cell by restricting it to meet your customizable conditions.
  - o Quick Tricks:
    - Use "$" character in front of a column and/or row cell reference to maintain static referencing.
    - Double-click the bottom right of a selected cell to quickly copy its contents downward.
      - This only works where cells in the column to the left are filled with values; any break in values will break the quick copy.
    - Use CTRL+A to quickly select an entire set of adjacent cells.
    - Use END key then an arrow key to quickly jump in the arrow's direction to the last cell containing values.
    - Use Paste-Special > Transpose to a set of values in the opposite direction (e.g., columns to rows).

Practical Application

- o Copy this data (at right) into Excel and try to follow these steps:
  - Add a filter to all of the columns.
    - Try filtering your data to just the month of May.
  - Create a pivot table based on the data.
    - Try to re-create the pivot table results shown below:

Salesperson	State	Sales	Month
Sally	FL	$ 500	April
Sally	FL	$ 600	May
Sally	FL	$ 450	June
Sally	FL	$ 650	July
Joe	FL	$ 500	April
Joe	FL	$ 450	May
Joe	FL	$ 525	June
Joe	FL	$ 575	July
Fred	CA	$ 300	April
Fred	CA	$ 375	May
Fred	CA	$ 425	June
Fred	CA	$ 450	July
Bill	CA	$ 625	April
Bill	CA	$ 575	May
Bill	CA	$ 550	June
Bill	CA	$ 650	July

Sum of Sales	Column L ▼				
Row Labels ▼	April	May	June	July	Grand Total
Bill	$625	$575	$550	$650	$2,400
Fred	$300	$375	$425	$450	$1,550
Joe	$500	$450	$525	$575	$2,050
Sally	$500	$600	$450	$650	$2,200
Grand Total	$1,925	$2,000	$1,950	$2,325	$8,200

- Add a new column to the data that only displays the first 2 letters of the Salesperson's name. (Hint: use LEFT function)
- In a new cell, calculate the average sales for all salespeople.
- In a new cell, calculate the median sales for all salespeople.
- Add conditional formatting to the cells in the sales column where any value less than $500 is red and any value greater than $500 is green.

Six Sigma-Measure – Lesson 6: Population vs. Sample Data

A review of population data and sample data and how we use them in statistical analysis.

Pre-Requisite Lessons:
- None

Population vs. Sample
- What is a population?
  - Represents every possible observation. It is ideal but very rare to get and often unnecessary.
- What is a sample?
  - A subset of the population that is generally a fair representation of the population.
    - A sample size calculator can help estimate how big a sample needs to be to fairly represent a population.
  - An adequate sample can allow someone to make inferences about the population.
    - It's kinda like "statistical prejudice", but that's too politically incorrect to say.
  - The difference between the conclusions from the sample vs. reality in the population is _RISK_.
    - Prudent statistical analysis demands we mitigate that risk as much as _necessary_ (as determined by VOC).
    - In sampling, we use precision or "margin of error" to account for that risk.

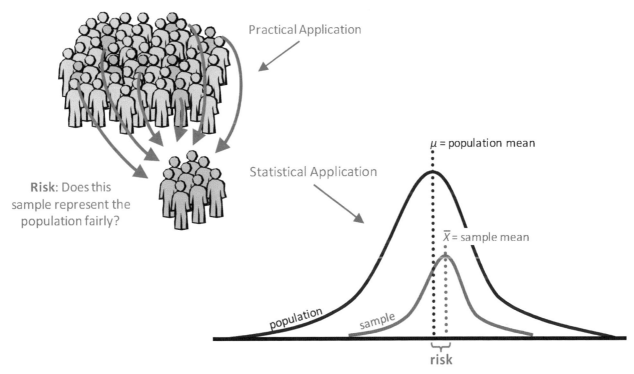

Practical Application
- Identify at least 3 metrics in your organization that rely on sampling.
  - What methods are used for selecting the sampled group?
    - Do you believe those methods are truly random? If not, then why not?
  - How accurate do you think those sampled metrics are in reflecting the population?
  - What is the risk if the sampled metrics do not accurately reflect the population?
  - What does your organization do to mitigate those potential risks?

Six Sigma-Measure – Lesson 7: Data Types

A review of discrete and continuous types of data and the differences between each type.

Pre-Requisite Lessons:
- None

Two Type of Data: Continuous & Discrete

- There are two primary types of data; below is a description of each:

Characteristics	Continuous Data	Discrete Data
Also known as	Variable data	Attribute data
Definition	Measured on a continuum; virtually infinite in scale or divisibility	Measured by counts or classifications; limited in scale and divisibility
General Examples	Numeric values like dollars, time, distance, or degrees	Yes/No, Pass/Fail, Colors, Locations, %'s
Business Examples	Revenue/Expenses, call duration, product specs	People (names or roles), product types, stores/offices, defects, % Performance
Advantages	Since it's infinitely divisible, the slightest defect can be detected & measured. This also allows for smaller sample sizes.	Due to its either/or quality, it's usually fast & easy to collect. It's also easy to understand since it can be measured on smaller scales (like yes/no or 1 to 5).
Disadvantages	Can be more difficult to measure which can require additional costs to collect data. The scale of scrutiny may be too granular or broad.	Data can be subjective. It only measures defect count and not severity. May require a large sample size.
Statistical Impact	Better measurement of variation; used with statistical tools that allow for more precision (e.g., regressions)	Not very effective for measuring variation; used with statistical tools that are less precise (e.g., Chi^2).

More Insight About Discrete Data

- How can discrete data include percentages since they're numeric?
  - Percentages are actually a measure of proportions for discrete data.
  - They're discretely limited between 0% to 100%.
  - Statistical tests can treat %'s like a continuous value, but use caution when doing so.
    - Statistical tests don't logically evaluate the types of data so it will accept %'s as continuous. The user should understand the potential risks of misinterpreting the results that are intended for continuous data.
  - Not all percentages are discrete.
    - If all the source data being measured are continuous, then the derived proportions (percentages) are also continuous.
    - If any of the source data being measured is discrete, then the derived proportions are discrete.
- There are two types of Discrete data:
  - Count Data:
    - Describes the frequency of an observable event or condition (e.g., a defect) that occurs within a process.
    - Typically used at the unit level such as for measuring a defect rate.

- Classification Data:
  - Describes the frequency of a characteristic attributable to a factor, part or output in a process.
  - Typically used within the unit level for measuring proportional defectiveness or p(d).

5 Units:

Defects:	Yes	Yes	Yes	No	Yes	**Defect Rate** = 80% (4/5)
Defectives:	2/9	3/9	1/9	0/9	3/9	**Defective Rate** = 20% (9/45)

Practical Application

- Find at least 10 metrics used in your organization and answer the following for each:
  - What kind of data type is it (i.e., discrete or continuous)?
  - For any percentage metrics (which are numerical representations of discrete values), what are the actual discrete values used to calculate the percent?
  - For any discrete values, is there a way that same information could be measured as a continuous value to allow for more advanced statistical analysis?

Six Sigma-Measure – Lesson 8: Distributions: Overview

A review of distributions and how they can be formed using dotplots and histograms.

Pre-Requisite Lessons:
- ○ Six Sigma-Measure #07 – Data Types

Building Distributions with Dotplots

- ○ What is a distribution?
  - • A distribution is created by plotting or distributing a set of data along a scale.
  - • The more data that's plotted, the more of a shape those data points display.
- ○ See the Dotplot examples at right:
  - • To build it in Minitab, go to *Graphs > Dotplots...*

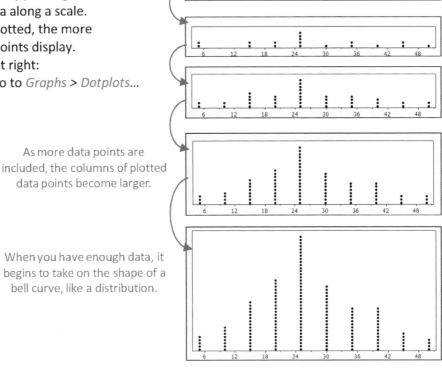

As more data points are included, the columns of plotted data points become larger.

When you have enough data, it begins to take on the shape of a bell curve, like a distribution.

Distributions displayed in Histograms

- ○ Limitations of Dot Plots
  - • Not all data points necessarily stack so neatly into columns like in the dotplot example.
  - • Since continuous data can be infinite in scale or divisibility, when there are more than 50 continuous data points, a Dot Plot can become less practical at displaying the values.
    - ▪ Instead, use a histogram.
- ○ What is a histogram?
  - • A histogram can take the same kind of data (and a lot more of it) and group the values into "bins".
    - ▪ In Minitab, go to *Graphs > Histogram...*

Vertical axis reflects the frequency or percent of data points in each bin

Each bin includes all data points that fall within a specified range

Horizontal axis reflects the scale for all data points being plotted.

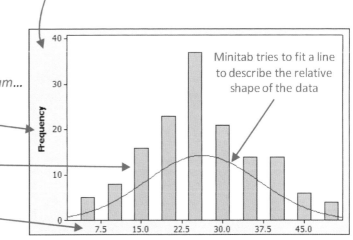

Minitab tries to fit a line to describe the relative shape of the data

SS: Measure

5

The Shape of Distributions

- o The shape of distributions are influenced by 2 characteristics:
  - Central Tendency
    - Refers to the location on the scale where the majority of data points are concentrated or centralized.
    - For normal distributions, the mean (or average) is the measurement for central tendency.
  - Variation or Spread
    - Refers to how dispersed the data points are spread across the scale.
    - For normal distributions, the standard deviation is the measurement for variation.

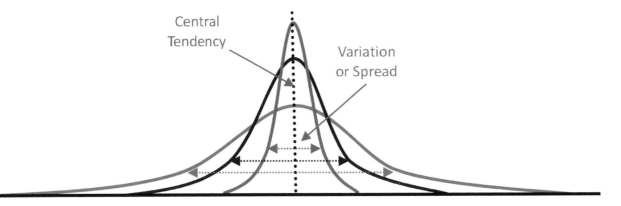

- What is kurtosis?
- It's a measure of the shape of the peak near the mean of the distribution.
  - A distribution with high or positive kurtosis (leptokurtic) has a sharp peak near the mean.
  - A distribution with low or negative kurtosis (platykurtic) appear flat with no peak near the mean.
- Which distribution above appears leptokurtic? Which appears more platykurtic?

Practical Application

- o Open the "Minitab Sample Data.MPJ" file and try to do the following:
  - Create a Dotplot each for Metric A and Metric B.
  - Create a Histogram each for Metric A and Metric B.
  - Which metric appears is more leptokurtic and which is more platykurtic?
- o Next, pull some historical data for at least 2 metrics used by your organization and try following the same steps described above.

Six Sigma-Measure – Lesson 9: Distributions: Normal

A review of normal distributions and how to test their normality using a normality test.
Pre-Requisite Lessons:
   o Six Sigma-Measure #08 – Distributions: Overview

Normal Distributions (bell curve)
   o Why is it called a "normal" distribution?
      • "Normal" implies the typical randomness that we expect to occur in life.
      • If there was no randomness, then we can presume there is some influence (bias or skewness).
      • We want the data that we analyze to be unbiased, therefore we need to ensure it reflects the "normal" randomness we would expect.
         ▪ Otherwise if the data is biased, then why analyze it if we can't be confident we'll find the right root cause?
   o A normal distribution is bell-shaped.
      • The bell shape is created because most of the data points fall in the middle.
      • The shape of the bell is influenced by the mean and standard deviation.
   o Characteristics of a normal distribution.
      • Completely described by its mean and standard deviation.
      • The tails on either end of the curve extend +/- infinity.

      • The area under the curve represents 100% of possible observations.
      • The curve is symmetrical where 50% of the data points fall on either side of the mean.
      • The mean (average) will be relatively equal to the median (50th percentile).

Normality Testing
   o A distribution with a bell curve doesn't necessarily mean it's "normal".
      • It's not uncommon for a distribution to appear normal, but it really isn't.
      • The normality of the distribution should be statistically tested.
   o Use the Anderson-Darling test of a Normality Test or Probability Plot.
      • A normality test or probability plot will plot the data on a logarithmic scale.
         ▪ In Minitab, go to *Stat > Basic Statistics > Normality Test* or go to *Graph > Probability Plot*
      • Normal data will appear like a straight line; Minitab will try to fit a line along the data points.
         ▪ A "fat pencil" test is if a fat pencil can lay across and cover all the data points, then it's probably a normal distribution.
      • A better test is to examine the p-value of the Anderson-Darling (AD) test.
         ▪ If p-value > 0.05, then it's normal.
         ▪ If p-value < 0.05, then it's *not* normal.
            – *In these examples, 0.05 is referring to the alpha risk which is the % chance of being right when concluding the data is normal. 5% is a commonly acceptable threshold.*

         This p-value is > 0.05 which means it's a normal distribution

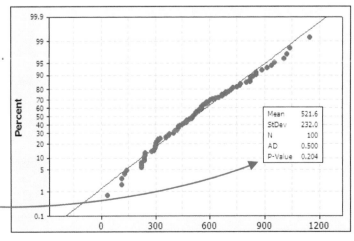

Practical Application

- o Open the "Minitab Sample Data.MPJ" file and try to do the following:
  - Run a normality test on each continuous metric.
  - Which metrics are normally distributed? How can you prove it?
- o Next, pull some historical data for at least 2 continuous metrics used by your organization and try following the same steps described above.

Six Sigma-Measure – Lesson 10: Distributions: Non-Normal

A review of non-normal and bi-modal distributions and how to test them using a normality test.
Pre-Requisite Lessons:
- o Six Sigma-Measure #09 – Distributions: Normal

Non-Normal Distributions
- o Non-normal distributions have bias or skewness.
  - • Since normal distributions reflect natural randomness in life, non-normal distributions are not random and therefore have something influencing its results.
  - • The bias in the data can be caused by two possible things:
    - ▪ The method for getting the sampled data was not random.
    - ▪ The process itself (from which the sample is pulled) has something skewing it.
  - • Example: Measuring the life of 1000 batteries.
    - ▪ What kind of distribution would you expect? If it's non-normal, then what may be causing it?
    - ▪ What are some things you would change to try to get a normal distribution?
- o Measure central tendency with the median.
  - • Bias in the data can cause the mean to shift.
  - • The median (50th percentile) never shifts.

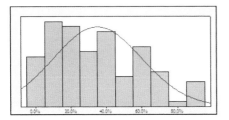

This distribution is non-normal because the p-value is < 0.05

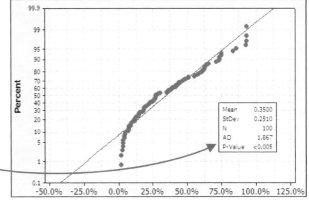

  - • What type of non-normal distribution is it?
    - ▪ Many types of non-normal distributions exist (e.g., weibull, lognormal, gamma, logistic, etc.).
      - – *To find out, go to Stat > Reliability/Survival > Distribution Analysis (Right) > Distribution ID Plot... (Not avail in Minitab 14 Student Version)*
      - – *Select the distribution type with the highest correlation coefficient; it can also be run for discrete factors in a variable.*

Bimodal Distribution
- o What is a bimodal distribution?
  - • These are distributions that appear to have two central tendencies (two bell curves).
    - ▪ It's possible to have more than two bell curves (multi-modality), but it's not as common.
  - • These occur when observations are taken from different populations.
    - ▪ Most things we measure don't have more than one central tendency. When we see this, it's most likely a sign we are measuring observations from more than one population.
  - • Example: Examine the graphical summary of data below.
    - ▪ What can you conclude from this?
    - ▪ Is it a normal or non-normal distribution?
    - ▪ What's the central tendency? Is it reliable?
    - ▪ How can this be fixed?

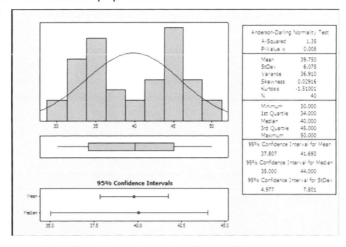

SS: Measure

5

Practical Application

- Open the "Minitab Sample Data.MPJ" file and try to do the following:
  - Run a normality test on each continuous metric.
  - Which metrics are non-normally distributed? How can you prove it?
  - Which metric (if any) has multi-modality?
- Next, pull some historical data for at least 2 continuous metrics used by your organization and try following the same steps described above.

Six Sigma-Measure – Lesson 11: Central Tendency

A review of the various measurements for central tendency, especially the mean and median.

Pre-Requisite Lessons:
  - o Six Sigma-Measure #10 – Distributions: Non-Normal

Characteristics of Distributions
  - o This topic reviewed here was originally covered on page 134.

Measurements of Central Tendency
  - o There are 3 primary measurements of central tendency:
    - Mean (μ "mu" or X "x-bar") – the average value within a set of continuous values.
      - The mean is considered the ideal measure of central tendency for normal distributions.
    - Median (η "eta") – 50th percentile or midpoint in a numerically sorted set of continuous data.
      - If there are an even # of values in the set, the median takes the average of the middle two values.
      - The median is considered the ideal measure of central tendency for non-normal distributions.
    - Mode – the most frequently occurring value in a set of continuous values.
      - A dataset can have more than one mode (multimodal).
  - o What is the age of people watching "Barney"?
    - In order to target their advertising, a TV network hired 3 statistical firms and asked them "What is the age of people watching Barney?"
      - 1st Firm – first to get results but didn't validate which "Barney" they wanted; they randomly surveyed a community which happened to be a retirement community.
      - 2nd Firm – next to get results and first validated it's the children's show "Barney"; they randomly surveyed a community and got the ages of all people who watch the show.
      - 3rd Firm – last to get results and first validated it's the children's show "Barney"; they randomly surveyed only the kids at daycare centers and in "young" communities.
    - What are the central tendencies for each group?
      - What are the risks each firm took in conducting their surveys?
      - What if the TV network wanted fast results? Which firm would've succeeded?

1st Firm	2nd Firm	3rd Firm
73	2	2
77	3	3
72	4	4
72	75	3
78	5	5
78	3	3
74	4	4
74	62	4
74	4	4
76	5	5
76	4	4
76	6	6
73	4	4
77	5	5
75	4	4
75	5	5
75	3	3
75	2	2
79	6	6
71	4	4

Practical Application
  - o Identify at least 3 metrics used by your organization that are based on central tendency (e.g., they use either an average or median value) and answer the following:
    - Is the metric a valid measurement of central tendency? To answer this, do the following:
      - Create a distribution of the data on which the metric is calculated.
      - Run a normality test on that data.
        - *If the distribution is normal, then it's valid to use either the average or median for the metric.*
        - *If the distribution is non-normal, then it's valid to only use the median for the metric (not the average).*
    - If the metric is not a valid measurement for central tendency, then do the following:
      - Re-calculate the metric using the valid measurement for central tendency.
      - Compare your result with the original metric.
        - *Are they significantly different?*
        - *If so, then how would that affect the actions normally taken from that metric? For example, would it change their targets or goals, or their processes that support that metric, or their behavior in how they measure performance, etc.?*

— Note: Before elevating issues like this with your organization's leadership, be sure to validate your calculations with others who have more experience in statistically analyzing data.

Six Sigma-Measure – Lesson 12: Spread

A review of the various measurements for spread or variation that include variance, standard deviation, inter-quartile range, etc.

Pre-Requisite Lessons:
- o Six Sigma-Measure #11 – Central Tendency

Characteristics of Distributions
- o This topic reviewed here was originally covered on page 134.

Spread or Variation Defined
- o What is variation or spread?
  - • It measures the distance each data point is from the central tendency (mean/median).
- o Why is variation so important?
  - • The central tendency only tells the output performance of all data points. It doesn't tell the _severity_ or _capability_ of the process itself.
    - ▪ "Place one foot on ice and one foot in the fire, then on the _average_ you should be warm."
- o Remember the two processes of throwing darts?

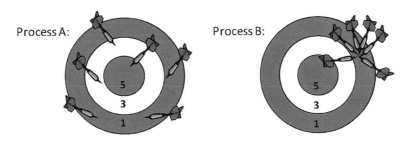

- • Which has a higher score? Which has a higher central tendency? Which is "better" and why?
- o Variation reflects where we have less control and where we feel the most pain.
  - • The degree of variation affects the degree of difficulty to correct/fix.
  - • The degree of predictability affects the degree of control and comfort.
    - ▪ Thermostat Calibration – consistently 3 degrees too low is easier to control than inconsistently high & low.
  - • To understand our data, we must understand both its central tendency and variation.

Measurements of Spread
- o There are several ways to measure variation or spread for normal distributions:
  - • Range – the entire extent of the dataset; the difference between the min and max data points.

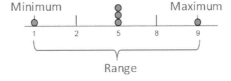

  - • Deviation – the distance a data point is from the mean or $(X - \mu)$.

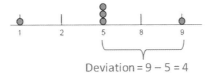

  - • Variance – the average squared deviation (or differences) about the mean or $(X - \mu)2 / N$ or σ^2.
    - ▪ The variance is intended to measure how spread out the distribution is from the mean.
  - • Standard Deviation (σ or s) – the square root of the variance or $\sqrt{(X - \mu)2 / N}$.

- The standard deviation measures the _average_ distance to the mean for all data points.
- It is the most common measure of variation across entire datasets that are normally distributed.
- How is variation measured for non-normal distributions (which don't use the mean)?
  - Stability Factor – the relative spread of data points about the median or *(Q1 / Q3)*
    - The closer the stability factor is to 1, the more likely there is little variation in the distribution.
    - The Inter-quartile Range (IQR), measured as *(Q3 – Q1)*, can also suggest the amount of variation by expressing the range of the middle 50% of the data points.

Practical Application
- What metrics (if any) does your organization use for measuring spread or variation?
  - Unfortunately, very few organizations use spread or variation as a critical metric.
- If your organization doesn't have metrics like this, then try doing the following:
  - Identify at least 3 metrics used by your organization that are based on continuous values.
  - Pull some historical data for each metric and run a normality test on the data.
    - If the distribution is normal, then calculate the variance and standard deviation.
    - If the distribution is non-normal, then calculate the IQR and stability factor.
  - What do these results tell you about the variation in each metric?
    - Which metric has the most variation?
    - Have you observed if your organization more frequently over-reacts to changes in that particular metric? If so, then it could indicate an ideal pain-point in your organization that needs to be addressed.

Six Sigma-Measure – Lesson 13: Comparing Distributions and Using the Graphical Summary

A review of the various measurements for spread or variation that include variance, standard deviation, inter-quartile range, etc.

Pre-Requisite Lessons:
  - o Six Sigma-Measure #12 – Spread

Characteristics of Distributions
  - o This topic reviewed here was originally covered on page 134.

Comparing Distributions
  - o The mean and standard deviation can make a difference when comparing distributions:
    - • Example 1: Different means and same standard deviations.

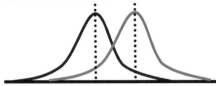

    - • Example 2: Same means and different standard deviations.

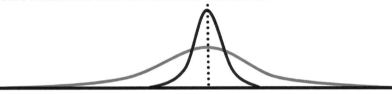

    - • Example 3: Different means and different standard deviations.

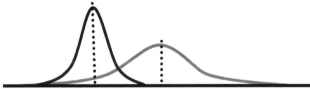

Graphical Summary
  - o Minitab's graphical summary provides a visual and statistical description of the data.
    - • In Minitab go to *Stat* > *Basic Statistics* > *Graphical Summary*...
      - ▪ "Variables" must be a continuous value in the dataset.
      - ▪ "By Variables" creates a separate graphical summary for each value in the selected column.

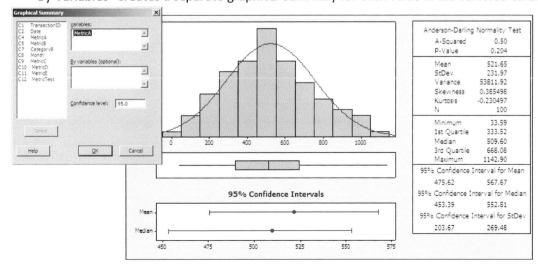

SS: Measure

Practical Application

- o Identify at least 3 metrics used by your organization based on continuous values.
  - Pull some historical data for each metric and run a graphical summary on each.
  - Answer the following questions for each metric:
    - Is the data normal or non-normal?
    - Is the data multi-modal?
    - What is the central tendency for each metric?
    - What is the spread or variation for each metric?

Six Sigma-Measure – Lesson 14: Variation Causes (Common vs. Special)

A review of the two main types of variation that can affect a process – common cause variation and special cause variation.

Pre-Requisite Lessons:
- o Six Sigma-Measure #13 – Comparing Distributions and using the Graphical Summary

Reviewing the Concept of Variation
- o This topic reviewed here was originally covered on page 86.

Types of Variation: Common vs. Special
- o Not all variation is necessarily bad – as long as it's controlled.
  - • Process variation can be related to the amount of control you have for that process.
  - • If we can understand and control our variation, we can have more control of the process.
- o There are two types of variation: Common vs. Special.

Characteristics	Common Cause Variation	Special Cause Variation
Also Known As	Noise	Signal or Anomaly
Variation Type	Natural & Random	Unnatural & Erratic
Distribution Type	Normal	Non-Normal
Source of Process "Pain"	Secondary	Primary
Process Impact	Generally from *within* the process	Generally from *outside* the process
Examples	•Poor design •Normal wear and tear •Poor environment (moisture, temp, etc.) •Poor maintenance	•Power surge •Extreme weather conditions •System/computer malfunction •Poor batch of raw materials

- • In the illustration at right, the two left darts may be worth the same points as the others, but their variation suggests something influenced their process:

Common Cause Variation:
The distance between these darts may represent natural, random variation in the process.

Special Cause Variation:
Their distance from the other darts may represent unnatural variation in the process causing them to land so far away.

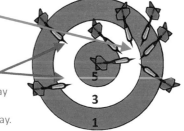

Practical Application
- o Identify at least 3 critical metrics used by your organization that tend to have volatility.
  - • Ask yourself the following for each metric:
    - ▪ What has the variation been like for the metric for the last year?
    - ▪ How does the organization typically respond to the variation? (E.g., over-react by quickly taking action, or over-analyzing by being slow to take action, etc.)
    - ▪ What has generally been the reason(s) for the variation observed in the metric?
    - ▪ Are the reasons more often common cause variation or special cause variation?
      - *– For example, many organizational leaders tend to find a reason for certain jumps or drops in a metric and in that sense are looking for a special cause; but in actuality, it may be a common cause that may not be so easy to identify and fix.*

Six Sigma-Measure – Lesson 15: Statistical Process Control (SPC)

An introduction to some of the concepts of statistical process control (SPC) and how it's used for measuring variation.

Pre-Requisite Lessons:
   o Six Sigma-Measure #14 – Variation Causes (Common vs. Special)

Types of Variation: Common vs. Special
   o This topic reviewed here was originally covered on page 145.

Statistical Process Control (SPC) Defined
   o What is Statistical Process Control (SPC)?
   • SPC is a method of measuring process data over time in order to find and fix special causes.
   • Control charts are used to help detect these special causes.
   • SPC also explores the Design of Experiments (DOE), but we won't cover that.
      ▪ DOE is generally a detailed method for designing tests or experiments for measuring variation.
   o Why should we only find and fix special cause variation?
   • Common cause variation appears normal and random, so it's harder to detect and fix.
   • Special cause variation appears inconsistent and unpredictable, so it's easier to detect and fix.
   o What if we identify the wrong type of variation?
   • It could lead to the Type I (α-alpha) or Type II (β-beta) risks analyzed with hypothesis testing.
      ▪ These two risks are covered more in-depth during hypothesis testing in the Analyze phase of DMAIC.
         – *Type I (α-alpha) Risk is the chance of treating something as guilty when it's really innocent (or convicting the innocent).*
         – *Type II (β-beta) Risk is the chance of treating something as innocent when it's really guilty (or letting the guilty go free).*

Actual Type of Variation...	⇨	Misinterpreted As...	⇨	Leads to Error Type...	⇨	Having this Outcome...
Common Cause		**Special** Cause		**Type I** (alpha risk)		**Wasted Time** (Problem doesn't exist)
Special Cause		**Common** Cause		**Type II** (beta risk)		**Problem Unresolved** (Condition still exists)

Impact of Variation to the Process
   o How can you tell the difference between good variation and bad variation?
   • Variation that is *within* the customer's requirements (VOC) is considered good or acceptable.
      ▪ This will generally include common cause variation and exclude any special cause variation.
   • Variation *outside* the customer's requirements is bad or unacceptable.
      ▪ This may include common cause variation, but will often include special cause variation.
   • Special cause variation is always "bad"; common cause variation is only bad when outside VOC.
   • Control charts are a primary tool for measuring and finding potentially bad variation.

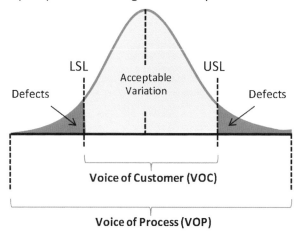

Practical Application

- Identify at least 3 critical metrics used by your organization that tend to have volatility.
  - Ask yourself the following for each metric:
    - What kind of variation (common or special) tends to cause the most "pain" felt by the organization?
    - Has the organization ever misinterpreted the variation (e.g., treating common cause as special cause)?
      - *If so, then what was the affect of that misinterpretation?*
      - *What could be done next time to validate the type of cause and prevent any misinterpretation?*

Six Sigma-Measure – Lesson 16: Testing for Special Cause Variation

A review of 8 different tests for special cause variation applied to an I-MR chart.

Pre-Requisite Lessons:
  o Six Sigma-Measure #15 – Statistical Process Control (SPC)

Reviewing Impact of Variation to the Process
  o This topic reviewed here was originally covered on page 147.

Control Charts Defined
  o How do you read a control chart?
  • Control charts plot the data points (continuous data) over time and define the following:
    ▪ Observations – the data points from the dataset that should be pre-sorted in date/time order.
    ▪ Mean – the average for all data points.
    ▪ LCL – Lower Control Limit defined as 3σ below the mean.
    ▪ UCL – Upper Control Limit defined as 3σ above the mean.
    ▪ Special Cause Tests – Any of 8 rules can be tested on the data to highlight potential special causes.
      – *We'll review later what these tests are and how to modify them.*
  • Below is an example of a control chart and its various components:

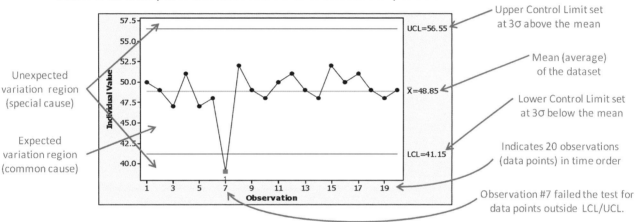

  • Control limits (LCL/UCL) are not the same as Specification limits (LSL/USL).
    ▪ Spec limits are tied to the VOC; a process can be "in control" but not meet customer requirements and vice versa.

Detecting Special Cause Variation
  o How do you detect special cause variation in a control chart?
  • Special cause variation may exist in a process that appears to be "in control" (within LCL/UCL).
    ▪ It may also be reflected in trends or behavior that appear non-normal.
  • There are 8 tests (general rules) for finding potential special cause variation.
    ▪ Some tests divide the "control region" of the chart into 3 zones (usually 1σ apart from each other).

Outside Control *(usually >3σ above mean)*	
	----- **UCL**
Zone A *(usually 3σ above mean)*	
Zone B *(usually 2σ above mean)*	
Zone C *(usually 1σ above mean)*	
	····· **Mean**
Zone C *(usually 1σ below mean)*	
Zone B *(usually 2σ below mean)*	
Zone A *(usually 3σ below mean)*	
	----- **LCL**
Outside Control *(usually >3σ below mean)*	

SS: Measure

o The 8 tests for Special Cause Variation:
1. One data point falls outside the control limits.

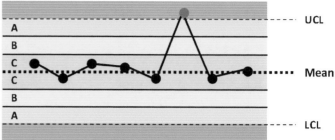

2. Nine data points in a row are on the same side of the mean.

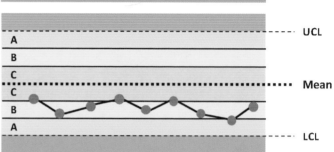

3. Six data points in a row are all increasing or decreasing.

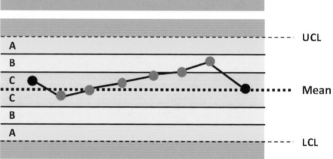

4. Fourteen data points in a row alternating up and down.

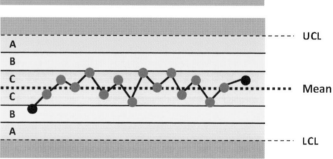

5. Two of three consecutive data points are on same side of the mean in zone A or beyond.

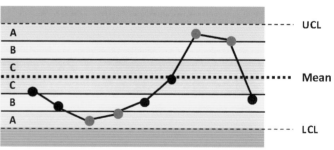

6. Four of Five consecutive data points are on same side of the mean in Zone B or beyond.

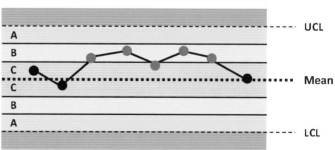

7. Fifteen consecutive data points within Zone C on either side of the mean.

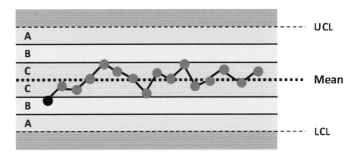

8. Eight consecutive data points outside of Zone C on either side of the mean.

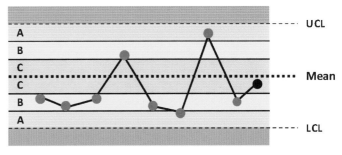

Finding the Special Cause Tests in Minitab

o How do I setup these special cause variation tests in Minitab?
  • In any of the control chart dialog boxes, select the "Chart Options…" button, then "Tests" tab.

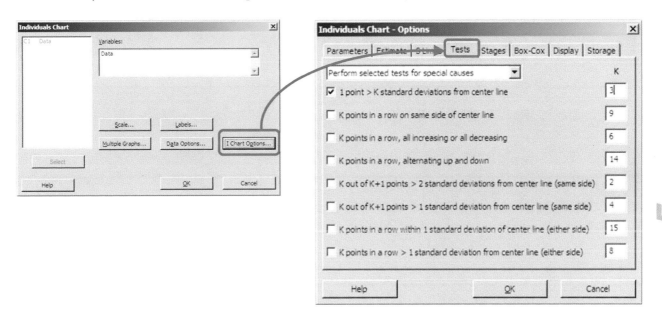

  • By default, the first test is applied for all control charts; check any others you want to run.
  • The "K" column allows you to modify the tests to be more or less restrictive than the standard.
  • When a test fails, the chart's data points will be red with a # referencing which test failed.
    ▪ Minitab's session window will also display which test failed and reference which observation(s) failed.

Practical Application

o Identify at least 2 metrics used by your organization that are continuous values and do the following:
  • Pull historical data for each metric (try to include at least 10 to 20 observations per metric).
  • For each metric, run all 8 of the variation tests from Minitab.
    ▪ In which of the 8 tests had each metric failed (if at all)?
    ▪ What is the reason for each failure?

- Which failures (if any) appear to be common or special cause variation? Which ones cannot be explained?
- What do those failures suggest about potential problems in the measured process?
- What actions should be taken (if any) to ensure those types of failures are prevented?

Six Sigma-Measure – Lesson 17: Variation Over Time (Short/Long Term Data)

A review of short and long term data and the impacts that variation has over time.

Pre-Requisite Lessons:
- o Six Sigma-Measure #16 – Testing for Special Cause Variation

Short/Long Term Data Defined
- o The timeframe for the collected data can significantly affect the analysis results.
  - What would happen if your data only included samples...
    - ...for only one day? Or only weekdays in a 7 day/wk process? Or only one shift of a 24 hr/day process?
  - The implications of these examples may be obvious, but what about when it's not so obvious?
    - How do you know what's a reasonable timeframe to include in your data?
    - Before we can answer this, we must first understand the two types of variation in a process.
- o Remember, there are two types of process variation: Common vs. Special.
  - This topic reviewed here was originally covered on page 145.
- o These different forms of process variation influence what type of data is collected.

Short Term Data	**Long Term Data**
• Collected from sub-groups in process • Captures only common cause variation • Data reflects a "snapshot" in time	• Collected across all sub-groups • Captures both common/special causes • Data reflects a full range of time.

Impact of Variation Over Time
- o Processes tend to show more variation in the long term than in the short term.
  - Long term variation is made up of both short term variation and process drift.
  - The shift between short and long term can be measured by taking samples of both short and long term data.
  - This shift of short term processes over a long term is about 1.5σ on average.
    - **Note**: this shift of 1.5σ is widely accepted in the Lean Six Sigma community, but there is also some strong debate as to its validity. For critical analyses, it may be best to do a separate analysis each for short and long term perspectives.
    - This is used more often when measuring process capability. We'll expand this discussion in the Analyze phase tools.
- o What timeframe should you use?
  - It depends on the data you're measuring and the amount of variation you expect in the process.
    - There isn't necessarily a "right or wrong" amount of time to reflect in your data.
    - The key is to be aware of how short term data is less likely to have special cause variation, but more likely to shift over time and affect your results.

Practical Application
- o Identify at least 2 metrics used by your organization that are continuous values and do the following:
  - Determine what may represent short vs. long term data for each metric.

- For example, how frequently is the metric data reported? If it's daily, then perhaps just a few weeks may represent short term and a few months may represent long term data. Or if it's reported monthly, then perhaps just a few months may represent short term and one year may represent long term.
- Pull enough historical data for each metric to account for at least long term data.
- Calculate the mean and standard deviation for all of the data across the long term.
- Calculate the mean and standard deviation for only about 25% of the data across a short term.
  - For example, if you have 24 weekly observations, then calculate them only using the first 6 observations, then next 6 observations, and so on.
- Compare the results between each short term sets of values and the long term values.
  - How do the short term values differ between each short term set?
  - How do those short term values differ from the long term values?
  - Which set of data appears to reflect the "true" mean and standard deviation for the process?

Six Sigma-Measure – Lesson 18: Rational Sub-Grouping

A review of how we sub-divide data for analysis using rational sub-grouping.

Pre-Requisite Lessons:
  o Six Sigma-Measure #17 – Variation Over Time (Short/Long Term Data)

Rational Sub-grouping Defined

  o What is rational sub-grouping?
    • It's the logical distinction of potential sub-processes that exist within an overall process.
    • These sub-processes are usually distinguished (or grouped) by a factor or category. Examples:
      ▪ Time (e.g., shift, time of day, day of month, etc.)
      ▪ Location (e.g., country, geographic region, metro/rural, native language, etc.)
      ▪ Processes (e.g., separating different processes or different methods of the same process, etc.)
      ▪ People (e.g., tenure, education level, etc.)
  o How do I know if I need rational sub-grouping?
    • Special cause variation may reveal the need for rational sub-grouping.
      ▪ If the same special cause tests tend to fail, then a sub-group may exist in the process.
    • Non-normal data can sometimes also indicate that sub-groups exist.
      ▪ A non-normal process may be caused by multiple, overlapping normal processes.
      ▪ From a normality plot, group the data points for each straight line in the plot to see if sub-groups exist.

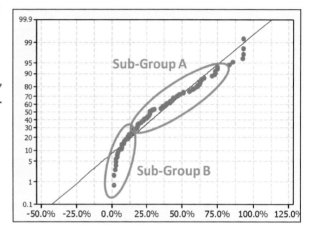

  o How do I know if I have the right rational sub-grouping?
    • Use ANOVA and HOV tests (Analyze phase) to confirm statistical differences between sub-groups.
      ▪ Keep the sub-grouping only if a statistical difference exists (low P value) between the sub-groups.

Practical Application

  o Identify at least 3 metrics used by your organization that are continuous values.
    • For each metric, identify at least 3 types of sub-groups currently used for reporting.
    • What are at least 2 other types of sub-groups that are possible, but improbable?
      ▪ How can you confirm if it's a rational sub-group that should be separately measured?

Six Sigma-Measure – Lesson 19: Calculating a Sample Size

A review of how to calculate a sample size using a Sample Size Calculator.
Pre-Requisite Lessons:
  o Six Sigma-Measure #18 – Rational Sub-Grouping

Sample Size Calculator Defined
  o What is a sample size calculator?
    • It helps determine how much data to collect in order to be confident in your results.
    • It is one of the easiest, most powerful and yet most neglected tools for basic data analysis.
  o What is the purpose of a sample size calculator?
    • Tells how much confidence or risk there is of accuracy in a given sample size.
    • Determines the amount of data necessary to sustain a certain level of confidence and accuracy.
    • Shows the amount of accuracy for a given sample size and confidence/risk level.

Sample Size Calculator Components
  o What are the different components of a sample size calculator?
    • There are actually two sample size calculators each having four key components:
      ▪ Discrete Data – use this calculator if the key metric you're evaluating is a discrete value.
        – *For example, polling which candidates are favored to win an election, measuring %'s or proportions of data, etc.*
        – *Components are 1) Defect Rate, 2) Confidence Level, 3) Precision, and 4) Sample Size.*
      ▪ Continuous Data – use this calculator if the key metric you're evaluating is a continuous value.
        – *For example, polling the age of customers, measuring call handle time, measuring average billing adjustments, etc.*
        – *Components are 1) Standard Deviation, 2) Confidence Level, 3) Precision, and 4) Sample Size.*
    • Each calculator shares 3 of the same components; below is a breakdown of all components:

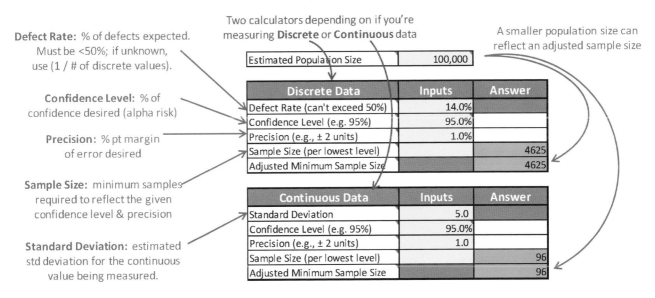

Defect Rate: % of defects expected. Must be <50%; if unknown, use (1 / # of discrete values).

Two calculators depending on if you're measuring **Discrete** or **Continuous** data

A smaller population size can reflect an adjusted sample size

Confidence Level: % of confidence desired (alpha risk)

Precision: % pt margin of error desired

Sample Size: minimum samples required to reflect the given confidence level & precision

Standard Deviation: estimated std deviation for the continuous value being measured.

Estimated Population Size		100,000

Discrete Data	Inputs	Answer
Defect Rate (can't exceed 50%)	14.0%	
Confidence Level (e.g. 95%)	95.0%	
Precision (e.g., ± 2 units)	1.0%	
Sample Size (per lowest level)		4625
Adjusted Minimum Sample Size		4625

Continuous Data	Inputs	Answer
Standard Deviation	5.0	
Confidence Level (e.g. 95%)	95.0%	
Precision (e.g., ± 2 units)	1.0	
Sample Size (per lowest level)		96
Adjusted Minimum Sample Size		96

How To Use the Calculator
  o How do you use the sample size calculator?
    • This particular sample size calculator allows you to enter any 3 of each calculator's required components and it returns the answer for the 4th missing value.
      ▪ This makes this calculator extremely effective for not only determining the necessary sample size, but to also return the confidence level or precision for an existing sample size.
      ▪ Simply type in a value in any 3 of the 4 yellow boxes for each calculator and keep any one yellow box empty. The answer will display at right in green for the missing, unknown value.

- NOTE: The sample size it returns is the minimum sample size for the lowest level measured.
    - For example, if you want to measure the average transactional errors at each of 100 stores, then the sample size should _not_ reflect the total transactions collected across all stores, but for _each_ store.
  - Sample size calculator steps:
    - Determine what data element to measure and it's data type (discrete vs. continuous).
    - Identify the estimated population size.
    - Based on the data type...
        - _Discrete Data – What is the defect rate? E.g., if the metric is 85%, then 1 – 85% is 15% as the defect rate. Or, if polling for 3 candidates, then 1 / 3 = 33%._
        - _Continuous Data – What is the metric's standard deviation? You may need to guess at first or pull a small sample to calculate a baseline._
    - How confident do you want to be in your sampled results? This is your alpha risk.
    - How precise do you want to be in your sampled results? This is your margin of error.

Estimated Population Size	100,000	②

Discrete Data	Inputs	Answer
Defect Rate (can't exceed 50%)	14.0%	
Confidence Level (e.g. 95%)	95.0%	
Precision (e.g., ± 2 units)	1.0%	
Sample Size (per lowest level)		4625
Adjusted Minimum Sample Size		4625

Continuous Data	Inputs	Answer
Standard Deviation	5.0	
Confidence Level (e.g. 95%)	95.0%	
Precision (e.g., ± 2 units)	1.0	
Sample Size (per lowest level)		96
Adjusted Minimum Sample Size		96

Examples Using a Sample Size Calculator

- Example 1: Polling for a local election in a city with 40,000 people
    - Scenario 1: If 2 candidates are running for local office, how many people should be surveyed of who they'll vote for in order to be 95% confident with +/- 3% margin (precision)?
        - After 300 surveys you find candidate A has 75% of votes; how does this change the total # to survey?
        - What if there were 3 candidates running for office; how does this change the total # to survey?
        - What if the city only had 12,000 people and you want 1% precision; how does this change the sample size?
    - Scenario 2: If 4 candidates are running for local office, how many people should be surveyed to find the age of the average voter and be 95% confident with +/- 1 year?
        - After 300 surveys you find the average so far is 42 with standard deviation of 12; what does that mean and how does this change the total # to survey?
        - What if you could only survey 400 people; how does this affect your confidence level and precision?
- Example 2: Call duration measurement at a Call Center
    - Scenario: How many samples are needed to measure each employee's call duration per month with 95% confidence and within 10 seconds of duration?
        - What if we only have 300 samples per employee; how does that affect our confidence or precision?

○ Example 3: Compare efficiency between two systems
  • Scenario: 90 similar transactions were each run through two different systems. System Alpha's time was 45 seconds and System Beta's time was 27 seconds (each had std dev of 1/3). Is System Beta statistically faster?
    ▪ What is the best/worst case difference in efficiency for System Beta?
    ▪ What if we only had 24 samples and System Alpha was at 180 seconds and System Beta at 160 seconds?

Practical Application
  ○ Identify at least 2 metrics used by your organization that are based on sampled data.
    • What is the ideal sample size for each metric to have 95% confidence (use the existing metric to determine the ideal precision typically used and the defect rate or standard deviation)?
      ▪ How does this compare to the actual sample size used for that metric?
        − *If the organization does not meet the ideal sample size, then what affect does that have on the confidence level and/or precision for each metric?*
    • Determine how the organization typically applies rational sub-grouping for the metric.
      ▪ How many levels exist for each type of sub-group?
      ▪ Does the organization have at least the ideal sample size calculated above for each sub-group level?
        − *If not, then what affect does this have on the confidence level and/or precision?*

Six Sigma-Measure – Lesson 20: Defining the Project Y

A review of why we need to define a project Y and some methods for ensuring we're defining the right project Y.

Pre-Requisite Lessons:
- o Introduction #04 – CTQ Drilldown
- o Six Sigma-Overview #04 – Transfer Function
- o Six Sigma-Define #02 – Building a Problem Statement

Review of the Transfer Function
- o This topic reviewed here was originally covered on page 89.

Defining the Project Y
- o In the Measure phase we define the project Y and identify all potential factors (X's).
  - • Remember, the goal for finding and fixing the root cause is to build a transfer function.
  - • To build that transfer function, we need to know the project Y and all possible X's in the process.
- o How do I find the project Y?
  - • Refer back to the problem statement in the Define phase.
    - ▪ How is the pain point in the problem statement being measured? That could be the project Y.
  - • Refer back to the CTQ drilldown.
    - ▪ The project Y may be a CTQ Level 3 metric that rolls directly up to CTQ Level 2 then CTQ Level 1.
- o What if the ideal project Y is not something currently measured?
  - • The project Y must always be measurable.
    - ▪ "You can't improve what you can't measure."
  - • If it's not a current metric, then a metric must be created for it ASAP.
    - ▪ It may require time and manual work, but the metric will serve as a baseline for measuring progress.
- o What are the characteristics of a good project Y?
  - • It should be a continuous value to allow for more powerful and flexible statistical tools.
  - • It should be clearly defined how it's calculated and what are its data sources & scale of scrutiny.
  - • It should be normalized or else you may risk a false-positive in the project progress.
    - ▪ For example, rather than tracking cost, should it be proportionate to revenue, or customers, etc.? What would happen if you only used cost and the project saw costs later decline? Did revenue decline too?

Practical Application
- o Identify at least 2 prior projects or initiatives you worked in your organization.
  - • What was the Y (critical output) for each project or initiative?
    - ▪ Remember, it should be the critical metric that was used to measure success of the project or initiative.
  - • Did the project Y reflect the pain felt that instigated the project or initiative in the first place?
    - ▪ If not, then what metric is better reflection of that pain being felt?
    - ▪ Why wasn't that other metric used?
  - • How does the project Y fit into the CTQ Drilldown?
    - ▪ If the project Y doesn't fall under a financial performance CTQ, then how was the financial impact measured for the project or initiative?

Six Sigma-Measure – Lesson 21: Defining the VOC and Defects

A review of what is the voice of the customer (VOC) and how it's used for defining various types of defect measurements.

Pre-Requisite Lessons:
- o Six Sigma-Measure #20 – Defining the Project Y

Starting with the VOC

- o The first step toward defining defects is to understand the voice of the customer (VOC).
  - Defects are like the symptoms of pain being felt in the project Y or problem statement.
    - ▪ Remember, they're not necessarily the root cause; we'll confirm that in the Analyze phase.
  - The VOC is generally represented as the customer's requirements.
    - ▪ What are the customer's expectations (typically expressed as goals or targets)?
    - ▪ What does the customer consider to be acceptable?
    - ▪ What is the customer willing to pay for?
  - Define the customer's requirements in terms of the project Y.
    - ▪ What are the customer's specific goals or targets for the project Y metric?
    - ▪ For a project Y that is a continuous value, these may be expressed in two ways (either one or both):
      - *– Upper Specification Limit (USL) – an upper level target such that anything exceeding it is considered a defect.*
      - *– Lower Specification Limit (LSL) – a lower level target such that anything beneath it is considered a defect.*
    - ▪ Below is an illustration how LSL and USL can be used to define defects.

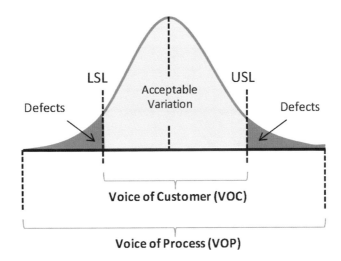

Testing a Customer's Requirements

- o Are the customer's requirements realistic?
  - Just because a customer may have a USL and/or LSL defined doesn't mean it's correct.
  - If the requirements seem unreasonable, then it may be necessary to test by asking the following:
    - ▪ If the customer has both a LSL and USL, then has the metric ever fallen within the acceptable range?
    - ▪ If the customer has either a LSL or USL, then has the metric ever achieved either target?
    - ▪ Has a competitor ever achieved the customer's requirements?
  - If "No" for any of the above questions, then consider doing the following:
    - ▪ Understand what the requirements are based on. Is there an existing benchmark? Is that benchmark valid?
    - ▪ Test the process to see if it's potentially capable of meeting the requirements.

o Example: Improving Customer Satisfaction (CSAT)
- What was the problem?
  - CSAT performance for issues handled via email was 26% pts worse than issues handled via phone calls.
- What were the Customer Requirements?
  - Email-based CSAT should perform within 3% pts of voice calls; they needed to improve about 23% pts.
- What was our approach?
  - Since this CSAT performance gap between email and calls seemed extreme, we explored how comparable the processes were to each other and found drastic differences.
  - Data was collected from both groups and an apples-to-apples comparison of sampled calls/emails was made to ensure they were in parity.
- What were our findings?
  - Email-based CSAT performance was within the acceptable 3% pt range.
    - *Despite this, we found the email-based productivity was far worse than voice and costing over $2M more per year.*
    - *The team changed the scope toward improving efficiency (higher productivity) instead of effectiveness (higher CSAT).*

Defects Defined

o Below is a list of some key terms used for measuring data.
- What is a unit?
  - It is something that can be quantified by the customer.
    - *It's the agreed upon scale of scrutiny representing the measurable and observable output of the process.*
    - *It may be a tangible object or intangible, like a service or transaction.*
- What is an opportunity?
  - It is the total number of chances per unit to have a defect.
    - *Each opportunity must be independent of other opportunities, measurable and observable, and tied to a customer CTQ.*
    - *The total count of opportunities indicates the complexity of a product or service.*
- What is a defect?
  - A single instance of non-conformance to a customer requirement (a metric outside USL or LSL).
    - *For example, in a call center it may be exceeding the call duration (USL) targets or below the CSAT (LSL) targets. In IT it may be dipping below the acceptable level (LSL) of system uptime.*
- What is a defective?
  - A unit containing one or more defects; measures the severity of how defective the unit is.
    - *For example, in a call center it may be a single call where the customer has multiple unresolved issues. In product design it may be a product having multiple failures. In billing it may be an invoice having multiple errors.*
- Below is an illustration comparing defects and defectives:

5 Units:					
Defects:	Yes	Yes	Yes	No	Yes	Defect Rate = 80% (4/5)
Defectives:	2/9	3/9	1/9	0/9	3/9	Defective Rate = 20% (9/45)

Example of Defining Defect Measurements
o Example: Performance Standards in a Billing Department

Measure Type	How it will be measured
Problem	"Customers call to complain about billing errors."
Project Y	Billing Accuracy Rate (BAR) – measured by a sample review from QA
Unit	A customer's invoice
Opportunity	An area defined as a critical factor in the invoice's quality (e.g., customer name/address, quantity ordered, unit price, taxes, etc.)
Opportunities per Unit	7 (as defined by the QA)
USL	None
LSL	98% (too many errors will cause too many customer calls/complaints)
Defect	A customer invoice with one or more opportunity failures
Defective Unit	% of failures found per invoice

Practical Application
o Identify at least 3 critical metrics used by your organization and answer the following:
- What are the targets or goals for each metric?
  - Is the goal a LSL,USL, or does the metric have both?
  - Who defined the goals?
  - How are the goals determined? Are they realistic?
- What are the other defect measurements for each metric?
  - What is a unit?
  - What is an opportunity?
  - How many opportunities are there per unit?
  - What would be a defect?
  - What would be a defective unit?
- How do your answers above differ from the typical perspective from others in the organization?

SS: Measure

5

Six Sigma-Measure – Lesson 22: Identify Root Causes – DCP Overview

A introduction to the extended topic on identifying root causes using a variety of tools that will help build a data collection plan (DCP).

Pre-Requisite Lessons:
- o Six Sigma-Measure #21 – Defining the VOC and Defects

Building a Data Collection Plan (DCP)

- o Remember, our goal is to build the transfer function, or *Y = f(X)*.
  - • By now, you should already have your project Y defined.
  - • Now, we need to find the potential X's for the transfer function.
    - ▪ "Potential" implies that we don't know for sure if nor by how much each factor (X) may be influencing Y.
    - ▪ The Analyze phase will help us answer that; for now, we just need to identify them to prepare for analysis.
- o The big question: "Do you have enough data measuring the Y and every X?"
  - • To answer this, the Team needs to build a plan of what data to collect and how to collect it.
    - ▪ This is called the "Data Collection Plan" or DCP.
- o How do I build a Data Collection Plan (DCP)?
  - • When working toward a goal, define the steps by starting at the goal and working backwards:

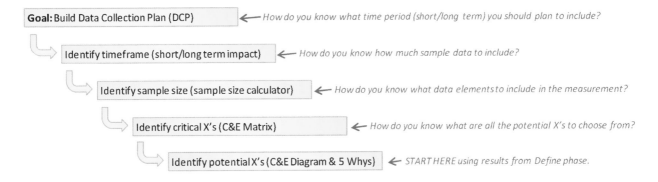

One Method for Building the DCP

- o What is the overall process for building the Data Collection Plan (DCP)?
  - • It can be built fairly quickly by conducting a meeting with the Team (about 2 – 4 hours).
  - • Below are the 5 general steps (using the IPO format) for leading that team meeting:

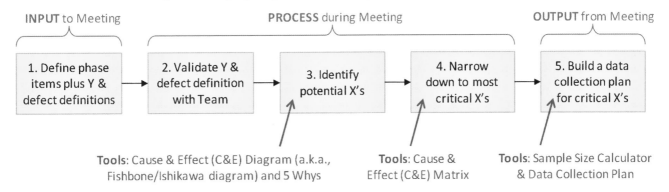

- o Are these steps required before collecting data?
  - • Not necessarily. But before quickly dismissing these steps, ask yourself the following:
    - ▪ Do I have a limited knowledge of or access to all data for the Y and every potential X?
    - ▪ Is there a moderate to high risk I may miss collecting data for a potentially critical X?
    - ▪ Is the Team commitment to the project unknown or relatively low?

- "Yes" to any of these questions may put the project at risk of failure.
  - Setting up a formal Team meeting and following the 5 steps above can help mitigate that potential risk.

DCP Meeting Details and Duration
- INPUT to Meeting
  - #1 – Define phase items plus Y & defect definitions.
    - At this point, this step should already be complete.
      - *The critical components of the Define phase that would help with this meeting include the problem statement, scope, and possibly a high-level process map or SIPOC.*
- PROCESS During Meeting
  - Meeting Kick-Off (~15 min)
    - The Sponsor/Champion may want to kick-off the meeting and return at the end to review the results.
  - #2 – Validate Y & defect definition with Team (~15 – 30 min)
    - The Team should review the following to ensure everyone agrees:
      - *Problem Statement & Scope.*
      - *Project Y – the critical metric(s) that will dictate the success or failure of the project.*
      - *Defect Definitions – these will help ensure you're targeting the right data for measuring the defects.*
  - #3 - Identify potential X's (~30 – 60 min)
    - Begin with the Cause & Effect (C&E) diagram (a.k.a., Fishbone or Ishikawa diagram).
    - Use the 5 Whys tool to drill down further within in each potential cause.
    - Use a combination of a simplified version of the C&E diagram with the 5 Whys tool .
  - #4 –Narrow down to most critical X's (~20 – 30 min)
    - Use the Cause & Effect (C&E) Matrix to filter all causes to the most likely root causes.
- OUTPUT From Meeting
  - #5 – Build a data collection plan for critical X's (~45 – 90 min)
    - Work through each potential root cause individually to assess how to measure the data.
    - Use a sample size calculator to validate the amount of data necessary for the ideal sample size.

Practical Application
- Identify at least 2 prior projects or initiatives you worked in your organization.
  - How was the data collected for each project or initiative?
    - Was there a formal plan defining what data to collect and how to collect it?
      - *If not, then was there any reason any of the data had to be re-collected (e.g., some data was missing, or didn't cover enough of a time period, or didn't include enough samples, etc.)?*
      - *How would the project or initiative have benefited (if at all) if a formal plan was defined for how to collect the data?*
      - *Why wasn't a formal plan created for collecting the data? (e.g., was it presumed that it would take too long, or the people involved didn't know how to do it, or not everyone thought it was necessary, etc.?)*
    - If there was a formal plan for collecting data, how did it affect the outcome of the project or initiative?

Six Sigma-Measure – Lesson 23: Identify Root Causes – C&E Diagram

An extension of the topic on identifying root causes using a cause & effect (C&E) diagram that will lead toward building a data collection plan (DCP).

Pre-Requisite Lessons:
  o Six Sigma-Measure #22 – Identify Root Causes – DCP Overview

Why Do We Need This Tool?
  o This topic reviewed here was originally covered on page 167.

C&E Diagram Defined
  o What is a Cause & Effect (C&E) Diagram?
  - It's a collaborative tool (a.k.a., Fishbone diagram or Ishikawa diagram) used by a team to help identify all possible causes for a particular undesirable effect.
  o What is the purpose of a C&E Diagram?
  - Helps a team focus on a problem's content and not its history.
  - Keeps the team focused on the problem's causes instead of the symptoms.
  - Uses a team's collective knowledge to build a holistic view and create team consensus of all possible causes affecting a problem.
  o Below is an example of a C&E Diagram built in Minitab:

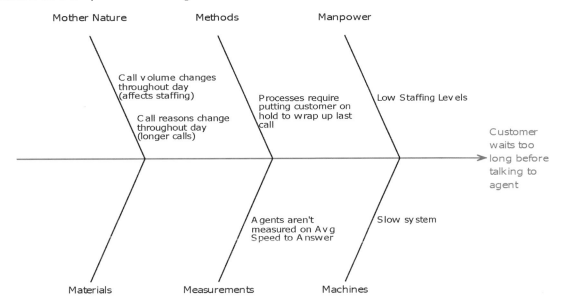

Building a C&E Diagram
  o How do you build the C&E Diagram?
  - Gather the team to build it together.
    - The C&E Diagram should be a collaborative, team product; it shouldn't be created by just one person.
    - Build the diagram with the team on a dry erase board or flip chart using post-it notes.
      - *There are many useful tools for building the diagram (e.g., Minitab, Excel, Visio, etc.); however, when working with a team, it can be more effective to build it manually first using post-it notes and using software later to document it.*
  - Define the "Effect".
    - This will most likely be the defects that were defined (or somehow tied to the problem statement).
      - *If you have multiple defects defined, then each unique defect can be an "effect" for multiple C&E diagrams.*

- Draw and label the diagram's "bones".
  - Below are common sources of variation that can be a suggested list of labels for each "bone":
    - *Manpower – Personnel issues like turnover, training, etc.*
    - *Machine - Issues related to equipment, hard/software, etc.*
    - *Method - Issues related to policies, SOPs, regulations, etc.*
    - *Measurement - Issues related to how things are measured like standards, performance, goals, etc.*
    - *Materials - Issues related to documentation, forms, etc.*
    - *Mother Nature - Issues related to outside influences like the economy, customers, vendors, etc.*

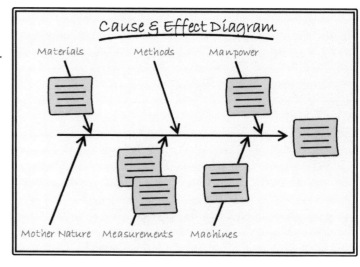

  - These labels can be modified and should be limited to just 4 to 6 unique labels.
    - *The labels help categorize possible causes so it's important that they are unique and relevant to the identified "effect".*
- Brainstorm potential causes for each of the "bone" categories.
  - Write on a post-it note a potential cause and stick it to each category. Move them around as necessary.
- Identify sub-causes by drilling more deeply into each cause by asking "Why does this happen?"
  - Notate each sub-cause as another "bone" extending off the main "bones".

Documenting a C&E Diagram
  o How do you document the C&E Diagram?
  - After the team manually builds the C&E diagram, it should be documented using various software tools to make it easily accessible and to embed it into the project storyboard.
  - Below are the instructions for building the diagram into Minitab:
    - Begin by typing the identified causes into different columns in Minitab's worksheet.
    - In Minitab go to *Stat > Quality Tools > Cause and Effect...*
    - Update the "Label" section to reflect the "bone" labels used in the diagram.
    - For the "Causes", assign the column title respective to the label you noted.
      - *If you have sub-causes, change the "In Column" drop-down to "Constant" to reflect the name of the new bone extension.*
      - *Then click the "Sub..." button and assign the column title respective to the newly created label.*
    - Type in the "Effect".
    - Add a new title as needed, otherwise Minitab will entitle it "Cause and Effect Diagram".
    - The dialog example (at right) is what was used to create the previously shown C&E diagram.

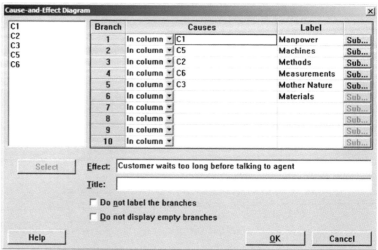

Practical Application

- o Identify a prior project or initiative you worked in your organization.
  - Try building a C&E Diagram for that project or initiative by answering the following:
    - What was used as the critical metric (project Y)?
    - How would you define a defect?
      - *This would be the ultimate "effect" used in the C&E Diagram.*
    - Review each source of variation listed below and notate any related causes leading to the effect.
      - *Manpower*
      - *Machine*
      - *Method*
      - *Measurement*
      - *Materials*
      - *Mother Nature*
    - Notate any additional sub-causes that also eventually lead to the ultimate effect.
  - Try building the C&E Diagram in an online tool like Minitab, Visio, PowerPoint, etc.

Six Sigma-Measure – Lesson 24: Identify Root Causes – 5 Whys

An extension of the topic on identifying root causes using a 5 Whys approach that will lead toward building a data collection plan (DCP).

Pre-Requisite Lessons:
- o Six Sigma-Measure #23 – Identify Root Causes – C&E Diagram

Why Do We Need This Tool?
- o This topic reviewed here was originally covered on page 167.

5 Whys Defined
- o What is 5 Whys?
  - It's a method of asking "Why?" about 5 times for each cause to drill down to the potential root cause. It doesn't have to be 5 questions if the team believes they drilled to a reasonable depth.
- o Below is an example of 5 Whys:
  - In the 1960's, Washington DC officials in charge of the Jefferson Memorial feared Jefferson's statue would be damaged by constantly washing off bird droppings. Their plan was to encase the statue in a thick layer of plastic costing $300K for the encasement and $20K/yr to maintain it. A GAO auditor came to ask "why".

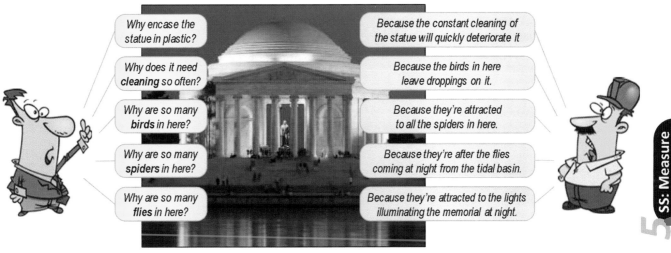

- The auditor bought a $2 solenoid to delay the lights until 30 minutes after dark. The flies were attracted to other light sources so the spiders and birds left and it was no longer necessary to encase the statue.

Practical Application
- o Identify a prior project or initiative you worked in your organization.
  - Try using the 5 Whys approach for that project or initiative by answering the following:
    - What was used as the critical metric (project Y)?
    - How would you define a defect?
      - *This would be the ultimate "effect" for which you're trying to find a cause.*
    - Why did the organization experience that effect?
    - Continue asking a series of "Why" questions until you reach a reasonable level that could represent the root cause for that undesirable effect.

Six Sigma-Measure – Lesson 25: Identify Root Causes – Combining the C&E Diagram and 5 Whys

An extension of the topic on identifying root causes by showing how the C&E diagram and 5 Whys approach can be combined for building a DCP.

Pre-Requisite Lessons:
- Six Sigma-Measure #24 – Identify Root Causes – 5 Whys

Why Do We Need This Tool?
- This topic reviewed here was originally covered on page 167.

Combining the C&E Diagram and 5 Whys
- Save time by building the C&E Diagram using 5 Whys.
  - Rather than building the C&E Diagram in the traditional fishbone format, follow these steps:
    - Layout what would be the "bone" labels as column labels in a spreadsheet.
      - *You can do this on a dry erase board or flipchart, but by doing it in a spreadsheet, it saves time for future documentation.*
    - For each column, brainstorm with the team all possible causes for the effect you're exploring.
    - As each potential cause is suggested, before writing it, use the 5 Whys to get to a root cause.
      - *For example, if the effect is long hold times for customers to talk to an agent and someone suggests a potential cause is because agents are too busy, then ask "why are they too busy?" and continue asking "why" to a reasonable root cause.*
    - Once the lowest reasonable level of a root cause is found, then write that in the respective column.
      - *Multiple causes may answer the same "why" question, so be sure to notate them all separately in the respective column.*
    - Continue for each column until all potential root causes are noted.
      - *It's OK if the same root cause is noted in more than one column or if it doesn't perfectly match that column's title.*
  - Below is an example of how the 6M "bone" labels can be documented with the root causes:

Effect or Defect: Too many billing errors

Manpower	Machine	Method	Measurement	Mother Nature	Materials
Issues related to people like turnover, poor training, etc.	*Issues related to equipment, hardware/software, fax machines, scanners, etc.*	*Issues related to policies, SOPs, regulations, etc.*	*Issues related to how things are measured like standards, performance, goals, etc.*	*Issues related to outside influences like the economy, customers, vendors, etc.*	*Issues related to documentation, forms, backup, etc.*
Employees entering wrong rates > new employees are more prone to make mistakes	Billing system is slow to update rates > New rates are effective before they're loaded into billing system> New rates don't have enough lead time.	Employees entering wrong rates > employees learning an outdated process in training > training materials don't account for current methods	Quality Assurance (QA) doesn't audit enough bills > QA doesn't have enough auditors > vacant QA positions were never back-filled due to budget cuts	Billing system outages jumble billing info > power surges cause outages	Employees entering wrong rates > billing docs have old rates > billing docs not updated in system
Billing system is slow to update rates > Commercial Sales Reps are slow at entering contract changes > Reps aren't incented to enter contract changes quickly			Quality Assurance (QA) doesn't audit enough bills > QA doesn't collect a random nor sizeable sample > QA doesn't know how to collect a random sizeable sample.		Employees entering wrong rates > customer contract data is old > contract data not updated

Practical Application
- Try combining the C&E Diagram and 5 Whys concept using the previous example.
  - In a new spreadsheet, notate how the effect to explore is "Fuel expense is too high".
    - Or you can change this to another type of expense like groceries, entertainment, phone, etc.
  - Next, notate each source of variation (6Ms) as a column heading.
  - Try answering "Why is my expense too high?"
    - For each potential cause you think of, ask yourself more "Why" questions until you reach what feels like a reasonable depth. Notate that as a possible root cause for that source of variation.
    - Repeat this process until you have explored and notated every possible cause.

Six Sigma-Measure – Lesson 26: Identify Root Causes – C&E Matrix

An extension of the topic on identifying root causes by showing how the C&E Matrix is used after a C&E diagram and 5 Whys for building a DCP.

Pre-Requisite Lessons:
   o Six Sigma-Measure #25 – Identify Root Causes – Combining the C&E Diagram and 5 Whys

Why Do We Need This Tool?
   o This topic reviewed here was originally covered on page 167.

C&E Matrix Defined
   o What is a C&E Matrix?
   - It's a tool that helps evaluate and prioritize all potential root causes.
   - Similar to a QFD tool, it objectively evaluates the team's subjective opinion about the causes.
   o What is the purpose of a C&E Matrix?
   - Narrows down all potential causes to just the critical few that are most likely the root causes.
   - Focuses the team on evaluating each cause individually and its direct impact to the effect.
   - Allows for an objective comparison of how each potential cause influences each effect.
   o Example of a C&E Matrix built in Excel:

Rating of Importance (0, 1, 3, 9)	9	3			
Process Outputs / **Process Inputs**	Billing Errors	Billing Credits		Total	Potential Data Collection Logic for each Cause
1 Employees entering wrong rates > new employees are more prone to make mistakes	3	1		30	Compare billing error rate between new and experienced employees
2 Billing system is slow to update rates > Commercial Sales Reps are slow at entering contract changes > Reps aren't incented to enter contract changes quickly	9	9		108	Compare billing error rate between customers having recently updated contracts and those not updated; compare differences between commercial vs. non-comm customers.
3 Billing system is slow to update rates > New rates are effective before they're loaded into billing system > New rates don't have enough lead time.	9	3		90	Compare billing error rate between bills affected by new rates and those unaffected by new rates.
4 Employees entering wrong rates > employees learning an outdated process in training > training materials don't account for current methods	3	9		54	See #1 (outdated training materials should primarily affect new employees coming out of training)
5 Quality Assurance (QA) doesn't audit enough bills > QA doesn't have enough auditors > vacant QA positions were never back-filled due to budget cuts	3	3		36	Compare billing error rate as monitored by QA rep between current bills and a previous time when QA had more reps.

Building the C&E Matrix

- o How do you build the C&E Matrix?
    - It's built collaboratively with the team and can be the natural next step from the C&E diagram.
    - Get the C&E diagram and follow the steps as prioritized below:

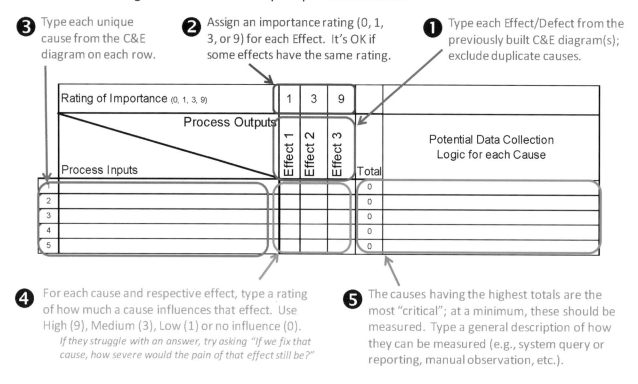

3 Type each unique cause from the C&E diagram on each row.

2 Assign an importance rating (0, 1, 3, or 9) for each Effect. It's OK if some effects have the same rating.

1 Type each Effect/Defect from the previously built C&E diagram(s); exclude duplicate causes.

4 For each cause and respective effect, type a rating of how much a cause influences that effect. Use High (9), Medium (3), Low (1) or no influence (0).
If they struggle with an answer, try asking "If we fix that cause, how severe would the pain of that effect still be?"

5 The causes having the highest totals are the most "critical"; at a minimum, these should be measured. Type a general description of how they can be measured (e.g., system query or reporting, manual observation, etc.).

Practical Application

- o Refer to the practical application from the pre-requisite lesson about combining the C&E Diagram and 5 Whys concept.
    - In that prior application, you should have identified some potential root causes (based on the effect of having too high of an expense, such as fuel expense).
    - Open the spreadsheet template for the C&E Matrix and begin to fill in the various components:
        - Type in the name of the effect that you used.
        - Assign an importance rating for each effect (if only one effect was used, then this step may be skipped).
        - Type into the designated area each of the causes you identified from the prior lesson.
        - Identify and type in the level of impact (9=High, 3=Medium, 1=Low) for each effect.
        - Select the top causes that have the highest result in the total column.
            - *These represent your narrowed down list of most likely causes to the undesired effects.*
    - Do these top causes seem logical that they would be the top?
        - If not, then there may have been some subjective bias in the results; these should be explored further.
    - If you only had one effect in this exercise, then the formal C&E Matrix may seem unnecessary.
        - The greatest value from the C&E Matrix is evident when you're evaluating multiple effects across multiple causes. To test that, just run through the exercise again by adding more effects and causes.

Six Sigma-Measure – Lesson 27: Identify Root Causes – Building the DCP

The last extension of the topic on identifying root causes by showing how to take the information gathered so far and build the DCP.

Pre-Requisite Lessons:

- ○ Six Sigma-Measure #26 – Identify Root Causes – C&E Matrix

Why Do We Need This Tool?

- ○ This topic reviewed here was originally covered on page 167.

DCP Defined

- ○ What is a Data Collection Plan (DCP)?
  - • It's a detailed plan describing exactly what data elements are necessary and who will acquire the data in order to properly measure the potential root causes that were identified.
- ○ What is the purpose of a DCP?
  - • Defines what data is to be collected and the precise method for collecting it.
  - • Unifies the team around the purpose for collecting the data and how it aligns to the causes.
  - • Keeps the team accountable for ensuring the data is collected in the prescribed manner.
- ○ Example of a DCP built in Excel:

Type of Sample Data	Dataset includes all bills for all types of customers.
Identifying Sample Data	N/A
Timeframe of Sample Data	Minimum of 2 years (to include historical data for QA rep staffing changes)
Sample Size	5000+ records

C&E #	Process Input/Output	Collection Logic	Item	Data Element	Data Type	Source	Priority	Collection Method	SME
1	New employees are more prone to make mistakes	Compare billing error rate between new and experienced employees	1	Billing Rep Tenure	Continuous	HR	Medium	Calculate tenure based on hire date and current date	Smith
2	Commercial Sales Reps aren't incented to enter contract changes quickly	Compare billing error rate between customers having recently updated contracts and those not updated; compare differences between commercial vs. non-comm customers.	2	Contract modification date	Discrete	Customer System	High	Automatic; pull all dates when a contract was modified within the analysis period (may include multiple updates per customer).	Jones
			3	Customer type	Discrete	Customer System	High	Automatic; identify per customer if they are commercial or non-commercial	Jones
3	New rates don't have enough lead time.	Compare billing error rate between bills affected by new rates and those unaffected by new rates.	4	Rate modification date	Discrete	Customer System	High	Automatic; pull all dates when a rate plan was modified within the analysis period (may include multiple updates per plan).	Jones
4	Training materials don't account for current methods	See #1 (outdated training materials should primarily affect new employees coming out of training)	5	Billing Rep Tenure	Continuous	HR	Medium	Same as item #1	Smith
5	Vacant QA positions were never back-filled due to budget cuts	Compare billing error rate as monitored by QA rep between current bills and a previous time when QA had more reps.	6	QA production rate	Continuous	QA Tracker	Medium	Manual; Collect historical rate at the lowest level (day/wk/mo) for last 2 years	Johnson
			7	QA staffing level	Continuous	QA Tracker	Medium	Manual; Identify # of QA reps for last 2 years at the same level of frequency as item #7	Johnson

Building a DCP

- ○ How do you build a Data Collection Plan (DCP)?
  - • The DCP can get *very* detailed, so try to move quickly to maintain momentum in the meeting.
  - • An effective method is to fill in the DCP one section at a time in the following order:
    1. Causes to Measure – This section ties the DCP to the list of causes from the C&E Matrix.
    2. Data Sources – This is the heart of the DCP prescribing what data to collect and how to get it.
    3. Data Collection Summary – This section summarizes the entire plan by describing the general source and context for the collected data and any relevant information about the sample size.
    4. Status – This section is reserved for future use to track the status for collecting the data.

Type of Sample Data									
Identifying Sample Data									
Timeframe of Sample Data		**3. Data Collection Summary**							
Sample Size									

C&E #	Process Input/Output	Collection Logic	Item	Data Element	Data Type	Source	Priority	Collection Method	SME	Data Collection Status
1. Causes to Measure				**2. Data Sources**						**4. Status**

- o Populating the (1) Causes to Measure section.
  - Get the C&E Matrix and for the causes that had high totals (more critical) fill in the following:
    - The C&E Matrix reference # - makes it easier to tie the DCP backwards to find out why it's on the DCP.
    - Process Input/Output – this is the respective cause description.
    - Collection Logic – A general description to remind how the data will probably need to be collected.
- o Populating the (2) Data Sources section.
  - Begin with the first cause in the list and identify each of the following:
    - Item – type an incrementing # in order to track and reference each data element separately.
    - Data Element – this can either be a data field in a system or an existing or new metric.
      - *Data Field – This can be the easiest to get; just type the name of the field/column to pull from the system.*
      - *Existing Metric – This may be easy to get; just type the name of the metric and include a description about it, as needed.*
      - *New Metric – This is the hardest to get; type a name to call the metric and include a brief description about it. This metric may require collecting and factoring multiple data elements.*
    - Data Type – this will either be "discrete" or "continuous" (see Measure module #5).
    - Source – Where will that data element be collected from? Identify a system name, report name or a brief, general description of where that data will be collected.
    - Priority – How essential is the data element for measuring the root cause? Type High, Medium, or Low.
    - Collection Method – Describe in more detail how to collect that data element depending on its type:
      - *Data Field – Describe the system table and field name(s) and any other relevant info for how to pull it from the system.*
      - *Existing Metric – Describe the specific method for pulling the metric including a report name or location, a page or reference from a report, a time period for the report (e.g., daily, weekly or monthly report), etc.*
      - *New Metric – Describe exactly how this new metric will be calculated, the data sources used, the equation or logic for calculating it, etc. If there are multiple collection methods, consider splitting the cells/rows to track them separately.*
    - SME – Identify the primary person who is responsible for collecting the respective data element.
  - What if there are multiple data elements needed for each potential root cause?
    - Split the cells or rows to reflect the multiple data elements per cause.
  - What if the same data element is necessary for more than one potential root cause?
    - It should still be identified in the plan, so simply reference the data element item # that was already noted so that it's later understood the same data element can be used for testing multiple root causes.
    - It may be helpful to change the cell color for those duplicate data elements to easily find them.
- o Populating the (3) Data Collection Summary section.
  - After all of the data elements have been identified, define the following summary elements:
    - Type of Sample Data – A general description of what the final dataset should include for analysis.
    - Identifying Sample Data – This is not required; it could describe the general method, logic or intent for the dataset in how the data will be evaluated and analyzed.
    - Timeframe of Sample Data – Describes the beginning and ending time period represented in the sample data. This is essential to ensure the sample data isn't bias and includes all potential variation.
      - *This will be discussed in more detail later in this module.*

- Sample Size – Prescribes the appropriate sample size to collect for all the data. This may vary by data element and need to be clarified in its respective "Collection Method" cell.
  - *This will be discussed in more detail later in this module.*
- At this point, the DCP can be considered complete.
  - Ensure the entire team agrees with the DCP and understands their responsibility in collecting the data.
  - If there are any "TBD" items identified, be sure the team is committed to discussing these further as needed to ensure all necessary data elements are collected.
- Populating the (4) Status section.
  - This section is merely for tracking the progress of collecting data.
  - Consider scheduling recurring team meetings to track the data collection process.
    - This will help keep the SMEs accountable for collecting the data they committed to get.
    - Keep the DCP as a consistent team document to help remind them why the data collection is necessary.

Practical Application
- Refer to the practical application from the pre-requisite lesson about narrowing down the potential root causes by building the C&E Matrix.
  - In that prior application, you should have identified and narrowed down some potential root causes (based on the effect of having too high of an expense, such as fuel expense).
  - Open the spreadsheet template for the DCP and begin to fill in the various components:
    - Section 1 – Causes to Measure
      - *This is the information that comes from the C&E Matrix.*
    - Section 2 – Data Sources
      - *This is the critical portion of the DCP that defines exactly what data to collect, where to collect it from, how to collect it, and who will be collecting it.*
      - *Though this portion may be difficult to complete since it's a small, fictitious example, try to work through it as if it were a large, major expense for your organization.*
    - Section 3 – Data Collection Summary
      - *Remember, this information would just give a high level summary about all the data that you plan to collect.*
    - Section 4 – Status
      - *There's nothing to add here for this fictitious example.*

Six Sigma-Measure – Lesson 28: MSA - Overview

The first of an extended series on conducting a measurement system analysis (MSA) to help test the reliability of collected data.

Pre-Requisite Lessons:
- o Six Sigma-Overview #2 – Risk Analysis – The Reason We Use Statistics
- o Six Sigma-Measure #2 – The Necessity of the Measure Phase

Measurement System Defined
- o What is a measurement system?
  - • It refers to the method used for collecting data or calculating metrics.
  - • Some examples of measurement systems include the following:

Churn
# of customer cancellations / Total # of subscribed customers

OIBDA
Operating Income + Depreciation + Amortization + Tax + Interest
("OIBDA" stands for "Operating Income Before Depreciation & Amortization".)

Average Revenue per Unit (ARPU)
Total Revenue / Total # of Units
(A unit can be a customer, product, etc.)

Average Call Duration
Total Call Duration / Call Volume

- o How do you know you can trust the measurement system?
  - • Many metrics are taken for granted; but how do you know they're accurate?
  - • What is the risk of having errors in the measurement system?
  - • What if no measurement system exists for what you need to measure? How do you create it?

MSA Defined
- o What is a measurement system analysis (MSA)?
  - • It is a method for testing and validating the accuracy & precision of a measurement system.
  - • It measures the level of risk in the reliability of a measurement system.
  - • It's *not* just calibration; it's a more formal and methodical analysis of the measurement system.
- o What's the difference between Accuracy & Precision?
  - • **Accuracy** measures how correct a measurement is to a known standard or "master".
  - • **Precision** measures variation *within* the same and *between* different operators.

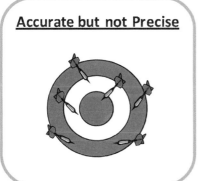

Accurate but not Precise

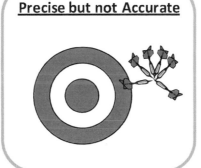

Precise but not Accurate

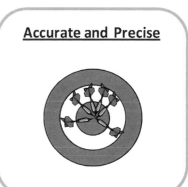

Accurate and Precise

Measuring Accuracy and Precision

- ○ How do we measure accuracy & precision in a MSA?
  - Accuracy and precision are measured from 3 perspectives:

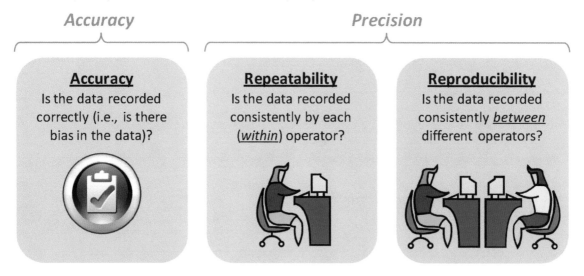

- ○ Some MSA tools can also measure by additional perspectives:
  - Linearity – is there bias over the operating range?
  - Stability – is there variation over time in the data process or measurement system?
  - Resolution/Discrimination – is the measure granular enough to detect small bias or variation?

General Flow of the MSA

- ○ Below is an overview of how a MSA is conducted and the 3 perspectives analyzed.
  - MSAs generally involve 3+ operators doing 3+ review trials of the same items.

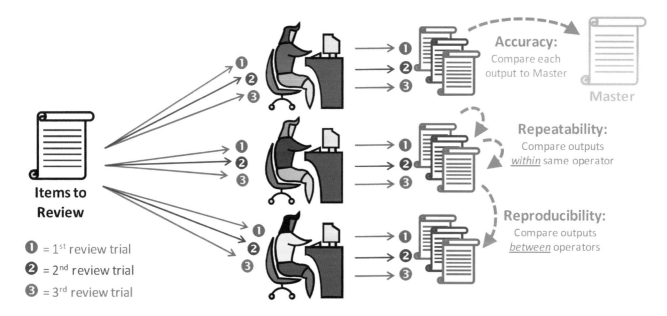

- This represents a blind study where the operators don't know they're processing the same info.
- This example is what is commonly used in a transactional environment.
  - Transactions to review may include customer calls, invoices, purchases, etc.
  - In a manufacturing environment, it would be a part or product that is reviewed by each operator.

Is the MSA Necessary?

- A Measurement System Analysis (MSA) can get very complex and take extra time.
  - The more complex (a lot of variables) and more operator-dependent (manual processes & measurements) in the measurement system, then the more time is required to do the MSA.
- If it takes so much time, then is a MSA really necessary?
  - Maybe. Like everything else, it depends on **_RISK_**. That is, what is the risk of _not_ doing a MSA?
- How do I measure the risk of not doing a MSA?
  - You can't; there isn't a formal, objective way to measure the risk of not doing a MSA.
  - Even so, you can subjectively assess the risk by asking yourself the following:
    - Are you at least 90% confident you can trust the accuracy of the measurement system?
    - Are you at least 90% confident you can trust the precision (lack of variation) of the measurement system?
    - Is the measurement system _not_ based on human involvement (e.g., time & motion, tick sheets, etc.)?
    - Is the speed of finishing the project more important than the accuracy or quality of the analysis?
      - _This is a balance of comparing risk vs. reward._
    - If you later discover the data was unreliable, would it be acceptable to redo the data collection & MSA?
  - If the team answers "Yes" to these questions, then it may be acceptable to skip the MSA.
    - This should be reviewed with the Champion & Sponsor so they're aware of the risks of skipping the MSA.
- Since MSAs can take on many forms and get very complex; let's keep it simple.
  - This module introduces the concepts and use of simple MSA tools that are most common.

Overview of Building the MSA

- There are 4 general steps for building the MSA:

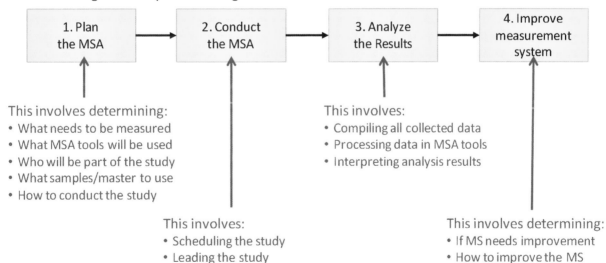

This involves determining:
- What needs to be measured
- What MSA tools will be used
- Who will be part of the study
- What samples/master to use
- How to conduct the study

This involves:
- Scheduling the study
- Leading the study
- Collecting data from the study

This involves:
- Compiling all collected data
- Processing data in MSA tools
- Interpreting analysis results

This involves determining:
- If MS needs improvement
- How to improve the MS
- Redoing MSA (as needed)

Practical Application

- Identify at least 3 completed projects or initiatives you worked in your organization.
  - At any point was there any data or critical information that was accused of being unreliable?
    - If so, what caused the accusation to be raised?
    - Was the accusation true (i.e., was it true that the data was unreliable)?
      - _If so, why wasn't the reliability of the data tested in advance?_
      - _How could a MSA have helped catch or prevent the unreliability of the data?_

- *Otherwise if the data was reliable after all, then what could've been done differently to prevent the accusation?*
- If there was no accusation at all, then why not (i.e., what kept anyone from challenging the data)?
  - *Should the data have been challenged, but perhaps no one was willing nor knowledgeable enough to challenge it?*

Six Sigma-Measure – Lesson 29: MSA – Planning & Conducting the MSA

An extended review on the series on building a MSA that covers the first two steps on how to plan and conduct the MSA.

Pre-Requisite Lessons:
  o Six Sigma-Measure #28 – MSA - Overview

Overview of Building the MSA
  o This topic reviewed here was originally covered on page 185.

1. Planning the MSA
  o What needs to be measured?
    • Begin with the project Y (output).
      ▪ Since the Y is the most critical metric for the project, it should be included in the MSA.
    • Include potentially high impacting X's that were identified in the Cause & Effect (C&E) Matrix.
    • Include any additional metrics that are considered essential for analysis.
    • Do measurements from a system need to be included in the MSA?
      ▪ Maybe. System-generated measurements generally have better precision than manually-based measurements. Many prudently managed systems normally undergo accuracy & precision validations. However, if there is a potential risk in the system's integrity, the MSA can help measure that risk.
  o What MSA tools will be used?
    • There are two basic tools we'll review that will depend on the type of data you're analyzing.
      ▪ Discrete Data = Attribute Agreement Analysis or Multiple Attribute R & R
      ▪ Continuous Data = Gage R & R Study
    • If you require a MSA on both data types, then both types of tools will be necessary.
      ▪ The difference may affect how you collect the data and eventually set it up for analysis in the tools.
  o Who will be part of the study?
    • You will need to decide who is responsible for recording and collecting the data.
    • A general rule for testing reproducibility is to use 3 different operators.
      ▪ The operators should represent a typical skill level (if possible, exclude strong experts and novices).
  o What samples/masters will be used?
    • "Masters" refer to a known set of accurate items to measure. They will serve as the standard for validating accuracy & precision.
      ▪ In a manufacturing environment, it can be sample products or customer production requirements.
      ▪ In a transactional environment, it can be a set of existing transactions/measures approved as accurate.
    • The "master" process outputs should be randomly selected so they represent process variation.
    • A general rule for testing is to use 10 to 20 different process outputs.
      ▪ If that's not possible, then a general rule is to select enough samples so that the (# of samples) x (# of operators) ≥ 14.
  o How will you conduct the study?
    • A plan should be developed that outlines the following:
      ▪ When will the MSA begin?
      ▪ Who are the operators that are part of the MSA?
      ▪ How will the process outputs to test be distributed to each operator?
      ▪ When will the process outputs be distributed to the operators for each review trial?
      ▪ When are the operators expected to return the results for each review trial?
      ▪ What processes are the operators expected to follow for their review process?

— *Is there a specific SOP that should be referenced?*

— *Are there specific criteria or requirements they are expected to follow?*

- Will calibration be done before the MSA begins? If so, when will it begin?
  - *Calibration should NOT be performed <u>during</u> the MSA. It should only be done before the MSA, if at all.*
  - *If no calibration is done before the MSA, the MSA results will more likely reflect the true As-Is process.*
- Build the document or template that the operators will use for collecting the data.
  - This will probably require understanding what data is collected and what MSA tools will be used.
    - *This will be reviewed in more detail in step #3 – Analyze the Results.*

2. Conduct the MSA

- Schedule the MSA
  - Begin to execute the MSA plan.
    - Begin to coordinate and schedule the MSA with all operators and analysts.
    - Pull the sample that will be used as the master dataset.
    - Distribute to the operators the document or method the operators will use to record the data.
      - *Ensure the operators have full understanding of what data to record for the study and how to record it.*
      - *Ensure the operators understand the deadlines for providing the data.*
- Leading and collecting data from the study
  - If observing the collection of the data, try to observe and document the following:
    - Process deviations
    - Environmental changes
    - Differences in skills or behaviors between operators
    - Observable errors in data entry
    - Observable errors in use of the measurement tool
  - Important: Do <u>NOT</u> calibrate nor make any process changes during the MSA!

Practical Application

- Due to the nature of a MSA, there isn't a practical application for the first two steps of planning and conducting the MSA.
  - Despite this, please review the suggested steps for planning and conducting the MSA.
    - How do these steps differ from other methods you may have seen for validating the reliability of data?

Six Sigma-Measure – Lesson 30: MSA – Attribute ARR Test

An extended review on the series on building a MSA, this covers the 3rd step of analyzing the results by using the Attribute ARR test.

Pre-Requisite Lessons:
- o Six Sigma-Measure #29 – MSA – Planning & Conducting the MSA

Overview of Building the MSA
- o This topic reviewed here was originally covered on page 185.

3. Analyze the Results
- o Compiling all collected data
  - As each trial of data is returned by each operator, be sure to clearly define and store them before compiling them.
  - Once all data is collected from each operator from each trial, begin to compile the data.
    - The method for compiling the data depends on the MSA tool to be used (based on below examples).
- o Processing data in MSA tools and Interpreting Analysis Results
  - There are two basic types of MSA tools we'll review that depend on the data being analyzed:
    - Discrete Data = Attribute ARR
    - Continuous Data = Gage R & R
  - The next few slides will review the Attribute ARR tool and how to interpret the results.

3. Analyze the Results: Attribute ARR Tool
- o Single Attribute ARR
  - This MSA tool does a simple analysis on a single set of discrete values (e.g., yes/no, good/bad, on/off, etc.).
    - This example is from the Minitab worksheet file "*MSA Example 01.mtw*".
    - This tool is not available in Minitab 14 Student Version.

A reference for each item being reviewed.

The "master" (correct answer)

The answer from each operator

A reference for each operator

A reference for each trial run. Minitab doesn't require this but it's helpful to track it in the data.

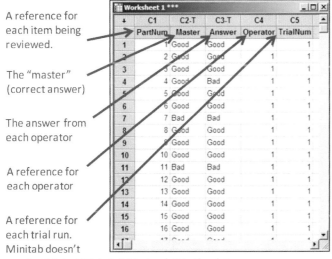
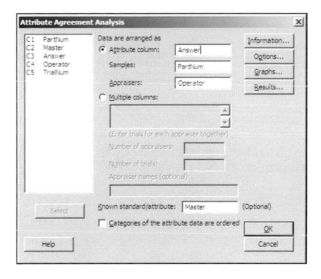

- Minitab outputs 4 types of results:
  - Within Appraisers – This is the Repeatability perspective.
  - Each Appraiser vs. Standard – This is the Accuracy perspective per operator.
  - Between Appraisers – This is the Reproducibility perspective.
  - All Appraisers vs. Standard – This is the Accuracy perspective for all operators.

- In each output, pay closest attention to the "Percent" and "Kappa" based on this scale:

Acceptance: >90% 70% - 90% <70%

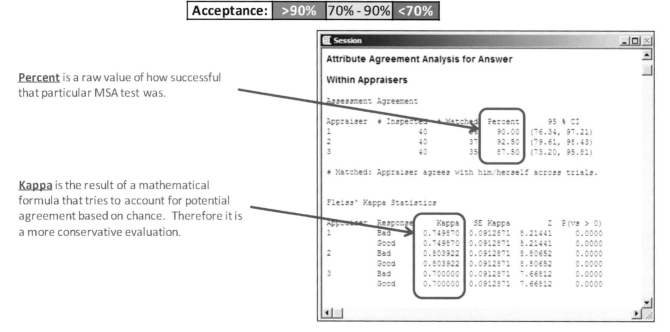

Percent is a raw value of how successful that particular MSA test was.

Kappa is the result of a mathematical formula that tries to account for potential agreement based on chance. Therefore it is a more conservative evaluation.

o Multiple Attribute ARR
  • This MSA tool can do a discrete analysis on a set of many values (both discrete and continuous).
    ▪ A blank template can be used from the Excel file "*MSA Multiple Attribute ARR.xls*" which is setup to analyze 40 different "parts" having 20 different attributes for up to 3 different trials.
    ▪ The below example is from the Excel file "*MSA Example 02.xls*" which analyzes only 4 unique values.

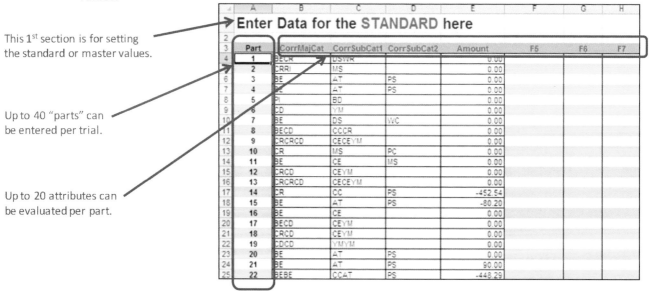

This 1st section is for setting the standard or master values.

Up to 40 "parts" can be entered per trial.

Up to 20 attributes can be evaluated per part.

  • Typing in the "Data Entry Tables"
    ▪ The data should align to the right operator/trial in the "Data Entry Tables" tab.
      – First, enter the "STANDARD" or master values. This is only entered once; it doesn't have multiple trials.
      – Next, enter the data for "Operator 1 – Trial 1", "Operator 1 – Trial 2", then "Operator 1 – Trial 3". Repeat per Operator.
      – If you neither have 40 parts nor 20 attributes per Operator/Trial, then leave those cells blank.

> The # of parts & attributes should at least be consistent with what was entered as the "Standard" or master.

- Go to the "Report" tab and click the "Run ARR Report" button. Below is an example output:

Click here once all values are entered in the "Data Entry Tables" tab

This section evaluates the Accuracy, Repeatability & Reproducibility.

This breaks down the analysis by row as a total (at top) and per attribute.

The MSA may fail overall...

...even though it may pass for one or more attributes.

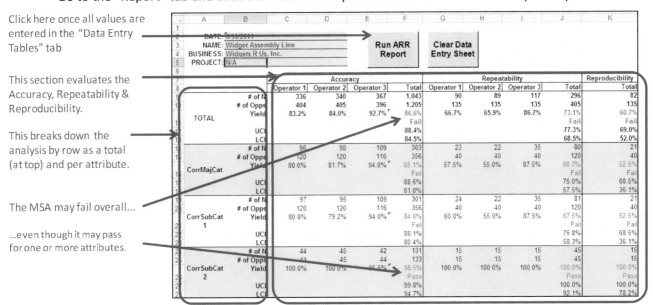

Practical Application

o Open the "*MSA Example 01.mtw*" file in Minitab.
   - Run the Attribute Agreement Analysis in Minitab as instructed in this lesson.
     - Do your results look the same as those described in the lesson?
   - Randomly select at least 10 of the values in the "Answer" column and change the good/bad value.
     - Re-run the analysis and compare the results from that last set of results. How do they differ?
o Open the "*MSA Example 02.xls*" file in Excel.
   - Go to the "Data Entry Tables" tab. Randomly select at least 20 of the values for any Operator and any Trial and change any of the provided values.
     - Go to the "Report" tab and click the "Run ARR Report" to re-run the analysis. How do the results differ from those provided in this lesson?

SS: Measure

5

Six Sigma-Measure – Lesson 31: MSA – Gage R&R Test

An extended review on the series on building a MSA, this covers the 3rd step of analyzing the results by using the Gage R&R test.

Pre-Requisite Lessons:
- o Six Sigma-Measure #30 – MSA – Attribute ARR Test

Overview of Building the MSA
- o This topic reviewed here was originally covered on page 185.

3. Analyze the Results
- o This topic reviewed here was originally covered on page 189.

3. Analyze the Results: Gage R&R Tool
- o Gage (Variable) R&R
  - • This MSA tool analyzes continuous data.
    - ▪ There are 2 types of Gage R&R studies; the difference depends on the parts used in the MSA:
      - **– Crossed Gage R&R Study** *– use this when the same parts are used by each operator for each trial.*
      - **– Nested Gage R&R Study** *– use this when different parts are used by each operator for each trial.*
    - ▪ Neither study analyzes accuracy; they only target precision (repeatability & reproducibility).
    - ▪ The below example is from the Minitab worksheet file *"MSA Example 03.mtw"*.
      - *– This tool is not available in Minitab 14 Student Version.*

A reference for each item being reviewed.

The "master" (correct answer)

The answer from each operator

A reference for each operator

A reference for each trial run. Minitab doesn't require this but it's helpful to track it in the data.

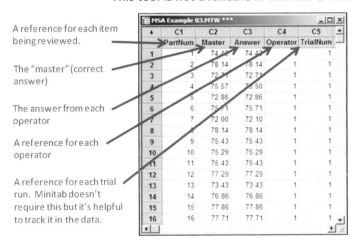

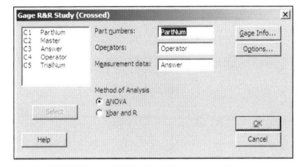

- Minitab outputs results in 2 forms:
  - Session Window – this *descriptively* displays the statistical results of the MSA.
  - Graphs Window – this *visually* displays the statistical results of the MSA.
- We'll examine how to interpret the results from both of these types of outputs.

Session Window	Graphs Window
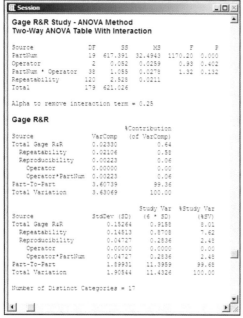	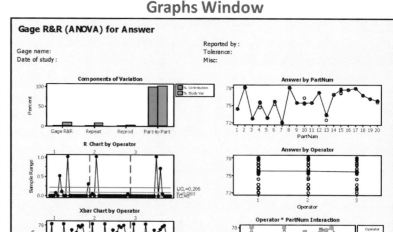

- Below is how to interpret the descriptive display of the MSA's results – shown in Minitab's session window.

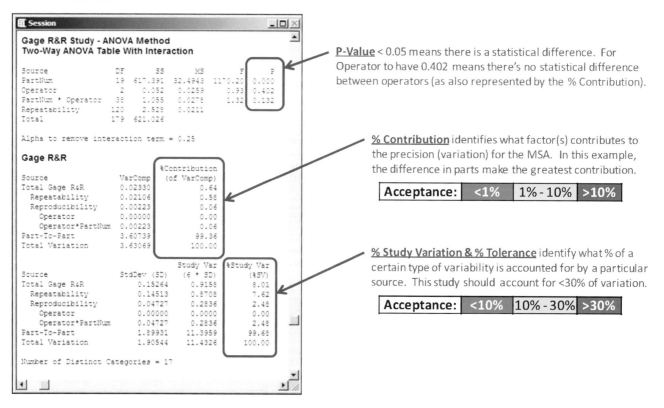

P-Value < 0.05 means there is a statistical difference. For Operator to have 0.402 means there's no statistical difference between operators (as also represented by the % Contribution).

% Contribution identifies what factor(s) contributes to the precision (variation) for the MSA. In this example, the difference in parts make the greatest contribution.

Acceptance:	<1%	1% - 10%	>10%

% Study Variation & % Tolerance identify what % of a certain type of variability is accounted for by a particular source. This study should account for <30% of variation.

Acceptance:	<10%	10% - 30%	>30%

- Below is how to interpret the graphical display of the MSA's results – shown in Minitab as a separate graph.

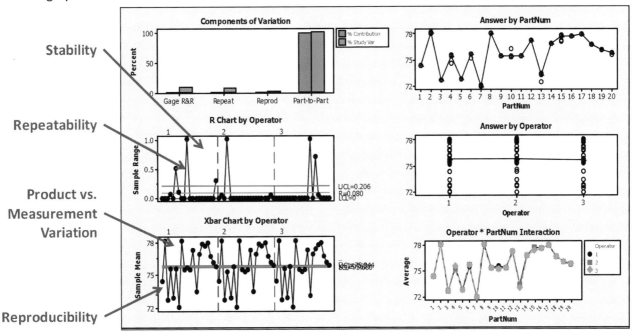

Stability

Repeatability

Product vs. Measurement Variation

Reproducibility

o Stability & Repeatability Range Chart
  - What does it do?
    - Identifies within operator variability.
    - Reflects variation between different measurements made by the same operator for the same part used by the same measurement tool/method.

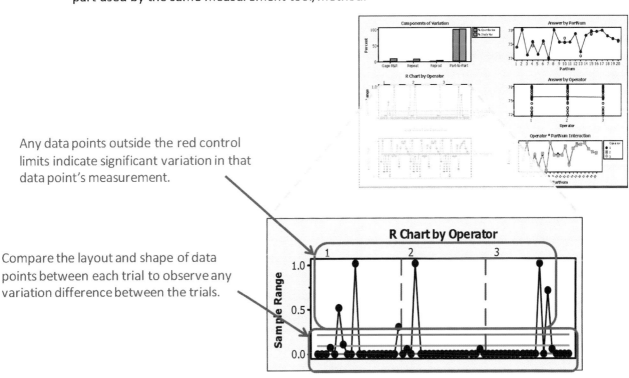

Any data points outside the red control limits indicate significant variation in that data point's measurement.

Compare the layout and shape of data points between each trial to observe any variation difference between the trials.

o Part vs. Measurement Variation and Reproducibility Xbar Chart
   • What does it do?
      ▪ Identifies measurement system variation as compared to part variation.
      ▪ Also identifies the difference between the average measures of different operators.

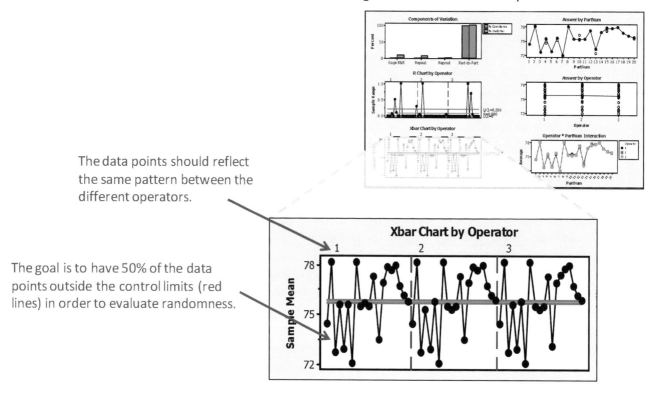

The data points should reflect the same pattern between the different operators.

The goal is to have 50% of the data points outside the control limits (red lines) in order to evaluate randomness.

Practical Application

o Open the "*MSA Example 03.mtw*" file in Minitab.
   • Run the Gage R&R Analysis in Minitab as instructed in this lesson.
      ▪ Do your results look the same as those described in the lesson?
   • Randomly select at least 10 of the values in the "Answer" column and change their values.
      ▪ Re-run the analysis and compare the results from that last set of results. How do they differ?

Six Sigma-Measure – Lesson 32: MSA – Improving the Measurement System

The last part of an extended review on the series on building a MSA, this covers the 4th step of improving the measurement system if the MSA fails.

Pre-Requisite Lessons:
- Six Sigma-Measure #31 – MSA – Gage R&R Test

Overview of Building the MSA
- This topic reviewed here was originally covered on page 185.

4. Improve Measurement System
- Did the MSA fail?
  - You may need to improve the measurement system depending on what part of the MSA failed and how severely it failed.
    - How did the MSA fail? How can the problem be fixed where it failed?
    - Use the list below to troubleshoot how to fix where the MSA failed:

Failure	How did it fail?	How can it be fixed?
Stability	• Lack of procedures	• Write clear & simple SOPs
	• Measurement device reacts differently to variation when used	• Verify measurement device functions properly and can handle procedure variation
	• Non-standardized steps in process	• Standardize and bring compliance to SOPs
	• Changed measurement method during MSA	• Re-run MSA with a consistent measurement method
Repeatability	• Operator error	• Develop process maps for most repeatable operator
	• Measures are rounded by system, operator or measuring device	• Replace/adjust measurement device to allow for smaller units
	• Differences in operator technique between measurements	• Instruct operator about entire measurement device scale
Reproducibility	• Operator bias (e.g., operator not following SOP)	• Find & remove operator bias (e.g., enforce SOP)
	• Rounding up/down of measurement, or inverting or forgetting sign for measurement	• Implement consistent procedures (SOP)

- What do you do after the MSA failure has been identified and fixed?
  - Ensure the improvements were effective; it may be necessary to re-run the MSA.
    - If possible, use the same parts from the first MSA.
    - If the MSA isn't re-run, the same original risks may exist as if the MSA was never run in the first place.

Practical Application
- Due to the nature of a MSA, there isn't a practical application for the last step of improving the measurement system when running the MSA.
  - Despite this, please review the prior suggestions answering "How can it be fixed?"
    - What additional ways would you recommend for fixing the different areas where the MSA failed?

Unit 6: Six Sigma Analyze Phase

The most common tools and concepts that pertain to the Analyze phase of the DMAIC methodology of Six Sigma which is intended to help us apply analytical tests on the collected data for finding the root cause of the problem we're trying to solve.

Six Sigma-Analyze – Lesson 1: Analyze Phase Roadmap (Level 3)

A deeper look into level 3 of the DMAIC roadmap that identifies critical steps and tools for navigating a project through the Analyze phase.

Pre-Requisite Lessons:
- Six Sigma Overview #05 – DMAIC Roadmap (Levels 1 & 2)

DMAIC Roadmap (Level 1)
- This topic reviewed here was originally covered on page 91.

DMAIC Roadmap (Level 2)
- This topic reviewed here was originally covered on page 91.

Analyze Phase Roadmap (Level 3)
- The DMAIC roadmap can be drilled down even deeper to a 3rd level for each phase.
  - Level 3 questions can guide someone to the specific tool(s) for navigating a project or initiative.

	Question Levels 1 to 3	Tool/Resource
Analyze	**Can you statistically validate what are the root causes (inputs or Xs)?**	
	Do you know what the process capability is (a.k.a. Voice of Process or VOP)?	
	Have you assessed the statistical characteristics of your data (i.e., mean, standard deviation, median, mode, etc.)?	Descriptive Statistics
	Do you know if your process is stable?	I-MR chart
	Do you know if your process distribution is normal or non-normal?	Normality Plot (AD test)
	Do you know what your key process capability measurements are (i.e., DPMO, DPU, Z score, sigma level, p(d), Cpk, etc.)?	Process Capability (with six pack)
	Do you know what the target sigma level or performance objectives are for the project?	Performance Objectives
	Have you done hypothesis testing to identify which potential Xs are statistically significant?	
	Have you identified the yes/no question for the practical problem of each potential X?	Hypothesis Testing
	Have you converted the practical problem into a statistical problem for each potential X?	Hypothesis Testing
	Have you identified for every potential X the right statistical test based on data type (e.g. continuous vs. discrete), test type (e.g., proportions, central tendency, spread, or relationships), and comparison level (e.g., 1:Standard, 1:1, or 2+ factors)?	Hypothesis Testing
	Have you interpreted the statistical results for the test on each potential X?	Hypothesis Testing
	Have you translated the statistical results into a practical solution that answers the original practical problem for each potential X?	Hypothesis Testing
	OUTPUTS: Updated Project Storyboard, key process capability metrics, and hypothesis testing results	

Practical Application
- Identify at least 2 projects you led or worked on in the past.
  - For each project, review all the questions in the Analyze phase level 3 roadmap.
    - What questions and related tools/resources were not addressed in the project?
    - Why were they not addressed?
    - What different outcome or results could've been realized if they were addressed in the project?

SS: Analyze

6

Six Sigma-Analyze – Lesson 2: Descriptive Statistics

An introduction to some less common yet very useful statistics that help to describe the data we're analyzing.
Pre-Requisite Lessons:
- Six Sigma-Measure #08 – Distributions: Overview
- Six Sigma-Measure #11 – Central Tendency
- Six Sigma-Measure #12 – Spread

Descriptive Statistics Defined
- What are descriptive statistics?
  - They are a variety of standard statistical metrics that describe the data you're analyzing.
    - These standard statistical metrics include the mean, standard deviation, median, mode, etc.
  - Minitab can also show descriptive statistics along with a graphical summary (shown below).
    - The examples below are run on "MetricA" field in the *Minitab 14 Sample Data v1.MPJ* file:

From *Stat > Basic Statistics > Graphical Summary...*   From *Stat > Basic Statistics > Display Descriptive Statistics...*

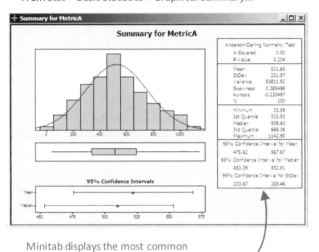

Minitab displays the most common
descriptive statistics with the graphical summary....

...or a full list of them without the graphical summary

Type of Descriptive Statistics
- Descriptive statistics can be categorized based on what they're measuring.
  - They're either a measurement of central tendency or variation (or spread).
  - Below is a chart of the descriptive statistics grouped by how frequently they're used:

Usage	Central Tendency	Variation or Spread
Common	• Mean or Average (μ) • Median (50th percentile) • Mode	• Range (Min and Max) • Deviation • Variance • Standard Deviation (σ) • Stability Factor • Interquartile Range (IQR)
Less Common	• Standard Error of the Mean (SE Mean) • Trimmed Mean • Mean of the Squared Successive Differences (MSSD)	• Coefficient of Variance (COV) • Skewness • Kurtosis

- Review of distributions.
  - As part of this discussion on descriptive statistics, we'll briefly review the different types of distributions (previously discussed in the Measure phase).

Distributions
- This topic reviewed here was originally covered on page 134, 135 and 137.

Central Tendency: Less Common Statistics

o Standard Error of Mean (SE Mean)

Question	Answer
How is it calculated?	$$\frac{\sigma}{\sqrt{n}}$$
What is its purpose?	It's used to determine the confidence interval of the mean.
How is it interpreted?	A smaller SE Mean is better, indicating more confidence of the mean.
What is a practical application?	Multiply the SE Mean by the # of standard deviations for which you want your confidence interval. For example, to get a 95% confidence interval around the mean, calculate as follows (or use 3 to calculate 99% confidence interval): *(μ − (SE Mean x 2))* and *(μ + (SE Mean x 2))* The result tells you that for every data sample you take of that same population, there's a 95% chance your mean for that future sample will fall somewhere within that confidence interval. The smaller the interval, then the more confident you can be about your mean. How can you make your SE Mean smaller? Either decrease your standard deviation or increase your sample size.

o Trimmed Mean

Question	Answer
How is it calculated?	Recalculate the mean using only data points between the 5th and 95th percentiles.
What is its purpose?	It's used to recalculate the mean without considering outliers that may be significantly influencing it.
How is it interpreted?	If the trimmed mean is very different from the mean, then there are severe outliers influencing the mean.
What is a practical application?	Use the trimmed mean as a quick check to see how significant the outliers are influencing the overall mean. If the mean shifts a lot, then examine the outliers to see if they should be removed from the analysis as anomalies. If the mean doesn't shift much, then the outliers in the data should probably not be removed from the analysis.

o Mean of the Squared Successive Differences (MSSD)

Question	Answer
How is it calculated?	$$\frac{\sum(X_{i+1} - Xi)^2}{2(n-1)}$$
What is its purpose?	It's used to validate the randomness of the sample dataset.
How is it interpreted?	The closer the MSSD is to the variance, then the more likely the sample data is truly random.
What is a practical application?	Variance is calculated by the deviation of each data point to the sample mean. However, MSSD is calculated by the deviation of one data point to another successively through the dataset (e.g., point 1 is compared to point 2, point 2 is compared to point 3, point 3 is compared to point 4, etc.). If the sequence of selected data is truly random, then they should arrive at about the same value. Despite the intimidating formula, just compare the MSSD and variance in the descriptive statistics results. If they are relatively close to each other (e.g., one is at least 90% to 95% of the other), then your dataset sequence is probably random.

Variation: Less Common Statistics

o Coefficient of Variance (COV)

Question	Answer
How is it calculated?	$\left(\dfrac{\sigma}{\mu}\right) x\ 100$
What is its purpose?	It normalizes the variability for a measurement.
How is it interpreted?	A smaller COV is better (closer to zero), meaning the variation isn't as significant relative to the mean.
What is a practical application?	Use this when wanting to compare the variation between two completely different measurements. For example, suppose you have the following call center measurements: **Metric** / **Mean** / **Std Deviation** Call Duration — 600 seconds — 100 seconds Customer Satisfaction (CSAT) — 85% — 15% At first glance, it seems CSAT may be smaller, but based on these measurements, the COV for Call Duration is 16.7 and the COV for CSAT is 17.6. Since the call duration COV is smaller, it has less variation relative to its mean than CSAT.

o Skewness

Question	Answer
What is its purpose?	Identifies how skewed (bias) the data is.
How is it interpreted?	Use the following scale to interpret skewness: 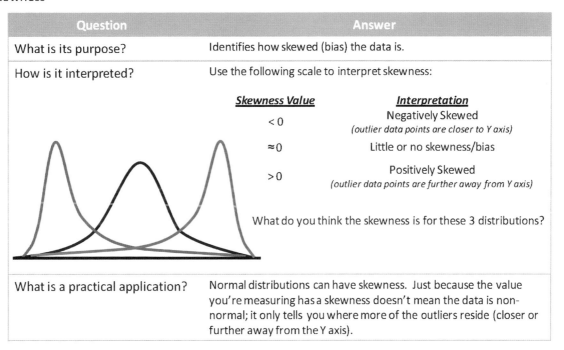 **Skewness Value** / **Interpretation** < 0 — Negatively Skewed *(outlier data points are closer to Y axis)* ≈ 0 — Little or no skewness/bias > 0 — Positively Skewed *(outlier data points are further away from Y axis)* What do you think the skewness is for these 3 distributions?
What is a practical application?	Normal distributions can have skewness. Just because the value you're measuring has a skewness doesn't mean the data is non-normal; it only tells you where more of the outliers reside (closer or further away from the Y axis).

o Kurtosis

Question	Answer
What is its purpose?	Measures the shape of your normal curve where your central tendency is.
How is it interpreted?	Use the following scale to interpret kurtosis:

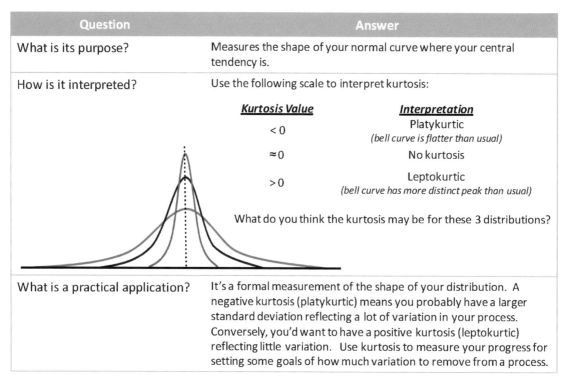

Kurtosis Value	Interpretation
< 0	Platykurtic (bell curve is flatter than usual)
≈ 0	No kurtosis
> 0	Leptokurtic (bell curve has more distinct peak than usual)

What do you think the kurtosis may be for these 3 distributions?

| What is a practical application? | It's a formal measurement of the shape of your distribution. A negative kurtosis (platykurtic) means you probably have a larger standard deviation reflecting a lot of variation in your process. Conversely, you'd want to have a positive kurtosis (leptokurtic) reflecting little variation. Use kurtosis to measure your progress for setting some goals of how much variation to remove from a process. |

Practical Application

o Identify at least 3 metrics used by your organization and do the following:
- For each metric, try to pull at least 15 to 20 data points (the frequency doesn't matter as much, so they can be daily, weekly, monthly, etc.).
- Run the descriptive statistics described in this lesson.
    - For example, add the data to Minitab and go to *Stat* > *Basic Statistics* > *Display Descriptive Statistics...*, and select at least the statistics discussed in this lesson.
- Answer these questions for each metric and identify which descriptive statistic answers it for you:
    - Does the metric have a right tail distribution, left tail distribution, or neither?
    - Are outliers significantly affecting your metric?
    - Is your data considered to be random?
    - Is the distribution curve relatively flat, peaked, or neither?
    - Of the 3 metrics, which one has the most variation around the mean, and which has the least?
    - Of the 3 metrics, which one has the biggest confidence interval and which has the smallest?

Six Sigma-Analyze – Lesson 3: Process Capability: Overview

The first of a series of lessons about process capability; this lesson defines what process capability is and reviews a method for calculating it.

Pre-Requisite Lessons:
  - ○ None

Process Capability Defined

- ○ What is process capability?
  - • As the term implies, it's a measurement of how capable a process is performing.
  - • It generally consists of a group of metrics that view the process from different perspectives.
  - • "Process Capability" is also referred to as the "Voice of the Process" or VOP.
    - ▪ The term VOP is in contrast to VOC which stands for "Voice of the Customer" and reflects the customer's requirements or expectations of the process.
- ○ Why do we need to measure the process capability?
  - • VOP is like an As-Is snapshot of how the process is performing. When comparing this to the customer's requirements (VOC), the performance gaps become the project opportunities.

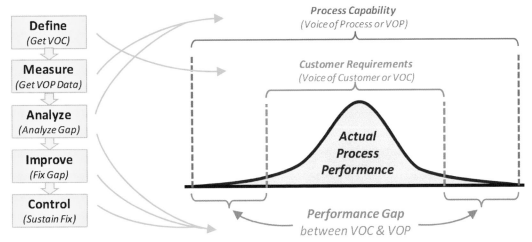

Process Capability Calculation Method

- ○ What is the method for calculating the process capability?
  - • There are a few steps and tools involved in the process. Below is an overview of the method:

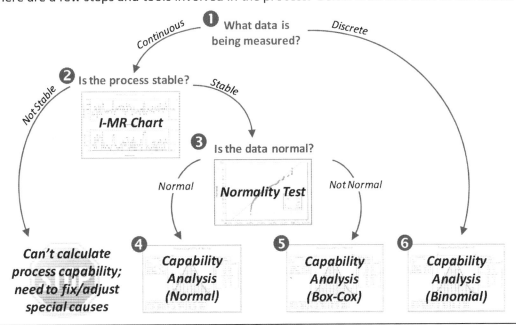

Practical Application

- o Identify at least 2 continuous metrics used by your organization.
  - We will use these metrics for the next few lessons discussing process capability.
  - To your knowledge, has the process capability already been calculated for either metric?
    - If so, what is it?
  - Do you (or your organization) consider each metric to be "capable"?
    - If so, how is that capability tested and validated?
  - If your organization found those metrics were not capable, what actions would be taken (if any)?
    - What other critical metrics or processes could be affected if these metrics were not capable?

Six Sigma-Analyze – Lesson 4: Process Capability: Steps 1 to 3

As part of a series about process capability, this lesson reviews the first 3 steps for following a method for calculating the capability of a process.

Pre-Requisite Lessons:
- o Six Sigma-Measure #07 – Data Types
- o Six Sigma-Measure #09 – Distributions: Normal
- o Six Sigma-Measure #10 – Distributions: Non-Normal
- o Six Sigma-Measure #16 – Testing for Special Cause Variation
- o Six Sigma-Measure #21 – Defining Defects

Process Capability Review
- o This topic reviewed here was originally covered on page 207.

1. What data is being measured?
- o To answer this, define the type of data and key data characteristics.
- o Review from the Measure phase lesson on "Data Types".
  - • This topic reviewed here was originally covered on page 131.
- o Review from the Measure phase lesson on "Defining Defects".
  - • This topic reviewed here was originally covered on page 164.

2. Is the process stable?
- o To answer this, use control charts to assess the stability of the process.
- o Review from the Measure phase lesson on "Testing for Special Cause Variation".
  - • This topic reviewed here was originally covered on page 149.

3. Is the data normal?
- o To answer this, test the data's normality.
- o Review from the Measure phase lessons on normal and non-normal distributions.
  - • This topic reviewed here was originally covered on page 135 and 137.

Practical Application
- o Refer to the 2 continuous metrics identified in the first lesson about process capability.
  - • For each metric, answer the first 3 steps of this process capability calculation method:
    - ▪ What data is being measured (i.e., the type of data)?
      - – *If it's discrete, then plan to advance to the step 6 about the capability analysis (binomial) test.*
      - – *If it's continuous, then continue to the next question.*
      - – *In either case above, be sure to also identify what is a unit, an opportunity, a defect, and a defective.*
    - ▪ Is the process stable?
      - – *If it's not stable, then plan to stop further analysis for that metric until you can collect data that reflects a stable process.*
      - – *If it is stable, then continue to the next question.*
    - ▪ Is the data normal?
      - – *If it's normal, then plan to advance to step 4 about capability analysis (normal).*
      - – *If it's not normal, then plan to advance to step 5 about capability analysis (Box-Cox).*

Six Sigma-Analyze – Lesson 5: Process Capability: Step 4 (Normal Dist)

As part of a series about process capability, this lesson shows how to assess the capability of a process that's based on a normal distribution.

Pre-Requisite Lessons:
  - Six Sigma-Analyze #04 – Process Capability: Steps 1 to 3

Process Capability Review
  - This topic reviewed here was originally covered on page 207.

Capability Analysis (Normal Dist)
  - Follow the next set of steps when the following conditions exist in the data:
    - Data type = Continuous
    - Process = Stable
    - Distribution = Normal
  - How do I calculate the process capability?
    - The example below is run on "MetricA" field in the *Minitab 15 Sample Data v1.MPJ* file:
      - NOTE: Minitab 14 Student Version does not support this process capability calculation. Follow instructions later on how to manually calculate the process capability.

From *Stat > Quality Tools > Capability Analysis > Normal...*

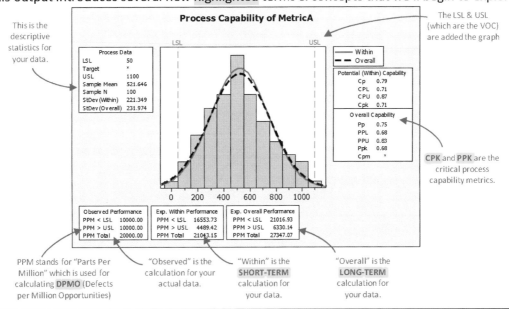

Identify the field used for measuring the process (probably the project Y).

Use "1" for subgroup size. See the Measure phase lesson on "Rational Sub-Grouping" for more details.

Type in the customer's requirements (VOC) in terms of an upper and/or lower spec limit.

An Example from Minitab
  - Below is the output from Minitab.
    - This output introduces several new highlighted terms & concepts that we'll begin to explore.

This is the descriptive statistics for your data.

The LSL & USL (which are the VOC) are added the graph

CPK and PPK are the critical process capability metrics.

PPM stands for "Parts Per Million" which is used for calculating DPMO (Defects per Million Opportunities)

"Observed" is the calculation for your actual data.

"Within" is the SHORT-TERM calculation for your data.

"Overall" is the LONG-TERM calculation for your data.

Process Capability (DPMO)

- o What is DPMO?
  - It's a count of the number of defects expected to occur for every one million opportunities run in the process.
    - It's essentially like a percent defective or p(d) that's carried out to the 4th decimal place.
- o How is it calculated?
  - The equation for DPMO is as follows:

$$\left(\frac{Total\ Defects}{Total\ Units \times Opportunities\ per\ Unit} \right) \times 1,000,000$$

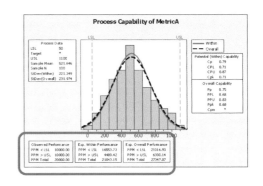

- o How is it interpreted? (using the Minitab example)

In the actual dataset that was "observed", 1% (or 10,000 out of 1,000,000) of the data points each fell below the LSL and above the USL; together 2% (or 20,000 out of 1,000,000) of the data points are defects

By calculating for the short-term, 1.66% of the data points would fall below the LSL and only 0.45% would lie above the USL leaving a total p(d) of 2.1% (or 97.9% success).

By calculating for the long-term, 2.1% of the data points would fall below the LSL and only 0.63% would lie above the USL leaving a total p(d) of 2.73% (or 97.27% success).

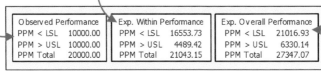

Observed Performance		Exp. Within Performance		Exp. Overall Performance	
PPM < LSL	10000.00	PPM < LSL	16553.73	PPM < LSL	21016.93
PPM > USL	10000.00	PPM > USL	4489.42	PPM > USL	6330.14
PPM Total	20000.00	PPM Total	21043.15	PPM Total	27347.07

What can we conclude from this? Based on the short & long term calculations, it appears the process is more likely to fail (create defects) that fall below the LSL.

Process Capability (Z score or sigma level)

- o What is a Z Score (a.k.a. sigma level)?
  - Practically, Z score measures the VOP in relation to the VOC. In a sense, it measures the "severity of pain" in the process not meeting the customer's requirements.
  - Technically, Z score measures the number of standard deviations (σ) a data point (like USL) is from the mean.
- o How is it calculated?
  - The equation for Z score is as follows ("X" is generally an observation like USL): $Z = \left(\frac{X - \mu}{\sigma} \right)$

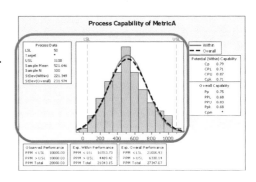

- o How is it interpreted?
  - From the Minitab example, use USL as "X":

$$Z = \left(\frac{X - \mu}{\sigma} \right) = \left(\frac{1100 - 521.6}{221.3} \right) = \left(\frac{578.4}{221.3} \right) = 2.61$$

- What can we conclude from this?
  - If a capable process has at least 3 σ between the spec limit and mean, then this process is not quite capable.
- How is short vs. long term data accounted for in the Z score?
  - If the data is short term (Z_{st}) and you want to calculate long term capability (Z_{lt}) then subtract 1.5σ from Z.
  - If the data is long term (Z_{lt}) and you want to calculate short term capability (Z_{st}) then add 1.5σ to Z.
  - Therefore, a formula we can derive from this is: $Z_{lt} = Z_{st} - Z_{shift}$ (or 1.5)

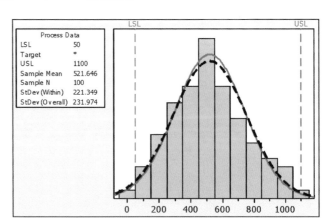

- **Note**: this shift of 1.5σ is widely accepted in the Lean Six Sigma community, but there is also some strong debate as to its validity. For critical analyses, it may be best to do a separate analysis each for short and long term perspectives.

Process Capability (Convert Z to Probability)

- o What is cumulative probability?
    - It refers to the portion of your distribution (area under the curve) derived by your Z score.
    - It's a calculation converting the Z score into a p(d), which is used for calculating the DPMO.
        - For example, having the short term Z scores (sigma levels) shown at right, then the DPMO can be determined.
- o How is it calculated?

Sigma$_{ST}$	% Success	DPMO
1σ	30.9%	691,462
2σ	69.1%	308,538
3σ	93.3%	66,807
4σ	99.38%	6,210
5σ	99.977%	233
6σ	99.9997%	3.4

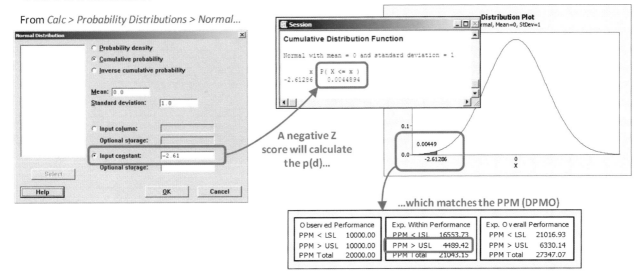

From *Calc > Probability Distributions > Normal...*

A negative Z score will calculate the p(d)...

...which matches the PPM (DPMO)

Process Capability (Cpk & Ppk)

- o What is Cpk & Ppk?
    - These measure short-term (Cpk) and long-term (Ppk) process performance (VOP) in relation to the spread (or total tolerance) between LSL & USL (VOC).
- o How is it calculated?
    - The equation for Cpk is as follows (Ppk is similar):

$$C_{pk} = \min\left(\frac{USL - \mu}{3\sigma_{st}}, \frac{\mu - LSL}{3\sigma_{st}}\right) = \min\left(\frac{Z_{usl}}{3}, \frac{Z_{lsl}}{3}\right)$$

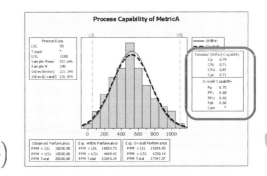

- o How is it interpreted? (using the Minitab example)
    - Cp represents the process *potential* while Cpk is the process *performance*.
    - If Cpk < 1, the process is not capable within the tolerance (LSL & USL).
    - The higher Cpk is above 1, the more capable the process is of achieving results within tolerance.
    - If Cp is much greater than Cpk, then the process mean is missing the target.
        - If they are both <1, then it may be better to focus on shifting the mean *before* reducing variation in order to get faster improvements.
    - Ppk will always be lower than Cpk. But if it's significantly lower, then it's driven by the long term variation (mean shift) between sub-groups.

Potential (Within) Capability	
Cp	0.79
CPL	0.71
CPU	0.87
Cpk	0.71
Overall Capability	
Pp	0.75
PPL	0.68
PPU	0.83
Ppk	0.68
Cpm	*

- In these cases, focus on reducing that sub-group variation knowing that the long-term process capability (Ppk) has the potential of improving closer to the Cpk.

Minitab's Process Capability Sixpack™

- Minitab combines the tests for stability, normality & process capability into one chart.
    - Go to *Stat > Quality Tools > Capability Sixpack > Normal...*
        - NOTE: Minitab 14 Student Version does not support this process capability tool.

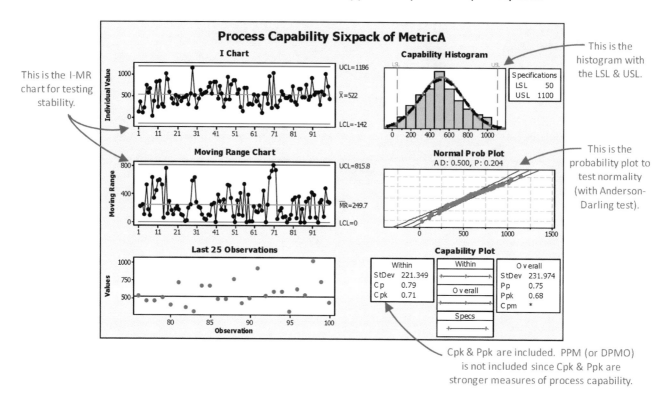

This is the I-MR chart for testing stability.

This is the histogram with the LSL & USL.

This is the probability plot to test normality (with Anderson-Darling test).

Cpk & Ppk are included. PPM (or DPMO) is not included since Cpk & Ppk are stronger measures of process capability.

Practical Application

- Refer to the 2 continuous metrics identified in the first lesson about process capability.
    - For each metric, answer the following:
        - Was the metric a continuous value, from a stable process having a normal distribution?
            - *These attributes are based on the first 3 steps of the process capability calculation method.*
        - If so, then run a capability analysis for a normal distribution and answer the following:
            - *What is the DPMO?*
            - *What is the Z score?*
            - *What is the cumulative probability or p(d)?*
            - *What are the Cpk and Ppk?*
        - Based on the above findings, is the process capable?

Six Sigma-Analyze – Lesson 6: Process Capability: Step 5 (Non-Normal Dist)

As part of a series about process capability, this lesson shows how to assess the capability of a process that's based on a non-normal distribution.

Pre-Requisite Lessons:

  o Six Sigma-Analyze #05 – Process Capability: Step 4 (Normal Dist)

Process Capability Review

  o This topic reviewed here was originally covered on page 207.

Review of Capability Analysis Metrics

  o Below are the metrics previously reviewed when calculating process capability:
  - Defects per Million Opportunities (DPMO)
    - This topic reviewed here was originally covered on page 212.
  - Z score or sigma level
    - This topic reviewed here was originally covered on page 212.
  - Cpk and Ppk
    - This topic reviewed here was originally covered on page 213.

Capability Analysis (Non-Normal Dist)

  o How do you measure process capability for non-normal data?
  - Use the same process capability tool in Minitab, but transform the data first.
    - A Box-Cox transformation will raise the data to the power λ (lambda) – a number between -5 and 5.
    - This method will "normalize" the non-normal data in order to calculate the process capability metrics.
  - In the "Capability Analysis (Normal Distribution)" box, click the "Box-Cox..." button.

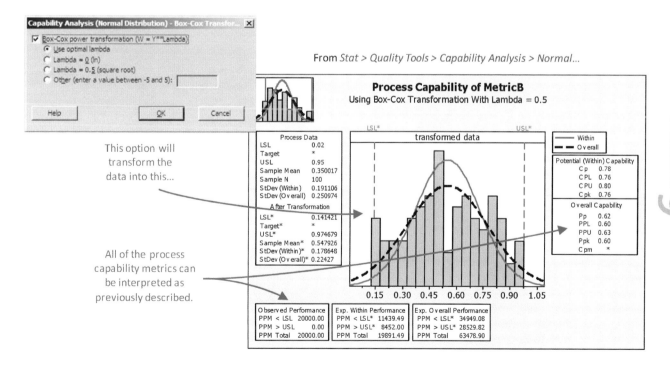

Practical Application

  o Refer to the 2 continuous metrics identified in the first lesson about process capability.
  - For each metric, answer the following:
    - Was the metric a continuous value, from a stable process having a non-normal distribution?

- *These attributes are based on the first 3 steps of the process capability calculation method.*
- If so, then run a capability analysis for a non-normal distribution and answer the following:
  - *What is the DPMO?*
  - *What is the Z score?*
  - *What is the cumulative probability or p(d)?*
  - *What are the Cpk and Ppk?*
- Based on the above findings, is the process capable?

Six Sigma-Analyze – Lesson 7: Process Capability: Step 6 (Binomial)

As part of a series about process capability, this lesson shows how to assess the capability of a process that's based on discrete or binomial data.

Pre-Requisite Lessons:
- o Six Sigma-Analyze #05 – Process Capability: Step 4 (Normal Dist)
- o Six Sigma-Analyze #06 – Process Capability: Step 5 (Non-Normal Dist)

Process Capability Review
- o This topic reviewed here was originally covered on page 207.

Review of Capability Analysis Metrics
- o Below are the metrics previously reviewed when calculating process capability:
  - • Defects per Million Opportunities (DPMO)
    - ▪ This topic reviewed here was originally covered on page 212.
  - • Z score or sigma level
    - ▪ This topic reviewed here was originally covered on page 212.
  - • Cpk and Ppk
    - ▪ This topic reviewed here was originally covered on page 213.

Process Capability (Discrete Data)
- o How do you measure process capability for discrete data?
  - • There are two tools that you can use; the one you use will depend on how your data is setup:
    - ▪ Binomial Analysis – Uses P chart for measuring the # of defectives out of a total sample.
      - – *For example, measuring unresolved calls, broken products, erroneous bills, etc.*
    - ▪ Poisson Analysis – Uses U chart for measuring the # of defects per unit (DPU).
      - – *For example, measuring # of errors a phone rep made per call, # of errors appearing on each bill, etc.*
  - • The example below is run on "MetricB" field in the *Minitab 15 Sample Data v1.MPJ* file:

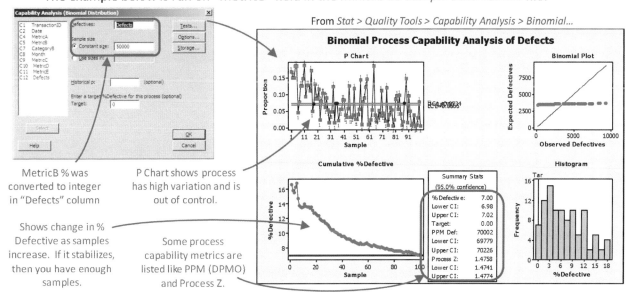

MetricB % was converted to integer in "Defects" column

P Chart shows process has high variation and is out of control.

Shows change in % Defective as samples increase. If it stabilizes, then you have enough samples.

Some process capability metrics are listed like PPM (DPMO) and Process Z.

Practical Application
- o Identify at least 2 discrete metrics used by your organization.
  - • Run each metric through the capability analysis for binomial data and answer the following:
    - ▪ What is the DPMO?
    - ▪ What is the Z score?
  - • Based on the above findings, is the process capable?

Six Sigma-Analyze – Lesson 8: Defining Performance Objectives

A review of how to define the performance objectives based on the results of a process capability analysis.
Pre-Requisite Lessons:
  o Six Sigma-Analyze #05 – Process Capability: Step 4 (Normal Dist)
  o Six Sigma-Analyze #06 – Process Capability: Step 5 (Non-Normal Dist)

Defining Performance Objectives
  o How do you define performance objectives?
    • At this point, you should know the Performance Gap (difference between VOC & VOP).
    • Review the analysis and Performance Gap with the team and consider the following:
      ▪ How severe is the performance gap?
      ▪ Are the customer requirements (VOC) realistic?
        – *Should they be re-evaluated or adjusted in consideration of the VOP?*
      ▪ What constraints (equipment, people, cost, etc.) may limit the opportunity to improve the gap (or VOP)?
    • Based on a team review of the gap, determine the following:
      ▪ What is a reasonable objective for improving the VOP?
        – *Can it be defined in terms of DPMO, p(d), Z score, Cpk/Ppk, etc.*
      ▪ How should the scope be modified to account for meeting these new performance objectives?
    • Ensure the team (especially the Sponsor & Champion) agree with the performance objectives and any potential changes made to the scope.

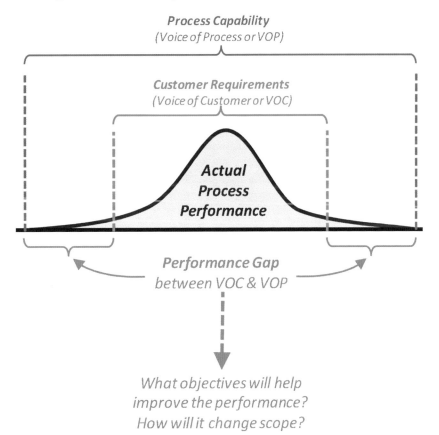

Practical Application
  o Refer to the 2 continuous metrics identified in the lessons about process capability.
    • For each metric, answer the following:
      ▪ Restate the key process capability values for each metric as previously defined:
        – *What is the DPMO?*

- *What is the Z score?*
- *What is the cumulative probability or p(d)?*
- *What are the Cpk and Ppk?*

- Based on the above findings, what is the performance gap between the VOC and VOP?
- What is a reasonable objective for improving that performance gap?
  - *How would you define that objective in terms of process capability? (e.g., how much can the DPMO or p(d) be reduced? Or how much can the Cpk and Ppk be improved?)*

Six Sigma-Analyze – Lesson 9: Hypothesis Testing: Overview

An introductory overview to an extended series about hypothesis testing. This lesson includes the general 4 step process used for hypothesis testing.

Pre-Requisite Lessons:

  o None

An Example from our Judicial System

  o To understand hypothesis testing, let's first look at an example of our judicial system.
    • An entire Lean or Six Sigma project can be compared to a courtroom trial as described below:

Jury = **Sponsor/Champion**
Make final decision and determine consequences/actions.

Judge = **Peers, Mentor or MBB**
Reviews process to ensure methodology is followed and sufficient evidence is provided.

Prosecutor = **Six Sigma Black Belt**
Primary leader for evaluating evidence and proving to the jury the Defendant's guilt.

Defendant = **Root Cause**
Represents the source of the problem and why there's a case in the first place.

Witness/Evidence = **Data Analysis**
The proof used by the Prosecutor to demonstrate the Defendant's guilt beyond "a reasonable doubt" .

Hypothesis Testing Defined

  o What is hypothesis testing?
    • It's a formal method of statistically testing and validating data for differences between factors.
    • It's a method of testing one factor (X) at a time to see if/how it influences the output (Y).
  o What is the purpose of hypothesis testing?
    • To find evidence that statistically proves what is the root cause for the original problem in the project.
  o How does it fit into our judicial system example?

    • It represents all the testing and analysis done on the evidence *before* the trial.
    • The burden of proof is on the prosecution; they must provide sufficient evidence to convict the Defendant.
    • Likewise, hypothesis testing is used to validate if the evidence is sufficient to prove what is the root cause.
  o What if the prosecution doesn't have evidence?
    • Generally, if the prosecution can't fulfill their burden of proof, their case is dismissed.
    • Likewise, if there's insufficient evidence to prove the root cause, the project may be at risk.
      ▪ At a minimum there is no data to validate the root cause so the risks of continuing should be considered.

Gathering the Evidence

o The police gather and analyze evidence the same way we do in DMAIC.
  • The DMAIC methodology of Six Sigma is used for solving a problem with an unknown root cause.
  • Likewise, the police use a similar method to solve a crime having an unknown suspect.

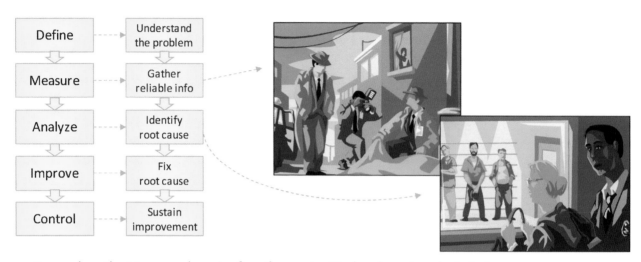

o Remember, the Measure phase is often the most critical and most neglected phase.
  • The Measure phase was when we gathered the data that may become evidence.
  • In solving a crime, if the evidence is not reliable, then it can't be used to convict.
  • Likewise, validating the evidence using hypothesis testing is useless if the data isn't reliable.

Examining the Evidence

o How do we examine the evidence?
  • Again, the approach is very similar to how the police examine evidence as described below:

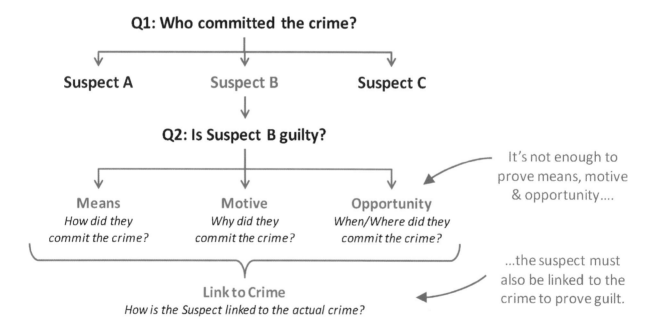

  • Just as evidence is examined for each suspect, each factor (X) is examined in the data.
  • Just as evidence must link the suspect to the crime, hypothesis testing may similarly prove the "means, motive & opportunity", but the compiled evidence must link the suspected factor (X) as the true root cause of the problem.

Proof Beyond a Reasonable Doubt

- o How much proof is needed for "convicting" the root cause?
  - In our judicial system, a suspect is innocent until proven guilty "beyond a reasonable doubt".
  - Likewise, prudent data analysis presumes innocence on each factor (X) until proven "guilty".
    - Hypothesis testing does this by starting the test with a null (innocent) and alternative (guilty) hypothesis.
    - It measures "reasonable doubt" using alpha (α) and beta (β) error types (more on this later).
- o How much evidence is needed for proof beyond reasonable doubt?
  - It doesn't require 100% facts, but it depends on the "jury" (i.e., the Sponsor & Champion).
    - Refer to the ABC model on page 37:

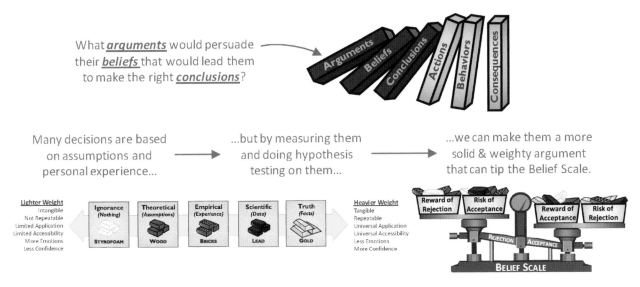

What **_arguments_** would persuade their **_beliefs_** that would lead them to make the right **_conclusions_**?

Many decisions are based on assumptions and personal experience...

...but by measuring them and doing hypothesis testing on them...

...we can make them a more solid & weighty argument that can tip the Belief Scale.

Measuring Statistical Risk

- o Statistics generally use two measurements for risk: Alpha (α) and Beta (β).
  - To explain these, let's assume that all possible evidence is represented as an empty glass.
    - The glass is filled with what data/evidence we have.
    - How full should the glass be for me to make a reasonable conclusion?

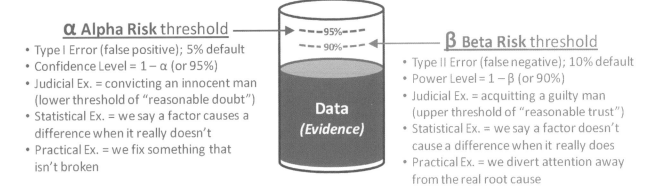

α Alpha Risk threshold
- Type I Error (false positive); 5% default
- Confidence Level = $1 - α$ (or 95%)
- Judicial Ex. = convicting an innocent man (lower threshold of "reasonable doubt")
- Statistical Ex. = we say a factor causes a difference when it really doesn't
- Practical Ex. = we fix something that isn't broken

β Beta Risk threshold
- Type II Error (false negative); 10% default
- Power Level = $1 - β$ (or 90%)
- Judicial Ex. = acquitting a guilty man (upper threshold of "reasonable trust")
- Statistical Ex. = we say a factor doesn't cause a difference when it really does
- Practical Ex. = we divert attention away from the real root cause

- o What is the ideal level of risk I need?
  - It depends on the inherent risks of what's being analyzed.
    - Would you want 5% risk for pharmaceutical testing, surgical equipment, or nuclear engineering?
  - Most statistical tests require a confidence level (1-α), but not many require a power level (1-β).
- o **Bottom Line**: if the test results are unexpected or fall between the alpha & beta risks, then test again with more samples.

Hypothesis Testing: 4 Step Process

o The 4 step process for hypothesis testing begins and ends with keeping it practical:

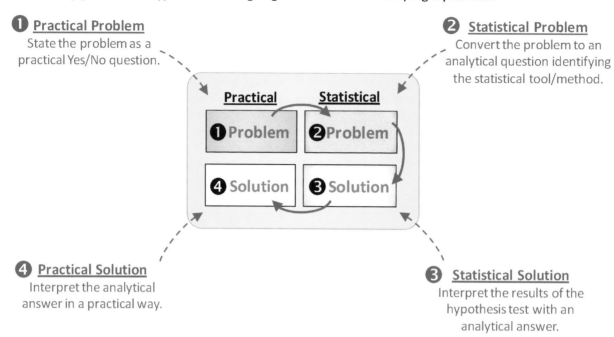

❶ Practical Problem
State the problem as a practical Yes/No question.

❷ Statistical Problem
Convert the problem to an analytical question identifying the statistical tool/method.

❹ Practical Solution
Interpret the analytical answer in a practical way.

❸ Statistical Solution
Interpret the results of the hypothesis test with an analytical answer.

o Steps 2 & 3 are the heart of hypothesis testing where we'll spend the most time.

Practical Application

o Think of at least 2 prior projects or initiatives you worked in your organization.
- How confident are you that the results (i.e., your conclusions) from those examples were right?
  - What are you basing that confidence on?
  - If your confidence for either example is less than 95%, then what are some of the "reasonable doubts" you have about the accuracy of those results?
  - If you were asked to present those examples for a real legal case in court, would you have the same level of confidence?
    – *If not, then why not?*
  - Would you change the data or analysis that was done before submitting it as evidence?
    – *What changes would you make and why?*
    – *Are these changes indicative of risks that you or others overlooked in the project or initiative? If so, then why were these overlooked and not further analyzed or validated to mitigate that risk?*

Six Sigma-Analyze – Lesson 10: Hypothesis Testing: Formal and Informal Sub-Processes

An extension on a series about hypothesis testing, this lesson builds on the prior 4 steps for hypothesis testing by looking at the 6 basic sub-steps.
Pre-Requisite Lessons:
   o Six Sigma-Analyze #09 – Hypothesis Testing - Overview

Hypothesis Testing: 4 Step Process
   o This topic reviewed here was originally covered on page 224.

Formal & Informal Sub-Processes Defined
   o How do I define a statistical problem?
      • There are two ways to define a statistical problem for hypothesis testing: formally or informally.
         ▪ **Formal**: Stringent process used with high risk situations and/or highly precisioned instruments.
         ▪ **Informal**: Less stringent process used in general business operations.
      • We'll review the formal method to be familiar with the concepts, but most of the training will use the informal method.
   o Formal Hypothesis Testing generally follows these 6 steps:

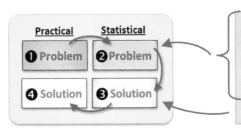

1. Define the objective.
2. State the Null Hypothesis (H_0) and Alternative Hypothesis (H_a).
3. Define the confidence ($1-\alpha$) and power (beta or $1-\beta$).
4. Collect the sample data.
5. Calculate the P-value.
6. Interpret the results: accept or reject the null hypothesis (H_0).

   o Informal Hypothesis Testing accelerates the same basic concepts of the formal testing:
      • The informal way is not a reason to dilute the analysis or ignore any potential risks.
      • It merely accelerates some steps by not formally documenting the details.

1. Define the objective. *(combined with "practical problem")*
2. ~~State the Null Hypothesis (H_0) and Alternative Hypothesis (H_a).~~
3. ~~Define the confidence ($1-\alpha$) and power (beta or $1-\beta$).~~ *($\alpha = 5\%$)*
4. Collect the sample data.
5. Calculate the P-value. *(combined with "practical solution")*
6. ~~Interpret the results: accept or reject the null hypothesis (H_0).~~

Formal Hypothesis Testing (steps 1 & 2)
   1. Define the Objective.
      • What is the question you're trying to answer?
         ▪ State this objective as a Yes/No question.
         ▪ Emphasize the difference between values.
            – Example: *"Is there a difference between A and B?"*
         ▪ Include more specific detail such as referencing the data elements that will be analyzed.
            – Example of Practical Problem: *"Does it cost more to use a vendor to run our call center?"*
            – Translated to objective: *"Is there a difference in cost between a vended and internally operated call center?"*
   2. State the Null Hypothesis (H_0) and Alternative Hypothesis (H_a).
      • The Null Hypothesis (H_0) assumes innocence, i.e., no difference between the factors.
      • The goal in hypothesis testing is to test the Null Hypothesis (H_0) to see if it's true:
         ▪ If *true*, then H_0 is *accepted*, i.e., the analyzed factor is "innocent" – there is no difference.
         ▪ If *false*, then H_0 is *rejected*, i.e., the analyzed factor is presumed "guilty" – there is a difference.

— In this latter case, the Alternative Hypothesis (H_a) is accepted when the Null Hypothesis is rejected.

- Example: "Is there a difference in cost between a vended and internally operated call center?"

$$(H_0): \mu_{vendor} = \mu_{internal} \quad \textit{(i.e., \underline{no difference} between mean cost)}$$

$$(H_a): \mu_{vendor} \neq \mu_{internal} \quad \textit{(i.e., \underline{difference} between mean cost)}$$

- Here's this example in the form of distributions:

Formal Hypothesis Testing (step 3)

3. Define the confidence ($1-\alpha$) and power ($1-\beta$).
   - This topic reviewed here was originally covered on page 223.

Formal Hypothesis Testing (steps 4 & 5)

4. Collect the sample data.
   o In the Measure phase of DMAIC, we reviewed:
     - Data Collection Plan (DCP) in Measure phase (see page 167).
     - Sample Size Calculator in Measure phase (see page 157).
     - Measurement System Analysis (MSA) in Measure phase (see page 183).
   - In following these, you should now have a reliable dataset that includes all potential root causes (factors or "suspects") that you need to analyze.
   - Before you begin analysis, just be sure to do the following:
     - Determine what specific factors will be tested.
       - *In our example, "Is there a difference in cost between a vended and internally operated call center?", what factors in the data are necessary to test this question?*
     - Determine if the data contains sufficient samples for the analysis.
       - *If the data only contains a subset of the factors to be tested, re-run the sample size calculator to ensure it's sufficient.*
   - What if the collected data to use for this test does not meet the required sample size?
     - What are the risks?
     - How can the risks be mitigated?
5. Calculate the P-value.
   - What is the P-value?
     - Technically, it's the probability of getting a sample statistic like one that's observed if the H_0 is true.
     - Practically, it's the percent chance or risk of being <u>wrong</u> when concluding a difference between the factors.
       - *Or if you calculate 1 – P-value, it's the % chance of being <u>right</u> that there's a difference in the tested factors.*
   - How do I calculate the P-value?
     - Most statistical tests that we'll be reviewing in Minitab will automatically calculate the P-value for you.

Formal Hypothesis Testing (step 6)

6. Interpret: Accept or Reject Null Hypothesis (H_0).
   - Compare the P-value with your alpha risk (α):
   - What does this mean as a statistical solution?

- Accepting the H_0 validates that there is no statistical difference between the tested factors.
- Rejecting the H_0 validates that there is a statistical difference between the tested factors.
  o How do I interpret this information into a practical solution?
- Example: "Is there a difference in cost between a vended and internally operated call center?"
  - If p-value < α, then we conclude "there is a statistically significant difference in the average cost between vended and internally operated call centers".
  - However, don't forget to consider the _practical implications_.
    - _What if the cost difference is $1/call?_
    - _What if the cost difference is only $0.05/call?_
    - _What if your α is 5% and the p-value was 0.08?_

Practical Application
  o Identify at least 1 critical metric used by your organization and do the following:
- We'll use that metric as the "output Y" for most of our future lessons on hypothesis testing.
  - The output Y should be a continuous (numeric) value; it's acceptable if it's a percentage (a discrete value).
- Identify at least 5 other factors related to that output Y metric; these will serve as the input X's.
  - These other factors should include at least two continuous and two discrete types of values.
  - Label each factor as X_1, X_2, X_3, and so on.
- Get the data for the Y and all X's for a reasonable timeframe at a reasonable level of detail.
  - The data should include at least 30 to 50 observations. The more granular the data, then the more observations you should have collected.
    - _E.g., if collecting daily values, then there should probably be several months worth of values, which could easily be 200 or more observations. But if collecting monthly values, then there should be several years' worth of values (3 years will cover 36 monthly observations)._
  - If using sampled data, then ensure the data is randomly collected.
  - Ensure you can trust the reliability of the collected data (i.e., conduct a MSA, if necessary).
- Keep these factors on hand while reviewing the practical applications in future lessons on hypothesis testing.

Six Sigma-Analyze – Lesson 11: Hypothesis Testing: Statistical Laws and Confidence Intervals

An extension on a series about hypothesis testing, this lesson introduces some statistical concepts that are fundamental to most hypothesis testing.

Pre-Requisite Lessons:
- o Six Sigma-Analyze #10 – Hypothesis Testing – Formal and Informal Sub-Processes

Some Statistical Laws
- o There are 3 general laws commonly associated with statistics:
  - • The Law of Averages, the Law of Large Numbers (LLN), and the Central Limit Theorem (CLT).
- o Law of Averages
  - • This is actually not a law but a lay term generally applied by people unfamiliar with statistics.
  - • It is a belief that the outcome of random events will eventually "even out".
    - ▪ Example 1: Belief an event is "due" to happen.
      - – *If you flip a coin 10 times and get heads all 10 times, this belief presumes that you're "due" to get tails next. However, the probability of getting tails doesn't change; it's still 50/50.*
      - – *However, since getting heads 10 straight times is unexpected, then it's more likely that the coin is unevenly weighted (bias). If so, there's a greater probability of getting heads again.*
    - ▪ Example 2: Belief a sample's average must equal its expected value.
      - – *If you flip a coin 100 times, there's only an 8% chance there will be exactly 50 heads.*
    - ▪ Example 3: Belief that a rare occurrence will happen given enough time.
      - – *"If I send my résumé to enough places, someone will eventually hire me."*
      - – *This may actually be true assuming nonzero probabilities and that the number of trials is really large enough; the law of averages is then simply the Law of Large Numbers (LLN).*
- o Law of Large Numbers (LLN)
  - • This is a legitimate theorem that the average of the results obtained from a large number of samples will be close to the expected value and will get closer as you obtain more samples.
    - ▪ Example: The expected average value of a six-sided die is $(1 + 2 + 3 + 4 + 5 + 6) \div 6 = 3.5$.
      - – *Roll the die 10 times, the average of those 10 rolls will be close to 3.5.*
      - – *The more trials or sets of 10 rolls you record, then the closer the cumulative average will be to 3.5.*
  - • This law is the premise for the Central Limit Theorem (CLT) applied in statistical testing.

Central Limit Theorem (CLT)
- o The statistical tests used in hypothesis testing are founded on the CLT.
  - • Understanding this theorem can help you understand the basis for most statistical tests.
- o What is the Central Limit Theorem (CLT)?
  - • Technically, the means of random samples from <u>any</u> distribution (normal or non-normal) with a mean of μ and a variance of σ^2 will have the following:
    - ▪ An approximately normal distribution.
    - ▪ A mean equal to μ.
    - ▪ A variance equal to σ^2/n.
- o Example: Rolling Dice
  - • Suppose you roll a pair of dice 10 times and write down the average of all the rolls. If you continue rolling the dice and writing down the average value after each set of 10 rolls, then:
    - ▪ The averages of each of those sets of rolls will be about the same.
    - ▪ The more you roll, the variance between the values will become more & more narrow (less variation).
  - • What if the dice are weighted (bias)?
    - ▪ The theorem results are the same, except the average will shift.

- What can we conclude from the CLT?
  - The more samples you collect, the more _confident_ you can be about what the mean is for all samples of the population.

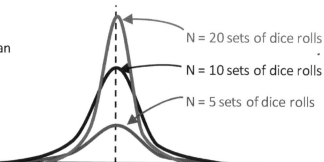

N = 20 sets of dice rolls

N = 10 sets of dice rolls

N = 5 sets of dice rolls

Confidence Intervals (CI)
- What is a confidence interval (CI)?
  - It represents the range (lower & upper bounds) in which the population mean should reside based on the data in the sample.
  - Let's look at the impact of the CI using the prior dice example:

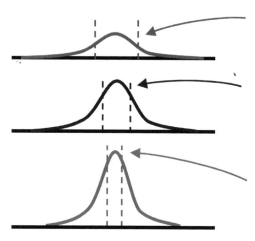

Based on 5 sets of dice rolls, the population mean should fall within this interval.

Based on 10 sets of dice rolls, the population man should fall within this more narrow interval.

Based on 20 sets of dice rolls, the population man should fall within this more narrow interval.

- The spread of the range is dependent on the size of the sample (more samples will reduce the interval) and the desired confidence (95% confidence will be more narrow than 99%).
  - Remember the Standard Error of the Mean (SE Mean)? It is the descriptive statistic used to calculate the confidence interval. To get 95% CI, calculate SE Mean by 2, or by 3 to get 99%.
- Remember, statistics are intended to help you make inferences about a population.
  - A mean of 57 with a 95% confidence interval of 55 and 59 implies that although the sample mean is only 57, you can be 95% confident that the population mean will fall somewhere between 55 and 59.

Using CIs in Statistical Tests
- How do statistical tests use the confidence intervals (CI)?
  - Statistical tests generally compare the different CIs between factors to see if a difference exists.

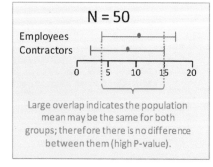

N = 50

Employees
Contractors

0   5   10   15   20

Large overlap indicates the population mean may be the same for both groups; therefore there is no difference between them (high P-value).

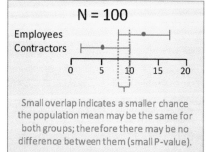

N = 100

Employees
Contractors

0   5   10   15   20

Small overlap indicates a smaller chance the population mean may be the same for both groups; therefore there may be no difference between them (small P-value).

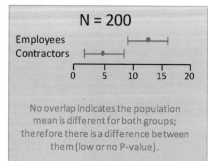

N = 200

Employees
Contractors

0   5   10   15   20

No overlap indicates the population mean is different for both groups; therefore there is a difference between them (low or no P-value).

- Example: Compare efficiency between two systems
- Scenario: 50 similar transactions were each run through two different systems. System A's time was 180 seconds and System B's time was 160 seconds (assume standard deviation of about 1/3).

- Is System B statistically faster? What is the best/worst case difference in efficiency for System B?

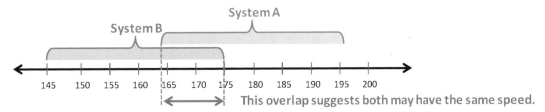

- Bottom Line: Increase your sample size to decrease (narrow) your confidence interval.

Practical Application

o Scenario:
- You have two sets of continuous data that you're comparing; each set has 100 values. The first dataset has an average value of 127 with a confidence interval of 117 to 137, and the second dataset has an average value of 132 with a confidence interval of 123 and 140.

o Try to answer the following questions based on the above scenario:
- Would you consider the confidence intervals to be wide or narrow?
- Would you expect the P-value to be high, medium, or low?
- Is there a statistical difference between these two datasets?
  - How confident (roughly) would you be in your conclusion?
- How would the analysis change if you were only able to collect 50 samples per dataset?
- How would the analysis change if you collect 300 samples per dataset?

Six Sigma-Analyze – Lesson 12: Hypothesis Testing: Finding the Right Statistical Test

An extension on a series about hypothesis testing, this lesson reviews a chart that can help you find the right statistical test for your analysis.

Pre-Requisite Lessons:
  o Six Sigma-Analyze #11 – Hypothesis Testing – Statistical Laws and Confidence Intervals

What Statistical Test Do I Use?
  o The type of statistical test depends on the data to be tested.
  • Use the chart below to help you find the right statistical test for your hypothesis testing.
    ▪ Note: The values being reviewed for the hypothesis test are the output Y and one of the input X's (which may consist of one or more groups or factors).

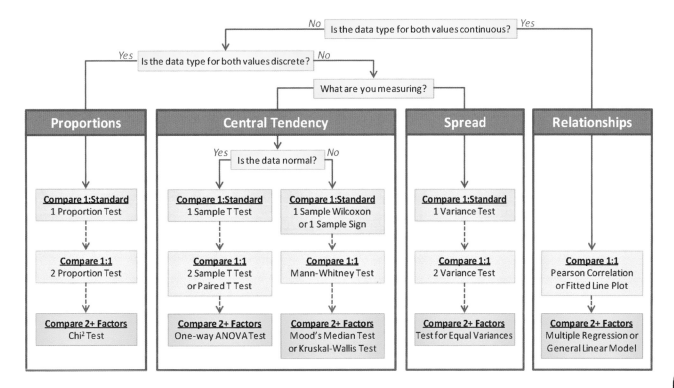

Practical Application
  o Refer to the critical metric (output Y) and at least 5 factors (input X's) you identified in a previous lesson for applying to this hypothesis testing.
  • Based on the chart in this lesson, what statistical tests would you possibly use for analysis?
    ▪ You may need to run a normality test on your output Y.

Six Sigma-Analyze – Lesson 13: Hypothesis Testing: Proportions (Compare 1:Standard)

An extension on a series about hypothesis testing, this lesson reviews the 1 Proportion Test as a measurement of proportions.

Pre-Requisite Lessons:
- o Six Sigma-Analyze #12 – Hypothesis Testing – Finding the Right Statistical Test

Why do we need hypothesis testing?
- o Remember, our project goal is to resolve a problem by first building a transfer function.
  - We don't want to just alleviate symptoms, we want to resolve the root cause.
    - Remember Hannah? We don't want to alleviate the arthritis pain in her leg, but heal the strep throat.
  - If we don't know what the root cause is, then we need to *build a transfer function*.
    - By building a transfer function, we can know what changes (improvements) should fix the root cause.
- o Remember, the Transfer Function is defined as $Y = f(X)$.
  - This is described as "output response Y is a function of one or more input X's".
  - It's part of the IPO flow model where we described the IPO flow model as one or more inputs feeding into a process that transforms it to create a new output.

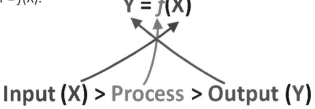

- o How does a transfer function fit with hypothesis testing?
  - Hypothesis testing tells us which X's (inputs) are independently influencing the Y (output).
    - When we reject a null hypothesis, we're building evidence proving which X's are "guilty" of driving the Y.
    - We'll compile all the evidence in the Improve phase of DMAIC and begin to fix those root causes.

Review Hypothesis Testing: 4 Step Process
- o Remember, the 4 high-level steps for hypothesis testing begin/end with being practical:
  - This topic reviewed here was originally covered on page 224.
- o As the heart of hypothesis testing, steps 2 & 3 can be drilled to the following 6 steps:
  - This topic reviewed here was originally covered on page 225.

Review Finding the Right Statistical Test
- o This topic reviewed here was originally covered on page 233.

Proportions Redefined
- o What are proportions?
  - They are a measurement of discrete values.
  - They are generally measured as percentages.
    - Though percentages are numeric, they are not considered continuous values.
      - *Although they can still be used in non-proportional statistical tests that require continuous values, it's important to understand that doing so may put your analysis at risk. Be sure any potential findings from it are fully validated.*

o Defects and Defectives are proportional measurements.
  • Below are some examples of how proportions can be measured:

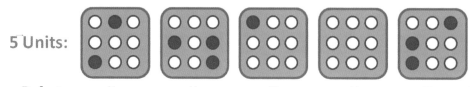

Defects:	Yes	Yes	Yes	No	Yes	**Defect Rate** = 80% (4/5)
Defectives:	2/9	3/9	1/9	0/9	3/9	**Defective Rate** = 20% (9/45)

o Why are statistical tests needed for proportions?
  • Simple proportions using percentages may be insufficient.
  • Statistical tests on proportions help assess the level of confidence we can have in them.
  • For example, a 50% proportion of 100,000 records can have very different implications from a sample that only has 100 records.

1 Proportion Test: Introduction

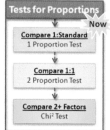

o When should I use it?
  • To compare one proportion value with a standard or target value.
o How do I find it in Minitab?
  • *Stat > Basic Statistics > 1 Proportion...*
o What are the inputs for the test?

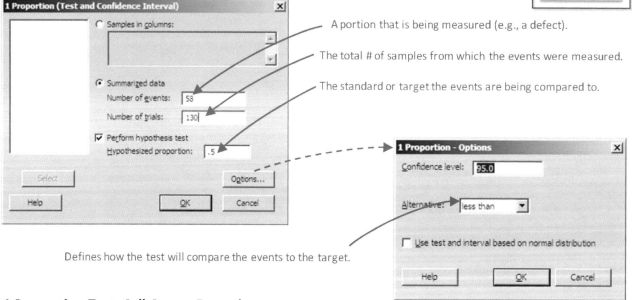

A portion that is being measured (e.g., a defect).

The total # of samples from which the events were measured.

The standard or target the events are being compared to.

Defines how the test will compare the events to the target.

1 Proportion Test: Call Center Example

o Example: Repeat Calls in a Call Center Meeting a Target
  • Background:
    ▪ A call center in Phoenix wants to know if they're meeting their goal where 60% of their calls do not have a repeat call within 2 days. They sampled 130 calls and found 82 did not have repeat calls. Though that's 63%, does it meet their goal?
  • Practical Problem:
    ▪ Do the 82 of 130 sampled calls prove the Phoenix call center is meeting their goal?
  • Statistical Problem:
    ▪ State the null (H_0) and alternative (H_a) hypotheses:
      – H_0: *the proportion <= 60% (or 0.60) and H_a: the proportion > 60% (or 0.60)*

- *What does this mean? If the goal is met, then we expect to reject the H_0 and accept the H_a proving they met the goal.*
  - Define the confidence (1-α) and power (1-β):
    - *For confidence, we'll accept the default of 95% (which means α = 5%) and power of 90% (which means β = 10%).*
  - Type the statistical problem into Minitab:
    - *In Minitab, go to Stat > Basic Statistics > 1 Proportion…*
    - *Select "Summarized data", and type **82** for "Number of events" and **130** for "Number of trials".*
    - *Check the box to "Perform Hypothesis Test" and type in the goal of **0.60**.*
    - *Click "Options…" and ensure the "Confidence Level" is **95.0** and "Alternative" is **"greater than".***
- Statistical Solution:
  - Refer to the session window results. What does this mean?
    - *Since P-value is > 0.05 (α), then we fail to reject H_0.*
    - *"95% Lower Bound" is a confidence internal; what does it mean?*
- Practical Solution:
  - The sample is insufficient to prove that the Phoenix call center is meeting its goal of 60%.
  - Why did this happen? How can you change the results?

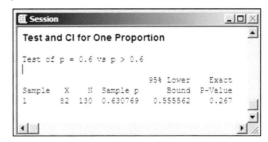

1 Proportion Test: Billing Example

o Example: Billing Quality Meeting a Target
  - Background:
    - The Billing department has a goal of 98% accuracy for customer bills which each have multiple opportunities for error. A sample of 1000 bills found only 17 errors.
  - Practical Problem:
    - Do the 17 of 1000 sampled bills prove the Billing dept. is meeting their goal?
  - Statistical Problem:
    - State the null (H_0) and alternative (H_a) hypotheses:
      - *H_0: the proportion <= 98% and H_a: the proportion > 98%*
      - *What does this mean? If the goal is met, then we expect to reject the H_0 and accept the H_a proving they met the goal.*
    - Define the confidence (1-α) and power (1-β):
      - *For confidence, we'll accept the default of 95% (which means α = 5%) and power of 90% (which means β = 10%).*
    - Type the statistical problem into Minitab:
      - *In Minitab, go to Stat > Basic Statistics > 1 Proportion…*
      - *Select "Summarized data", and type **983** for "Number of events" and **1000** for "Number of trials". Why 983 and not 17?*
      - *Check the box to "Perform Hypothesis Test" and type in the goal of **0.98**.*
      - *Click "Options…" and ensure the "Confidence Level" is **95.0** and "Alternative" is **"greater than".***
  - Statistical Solution:
    - Refer to the session window results. What does this mean?
      - *Since P-value is > 0.05 (α), then we fail to reject H_0.*
      - *"95% Lower Bound" is a confidence internal; what does it mean?*

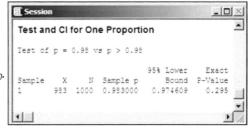

> — *What happens if you use 2% goal and 17 errors in the test?*
- Practical Solution:
    - The sample is insufficient to prove that the Billing dept is meeting its goal of 98%.
    - Why did this happen? How can you change the results?

Practical Application
- o Refer to the critical metric (output Y) and at least 5 factors (input X's) you identified in a previous lesson for applying to this hypothesis testing.
    - For any factor that is a percentage value, try applying the 1 Proportion Test.
        - To do this, you'll need to compare that factor with a goal for that factor typically set by the organization.
        - Other factors in your organization can be used for this exercise.
    - Before running the 1 Proportion Test, does the factor meet or exceed the goal?
    - After running the 1 Proportion Test, does the factor statistically meet or exceed the goal?
    - If the answers to the above 2 questions are different, then how does that affect how you'd typically measure and communicate that factor in the organization?
        - For example, does that factor meeting or not meeting the goal affect financial decisions (e.g., how people are compensated), or process changes (e.g., how the process may be modified), or other critical actions?
        - If so, then how should the results from this 1 Proportion Test be used to influence your organization?
            - *Should they change how the goals are set?*
            - *Should they change how the factor is measured?*
            - *Should they change how they react when they compare the metric to the goal?*

Six Sigma-Analyze – Lesson 14: Hypothesis Testing: Proportions (Compare 1:1)

An extension on a series about hypothesis testing, this lesson reviews the 2 Proportions Test as a measurement of proportions.

Pre-Requisite Lessons:

o Six Sigma-Analyze #13 – Hypothesis Testing: Proportions (Compare 1:Standard)

Why do we need hypothesis testing?

o This topic reviewed here was originally covered on page 235.

Review Hypothesis Testing: 4 Step Process

o Remember, the 4 high-level steps for hypothesis testing begin/end with being practical:
  • This topic reviewed here was originally covered on page 224.
o As the heart of hypothesis testing, steps 2 & 3 can be drilled to the following 6 steps:
  • This topic reviewed here was originally covered on page 225.

Review Finding the Right Statistical Test

o This topic reviewed here was originally covered on page 233.

Proportions Redefined

o This topic reviewed here was originally covered on page 235.

2 Proportions Test: Introduction

o When should I use it?
  • To compare one proportion value with another proportion value to determine of there is a statistical difference between them.
o How do I find it in Minitab?
  • *Stat > Basic Statistics > 2 Proportions…*
o What are the inputs for the test?

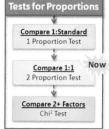

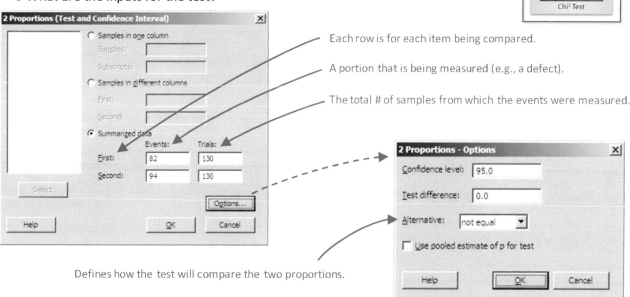

Each row is for each item being compared.

A portion that is being measured (e.g., a defect).

The total # of samples from which the events were measured.

Defines how the test will compare the two proportions.

2 Proportions Test: Call Center Example

o Example: Repeat Calls Between Two Call Centers
  • Background:
    ▪ The Phoenix and Reno call centers handle different kinds of customer issues but both try to reduce customers' repeat calls within 2 days. 130 calls were sampled from each with 82 from Phoenix and 94 from Reno that didn't have repeat calls.

- Practical Problem:
  - Is there a statistical difference in repeat calls between the call centers?
- Statistical Problem:
  - State the null (H_0) and alternative (H_a) hypotheses:
    - H_0: *Phoenix Proportion = Reno Proportion and* H_a: *Phoenix proportion ≠ Reno Proportion*
  - Define the confidence (1-α) and power (1-β):
    - *For confidence, we'll accept the default of 95% (which means α = 5%) and power of 90% (which means β = 10%).*
  - Type the statistical problem into Minitab:
    - *In Minitab, go to* Stat > Basic Statistics > 2 Proportions...
    - *Select "Summarized data". For "Events" type* **82** & **94** *respectively for the first & second boxes and* **130** *for both "Trials".*
    - *Click "Options..." and ensure the "Confidence Level" is* **95.0** *and "Alternative" is "**not equal**".*
- Statistical Solution:
  - Refer to the session window results. What does this mean?
    - *Since P-value is > 0.05 (α), then we fail to reject H_0.*
    - *"95% CI for difference" shows the lower & upper bounds of the confidence interval. If it spans across zero, then there's less difference between the compared values.*
- Practical Solution:
  - The sample doesn't prove a statistical difference in repeat calls between the two call centers.
  - Why did this happen? What if α = 1%?

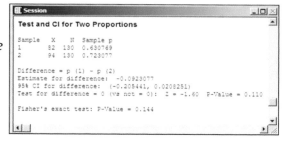

2 Proportions Test: Billing Example
  - Example: Billing Quality Between Different Bill Entry Locations
    - Background:
      - The Billing department has a goal of 98% accuracy for customer bills. The billing information is entered either at Chicago or Miami. A sample of 1000 bills at each location found Chicago had 17 errors and Miami had 28 errors.
    - Practical Problem:
      - Is there a statistical difference in billing quality between the billing locations?
    - Statistical Problem:
      - State the null (H_0) and alternative (H_a) hypotheses:
        - H_0: *Chicago Proportion = Miami Proportion and* H_a: *Chicago proportion ≠ Miami Proportion*
      - Define the confidence (1-α) and power (1-β):
        - *For confidence, we'll accept the default of 95% (which means α = 5%) and power of 90% (which means β = 10%).*
      - Type the statistical problem into Minitab:
        - *In Minitab, go to* Stat > Basic Statistics > 2 Proportions...
        - *Select "Summarized data". For "Events" type* **17** & **28** *respectively for the first & second boxes and* **1000** *for both "Trials".*
        - *Click "Options..." and ensure the "Confidence Level" is* **95.0** *and "Alternative" is "**not equal**".*
    - Statistical Solution:
      - Refer to the session window results. What does this mean?
        - *Since P-value is > 0.05 (α), then we fail to reject H_0.*
        - *What does P-value of 0.097 really mean in terms of risk?*

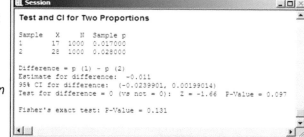

- Practical Solution:
  - The sample doesn't prove a statistical difference in billing quality between the two locations.
    - *However, we can be 90% confident there is a difference.*
  - Why did this happen? How can you change the results?

2 Proportions Test: Excel Template
- This statistical test can be run from within Excel instead of Minitab.
  - This Excel template is in the "*ProportionsTest.xlsb*" file and was built by Matt Hansen.
    - The formulas in the Excel file require Excel 2010 or higher.
  - The Excel template includes two sections for running the test as described below.
- Simple 2 Proportions Test in Excel.
  - Use this section for doing a quick test just as you would in Minitab.

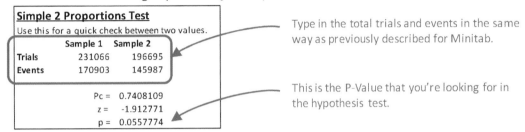

Type in the total trials and events in the same way as previously described for Minitab.

This is the P-Value that you're looking for in the hypothesis test.

- Dynamic 2 Proportions Test in Excel.
  - Use this section for copying/pasting into other files for quickly running the test on many metrics.

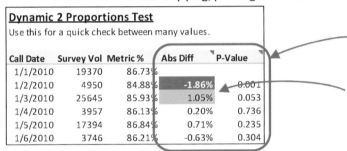

Copy/paste the formulas from these two columns into your own report. Be sure the two columns to the left of these ("Survey Vol" and "Metric %") are in the same position as this example or else the formulas won't work.

The "Abs Diff" is the key value to look for. It calculates the absolute difference between the current "Metric %" and the one above it. If it's **red**, then the P-value is below 0.05 and the "Abs Diff" is statistically significant. If it's orange, then the P-value is between 0.05 and 0.10, a Beta risk.

Practical Application
- Refer to the critical metric (output Y) and at least 5 factors (input X's) you identified in a previous lesson for applying to this hypothesis testing.
  - For any factor that is a percentage value, try applying the 2 Proportions Test.
    - To do this, you'll need to compare at least two different sets of that same factor (e.g., across multiple periods of time, or by different locations, or by different groups, etc.).
    - Other factors in your organization can be used for this exercise.
  - Before running the 2 Proportions Test, do the factors appear to be different?
  - After running the 2 Proportions Test, are the factors statistically different?
  - If the answers to the above 2 questions are different, then how does that affect how you'd typically measure and communicate that in the organization?
    - For example, does the difference between the factors affect financial decisions (e.g., how people are compensated), or process changes (e.g., how the process may be modified), or other critical actions?
    - If so, then how should the results from this 2 Proportions Test be used to influence your organization?
      - *Should they change how the factors are compared (e.g., across different times, locations, groups, etc.)?*
      - *Should they change how the factor is measured?*
      - *Should they change how they react when they compare the metric this way?*

Six Sigma-Analyze – Lesson 15: Hypothesis Testing: Proportions (Compare 2+ Factors)

An extension on a series about hypothesis testing, this lesson reviews the Chi^2 Test (Goodness-of-Fit & Association) as a measurement of proportions.

Pre-Requisite Lessons:
  o Six Sigma-Analyze #14 – Hypothesis Testing: Proportions (Compare 1:1)

Why do we need hypothesis testing?
  o This topic reviewed here was originally covered on page 235.

Review Hypothesis Testing: 4 Step Process
  o Remember, the 4 high-level steps for hypothesis testing begin/end with being practical:
     • This topic reviewed here was originally covered on page 224.
  o As the heart of hypothesis testing, steps 2 & 3 can be drilled to the following 6 steps:
     • This topic reviewed here was originally covered on page 225.

Review Finding the Right Statistical Test
  o This topic reviewed here was originally covered on page 233.

Proportions Redefined
  o This topic reviewed here was originally covered on page 235.

Chi^2 Test: Introduction
  o When should I use it?

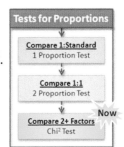

     • To compare proportions between more than 2 factors or groups.
        ▪ "Chi" refers to the Greek small letter "χ" (pronounced Kye) often written as χ^2.
        ▪ The test compares the _actual_ frequency/proportion of observations to an _expected_ frequency/proportion of those observations.
  o There are two types of Chi^2 tests:
     • Test for Goodness-of-Fit (One Variable)
        ▪ Compares an observed factor with that factor's fixed or evenly proportionate set of outcomes.
           – *A coin has only two types of outcomes so if it's unbiased, then the expected outcome should be about 50:50.*
           – *A die has six sides so if it's unbiased, then the expected outcome for each side is about 1/6.*
           – *If there are 4 candidates running for office, then the expected outcome per candidate is about 25%.*
        ▪ How do I find it in Minitab?
           – *Go to Stat > Tables > Chi-Square Goodness-of-Fit Test (One Variable)…*
     • Test for Association (Two way table)
        ▪ Compares two factors where neither has a fixed or evenly proportionate set of outcomes.
           – *Comparing the gender vs. political affiliation for a group of surveyed people. Though each group may itself have a fixed set of outcomes (like gender is either male or female), they're not being compared to themselves but to a different factor.*
           – *Comparing the amount of training vs. performance metrics for a group of employees.*
        ▪ How do I find it in Minitab?
           – *Go to Stat > Tables > Chi-Square Test (Two Way Table in Worksheet)… or Cross Tabulation and Chi-Square…*

Chi² Test Statistic for Goodness-of-Fit

o What is the Chi² test statistic?

$$\chi^2 = \sum_{j=1}^{g} \frac{(f_o - f_e)^2}{f_e}$$

where f_e is frequency expected
and f_o is frequency observed

o How does the Chi² test statistic work for goodness-of-fit tests?
   • Example: A coin is tossed 100 times with the results of 64 heads and 26 tails.

	Observed (f_o)	Expected (f_e)	$\frac{(f_o - f_e)^2}{f_e}$
Heads	64	50	3.92
Tails	36	50	3.92
χ^2			7.84

   ▪ The P-value is calculated separately by looking up the Chi² distribution using the Chi² statistic (7.84) and degrees of freedom calculated as: (# of rows − 1) * (# of columns − 1). Minitab calculates this for you.

Chi² Test (Goodness-of-Fit): Coin Example

o Example: A coin toss
   • Background:
      ▪ A coin is tossed 100 times with the results of 64 heads and 36 tails.
   • Practical Problem:
      ▪ Is the coin unbiased with results of 64 heads out of 100 coin tosses?
   • Statistical Problem:
      ▪ State the null (H_0) and alternative (H_a) hypotheses:
         − H_0: Probability of Heads or Tails = 0.5 and H_a: Probability of Heads or Tails ≠ 0.5
      ▪ Define the confidence (1-α) and power (1-β):
         − For confidence, we'll accept the default of 95% (which means α = 5%) and power of 90% (which means β = 10%).
      ▪ Type the statistical problem into Minitab:
         − The data may be typed into a worksheet like in the example.
         − In Minitab, go to Stat > Tables > Chi-Square Goodness-of-Fit Test (One Variable)...

Category	Observation
Heads	64
Tails	36

         − Select "Observed Counts" and select the "**Observation**" column.
         − If a category is included, then select the "**Category**" column for "Category names".
         − Select "**Equal proportions**" under "Test" since the proportions for a coin toss are expected to be equal.
   • Statistical Solution:
      ▪ Refer to the session window results.
         − Since P-value is < 0.05 (α), we reject H_0.
         − Both categories (heads & tails) equally contribute to the Chi² statistic.

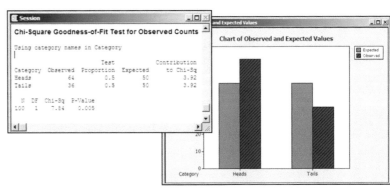

- Practical Solution:
  - No, the coin is not unbiased; it does appear to favor heads more than tails.
  - The graph at right visually displays the comparison between the actual observations and expected results.

Chi² Test (Goodness-of-Fit): Die Example
- Example: Rolling a Die
  - Background:
    - A die is rolled 120 times with these results.
  - Practical Problem:
    - Is the die unbiased based these results?
  - Statistical Problem:
    - State the null (H_0) and alternative (H_a) hypotheses:
      - H_0: *Probability of any die face = 0.167 and H_a: Probability of any die face ≠ 0.167*
    - Define the confidence (1-α) and power (1-β):
      - *For confidence, we'll accept the default of 95% (which means α = 5%) and power of 90% (which means β = 10%).*
    - Type the statistical problem into Minitab:
      - *Using the datasheet above in Minitab, go to Stat > Tables > Chi-Square Goodness-of-Fit Test (One Variable)...*
      - *Select "Observed Counts" and select the "**Observation**" column.*
      - *If a category is included, then select the "**Face**" column for "Category names".*
      - *Select "**Equal proportions**" under "Test" since the proportions for rolling a die are expected to be equal.*
  - Statistical Solution:
    - Refer to the session window results.
      - *Since P-value is > 0.05 (α), then we fail to reject H_0.*
      - *Face value of 4 contributes the most to the Chi² statistic.*
  - Practical Solution:
    - Yes, the die appears unbiased.
    - The graph at right compares actual vs. expected results.
      - *Since face value 4 appears to stand out, what would happen if you multiply each value by 10 (increase sample size)?*

Face	Observation
1	16
2	21
3	18
4	30
5	20
6	15

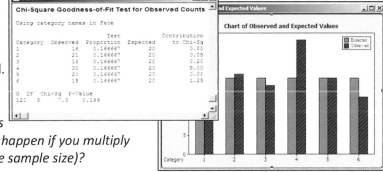

Chi² Test (Goodness-of-Fit): Call Center Example
- Example: Call Volume between Call Centers
  - Background:
    - The call volume at 5 different call centers has changed over time. The chart at right shows the current call volume and prior proportions per call center.
  - Practical Problem:
    - Has the volume proportion changed significantly between call centers?
  - Statistical Problem:
    - State the null (H_0) and alternative (H_a) hypotheses:
      - H_0: *Current Vol Portion = Prior Vol Portion and H_a: Current Vol Portion ≠ Prior Vol Portion*
    - Define the confidence (1-α) and power (1-β):

Call Center	Current Vol	Prior Vol
Phoenix	65000	30%
Miami	52000	25%
Chicago	27000	15%
Reno	42000	20%
St Louis	23000	10%

6 SS: Analyze

- For confidence, we'll accept the default of 95% (which means α = 5%) and power of 90% (which means β = 10%).
- Type the statistical problem into Minitab:
  - *Using the datasheet above in Minitab, go to Stat > Tables > Chi-Square Goodness-of-Fit Test (One Variable)...*
  - Select the "**Current Vol**" column for "Observed Counts" and select the "**Call Center**" column for "Category names".
  - Select "**Prior Vol**" under "Specific Proportions".
- Statistical Solution:
  - Refer to the session window results.
    - *Since P-value is < 0.05 (α), then reject H_0.*
    - *Chicago & St Louis contribute the most to the Chi^2 statistic. What does that mean?*
- Practical Solution:
  - Yes, the volume proportion has changed between the call centers.
  - The graph at right compares actual vs. expected results.
    - *Why do Phoenix & St Louis look the same but have different contributions?*

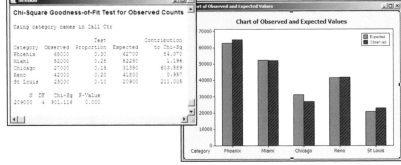

Chi^2 Test Statistic for Associations
- How does the Chi^2 test statistic work for associations?
  - Example: 1000 men and women surveyed about their political affiliation.
    - Below are the survey counts across a matrix of the two independent factors:

	Liberal	Moderate	Conservative	Total
Men	Lib. Men	Mod. Men	Conserv. Men	512
Women	Lib. Women	Mod. Women	Conserv. Women	488
Total	275	416	309	1000

- To build the Chi^2 test statistic, the _expected_ counts are calculated for the 6 factor combinations.
  - *For example, 51.2% of those surveyed are men and 27.5% of those surveyed are liberal. Therefore, by multiplying them together (51.2% * 27.5% = 14.1%), then 141 of those surveyed are expected to be liberal men.*

	Liberal	Moderate	Conservative	Total
Men	141	213	158	512
Women	134	203	151	488
Total	275	416	309	1000

- Below are the actual observations from the 1000 surveys that we'll analyze next.

	Liberal	Moderate	Conservative	Total
Men	125	244	143	512
Women	150	172	166	488
Total	275	416	309	1000

Chi^2 Test (Association): Political Example

o Example: Comparing gender vs. political affiliation.
   • Background:
      ▪ 1000 men and women were surveyed about their political affiliation.
   • Practical Problem:
      ▪ Is there a statistical difference in political affiliation between men and women?
   • Statistical Problem:
      ▪ State the null (H$_0$) and alternative (H$_a$) hypotheses:
         – *H$_0$: Proportions of political affiliation for men = Proportions of political affiliation for women and H$_a$: Proportions of political affiliation for men ≠ Proportions of political affiliation for women*
      ▪ Define the confidence (1-α) and power (1-β):
         – *For confidence, we'll accept the default of 95% (which means α = 5%) and power of 90% (which means β = 10%).*
      ▪ Type the statistical problem into Minitab:
         – *The data may be typed into a worksheet like the example on the prior page.*
         – *In Minitab, go to Stat > Tables > Chi-Square Test (Two Way Table in Worksheet)... Use this method when you have summary data in the worksheet.*
         – *In the "Columns containing the table" box, select the "**Liberal**", "**Moderate**", and "**Conservative**" columns.*

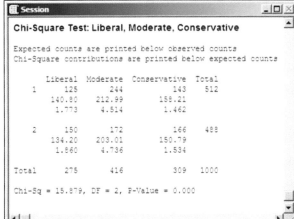

   • Statistical Solution:
      ▪ Refer to the session window results.
         – *Since P-value is < 0.05 (α), then we reject H$_0$.*
         – *Which group contributed the most to Chi^2?*
   • Practical Solution:
      ▪ Yes, there is a statistical difference in political affiliations between men and women.
         – *How would you interpret the results practically?*

Chi^2 Test (Association): Clerk Example

o Example: Comparing Clerks vs. Category A (Color).
   • Background:
      ▪ Use the arbitrary values in the "Clerk" and "CategoryA" columns of the Minitab Sample Data file.
   • Practical Problem:
      ▪ Is there a statistical difference between clerks and the colors noted in Category A?
   • Statistical Problem:
      ▪ State the null (H$_0$) and alternative (H$_a$) hypotheses:
         – *H$_0$: Proportion of each clerk & color = Proportion of each other clerk & color and H$_a$: Proportion of each clerk & color ≠ Proportion of each other clerk & color.*
      ▪ Define the confidence (1-α) and power (1-β):
         – *For confidence, we'll accept the default of 95% (which means α = 5%) and power of 90% (which means β = 10%).*

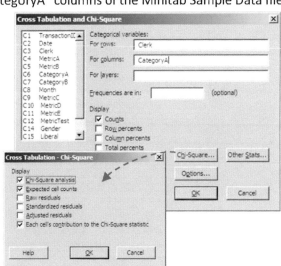

- Type the statistical problem into Minitab:
  - *In Minitab, go to Stat > Tables > Cross Tabulation and Chi-Square... Use this method when you have detail data.*
  - *In the "For rows" field, select the "**Clerk**" column.*
  - *In the "For columns" field, select the "**CategoryA**" column.*
  - *In the "Display" section, select the "**Counts**" box.*
  - *Click the "Chi-Square..." button and in the dialog box select "Chi-Square analysis", "Expected cell counts", "Each cell's contribution...".*
- What does the cross tabulation do?
  - *It takes the detailed worksheet data and builds a cross-tabulated table (like a pivot table) performing the same type of Chi^2 analysis comparing expected vs. actual observations.*
- Statistical Solution:
  - Refer to the session window results.
    - *Since P-value is > 0.05 (α), then we fail to reject H_0.*
- Practical Solution:
  - No, there is no statistical difference in the proportions between the clerks and colors.
  - However, how would you practically interpret the results of the P-value and Chi^2 statistic?

Session

Tabulated statistics: Clerk, CategoryA

Rows: Clerk   Columns: CategoryA

	Blue	Green	Red	White	Yellow	All
Bertha	2	4	2	3	4	15
	2.100	2.100	2.850	4.500	3.450	15.000
	0.0048	1.7190	0.2535	0.5000	0.0877	*
Fred	4	2	5	7	4	22
	3.080	3.080	4.180	6.600	5.060	22.000
	0.2748	0.3787	0.1609	0.0242	0.2221	*
George	4	2	2	4	6	18
	2.520	2.520	3.420	5.400	4.140	18.000
	0.8692	0.1073	0.5896	0.3630	0.8357	*
Mary	0	5	2	2	4	13
	1.820	1.820	2.470	3.900	2.990	13.000
	1.8200	5.5563	0.0894	0.9256	0.3412	*
Peter	1	0	6	10	1	18
	2.520	2.520	3.420	5.400	4.140	18.000
	0.9168	2.5200	1.9463	3.9185	2.3815	*
Sally	3	1	2	4	4	14
	1.960	1.960	2.660	4.200	3.220	14.000
	0.5518	0.4702	0.1638	0.0095	0.1889	*
All	14	14	19	30	23	100
	14.000	14.000	19.000	30.000	23.000	100.000
	*	*	*	*	*	*

Cell Contents: Count
                      Expected count
                      Contribution to Chi-square

Pearson Chi-Square = 28.190, DF = 20, P-Value = 0.105
Likelihood Ratio Chi-Square = 30.780, DF = 20, P-Value = 0.058

Practical Application

- Refer to the critical metric (output Y) and at least 5 factors (input X's) you identified in a previous lesson for applying to this hypothesis testing.
  - Select at least 3 factors that are discrete values.
    - Other factors in your organization can be used for this exercise.
  - Before running the Chi^2 Test, does any combination of the factors appear imbalanced?
  - After running the Chi^2 Test, what combination of factors are statistically different?
  - If the answers to the above 2 questions are different, then how does that affect how you'd typically measure and communicate that in the organization?
    - For example, does the difference affect financial decisions (e.g., how people are compensated), or process changes (e.g., how the process may be modified), or other critical actions?
    - If so, then how should the results from this Chi^2 Test be used to influence your organization?
      - *Should they change how the factors are compared (e.g., across different times, locations, groups, etc.)?*
      - *Should they change how the factors are measured?*
      - *Should they change how they react when they compare the factors this way?*

Six Sigma-Analyze – Lesson 16: Hypothesis Testing: Central Tendency – Normal (Compare 1:Standard)

An extension on a series about hypothesis testing, this lesson reviews the 1 Sample T test as a central tendency measurement for normal dist.

Pre-Requisite Lessons:
- o Six Sigma-Analyze #15 – Hypothesis Testing: Proportions (Compare 2+ Factors)

Why do we need hypothesis testing?
- o This topic reviewed here was originally covered on page 235.

Review Hypothesis Testing: 4 Step Process
- o Remember, the 4 high-level steps for hypothesis testing begin/end with being practical:
  - • This topic reviewed here was originally covered on page 224.
- o As the heart of hypothesis testing, steps 2 & 3 can be drilled to the following 6 steps:
  - • This topic reviewed here was originally covered on page 225.

Review Finding the Right Statistical Test
- o This topic reviewed here was originally covered on page 233.

Confidence Intervals (CI) Redefined
- o This topic reviewed here was originally covered on page 230.

1 Sample T Test: Introduction
- o When should I use it?
  - • To compare one mean value with a standard or target value.
- o How do I find it in Minitab?
  - • *Stat > Basic Statistics > 1 Sample T…*
- o What are the inputs for the test?

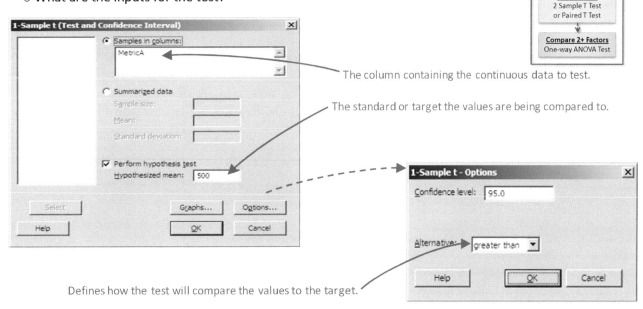

The column containing the continuous data to test.

The standard or target the values are being compared to.

Defines how the test will compare the values to the target.

1 Sample Test: MetricA Example
- o Example: MetricA sample values
  - • Background:
    - ▪ Use the arbitrary values in the "MetricA" column of the Minitab Sample Data file.

- Practical Problem:
  - Does the mean of MetricA exceed the target of 500?
- Statistical Problem:
  - State the null (H_0) and alternative (H_a) hypotheses:
    - H_0: μ <= 500 and H_a: μ > 500
    - *What does this mean? If the goal is met, then we expect to reject the H_0 and accept the H_a proving they met the goal.*
  - Define the confidence (1-α) and power (1-β):
    - *For confidence, we'll accept the default of 95% (which means α = 5%) and power of 90% (which means β = 10%).*
  - Type the statistical problem into Minitab:
    - *In Minitab, go to Stat > Basic Statistics > 1 Sample T...*
    - *Select "Samples in columns", and select **MetricA** from the list of columns.*
    - *Check the box to "Perform Hypothesis Test" and type in the goal of **500**.*
    - *Click "Options..." and ensure the "Confidence Level" is **95.0** and "Alternative" is **"greater than"**.*
- Statistical Solution:
  - Refer to the session window results. What does this mean?
    - *Since P-value is > 0.05 (α), then we fail to reject H_0.*
    - *"95% Lower Bound" is a confidence internal; what does it mean?*
- Practical Solution:
  - The sample is insufficient to prove that MetricA exceeds the target of 500.
  - Why did this happen? How can you change the results?

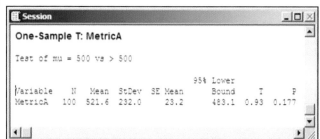

Practical Application

- Refer to the critical metric (output Y) and at least 5 factors (input X's) you identified in a previous lesson for applying to this hypothesis testing.
  - For any factor that is a continuous value, try applying the 1 Sample T Test.
    - To do this, you'll need to compare that factor with a goal for that factor typically set by the organization.
    - Other factors in your organization can be used for this exercise.
  - Before running the 1 Sample T Test, does the factor meet or exceed the goal?
  - After running the 1 Sample T Test, does the factor statistically meet or exceed the goal?
  - If the answers to the above 2 questions are different, then how does that affect how you'd typically measure and communicate that factor in the organization?
    - For example, does that factor meeting or not meeting the goal affect financial decisions (e.g., how people are compensated), or process changes (e.g., how the process may be modified), or other critical actions?
    - If so, then how should the results from this 1 Sample T Test be used to influence your organization?
      - *Should they change how the goals are set?*
      - *Should they change how the factor is measured?*
      - *Should they change how they react when they compare the metric to the goal?*

Six Sigma-Analyze – Lesson 17: Hypothesis Testing: Central Tendency – Normal (Compare 1:1)

An extension on a series about hypothesis testing, this lesson reviews the 2 Sample T & Paired T tests as central tendency measurements for normal dist.

Pre-Requisite Lessons:
- o Six Sigma-Analyze #16 – Hypothesis Testing: Central Tendency – Normal (Compare 1:Standard)

Why do we need hypothesis testing?
- o This topic reviewed here was originally covered on page 235.

Review Hypothesis Testing: 4 Step Process
- o Remember, the 4 high-level steps for hypothesis testing begin/end with being practical:
  - • This topic reviewed here was originally covered on page 224.
- o As the heart of hypothesis testing, steps 2 & 3 can be drilled to the following 6 steps:
  - • This topic reviewed here was originally covered on page 225.

Review Finding the Right Statistical Test
- o This topic reviewed here was originally covered on page 233.

Confidence Intervals (CI) Redefined
- o This topic reviewed here was originally covered on page 230.

Compare 1:1 Tests: Introduction
- o When should I use it?
  - • To compare one mean value with another mean value to determine if there is a statistical difference between them.
- o There are two types of tests for comparing two sets of means:
  - • 2 Sample T Test is a test for *Independent* variables.
  - • Paired T Test is a test for *dependent* variables.
  - • Both tests use μ_0 to represent the hypothesized "difference" in the means.
  - • The null hypothesis will stay the same, but the alternative hypotheses may vary:
    - ▪ $H_0: \mu_1 = \mu_2$
    - ▪ $H_a: \mu_1 \neq \mu_2$ ($\mu_0 = 0$), or...
    - ▪ $H_a: \mu_1 - \mu_2 < \mu_0$ (left-tailed), or...
    - ▪ $H_a: \mu_1 - \mu_2 > \mu_0$ (right-tailed), or...
    - ▪ $H_a: \mu_1 - \mu_2 \neq \mu_0$ (two-tailed)

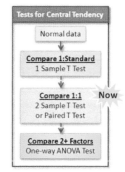

	2 Sample T Test	Paired T Test
Comparison	Means between <u>independent</u> variables	Means between <u>dependent</u> variables
Sample Sources	Same type of sample from <u>different</u> groups	Same type of sample from (possibly) <u>same</u> group
Examples	• Same type of output measurements from two different machines or manufacturing plants. • Same performance metrics between two different call centers. • Same sales metrics between reps from different stores.	• Measurements from the same machine before and after a system upgrade. • Performance metrics from the same call center before and after process changes. • Sales metrics from the same store before and after new training.

SS: Analyze

2 Sample T Test: MetricA & MetricD Example

- ○ Example: MetricA and MetricD sample values
  - • Background:
    - ▪ Use the arbitrary values in the "MetricA" and "MetricD" columns of the Minitab Sample Data file.
  - • Practical Problem:
    - ▪ Is the mean for MetricA greater than MetricD?
  - • Statistical Problem:
    - ▪ State the null (H_0) and alternative (H_a) hypotheses:
      - − H_0: $\mu_{MetricA} = \mu_{MetricD}$ and H_a: $\mu_{MetricA} - \mu_{MetricD} > \mu_0$
    - ▪ Define the confidence (1-α) and power (1-β):
      - − *For confidence, we'll accept the default of 95% (which means α = 5%) and power of 90% (which means β = 10%).*
    - ▪ Type the statistical problem into Minitab:
      - − *In Minitab, go to Stat > Basic Statistics > 2 Sample T...*
      - − *Select "Samples in different columns", and select **MetricA** for "First" and select **MetricD** for "Second".*
      - − *Click "Options..." and ensure the "Confidence Level" is **95.0** and "Alternative" is "**greater than**".*
  - • Statistical Solution:
    - ▪ Refer to the session window results. What does this mean?
      - − *Since P-value is < 0.05 (α), then we reject H_0.*
  - • Practical Solution:
    - ▪ The sample is sufficient to prove that the mean for MetricA is greater than MetricD.

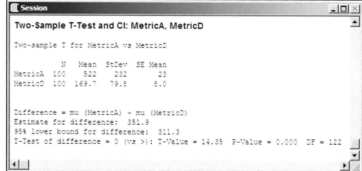

Paired T Test: MetricA by Month Example

- ○ Example: MetricA by Month sample values
  - • Background:
    - ▪ Use the values in the "MetricA" and "Month" columns of the Minitab Sample Data file.
  - • Practical Problem:
    - ▪ Is the mean for MetricA different between June and July?
  - • Statistical Problem:
    - ▪ State the null (H_0) and alternative (H_a) hypotheses:
      - − H_0: $\mu_{Metric(June)} = \mu_{MetricA(July)}$ and H_a: $\mu_{MetricA(June)} - \mu_{MetricA(July)} \neq \mu_0$
    - ▪ Define the confidence (1-α) and power (1-β):
      - − *For confidence, we'll accept the default of 95% (which means α = 5%) and power of 90% (which means β = 10%).*
    - ▪ Type the statistical problem into Minitab:
      - − *MetricA data will need to be split between the months of June & July. To do this, do the following:*
        - ➢ *Sort the data by going to Data > Sort..., select all columns to sort, select "**Month**" in the first "By Column" field and select "Original Columns". This will re-sort your data by the values in the Month column.*
        - ➢ *Copy/paste the first 46 records in MetricA associated with June to an empty column, then do the same for the remaining records associated with July.*
      - − *In Minitab, go to Stat > Basic Statistics > Paired T...*
      - − *Select "Samples in columns", and select the column for MetricA in June for "First" and select the MetricA for July for "Second".*

- *Click "Options..." and ensure the "Confidence Level" is **95.0** and "Alternative" is **"not equal"**.*
- Statistical Solution:
  - Refer to the session window results. What does this mean?
    - *Since P-value is > 0.05 (α), then we fail to reject H_0.*
- Practical Solution:
  - The sample is insufficient to prove that the mean for MetricA is different between June and July.

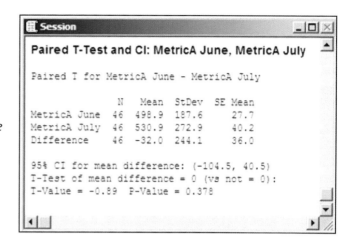

```
Session                                        _ □ ×

Paired T-Test and CI: MetricA June, MetricA July

Paired T for MetricA June - MetricA July

                   N   Mean   StDev   SE Mean
MetricA June      46   498.9  187.6     27.7
MetricA July      46   530.9  272.9     40.2
Difference        46   -32.0  244.1     36.0

95% CI for mean difference: (-104.5, 40.5)
T-Test of mean difference = 0 (vs not = 0):
T-Value = -0.89  P-Value = 0.378
```

Practical Application

- o Refer to the critical metric (output Y) and at least 5 factors (input X's) you identified in a previous lesson for applying to this hypothesis testing.
  - For any factor that is a continuous value, try applying the 2 Sample or Paired T Test.
    - To do this, you'll need to compare at least two different sets of that same factor (e.g., across multiple periods of time, or by different locations, or by different groups, etc.).
    - Other factors in your organization can be used for this exercise.
  - Before running the 2 Sample or Paired T Test, do the means of the factors appear to be different?
  - After running the 2 Sample or Paired T Test, are the means of the factors statistically different?
  - If the answers to the above 2 questions are different, then how does that affect how you'd typically measure and communicate that factor in the organization?
    - For example, do the differences between the compared factors affect financial decisions (e.g., how people are compensated), or process changes (e.g., how the process may be modified), or other critical actions?
    - If so, then how should the results from this statistical test be used to influence your organization?
      - *Should they change how the factors are compared (e.g., across different times, locations, groups, etc.)?*
      - *Should they change how the factor is measured?*
      - *Should they change how they react when they compare the metric this way?*

SS: Analyze

6

Six Sigma-Analyze – Lesson 18: Hypothesis Testing: Central Tendency – Normal (Compare 2+ Factors)

An extension on a series about hypothesis testing, this lesson reviews the ANOVA test as a central tendency measurement for normal dist.

Pre-Requisite Lessons:
- o Six Sigma-Analyze #17 – Hypothesis Testing: Central Tendency – Normal (Compare 1:1)

Why do we need hypothesis testing?
- o This topic reviewed here was originally covered on page 235.

Review Hypothesis Testing: 4 Step Process
- o Remember, the 4 high-level steps for hypothesis testing begin/end with being practical:
  - • This topic reviewed here was originally covered on page 224.
- o As the heart of hypothesis testing, steps 2 & 3 can be drilled to the following 6 steps:
  - • This topic reviewed here was originally covered on page 225.

Review Finding the Right Statistical Test
- o This topic reviewed here was originally covered on page 233.

Confidence Intervals (CI) Redefined
- o This topic reviewed here was originally covered on page 230.

One-Way ANOVA: Introduction
- o **When should I use it?**
  - • To compare mean values for multiple factors.
- o How do I find it in Minitab?
  - • *Stat > ANOVA > One-Way...*
- o What are the inputs for the test?

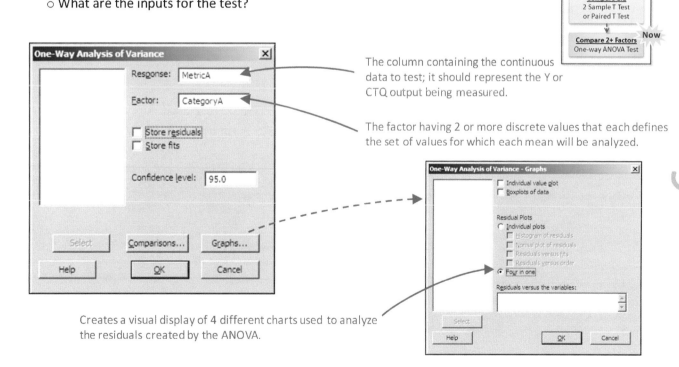

The column containing the continuous data to test; it should represent the Y or CTQ output being measured.

The factor having 2 or more discrete values that each defines the set of values for which each mean will be analyzed.

Creates a visual display of 4 different charts used to analyze the residuals created by the ANOVA.

One-Way ANOVA: Interpreting Results

- o How do I interpret the ANOVA results?
  - Below is an example of the output from an ANOVA test.
  - We'll separately explore each summary and detail portion.

Summary:
This portion summarizes
the results of the test.

Details:
This portion lists the
detailed results of the test.

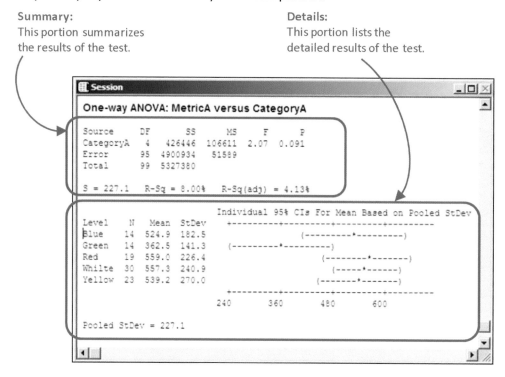

One-Way ANOVA: Summary Portion

- o What does the *summary* portion of the ANOVA results mean?

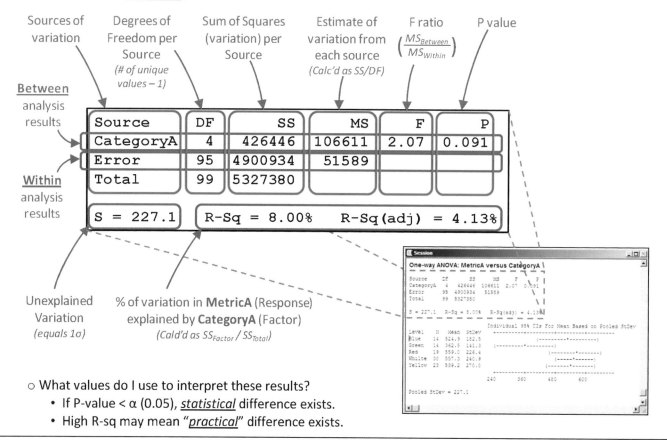

- o What values do I use to interpret these results?
  - If P-value < α (0.05), *statistical* difference exists.
  - High R-sq may mean "*practical*" difference exists.

One-Way ANOVA: Detail Portion

o What does the _detailed_ portion of the ANOVA results mean?

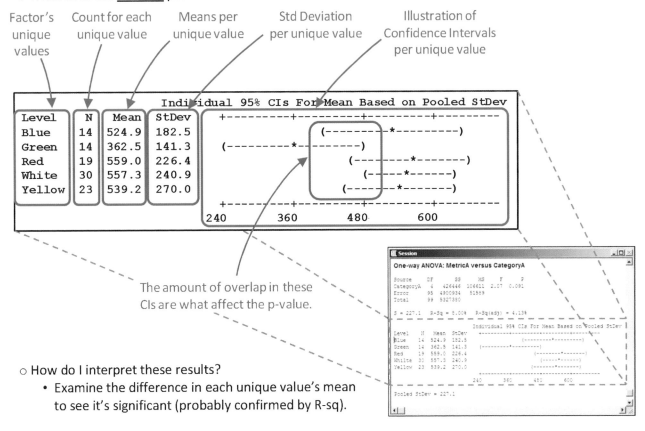

Factor's unique values

Count for each unique value

Means per unique value

Std Deviation per unique value

Illustration of Confidence Intervals per unique value

The amount of overlap in these CIs are what affect the p-value.

o How do I interpret these results?
  • Examine the difference in each unique value's mean to see it's significant (probably confirmed by R-sq).

One-Way ANOVA: Residuals Introduction

o What are residuals?
  • They represent all the deviations for each data point.
  • Remember, a deviation is the distance a data point is from the mean.

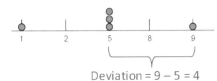

Deviation = 9 − 5 = 4

o Why are residuals used in an ANOVA test?
  • They help identify potential serious problems in the analysis.
  • It helps validate the ANOVA test to ensure the results are reliable.
o What do we look for in the residuals?
  • Residuals should have these characteristics:
    ▪ They should be normally distributed.
    ▪ They should be independent.
    ▪ They should have equal variances.
o How do I measure the residuals?
  • In the ANOVA dialog box, select "Graphs...".
  • In the Graphs box, select "Four in One" from the "Residual Plots" section (example at right).

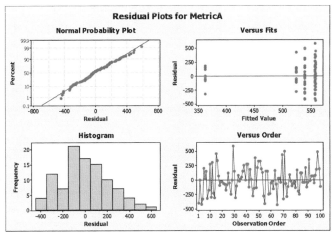

One-Way ANOVA: Residuals Interpretation

o Interpreting the residual plots for normality:
- These plotted residuals should be normally distributed.

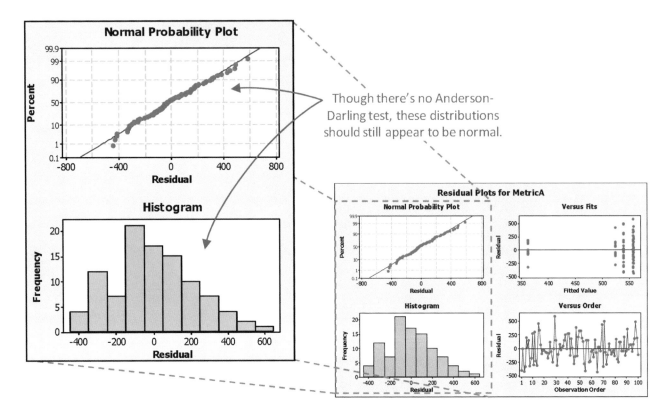

Though there's no Anderson-Darling test, these distributions should still appear to be normal.

o Interpreting the residual plots for equal variance and independence:
- These plotted residuals should appear random yet evenly spread.

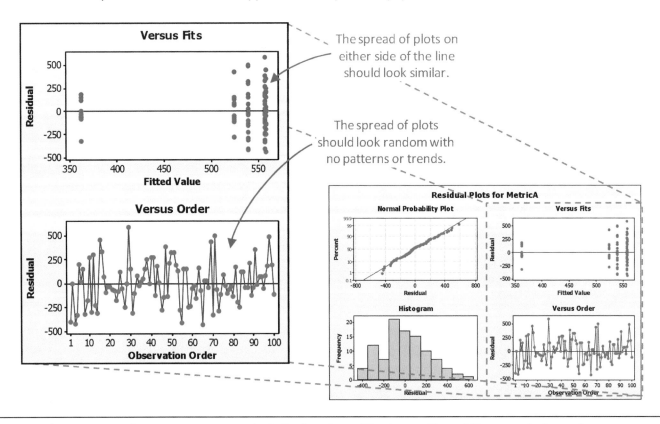

The spread of plots on either side of the line should look similar.

The spread of plots should look random with no patterns or trends.

One-Way ANOVA: Boxplots

o What are boxplots (a.k.a., "box and whiskers")?
  - A graphical summary of a distribution's shape, central tendency & spread.
  - They help compare multiple distributions and statistical characteristics.
  - It's like a birds-eye view (looking down from the top) of a distribution.

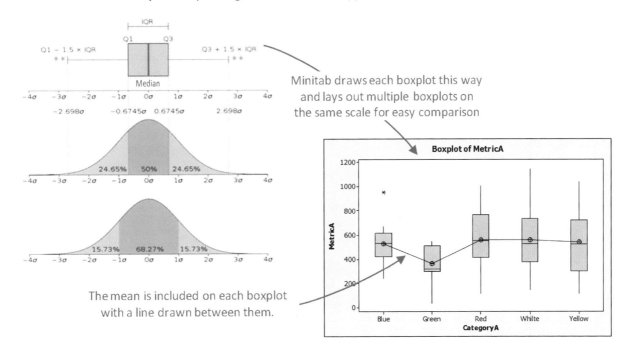

Minitab draws each boxplot this way and lays out multiple boxplots on the same scale for easy comparison

The mean is included on each boxplot with a line drawn between them.

ANOVA Test: MetricA & CategoryA Example

o Example: MetricA and CategoryA sample values
  - Background:
    ▪ Use the values in the "MetricA" and "CategoryA" columns of the Minitab Sample Data file.
  - Practical Problem:
    ▪ Is the mean for MetricA different between the various CategoryA values?
  - Statistical Problem:
    ▪ State the null (H_0) and alternative (H_a) hypotheses:
      − H_0: $\mu_{CategoryA1} = \mu_{CategoryA2} = \mu_{CategoryA3}$ etc., and H_a: = $\mu_{CategoryA1} \neq \mu_{CategoryA2} \neq \mu_{CategoryA3}$ etc.
    ▪ Define the confidence $(1-\alpha)$ and power $(1-\beta)$:
      − For confidence, we'll accept the default of 95% (which means α = 5%) and power of 90% (which means β = 10%).
    ▪ Type the statistical problem into Minitab:
      − In Minitab, go to Stat > ANOVA > One Way...
      − Select **MetricA** for "Response" and select **CategoryA** for "Factor".
      − Click "Graphs..." and for "Residual Plots" select **Four in one**.
  - Statistical Solution:
    ▪ Refer to the session window results.
      − Since P-value is > 0.05 (α), then we fail to reject H_0.
      − R-sq(adj) suggests only 4% of variation can be explained.
  - Practical Solution:

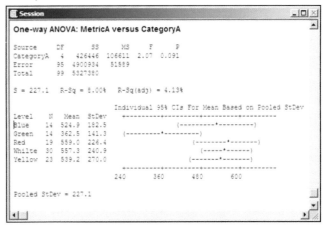

SS: Analyze

- The sample is insufficient to prove that the means for MetricA between each type of CategoryA value are different.
- If we assumed power=90% (β=10%), then how do we apply it to this test? What does it mean?

ANOVA Test: MetricA & CategoryB Example

○ Example: MetricA and CategoryB sample values
- Background:
    - Use the values in the "MetricA" and "CategoryB" columns of the Minitab Sample Data file.
- Practical Problem:
    - Is the mean for MetricA different between the various CategoryB values?
- Statistical Problem:
    - State the null (H_0) and alternative (H_a) hypotheses:
        - H_0: $\mu_{CategoryB1} = \mu_{CategoryB2} = \mu_{CategoryB3}$ etc., and H_a: $= \mu_{CategoryB1} \neq \mu_{CategoryB2} \neq \mu_{CategoryB3}$ etc.
    - Define the confidence (1-α) and power (1-β):
        - For confidence, we'll accept the default of 95% (which means α = 5%) and power of 90% (which means β = 10%).
    - Type the statistical problem into Minitab:
        - In Minitab, go to Stat > ANOVA > One Way...
        - Select **MetricA** for "Response" and select **CategoryB** for "Factor".
        - Click "Graphs..." and for "Residual Plots" select **Four in one**.
- Statistical Solution:
    - Refer to the session window results.
        - Since P-value is > 0.05 (α), then we fail to reject H_0.
        - R-sq(adj) suggests 0% of variation can be explained.
- Practical Solution:
    - The sample is insufficient to prove that the means for MetricA between each type of CategoryB value are different.
    - If we assumed power=90% (β=10%), then how do we apply that to this test?

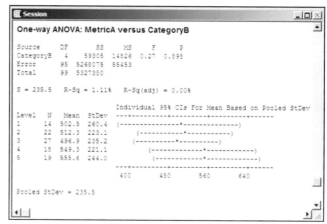

Practical Application

○ Refer to the critical metric (output Y) and at least 5 factors (input X's) you identified in a previous lesson for applying to this hypothesis testing.
- For any factor that is a continuous value, try applying the ANOVA Test.
    - To do this, you'll need a discrete factor that has 2 or more sets of values (e.g., across multiple periods of time, or different locations, or different groups, etc.).
    - Other factors in your organization can be used for this exercise.
- Before running the ANOVA Test, do the means for each factor group appear to be different?
- After running the ANOVA Test, are the means for each factor group statistically different?
- If the answers to the above 2 questions are different, then how does that affect how you'd typically measure and communicate that factor in the organization?
    - For example, does the difference in the means affect financial decisions (e.g., how people are paid), or process changes (e.g., how the process may be modified), or other critical actions?
    - If so, then how should the results from this statistical test be used to influence your organization?
        - Should they change how each factor group is compared (e.g., between different times, locations, groups, etc.)?
        - Should they change how each factor group is measured?
        - Should they change how they react when they compare the metric this way?

Six Sigma-Analyze – Lesson 19: Hypothesis Testing: Central Tendency – Non-Normal (Nonparametric Tests)

An extension on hypothesis testing, this lesson what nonparametric tests are and how they're used for non-normal dist.

Pre-Requisite Lessons:

o Six Sigma-Analyze #18 – Hypothesis Testing: Central Tendency – Normal (Compare 2+ Factors)

Review Finding the Right Statistical Test

o This topic reviewed here was originally covered on page 233.

Nonparametric Tests

o What are nonparametric tests?

- They are statistical tests that don't require the distribution to have certain parameters such as a normal distribution with the parameters of mean (μ) and standard deviation (σ).
    - Since nonparametric tests don't require these parameters typical for normal distributions, they can be very powerful when testing non-normal distributions.

o If non-normal distributions have bias, then why should we test them?

- For the most part, non-normal distributions may have bias or be skewed from the collected sample. But this may not always be the case.
    - It's more ideal to run statistical tests designed for normal distributions.
- Should the process being measured have a normal distribution?
    - If YES, then ask...
        - *Is the method used for collecting the sample data random and unbiased?*
        - *Does the measurement extend across multiple, different processes?*
        - *If YES to either of these questions, then fix the method for collecting the sample and re-collect it.*
    - If NO, then it may be appropriate to continue the hypothesis testing using nonparametric tests.
        - *Measurements that don't extend below zero are more likely to be non-normally distributed. For example...*
            - ➤ *Measurements of time that start at zero, like call duration or handle time.*
            - ➤ *Measurements of dollars that start at zero, like salaries or home values.*

Practical Application

o Refer to the critical metric (output Y) and at least 5 factors (input X's) you identified in a previous lesson for applying to this hypothesis testing.

- For any continuous factor that has a non-normal distribution, should the process that the metric is measuring have a normal distribution?
    - If YES, then...
        - *Is the method used for collecting the sample data random and unbiased?*
        - *Does the measurement extend across multiple, different processes?*
        - *If YES to either of these questions, then fix the method for collecting the sample and re-collect it.*
    - If NO, then it may be appropriate to continue the hypothesis testing using nonparametric tests.

Six Sigma-Analyze – Lesson 20: Hypothesis Testing: Central Tendency – Non-Normal (Compare 1:Standard)

An extension on hypothesis testing, this lesson reviews the 1 Sample Sign & Wilcoxon tests as central tendency measurements for non-normal dist.

Pre-Requisite Lessons:

o Six Sigma-Analyze #19 – Hypothesis Testing: Central Tendency – Non-Normal (Nonparametric Tests Overview)

Why do we need hypothesis testing?

o This topic reviewed here was originally covered on page 235.

Review Hypothesis Testing: 4 Step Process

o Remember, the 4 high-level steps for hypothesis testing begin/end with being practical:
  • This topic reviewed here was originally covered on page 224.
o As the heart of hypothesis testing, steps 2 & 3 can be drilled to the following 6 steps:
  • This topic reviewed here was originally covered on page 225.

Review Finding the Right Statistical Test

o This topic reviewed here was originally covered on page 233.

Confidence Intervals (CI) Redefined

o This topic reviewed here was originally covered on page 230.

Compare 1:Standard Tests: Introduction

o When should I use it?
  • To compare one median value with a standard (e.g., a target) or expected median value.
o There are two types of tests for comparing medians to a standard:
  • 1 Sample Sign Test is a test for *any* distribution (regardless of symmetry).
  • 1 Sample Wilcoxon Test is a test for *symmetric* distributions.
o How do you know if the data is symmetrical?
  • Use a symmetry plot by going to *Stat > Quality Tools > Symmetry Plot*…
  • The symmetry plot measures the distance of each data point to the median.

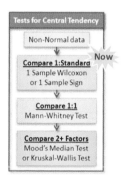

    ▪ If the distance is equal on either side of the median, then they would form a diagonal line when plotted.
    ▪ If the plotted data points deviate too far from the line, it is not symmetrical.
      – *In this case, don't use the 1 Sample Wilcoxon test.*

Although MetricA is normally distributed, it is not symmetrical.

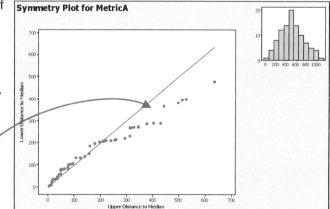

1 Sample Sign & Wilcoxon Test: Introduction

o When should I use it?
  • To compare one median value with a standard or target value for a symmetrical distribution or to find the confidence internal for a median.

- How do I find it in Minitab?
  - For the 1 Sample Sign test…
    - Go to *Stat > Nonparametrics > 1 Sample Sign…*
  - For the 1 Sample Wilcoxon test…
    - Go to *Stat > Nonparametrics > 1 Sample Wilcoxon…*
- What are the inputs for the test?
  - The inputs for both tests are identical:

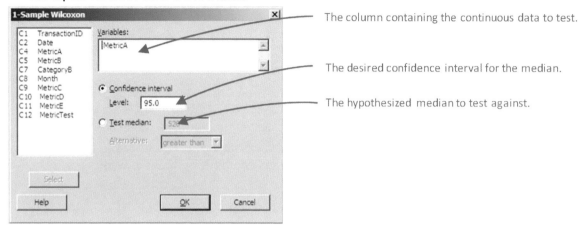

The column containing the continuous data to test.

The desired confidence interval for the median.

The hypothesized median to test against.

1 Sample Sign Test: MetricB Example

- Example: MetricB sample values
  - Background:
    - Use the arbitrary values in the "MetricB" column of the Minitab Sample Data file.
  - Practical Problem:
    - Is the median of MetricB greater than the LSL target of 25%?
  - Statistical Problem:
    - State the null (H_0) and alternative (H_a) hypotheses:
      - *H_0: η <= 0.25 and H_a: η > 0.25*
    - Define the confidence (1-α) and power (1-β):
      - *For confidence, we'll accept the default of 95% (which means α = 5%) and power of 90% (which means β = 10%).*
    - Type the statistical problem into Minitab:
      - *In Minitab, go to Stat > Nonparametrics > 1 Sample Sign…*
      - *In the "Variables" box, select **MetricB** from the list of columns.*
      - *Select "Test Median" and type in the goal of **0.25**.*
      - *In "Alternative" select **"greater than"**.*
  - Statistical Solution:
    - Refer to the session window results. What does this mean?
      - *Since P-value is > 0.05 (α), then we fail to reject H_0.*
  - Practical Solution:
    - The sample is insufficient to prove that MetricB is greater than the LSL target of 25%.
    - If we assumed power=90% (β=10%), then how do we apply that to this test? What does it mean?

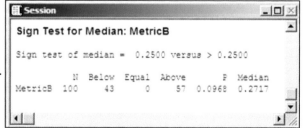

1 Sample Wilcoxon Test: MetricA Example

- Example: MetricA sample values
  - Background:
    - Use the arbitrary values in the "MetricA" column of the Minitab Sample Data file.

- Practical Problem:
  - Is the median of MetricA less than the USL target of 520?
- Statistical Problem:
  - State the null (H₀) and alternative (Hₐ) hypotheses:
    - H_0: $\eta >= 520$ and H_a: $\eta < 520$
  - Define the confidence (1-α) and power (1-β):
    - *For confidence, we'll accept the default of 95% (which means α = 5%) and power of 90% (which means β = 10%).*
  - Type the statistical problem into Minitab:
    - *In Minitab, go to Stat > Nonparametrics > 1 Sample Wilcoxon…*
    - *In the "Variables" box, select **MetricA** from the list of columns (use this even though MetricA is not symmetrical).*
    - *Select "Test Median" and type in the goal of **520**.*
    - *In "Alternative" select "**less than**".*
- Statistical Solution:
  - Refer to the session window results. What does this mean?
    - *Since P-value is > 0.05 (α), then we fail to reject H₀.*
- Practical Solution:
  - The sample is insufficient to prove that MetricA is less than the USL target of 520.

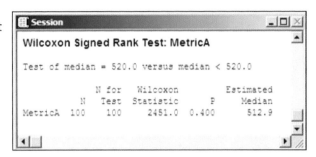

Session

Wilcoxon Signed Rank Test: MetricA

Test of median = 520.0 versus median < 520.0

	N	N for Test	Wilcoxon Statistic	P	Estimated Median
MetricA	100	100	2451.0	0.400	512.9

Practical Application
- Refer to the critical metric (output Y) and at least 5 factors (input X's) you identified in a previous lesson for applying to this hypothesis testing.
  - For any factor that is a continuous value, try applying both the 1 Sample Sign and 1 Sample Wilcoxon tests.
    - To do this, you'll need to compare that factor with a goal for that factor typically set by the organization.
    - These non-parametric tests are ideal for non-normal distributions, but you can still run them even if your continuous value has a normal distribution.
    - Other factors in your organization can be used for this exercise.
  - Before running either 1 Sample Test, does the factor meet or exceed the goal?
  - After running either 1 Sample Test, does the factor statistically meet or exceed the goal?
  - If the answers to the above 2 questions are different, then how does that affect how you'd typically measure and communicate that factor in the organization?
    - For example, does that factor meeting or not meeting the goal affect financial decisions (e.g., how people are compensated), or process changes (e.g., how the process may be modified), or other critical actions?
    - If so, then how should the results from this 1 Sample Test be used to influence your organization?
      - *Should they change how the goals are set?*
      - *Should they change how the factor is measured?*
      - *Should they change how they react when they compare the metric to the goal?*

SS: Analyze

6

Six Sigma-Analyze – Lesson 21: Hypothesis Testing: Central Tendency – Non-Normal (Compare 1:1)

An extension on hypothesis testing, this lesson reviews the Mann-Whitney test as a central tendency measurement for non-normal dist.

Pre-Requisite Lessons:

- Six Sigma-Analyze #20 – Hypothesis Testing: Central Tendency – Non-Normal (Compare 1:Standard)

Why do we need hypothesis testing?

- This topic reviewed here was originally covered on page 235.

Review Hypothesis Testing: 4 Step Process

- Remember, the 4 high-level steps for hypothesis testing begin/end with being practical:
  - This topic reviewed here was originally covered on page 224.
- As the heart of hypothesis testing, steps 2 & 3 can be drilled to the following 6 steps:
  - This topic reviewed here was originally covered on page 225.

Review Finding the Right Statistical Test

- This topic reviewed here was originally covered on page 233.

Confidence Intervals (CI) Redefined

- This topic reviewed here was originally covered on page 230.

Mann-Whitney Test: Introduction

- When should I use it?
  - To compare median values from two random samples from two populations having similar shape and variation.
  - It's also called the 2 Sample Rank test or 2 Sample Wilcoxon Rank Sum test.
- How do I find it in Minitab?
  - Go to *Stat* > *Nonparametrics* > *Mann-Whitney*...
- What are the inputs for the test?

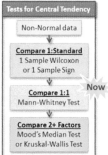

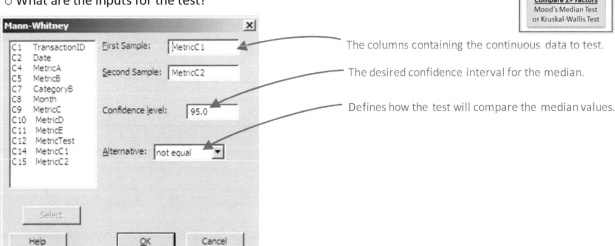

The columns containing the continuous data to test.

The desired confidence interval for the median.

Defines how the test will compare the median values.

Mann-Whitney Test: MetricC Example

- Example: MetricC sample values
  - Background:
    - Use the arbitrary values in the "MetricC" column of the Minitab Sample Data file.
    - Copy/paste the values of MetricC and split them 50/50 into two new columns.
      - *In this example, the first 50 were labeled "MetricC1" and the remaining 50 as "MetricC2".*

- Practical Problem:
  - Is the median of MetricC1 equal to the median of MetricC2?
- Statistical Problem:
  - State the null (H_0) and alternative (H_a) hypotheses:
    - H_0: $\eta_1 = \eta_2$ and H_a: $\eta_1 \neq \eta_2$
  - Define the confidence ($1-\alpha$) and power ($1-\beta$):
    - *For confidence, we'll accept the default of 95% (which means α = 5%) and power of 90% (which means β = 10%).*
  - Type the statistical problem into Minitab:
    - *In Minitab, go to Stat > Nonparametrics > Mann-Whitney…*
    - *In the "First Sample" box, select **MetricC1** from the list of columns and **MetricC2** as the "Second Sample".*
    - *Ensure the "Confidence Level" is **95.0** and alternative is "**not equal**".*
- Statistical Solution:
  - Refer to the session window results.
    - *P-value is the "Test is significant at" value.*
    - *Since P-value is > 0.05 (α), then we fail to reject H_0.*
- Practical Solution:
  - The sample is insufficient to prove that the median of MetricC1 is different than the median of MetricC2.

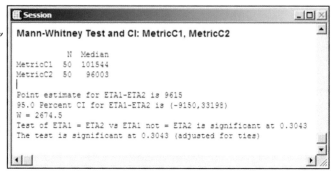

Practical Application

- o Refer to the critical metric (output Y) and at least 5 factors (input X's) you identified in a previous lesson for applying to this hypothesis testing.
  - For any factor that is a continuous value, try applying the Mann-Whitney test.
    - To do this, you'll need to compare at least two different sets of that same factor (e.g., across multiple periods of time, or by different locations, or by different groups, etc.).
    - A non-parametric test like this is ideal for non-normal distributions, but you can still run it even if your continuous value has a normal distribution.
    - Other factors in your organization can be used for this exercise.
  - Before running the Mann-Whitney Test, do the medians of the factors appear to be different?
  - After running the Mann-Whitney Test, are the medians of the factors statistically different?
  - If the answers to the above 2 questions are different, then how does that affect how you'd typically measure and communicate that factor in the organization?
    - For example, do the differences between the compared factors affect financial decisions (e.g., how people are compensated), or process changes (e.g., how the process may be modified), or other critical actions?
    - If so, then how should the results from this Mann-Whitney Test be used to influence your organization?
      - *Should they change how the factors are compared (e.g., across different times, locations, groups, etc.)?*
      - *Should they change how the factor is measured?*
      - *Should they change how they react when they compare the metric this way?*

Six Sigma-Analyze – Lesson 22: Hypothesis Testing: Central Tend. – Non-Normal (Compare 2+ Factors)

An extension on hypothesis testing, this lesson reviews the Mood's Median & Kruskal-Wallis tests as central tendency measurements for non-normal dist.

Pre-Requisite Lessons:
- o Six Sigma-Analyze #21 – Hypothesis Testing: Central Tendency – Non-Normal (Compare 1:1)

Why do we need hypothesis testing?
- o This topic reviewed here was originally covered on page 235.

Review Hypothesis Testing: 4 Step Process
- o Remember, the 4 high-level steps for hypothesis testing begin/end with being practical:
  - This topic reviewed here was originally covered on page 224.
- o As the heart of hypothesis testing, steps 2 & 3 can be drilled to the following 6 steps:
  - This topic reviewed here was originally covered on page 225.

Review Finding the Right Statistical Test
- o This topic reviewed here was originally covered on page 233.

Confidence Intervals (CI) Redefined
- o This topic reviewed here was originally covered on page 230.

Compare 2+ Factors Tests: Introduction
- o When should I use it?
  - To compare median values for multiple factors across different populations.
- o There are two types of tests to compare medians for multiple factors:
  - Mood's Median is a test when the population contains many outliers.
  - Kruskal-Wallis Test is a stronger test, except when there are many outliers.
- o How do you know if there are many outliers?
  - Use a boxplot to identify possible outliers (at right).
    - To create a boxplot, go to *Graph > Boxplot...*
- o What are the inputs for the test?
  - The inputs for both tests are identical:

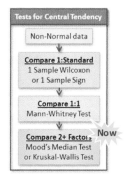

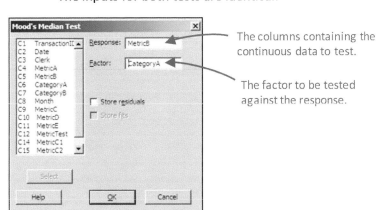

The columns containing the continuous data to test.

The factor to be tested against the response.

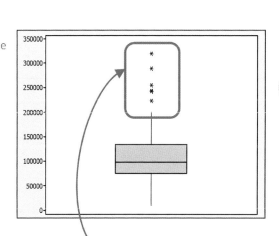

These outliers may be influencing the distribution. Therefore, you're better off using the Mood's Median test.

Mood's Median: Interpreting Results

o What do these results from the Mood's Median test mean?

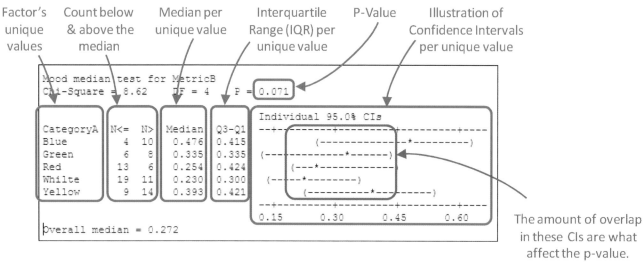

Factor's unique values | Count below & above the median | Median per unique value | Interquartile Range (IQR) per unique value | P-Value | Illustration of Confidence Intervals per unique value

```
Mood median test for MetricB
Chi-Square = 8.62     DF = 4     P = 0.071

                                   Individual 95.0% CIs
CategoryA  N<=  N>   Median  Q3-Q1  --+---------+---------+---------+----
Blue        4   10   0.476   0.415             (------------------*---------)
Green       6    8   0.335   0.335  (---------------*------)
Red        13    6   0.254   0.424     (---*-------------)
Whilte     19   11   0.230   0.300  (-----*---------)
Yellow      9   14   0.393   0.421       (-----------*----------)
                                    --+---------+---------+---------+----
                                    0.15      0.30      0.45      0.60

Overall median = 0.272
```

The amount of overlap in these CIs are what affect the p-value.

o How do I interpret these results?
  - If the P-value is less than the α risk, there's a statistical difference between the factor's values.
  - The IQR is a measurement of the spread for each factor, like a variance. A large difference in IQR between the values should be validated with a test for equal variances.

Mood's Median: MetricB Example

o Example: MetricB & CategoryA sample values
  - Background:
    - Use the arbitrary values in the "MetricB" and "CategoryA" columns of the Minitab Sample Data file.
  - Practical Problem:
    - Is there a difference in medians of MetricB for each CategoryA value?
  - Statistical Problem:
    - State the null (H_0) and alternative (H_a) hypotheses:
      - H_0: $\eta_{CategoryA1} = \eta_{CategoryA2} = \eta_{CategoryA3}$ etc., and H_a: $\eta_{CategoryA1} \neq \eta_{CategoryA2} \neq \eta_{CategoryA3}$ etc.
    - Define the confidence ($1-\alpha$) and power ($1-\beta$):
      - For confidence, we'll accept the default of 95% (which means α = 5%) and power of 90% (which means β = 10%).
    - Type the statistical problem into Minitab:
      - In Minitab, go to Stat > Nonparametrics > Mood's Median Test…
      - In the "Response" box, select **MetricB** from the list of columns.
      - In the "Factor" box, select **CategoryA** from the list of columns.
  - Statistical Solution:
    - Refer to the session window results.
      - Since P-value is > 0.05 (α), then we fail to reject H_0.
  - Practical Solution:
    - The sample is insufficient to prove that the medians of MetricB are different between the CatetoryA values.
    - If we assumed power=90% (β=10%), then how do we apply that to this test? What does it mean?
    - Which CategoryA values appear to drive what difference there is? How do you know it?

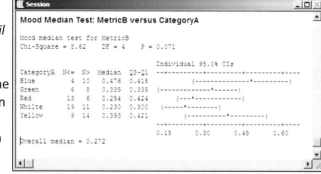

Kruskal-Wallis: Interpreting Results

o What do these results from the Kruskal-Wallis test mean?

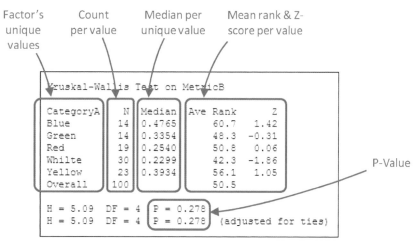

Factor's unique values | Count per value | Median per unique value | Mean rank & Z-score per value | P-Value

o How do I interpret these results?
- If the P-value is less than the α risk, there's a statistical difference between the factor's values.
- The factor having a Z-score furthest from zero (positive or negative) has the most difference (in mean rank) among all observations.
  - That is, if there is a statistical difference from this test, it's most likely affected by the factor(s) having a Z-value furthest from zero.

Kruskal-Wallis: MetricB Example

o Example: MetricB & CategoryA sample values
- Background:
  - Use the values in the "MetricB" and "CategoryA" columns of the Minitab Sample Data file.
- Practical Problem:
  - Is there a difference in medians of MetricB for each CategoryA value?
- Statistical Problem:
  - State the null (H_0) and alternative (H_a) hypotheses:
    - H_0: $\eta_{CategoryA1} = \eta_{CategoryA2} = \eta_{CategoryA3}$ etc., and H_a: $\eta_{CategoryA1} \neq \eta_{CategoryA2} \neq \eta_{CategoryA3}$ etc.
  - Define the confidence (1-α) and power (1-β):
    - For confidence, we'll accept the default of 95% (which means α = 5%) and power of 90% (which means β = 10%).
  - Type the statistical problem into Minitab:
    - In Minitab, go to Stat > Nonparametrics > Kruskal-Wallis...
    - In the "Response" box, select **MetricB** from the list of columns.
    - In the "Factor" box, select **CategoryA** from the list of columns.
- Statistical Solution:
  - Refer to the session window results.
    - Since P-value is > 0.05 (α), then we fail to reject H_0.
- Practical Solution:
  - The sample is insufficient to prove that the medians of MetricB are different between the CatetoryA values.
  - If we assumed power=90% (β=10%), then how do we apply that to this test? What does it mean?
  - Which CategoryA values appear to drive what difference there is? How do you know it?
  - Why is this so different from the Mood's Median test?

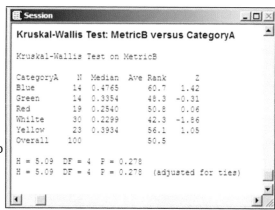

Practical Application

- o Refer to the critical metric (output Y) and at least 5 factors (input X's) you identified in a previous lesson for applying to this hypothesis testing.
  - For any factor that is a continuous value, try applying both the Mood's Median and Kruskal-Wallis tests.
    - To do this, you'll need a discrete factor that has 2 or more sets of values (e.g., across multiple periods of time, or different locations, or different groups, etc.).
    - Non-parametric tests like these are ideal for non-normal distributions, but you can still run them even if your continuous value has a normal distribution.
    - Other factors in your organization can be used for this exercise.
  - Before running either test, do the medians of the factors appear to be different?
  - After running either test, are the medians of the factors statistically different?
  - If the answers to the above 2 questions are different, then how does that affect how you'd typically measure and communicate that factor in the organization?
    - For example, does the difference between the compared factors affect financial decisions (e.g., how people are compensated), or process changes (e.g., how the process may be modified), or other critical actions?
    - If so, then how should the results from either test be used to influence your organization?
      - *Should they change how the factors are compared (e.g., across different times, locations, groups, etc.)?*
      - *Should they change how the factor is measured?*
      - *Should they change how they react when they compare the metric this way?*

Six Sigma-Analyze – Lesson 23: Hypothesis Testing: Spread (Compare 1:Standard)

An extension on hypothesis testing, this lesson reviews the 1 Variance test as a measurement of spread or variation.

Pre-Requisite Lessons:

o Six Sigma-Analyze #22 – Hypothesis Testing: Central Tendency – Non-Normal (Compare 2+ Factors)

Why do we need hypothesis testing?

o This topic reviewed here was originally covered on page 235.

Review Hypothesis Testing: 4 Step Process

o Remember, the 4 high-level steps for hypothesis testing begin/end with being practical:
  • This topic reviewed here was originally covered on page 224.
o As the heart of hypothesis testing, steps 2 & 3 can be drilled to the following 6 steps:
  • This topic reviewed here was originally covered on page 225.

Review Finding the Right Statistical Test

o This topic reviewed here was originally covered on page 233.

Confidence Intervals (CI) Redefined

o This topic reviewed here was originally covered on page 230.

1 Variance Test: Introduction

o When should I use it?
  • To compare one variance value with a standard or target value.
o How do I find it in Minitab?
  • *Stat > Basic Statistics > 1 Variance…*
o What are the inputs for the test?

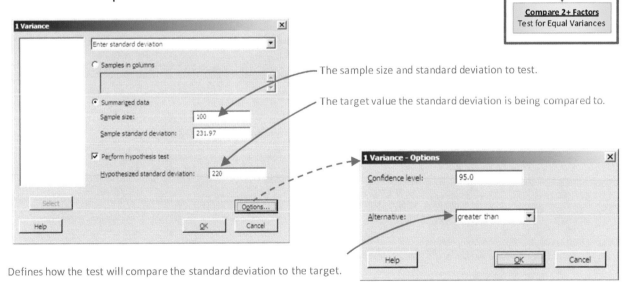

The sample size and standard deviation to test.

The target value the standard deviation is being compared to.

Defines how the test will compare the standard deviation to the target.

1 Variance Test: Call Center Example

o Example: Call Center Performance
  • Background:
    ▪ To ensure process stability, each call center is expected to have standard deviation of less than 5% for repeat calls from customers. A sample of 500 surveys for the Phoenix call center showed their rate was 85% with standard deviation of 4.8%.
  • Practical Problem:
    ▪ Is the standard deviation of 4.8% less than the USL target of 5%?

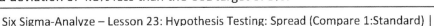

- Statistical Problem:
  - State the null (H₀) and alternative (Hₐ) hypotheses:
    - *– H₀: σ >= 0.05 and Hₐ: σ < 0.05*
  - Define the confidence (1-α) and power (1-β):
    - *For confidence, we'll accept the default of 95% (which means α = 5%) and power of 90% (which means β = 10%).*
  - Type the statistical problem into Minitab:
    - *In Minitab, go to Stat > Basic Statistics > 1 Variance…*
    - *Select "Enter Standard Deviation".*
    - *Select "Summarized Data", and select* **500** *for "Sample Size" and select* **0.048** *for "Sample Standard Deviation".*
    - *Check the "Perform Hypothesis Test" box and type* **0.05**.
    - *Click "Options…" and ensure the "Confidence Level" is* **95.0** *and "Alternative" is "**less than**".*
- Statistical Solution:
  - Refer to the session window results.
    - *Since P-value is > 0.05 (α), then we fail to reject H₀.*
- Practical Solution:
  - The sample is insufficient to prove that the Phoenix call center's standard deviation met the target of 5%.

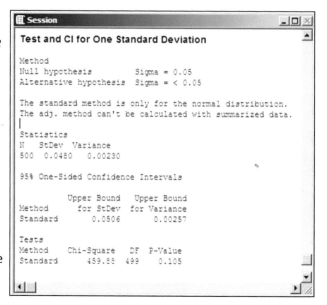

1 Variance Test: MetricA Example

- Example: MetricA sample values
  - Background:
    - Use the standard deviation of "MetricA" column of the Minitab Sample Data file.
  - Practical Problem:
    - Does the standard deviation of MetricA exceed the USL target of 220?
  - Statistical Problem:
    - State the null (H₀) and alternative (Hₐ) hypotheses:
      - *– H₀: σ <= 220 and Hₐ: σ > 220*
    - Define the confidence (1-α) and power (1-β):
      - *For confidence, we'll accept the default of 95% (which means α = 5%) and power of 90% (which means β = 10%).*
    - Type the statistical problem into Minitab:
      - *In Minitab, go to Stat > Basic Statistics > 1 Variance…*
      - *Select "Enter Standard Deviation".*
      - *Select "Summarized Data", and select* **100** *for "Sample Size" and select* **231.97** *for "Sample Standard Deviation".*
      - *Check the "Perform Hypothesis Test" box and type* **220**.
      - *Click "Options…" and ensure the "Confidence Level" is* **95.0** *and "Alternative" is "**greater than**".*

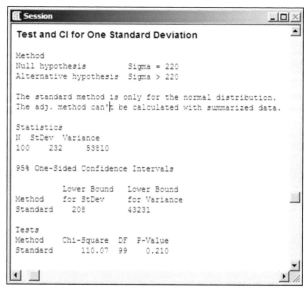

- Statistical Solution:
  - Refer to the session window results.
    - *Since P-value is > 0.05 (α), then we fail to reject H_0.*
    - *Lower Bound means it's possible for the standard deviation to be 208 which is below the USL target of 220.*
- Practical Solution:
  - The sample is insufficient to prove that MetricA standard deviation exceeds the target of 220.

Practical Application

- Refer to the critical metric (output Y) and at least 5 factors (input X's) you identified in a previous lesson for applying to this hypothesis testing.
  - For any factor that is a continuous value, try applying the 1 Variance test.
    - To do this, you'll need to compare that factor with a goal for that factor typically set by the organization.
    - Other factors in your organization can be used for this exercise.
  - Before running the 1 Variance Test, does the factor meet or exceed the goal?
  - After running the 1 Variance Test, does the factor statistically meet or exceed the goal?
  - If the answers to the above 2 questions are different, then how does that affect how you'd typically measure and communicate that factor in the organization?
    - For example, does that factor meeting or not meeting the goal affect financial decisions (e.g., how people are compensated), or process changes (e.g., how the process may be modified), or other critical actions?
    - If so, then how should the results from this 1 Variance Test be used to influence your organization?
      - *Should they change how the goals are set?*
      - *Should they change how the factor is measured?*
      - *Should they change how they react when they compare the metric to the goal?*

Six Sigma-Analyze – Lesson 24: Hypothesis Testing: Spread (Compare 1:1)

An extension on hypothesis testing, this lesson reviews the 2 Variance test as a measurement of spread or variation.

Pre-Requisite Lessons:

- o Six Sigma-Analyze #23 – Hypothesis Testing: Spread (Compare 1 to Standard)

Why do we need hypothesis testing?

- o This topic reviewed here was originally covered on page 235.

Review Hypothesis Testing: 4 Step Process

- o Remember, the 4 high-level steps for hypothesis testing begin/end with being practical:
  - This topic reviewed here was originally covered on page 224.
- o As the heart of hypothesis testing, steps 2 & 3 can be drilled to the following 6 steps:
  - This topic reviewed here was originally covered on page 225.

Review Finding the Right Statistical Test

- o This topic reviewed here was originally covered on page 233.

Confidence Intervals (CI) Redefined

- o This topic reviewed here was originally covered on page 230.

2 Variance Test: Introduction

- o When should I use it?
  - To compare two variance values from two random samples from two different, normal distributions.
- o How do I find it in Minitab?
  - *Stat > Basic Statistics > 2 Variances...*
- o What are the inputs for the test?

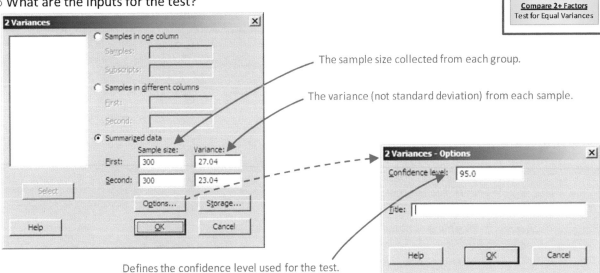

The sample size collected from each group.

The variance (not standard deviation) from each sample.

Defines the confidence level used for the test.

2 Variance Test: Call Center Example

- o Example: Comparison of Performance between Call Centers.
  - Background:
    - Each call center is expected to have a standard deviation of less than 5% for repeat calls from customers. A sample of 300 surveys each from the Phoenix & Reno call centers show their standard deviation was 4.8% & 5.2% respectively.

- Practical Problem:
  - Is there a difference in standard deviation between the two call centers?
- Statistical Problem:
  - State the null (H_0) and alternative (H_a) hypotheses:
    - H_0: $\sigma_{Phoenix} = \sigma_{Reno}$ and H_a: $\sigma_{Phoenix} \neq \sigma_{Reno}$
  - Define the confidence (1-α) and power (1-β):
    - *For confidence, we'll accept the default of 95% (which means α = 5%) and power of 90% (which means β = 10%).*
  - Type the statistical problem into Minitab:
    - *In Minitab, go to Stat > Basic Statistics > 2 Variances...*
    - *Select "Summarized Data".*
    - *Enter **300** for "Sample Size" for both "First" and "Second" and calculate and enter the variance for both call centers.*
    - *Click "Options..." and ensure the "Confidence Level" is **95.0**.*
- Statistical Solution:
  - Refer to the session window results.
    - *Since P-value is > 0.05 (α), then we fail to reject H_0.*
    - *A graph is generated to illustrate the CIs per call center.*
- Practical Solution:
  - The sample is insufficient to prove there's a difference in standard deviation between the two call centers.

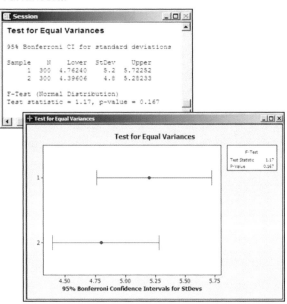

2 Variance Test: MetricA & CategoryA Example
- Example: MetricA and CategoryA sample values.
  - Background:
    - Use the standard deviation of "MetricA" column of the Minitab Sample Data file where "CategoryA" = Yellow and Green.
  - Practical Problem:
    - Is there a difference in MetricA's standard deviation when CategoryA is Yellow or Green?
  - Statistical Problem:
    - State the null (H_0) and alternative (H_a) hypotheses:
      - H_0: $\sigma_{Yellow} = \sigma_{Green}$ and H_a: $\sigma_{Yellow} \neq \sigma_{Green}$
    - Define the confidence (1-α) and power (1-β):
      - *For confidence, we'll accept the default of 95% (which means α = 5%) and power of 90% (which means β = 10%).*
    - Type the statistical problem into Minitab:
      - *Get the volume and variance for MetricA for both Yellow and Green for CategoryA. (Hint: Graphical Summary)*
      - *In Minitab, go to Stat > Basic Statistics > 2 Variances...*
      - *Select "Summarized Data" and enter the respective "Sample Size" and Variance for both "First" and "Second". Click "Options..." and ensure the "Confidence Level" is **95.0**.*

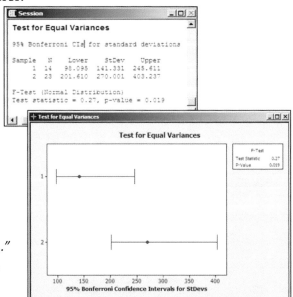

- Statistical Solution:
  - Refer to the session window results.
    - *Since P-value is < 0.05 (α), then we reject H_0.*
    - *A graph is generated to illustrate the CIs per CategoryA.*
- Practical Solution:
  - The sample is sufficient to prove there's a difference in standard deviation between Yellow & Green CategoryA.

Practical Application

- Refer to the critical metric (output Y) and at least 5 factors (input X's) you identified in a previous lesson for applying to this hypothesis testing.
  - For any factor that is a continuous value, try applying the 2 Variance test.
    - To do this, you'll need to compare at least two different sets of that same factor (e.g., across multiple periods of time, or by different locations, or by different groups, etc.).
    - Other factors in your organization can be used for this exercise.
  - Before running the 2 Variance Test, do the standard deviations appear to be different?
  - After running the 2 Variance Test, are the standard deviations statistically different?
  - If the answers to the above 2 questions are different, then how does that affect how you'd typically measure and communicate that factor in the organization?
    - For example, do the differences between the compared factors affect financial decisions (e.g., how people are compensated), or process changes (e.g., how the process may be modified), or other critical actions?
    - If so, then how should the results from this 2 Variance Test be used to influence your organization?
      - *Should they change how the factors are compared (e.g., across different times, locations, groups, etc.)?*
      - *Should they change how the factor is measured?*
      - *Should they change how they react when they compare the metric this way?*

SS: Analyze

6

Six Sigma-Analyze – Lesson 25: Hypothesis Testing: Spread (Compare 2+ Factors)

An extension on hypothesis testing, this lesson reviews the Test for Equal Variances as a measurement of spread or variation.

Pre-Requisite Lessons:
- o Six Sigma-Analyze #24 – Hypothesis Testing: Spread (Compare 1 to 1)

Why do we need hypothesis testing?
- o This topic reviewed here was originally covered on page 235.

Review Hypothesis Testing: 4 Step Process
- o Remember, the 4 high-level steps for hypothesis testing begin/end with being practical:
  - This topic reviewed here was originally covered on page 224.
- o As the heart of hypothesis testing, steps 2 & 3 can be drilled to the following 6 steps:
  - This topic reviewed here was originally covered on page 225.

Review Finding the Right Statistical Test
- o This topic reviewed here was originally covered on page 233.

Confidence Intervals (CI) Redefined
- o This topic reviewed here was originally covered on page 230.

Test for Equal Variances: Introduction
- o When should I use it?
  - To compare standard deviations or variances for multiple factors across different populations. It's also called "Homogeneity of Variance" (HOV).
- o How do I find it in Minitab?
  - *Stat > ANOVA > Test for Equal Variances…*
- o What are the inputs for the test?

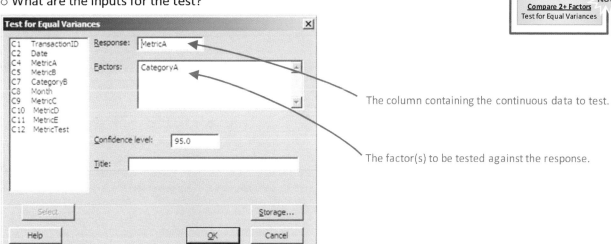

The column containing the continuous data to test.

The factor(s) to be tested against the response.

Test for Equal Variance: MetricA Example 1
- o Example: MetricA and CategoryA sample values.
  - Background:
    - Use the "MetricA" and "CategoryA" columns from the Minitab Sample Data file.
  - Practical Problem:
    - Is there a difference in standard deviation of MetricA for each CategoryA value?
  - Statistical Problem:
    - State the null (H_0) and alternative (H_a) hypotheses:

$- H_0: \sigma_{CategoryA1} = \sigma_{CategoryA2} = \sigma_{CategoryA3}$, etc. and $H_a: \sigma_{CategoryA1} \neq \sigma_{CategoryA2} \neq \sigma_{CategoryA3}$, etc.

- Define the confidence $(1-\alpha)$ and power $(1-\beta)$:
  - For confidence, we'll accept the default of 95% (which means $\alpha = 5\%$) and power of 90% (which means $\beta = 10\%$).
- Type the statistical problem into Minitab:
  - In Minitab, go to Stat > ANOVA > Test for Equal Variances...
  - Select **MetricA** for "Response" and **CategoryA** for "Factors".

- Statistical Solution:
  - Refer to the session window results.
    - Since P-value is > 0.05 (α), then we fail to reject H_0.
- Practical Solution:
  - The sample is insufficient to prove there's a difference in standard deviation between the CategoryA values.

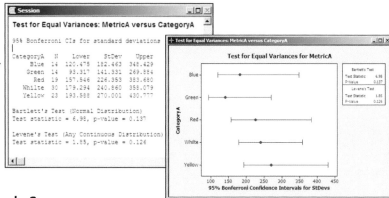

Test for Equal Variance: MetricA Example 2

o Example: MetricA and Month sample values.
- Background:
  - Use the "MetricA" and "Month" columns from the Minitab Sample Data file.
- Practical Problem:
  - Is there a difference in standard deviation of MetricA for each Month?
- Statistical Problem:
  - State the null (H_0) and alternative (H_a) hypotheses:
    - $H_0: \sigma_{June} = \sigma_{July}$ and $H_a: \sigma_{June} \neq \sigma_{July}$
  - Define the confidence $(1-\alpha)$ and power $(1-\beta)$:
    - For confidence, we'll accept the default of 95% (which means $\alpha = 5\%$) and power of 90% (which means $\beta = 10\%$).
  - Type the statistical problem into Minitab:
    - In Minitab, go to Stat > ANOVA > Test for Equal Variances...
    - Select **MetricA** for "Response" and **Month** for "Factors".

- Statistical Solution:
  - Refer to the session window results.
    - Since P-value is < 0.05 (α), then we reject H_0.
- Practical Solution:
  - The sample is sufficient to prove there's a difference in standard deviation between the months.
  - Could this have been tested in a 2 variance test?
    - Try using the "Samples in one column" section.

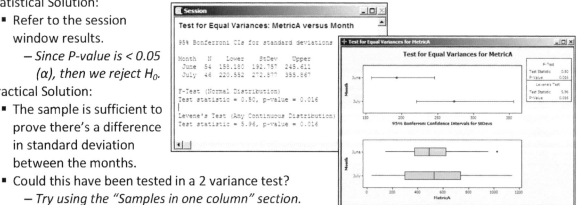

Practical Application

o Refer to the critical metric (output Y) and at least 5 factors (input X's) you identified in a previous lesson for applying to this hypothesis testing.
- For any factor that is a continuous value, try applying the Test for Equal Variances.
  - To do this, you'll need a discrete factor that has 2 or more sets of values (e.g., across multiple periods of time, or different locations, or different groups, etc.).

- Other factors in your organization can be used for this exercise.
- Before running the Test for Equal Variances, do the standard deviations for each factor group appear to be different?
- After running the Test for Equal Variances, are the standard deviations for each factor group statistically different?
- If the answers to the above 2 questions are different, then how does that affect how you'd typically measure and communicate that factor in the organization?
  - For example, does the difference between the compared factors affect financial decisions (e.g., how people are compensated), or process changes (e.g., how the process may be modified), or other critical actions?
  - If so, then how should the results from this statistical test be used to influence your organization?
    - *Should they change how each factor group is compared (e.g., between different times, locations, groups, etc.)?*
    - *Should they change how each factor group is measured?*
    - *Should they change how they react when they compare the metric this way?*

Six Sigma-Analyze – Lesson 26: Hypothesis Testing: Relationships (Overview)

An extension on hypothesis testing, this lesson introduces the concepts of a correlation and regression as part of measuring statistical relationships.

Pre-Requisite Lessons:

- o Six Sigma-Analyze #25 – Hypothesis Testing: Spread (Compare 2+ Factors)

Why do we need hypothesis testing?

- o This topic reviewed here was originally covered on page 235.

How are relationship tests different?

- o Relationship tests have a very different perspective from these other statistical tests.
  - It depends on the source (distribution) and what you're testing for (differences or similarities).

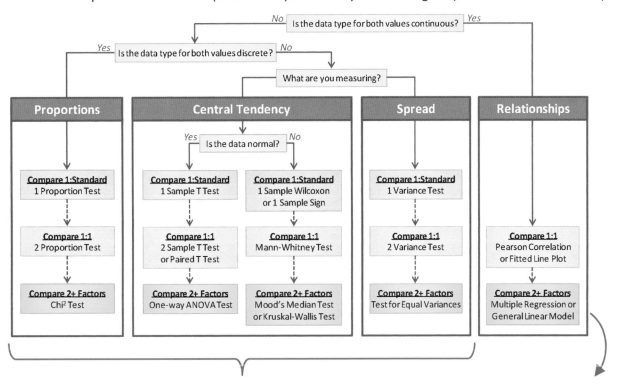

These tests look for ***differences*** within ***similar*** groups/distributions.

These tests look for ***similarities*** across ***different*** groups/distributions.

Correlation: Introduction

- o What is correlation?
  - It's a measure of linear association between two independent continuous values.
  - More specifically, it refers to how much can be explained by the linear association/relationship.
- o What is a correlation coefficient (a.k.a. Pearson correlation)?
  - It's a way of measuring the strength of correlation between two factors.
    - It does this by plotting the coordinates for the factors and trying to draw a line between those factors.
    - The distance the factors are from that line (errors or residuals) helps determine the correlation strength.
  - Correlation coefficient will fall on a scale between -1.0 and +1.0.
    - "r" = sample correlation coefficient.
    - "ρ" (rho) = population correlation coefficient.

- Below are examples of 3 different types of relationships and how we'd describe them:

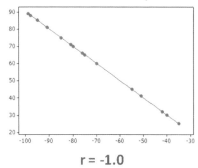
r = -1.0
100% of data points can be explained as a negative (inverse) relationship

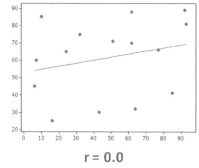
r = 0.0
0% of data points can be explained through a relationship.

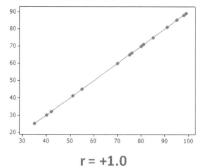
r = +1.0
100% of data points can be explained as a positive relationship

Determining Correlation Strength

- How do you determine the strength of a correlation?
  - The further the correlation (r) is away from zero, the stronger it is.
  - There is not a "perfect" threshold for determining if a correlation is weak or strong.
    - There have been many thresholds proposed, but it really depends on the factors you're using and what kind of relationship you'd expect between them.
  - Do you expect a relationship to exist between the factors?
    - If yes, then use the scale that is more strict.
    - Otherwise if you wouldn't have expected a relationship between the factors, use the other scale.

	-1.0	-0.75	-0.50	-0.25	0.0	+0.25	+0.50	+0.75	+1.0
Relationship Expected:	Strong	Moderate	Weak		None		Weak	Moderate	Strong
No Relationship Expected:	Strong			Moderate	Weak	Weak	Moderate	Strong	

- Remember, this scale is only intended as a general guide and not a formal rule.

Regression: Introduction

- What is a regression?
  - As previously noted, correlation (r) measures the linear association between two variables.
  - A regression builds an equation (or model) describing the nature of that relationship.
    - The equation will generally look like the following:

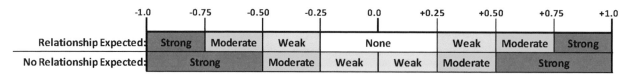

$$\text{Y-Response} = \text{Constant} + \text{Coefficient(X-Predictor)}$$

- The quality of the regression is measured by squaring the correlation coefficient, or r^2.
  - It measures the proportion of variation explained by the regression model.
- What can we do with a regression?
  - Build an equation (model), like a transfer function.
    - It allows us to explore the existence of the relationship between two or more variables.
  - Predict outcomes
    - With a regression equation, we can plug in other variables and to predict future results.
  - Validate equation
    - We can determine how accurate the equation's prediction was.
  - Determine driving factors
    - We can determine what key factors influence our output Y (response) the most.

Relationship Risk #1: Dealing with Sample Size
- Risk #1: A linear association (and correlation) can be drawn with only two data points.
  - Technically, the r^2 is 100%. But is this acceptable?

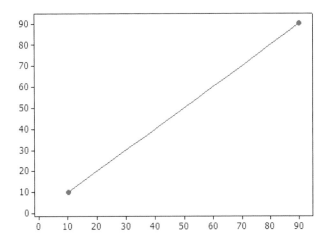

- How do you know if there are enough data points to trust the r^2 value?
  - Minitab will generally calculate a r^2(adj) value which accounts for the number of terms and data points in the regression model.
    - If there are too few data points, r^2(adj) will be smaller.
    - If there are enough data points, r^2(adj) will be closer to, but never exceed, the r^2 value.
  - As a rule of thumb, use the r^2(adj) from every test instead of just the r^2 value.

Relationship Risk #2: Correlation vs. Causation
- Risk #2: A relationship between factors doesn't mean one is causing/driving the other.
  - A relationship may exist between variables simply because they're both dependent on and influenced by another independent variable. See the example below...

Is there a relationship between shark attacks and ice cream sales?

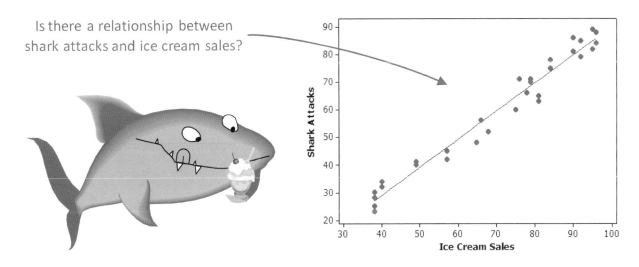

- If we didn't know better, we may be inclined to stop ice cream sales in order to prevent shark attacks.
  - *Does that make sense? Could there be another independent factor on which these two variables are dependent?*
- Always make sure any relationship between variables is *logical*.
- Any true causation should be able to be tested in additional ways in order to validate the cause.

Practical Application

- o Refer to the critical metric (output Y) and at least 5 factors (input X's) you identified in a previous lesson for applying to this hypothesis testing.
  - For any factors that are continuous values, consider the following:
    - Which sets of factors would you expect there to be some correlation? Why?
      - *What would you expect the correlation % (r) to be?*
      - *What could it mean if you actually found there was much less or no correlation as you expected?*
    - Which sets of factors would you expect there to be no correlation at all? Why?
      - *What could it mean if you found a correlation?*
  - It's helpful to consider the above types of questions *before* running the statistical tests.

Six Sigma-Analyze – Lesson 27: Hypothesis Testing: Relationships (Compare 1:1)

An extension on hypothesis testing, this lesson reviews the Pearson Correlation and Fitted Line Plot as part of measuring statistical relationships.

Pre-Requisite Lessons:
   o Six Sigma-Analyze #26 – Hypothesis Testing: Relationships (Overview)

Why do we need hypothesis testing?
   o This topic reviewed here was originally covered on page 235.

Review Hypothesis Testing: 4 Step Process
   o Remember, the 4 high-level steps for hypothesis testing begin/end with being practical:
      • This topic reviewed here was originally covered on page 224.
   o As the heart of hypothesis testing, steps 2 & 3 can be drilled to the following 6 steps:
      • This topic reviewed here was originally covered on page 225.

Review Finding the Right Statistical Test
   o This topic reviewed here was originally covered on page 233.

Pearson Correlation Test: Introduction
   o When should I use it?
      • To compare two continuous values to see if they are correlated.
   o How do I find it in Minitab?
      • *Stat > Basic Statistics > Correlation...*
   o What are the inputs for the test?

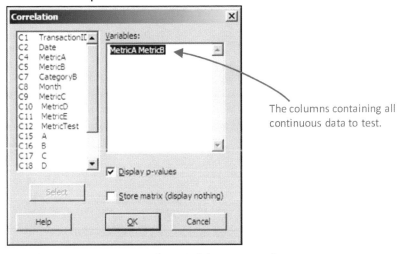

The columns containing all continuous data to test.

Pearson Correlation: Several Variables Example
   o Example: Several sample values
      • Background:
         ▪ Use all the arbitrary continuous values in Minitab Sample Data file.
      • Practical Problem:
         ▪ Is there a relationship between any of the continuous values? If so, how strong?
      • Statistical Problem:
         ▪ State the null (H_0) and alternative (H_a) hypotheses:
            — $H_0: \rho_1 = 0, \rho_2 = 0, \rho_3 = 0$, etc. and $H_a: \rho_1 > 0, \rho_2 > 0, \rho_3 > 0$, etc.
            — *What does this mean? If the correlation coefficient exceeds zero for any set of values, then the values are correlated.*
         ▪ Define the confidence (1-α) and power (1-β):

- *For confidence, we'll accept the default of 95% (which means α = 5%) and power of 90% (which means β = 10%).*
  - Type the statistical problem into Minitab:
    - *In Minitab, go to Stat > Basic Statistics > Correlation...*
    - *In the "Variables" box, select **MetricA, MetricB, MetricC, MetricD**, and **MetricE** from the list of columns.*
- Statistical Solution:
  - Refer to the session window results. What does this mean?
    - *Each continuous value is tested against every other continuous value, and the correlation coefficient and P-value are noted for each test.*
    - *Each test aligns with a row and column of metric values:*
      - ➤ *MetricA & MetricC have a P-value of 0.00 and correlation of 79%.*
      - ➤ *MetricB & MetricD have a P-value of 0.24 and correlation of 12%.*

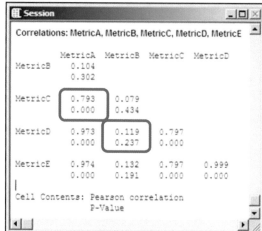

- Practical Solution:
  - What combination of metrics have a correlation?
  - Which combination of metrics has the strongest correlation?
  - Which combination of metrics has the weakest correlation?

Fitted Line Plot: Introduction
  - When should I use it?
    - To build a regression equation by comparing two continuous values to see how correlated they are.
  - How do I find it in Minitab?
    - *Stat > Regression > Fitted Line Plot...*
  - What are the inputs for the test?

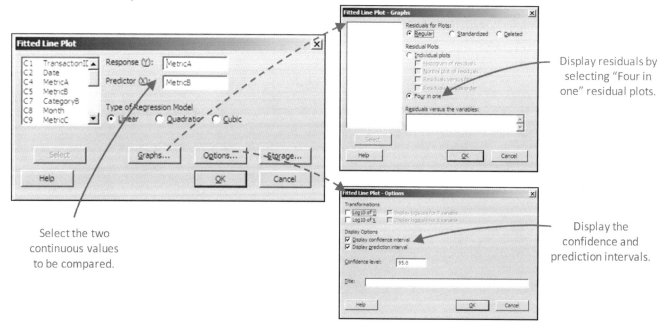

Fitted Line Plot: Confidence/Predictor Intervals

- o Remember, confidence intervals estimate a range around a mean.
  - Predictor Intervals are similar but give a range for predicting future data points.

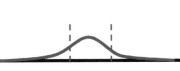

With fewer samples, the population mean falls within a wide interval.

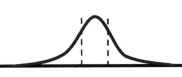

Add more samples and the population mean falls in a more narrow interval.

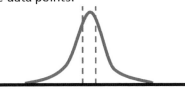

With more samples, the more confident (narrow) the mean interval becomes.

- Confidence and Predictor Intervals are drawn on the fitted line plot:

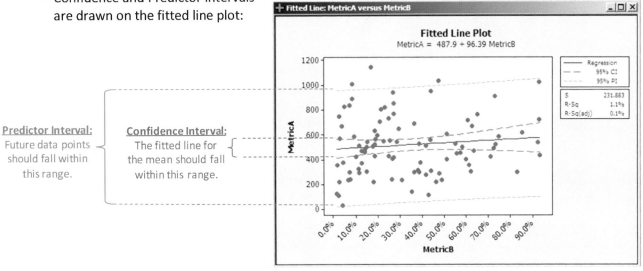

Predictor Interval: Future data points should fall within this range.

Confidence Interval: The fitted line for the mean should fall within this range.

Review of Residuals

- o This topic was originally covered on page 257.
- o What are residuals?
  - Remember, a deviation is the distance a data point is from the mean.
  - For regressions, residuals represent the deviation of each data point from the line being fit among the compared variables.
- o What do we look for in the residuals?
  - Residuals should have these characteristics:
    - ▪ They should be normally distributed, independent, and should have equal variances.

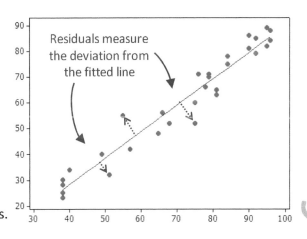

Residuals measure the deviation from the fitted line

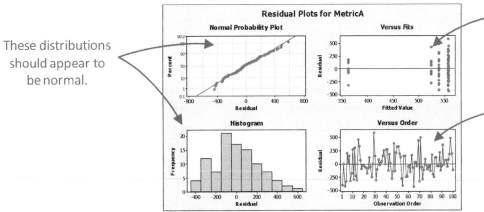

These distributions should appear to be normal.

The spread of plots on either side of the line should look similar.

The spread of plots should look random with no patterns or trends.

Fitted Line Plot: MetricA & MetricB Example

- o Example: MetricA & MetricB sample values
  - Background:
    - Use the arbitrary values in the "MetricA" and "MetricB" columns of the Minitab Sample Data file.
  - Practical Problem:
    - Is there a relationship between MetricA and MetricB? If so, how strong is it?
  - Statistical Problem:
    - State the null (H_0) and alternative (H_a) hypotheses:
      - $H_0: \rho = 0$ and $H_a: \rho > 0$
    - Define the confidence ($1-\alpha$) and power ($1-\beta$):
      - *For confidence, we'll accept the default of 95% (which means $\alpha = 5\%$) and power of 90% (which means $\beta = 10\%$).*
    - Type the statistical problem into Minitab:
      - *In Minitab, go to Stat > Regression > Fitted Line Plot...*
      - *Select **MetricA** as the "Response" and **MetricB** as the "Predictor" from the list of columns.*
      - *Click the "Graphs" button and select "**Four in one**".*
      - *Click the "Options" button and select "**Display Confidence Interval**" and "**Display Predictor Interval**".*

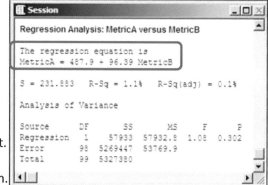

  - Statistical Solution:
    - Refer to the session window results.
      - *Since P-value is > 0.05 (α), then we fail to reject H_0.*
  - Practical Solution:
    - The sample is insufficient to prove that MetricA is correlated to MetricB. Therefore, the r^2 is irrelevant.
    - If there was a correlation between the variables, the regression equation could be used for prediction.

Practical Application

- o Refer to the critical metric (output Y) and at least 5 factors (input X's) you identified in a previous lesson for applying to this hypothesis testing.
  - For any set of factors that are continuous values, try applying the Pearson Correlation or Fitted Line Plot.
    - Other factors in your organization can be used for this exercise.
  - Before running either of these tests, do you expect there to be a relationship? If so, how strong?
  - After running either of these tests, does a statistical relationship exist? If so, how strong is it?
  - If the answers to the above 2 questions are different, then how does that affect how you'd typically measure and communicate the relationship of those factors in the organization?
    - For example, does the relationship between the factors affect financial decisions (e.g., how people are compensated), or process changes (e.g., how the process may be modified), or other critical actions?
    - If so, then how should the results from this test be used to influence your organization?
      - *Should they change how the factors are compared (e.g., across different times, locations, groups, etc.)?*
      - *Should they change how each factor is measured?*
      - *Should they change how they react when they compare these metrics this way?*

Six Sigma-Analyze – Lesson 28: Hypothesis Testing: Relationships (Compare 2+ Factors)

An extension on hypothesis testing, this lesson reviews the multiple regression and GLM as part of measuring statistical relationships.

Pre-Requisite Lessons:
- o Six Sigma-Analyze #27 – Hypothesis Testing: Relationships (Compare 1 to 1)

Why do we need hypothesis testing?
- o This topic reviewed here was originally covered on page 235.

Review Hypothesis Testing: 4 Step Process
- o Remember, the 4 high-level steps for hypothesis testing begin/end with being practical:
  - • This topic reviewed here was originally covered on page 224.
- o As the heart of hypothesis testing, steps 2 & 3 can be drilled to the following 6 steps:
  - • This topic reviewed here was originally covered on page 225.

Review Finding the Right Statistical Test
- o This topic reviewed here was originally covered on page 233.

Multiple Regression: Introduction
- o When should I use it?
  - • To build a regression equation by comparing more than two continuous values to see how correlated they are.
- o How do I find it in Minitab?
  - • *Stat > Regression > Regression…*
- o What are the inputs for the test?

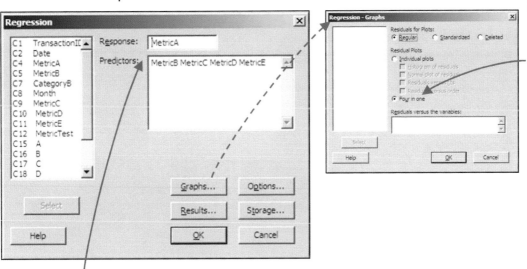

Select the continuous values to be compared.

Multiple Regression: Several Variables Example
- o Example: Several sample values
  - • Background:
    - ▪ Use all the arbitrary continuous values in Minitab Sample Data file.
  - • Practical Problem:
    - ▪ Is there a relationship between any of the continuous values? If so, how strong?
  - • Statistical Problem:
    - ▪ State the null (H_0) and alternative (H_a) hypotheses:

— $H_0: \rho_1 = 0$, $\rho_2 = 0$, $\rho_3 = 0$, etc. and $H_a: \rho_1 > 0$, $\rho_2 > 0$, $\rho_3 > 0$, etc.

- Define the confidence (1-α) and power (1-β):
  - *For confidence, we'll accept the default of 95% (which means α = 5%) and power of 90% (which means β = 10%).*
- Type the statistical problem into Minitab:
  - *In Minitab, go to* Stat > Regression > Regression...
  - *In the "Variables" box, select* **MetricA, MetricB, MetricC, MetricD,** *and* **MetricE** *from the list of columns.*
  - *Click the "Graphs" button and select* "**Four in one**".
- Statistical Solution:
  - Refer to the session window results.
    - *Each continuous value is tested against MetricA.*
    - *Since P-value is < 0.05 (α), then we reject H_0.*
    - *r^2(adj) of 94.84% suggests a strong correlation.*
    - *Of the variables tested, only MetricE has P-value < 0.05 (α).*
- Practical Solution:
  - About 95% of a relationship can be explained between the tested factors, but most of it is driven by MetricE.
  - This can be proven by re-running this test with just MetricE and the P-value and r^2 are likely to remain unchanged.

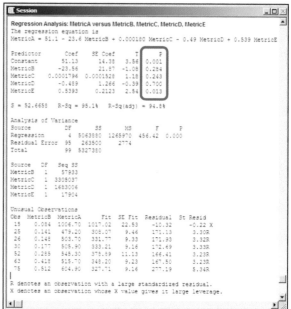

General Linear Model (GLM): Introduction

- When should I use it?
  - To evaluate the correlation between multiple factors - at least two continuous variables and any number of discrete factors.
- How do I find it in Minitab?
  - Stat > ANOVA > General Linear Model...
- What are the inputs for the test?

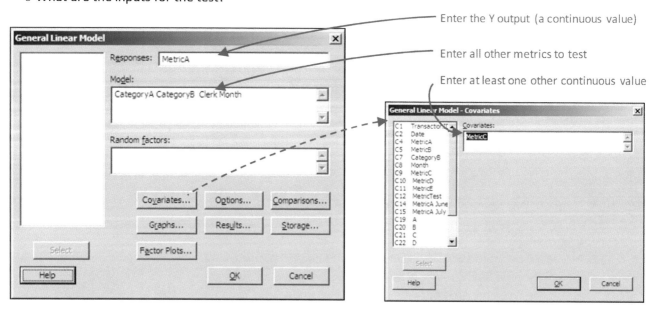

Enter the Y output (a continuous value)

Enter all other metrics to test

Enter at least one other continuous value

General Linear Model: Interpreting Results

○ How do I interpret the GLM results?
- Below is an example of the out from a GLM test.

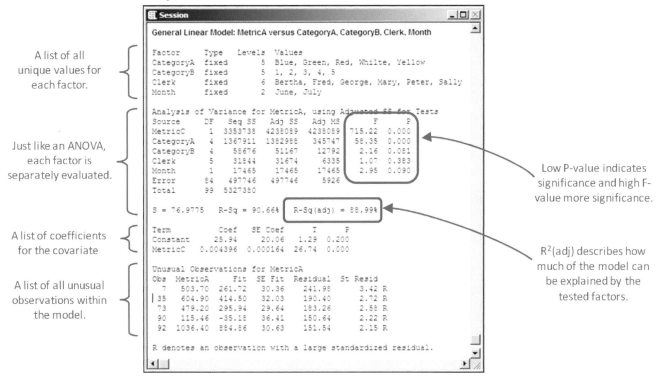

A list of all unique values for each factor.

Just like an ANOVA, each factor is separately evaluated.

A list of coefficients for the covariate

A list of all unusual observations within the model.

Low P-value indicates significance and high F-value more significance.

R^2(adj) describes how much of the model can be explained by the tested factors.

General Linear Model: Several Variables Example

○ Example: Several sample values
- Background:
  ▪ Use most of the arbitrary continuous & discrete values in Minitab Sample Data file.
- Practical Problem:
  ▪ Is there a relationship between the continuous & discrete values? If so, how strong?
- Statistical Problem:
  ▪ State the null (H_0) and alternative (H_a) hypotheses:
    − H_0: $\rho_1 = 0$, $\rho_2 = 0$, $\rho_3 = 0$, etc. and
      H_a: $\rho_1 > 0$, $\rho_2 > 0$, $\rho_3 > 0$, etc.
  ▪ Define the confidence (1-α) and power (1-β):
    − *For confidence, we'll accept the default of 95% (which means α = 5%) and power of 90% (which means β = 10%).*
  ▪ Type the statistical problem into Minitab:
    − *In Minitab, go to Stat > ANOVA > General Linear Model...*
    − *In the "Responses" box, select **MetricA**.*
    − *In the "Model" box, select **CategoryA**, **CategoryB**, **Clerk**, and **Month** from the list of columns.*
    − *Click the "Covariates" button and select **MetricC**.*
- Statistical Solution:
  ▪ Refer to the session window results.

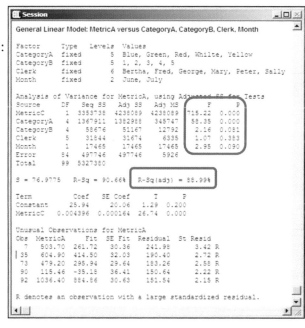

– Since only MetricC and CategoryA have P-value < 0.05 (α), then we reject H_0 for them; it's confirmed by high F-values.

– r^2(adj) of 88.99% suggests a strong correlation.

- Practical Solution:
    - About 89% of a relationship can be explained by the MetricC an CategoryA factors.

Practical Application

o Refer to the critical metric (output Y) and at least 5 factors (input X's) you identified in a previous lesson for applying to this hypothesis testing.

- For any all factors that are continuous values, try applying the multiple regression. Or if you have a least two continuous values, then try applying all factors to the general linear model (GLM).
    - Other factors in your organization can be used for this exercise.
- Before running either of these tests, do you expect there to be a relationship? If so, how strong?
- After running either of these tests, does a statistical relationship exist? If so, how strong is it?
- If the answers to the above 2 questions are different, then how does that affect how you'd typically measure and communicate the relationship of those factors in the organization?
    - For example, does the relationship between the factors affect financial decisions (e.g., how people are compensated), or process changes (e.g., how the process may be modified), or other critical actions?
    - If so, then how should the results from this test be used to influence your organization?
        – Should they change how the factors are compared (e.g., across different times, locations, groups, etc.)?
        – Should they change how each factor is measured?
        – Should they change how they react when they compare these metrics this way?

Unit 7: Six Sigma Improve Phase

The most common tools and concepts that pertain to the Improve phase of the DMAIC methodology of Six Sigma which is intended to help us find and pilot what improvements will fix the root cause of the problem we're trying to solve.

Six Sigma-Improve – Lesson 1: Improve Phase Roadmap (Level 3)

A deeper look into level 3 of the DMAIC roadmap that identifies critical steps and tools for navigating a project through the Improve phase.

Pre-Requisite Lessons:
- Six Sigma Overview #05 – DMAIC Roadmap (Levels 1 & 2)

DMAIC Roadmap (Level 1)
- This topic reviewed here was originally covered on page 91.

DMAIC Roadmap (Level 2)
- This topic reviewed here was originally covered on page 91.

Improve Phase Roadmap (Level 3)
- The DMAIC roadmap can be drilled down even deeper to a 3rd level for each phase.
  - Level 3 questions can guide someone to the specific tool(s) for navigating a project or initiative.

	Question Levels 1 to 3	Tool/Resource
Improve	**Do you know what improvements will fix the root causes (inputs or Xs) and by how much?**	
	Do you know which potential Xs are independent and statistically significant?	
	Have you compiled all your hypothesis testing results for the statistically significant Xs?	Compiling Statistical Test Results
	Do you know what the inter-relationship (multicollinearity) is between the significant Xs?	Compiling Statistical Test Results
	Have you built a transfer function? (if possible)	Transfer Function
	Does the team agree with the analysis results?	Buy-in/Sponsorship (CAP model)
	Do you know what improvements can be made to fix the root causes (inputs or Xs)?	
	Did you brainstorm potential improvements with the team?	Brainstorming Solutions
	Did you assess the impact/benefit vs. difficulty/complexity for each potential improvement?	Impact Matrix (PICK chart)
	Did you assess the potential risks for the key improvements?	Risk assessment (FMEA)
	Did you pilot the improvements and get successful results?	
	Did you build a pilot plan for the key improvements?	Pilot/Implementation Plan
	Did you define a time & location scope for the pilot?	Pilot Duration
	Did you build a scorecard for the pilot?	Scorecard
	Do you know if your scorecard data is accurate, and the method of collecting it (if manual) was repeatable and reproducible?	Measurement System Analysis (MSA)
	Did you get agreement from your team where the improvements will be piloted?	Buy-in/Sponsorship (CAP model)
OUTPUTS:	Updated Project Storyboard, list of improvements, data/charts (e.g., scorecard) validating the success of the pilot	

Practical Application
- Identify at least 2 projects you led or worked on in the past.
  - For each project, review all the questions in the Improve phase level 3 roadmap.
    - What questions and related tools/resources were not addressed in the project?
    - Why were they not addressed?
    - What different outcome or results could've been realized if they were addressed in the project?

Six Sigma-Improve – Lesson 2: Compiling Analysis Results

A review of how the various results from many hypothesis tests in the Analyze phase can be compiled in a simplified format.

Pre-Requisite Lessons:
- ○ Six Sigma-Analyze #09 through #28 – Hypothesis Testing

Compiling Analysis Results

- ○ Why should I compile my statistical test results from the Analyze phase?
  - • You need to validate your findings with the team, but you don't want to bore them with details.
  - • Compiling your prior analysis will help you quickly assess which inputs to review with the team.
  - • The compiled analysis will also serve as an excellent summary for project documentation.
- ○ How do I compile my analysis?
  - • One method is to build a chart defining all the inputs, the tests used, and the test results.
  - • Below is an example of how an analysis can be compiled in a spreadsheet:

What input was tested?	What is the source for the data so it can be re-tested?	What are the actual output results from the test (usually displayed in the Session window of Minitab)?						What conclusions would you and the team make based on these test results?

Input (X)	Dataset	Y (Response)	X (Factor)	Test	N	P-Value	R²(adj)	Results or Visual Display	Stat Sig?	Prac Sig Confid	Conclusion
Day of Week	DataSource.xls	Cycle Time	DOW	ANOVA	7718	0.000	1.11%	7 levels ranging 72 to 97 min	Yes	60%	Most likely to occur on Wed, then equally on Mon, Tue, or Thur, then Fri & Sun and least likely on Sat
				HOV	7718	0.000	n/a	7 levels ranging 60 to 80 min	Yes	60%	
Year & Month	DataSource.xls	Cycle Time	YearMonth	ANOVA	7718	0.000	0.76%	6 levels ranging 86 to 98 min	Yes	35%	Appears that it's higher in 1st month of each quarter and successively drops for subsequent months in qtr. Team thinks it may normally be higher at beginning of month, but not necessarily qtr; doesn't seem to be significant.
				HOV	7718	0.000	n/a	6 levels ranging 66 to 80 min	Yes	25%	
Year & Week	DataSource.xls	Cycle Time	YearWk	ANOVA	7718	0.000	1.38%	27 levels ranging 55 to 110 min	Yes	20%	ANOVA shows slight movement like in Month/Year test, but HOV shows a lot less variation; doesn't seem to stand out.
				HOV	7718	0.000	n/a	27 levels ranging 50 to 93 min	Yes	10%	
Hour Interval	DataSource.xls	Cycle Time	Hours	ANOVA	7718	0.009	0.19%	13 levels ranging 84 to 97 min	Yes	40%	In both tests, frequency was evenly spread across all hours, but hour 4 had highest minutes saved
				HOV	7718	0.001	n/a	13 levels ranging 68 to 84 min	Yes	40%	
Hour of Day	DataSource.xls	Cycle Time	Hour	ANOVA	7718	0.000	1.83%	24 levels ranging 81 to 120 min	Yes	40%	Hour 14 (2pm) stands out most for ANOVA & HOV & 16 (4pm) stands out in MM; nearly all the rest are a lot less; highest frequency (not min) occurs from 8pm - 12am.
				HOV	7718	0.000	n/a	24 levels ranging 46 to 92 min	Yes	40%	
				MM	7718	0.000	n/a	24 levels ranging 63 to 99 min	Yes	40%	
Employee Tenure	DataSource.xls	Cycle Time	AgentTen	ANOVA	7718	0.000	1.29%	3 levels ranging 76 to 99 min	Yes	70%	Agents with mid-range tenure (6 mos to 1 yr) have lowest cycle time. Does more tenure influence higher cycle time?
				HOV	7718	0.000	n/a	3 levels ranging 64 to 81 min	Yes	70%	

= Not Significant
= Probably Not Significant
= Probably Significant

Determining Practical Significance

- ○ Remember to follow the general order for testing significance:
  - • Statistical Significance: often done by checking the P value of the test result.
    - ▪ Example: if P value is less than alpha risk (usually .05), then it's considered statistically significant.
  - • Practical Significance: often done by checking the R^2(adj) value of the test result (if available)
    - ▪ Example: if P value shows it's statistically significant, then a high R^2(adj) generally means how much of that statistical significance can be explained (or how practical that significance may be).
- ○ No matter how you interpret your test results, *logic must always take precedent*!
  - • The test output results are only as reliable (and logical) as your input to the equations.
    - ▪ Example: a regression between ice cream sales and shark attacks has P = 0.00 and R^2(adj) = 82%.
    - ▪ Example: an ANOVA test had a P = 0.07 and R^2(adj) of 65%.
    - ▪ Example: a regression between Revenue and Sales Commissions has P = 0.00 and R^2(adj) = 77%.

Practical Application

- ○ Refer to the critical metric (output Y) and at least 5 factors (input X's) you identified in the Analyze phase for which you did hypothesis testing.
  - • Build a spreadsheet (like the example shown) for documenting the hypothesis test results.
    - ▪ Select at least 3 hypothesis test results and populate the values into the spreadsheet.
    - ▪ Try adding color to some cells to make the results easily stand out between the different tests.

SS: Improve

Six Sigma-Improve – Lesson 3: Testing for Multicollinearity

A review of how we can assess if the factors tested in the hypothesis tests in the Analyze phase have multicollinearity (i.e., interdependency).

Pre-Requisite Lessons:
  o Six Sigma-Analyze #09 through #28 – Hypothesis Testing

Why do we need hypothesis testing?
  o This topic reviewed here was originally covered on page 235.

Multicollinearity Defined
  o What is multicollinearity?
   • When building the transfer function, we expect each X (input) to be independent.
    ▪ If they're not, it could impede accurate control of the inputs to create the desired Y (output).
   • Multicollinearity is when two or more independent variables are found to have inter-dependency.
  o Multicollinearity Example:
   • Transfer Function: Fuel Efficiency (Y) = f(fuel price, speed, engine size, vehicle weight, etc.)
    ▪ Engine size and vehicle weight are considered independent factors that influence fuel efficiency.
    ▪ But the bigger the engine, the more it adds to the vehicle weight too.
  o How do we test for multicollinearity?
   • Use Multiple Regression Procedures.
    ▪ These consist of 7 general steps using correlation testing, matrix plots, regressions, etc.

Multiple Regression Procedures
  o The process for Multiple Regressions depends on the following assumptions:
   • The output (Y) is normal.
    ▪ Validate by the P value of a normality test or probability plot. If P > .05, then it's normal.
    ▪ If data isn't normal, consider transforming it to make it normal or assume risk of non-normality.
   • The correct sample size is used.
    ▪ Run a sample size calculation on the data to ensure there are enough data points.
   • Each X being tested is continuous.
    ▪ You can convert the X values to numeric to "fool" Minitab into treating them as continuous.
  o Step 1 – Test each X against the Y to ensure there is a relationship.
   • You should have already done this in the Analyze phase; check for high R^2(adj) value.
  o Step 2 – Run a Matrix Plot for all Xs and the Y
   • In Minitab, go to *Graph* > *Matrix Plot*; check for any linear relationships of possible collinearity.

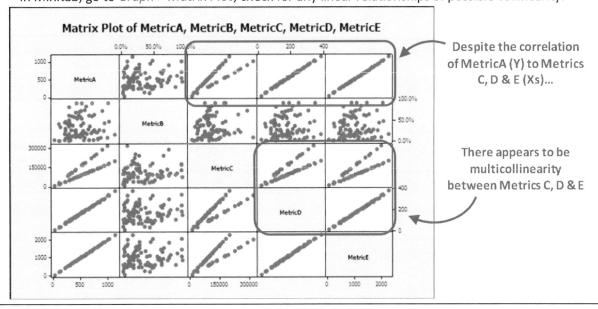

Matrix Plot of MetricA, MetricB, MetricC, MetricD, MetricE

Despite the correlation of MetricA (Y) to Metrics C, D & E (Xs)...

There appears to be multicollinearity between Metrics C, D & E

- Based on the above example Matrix Plot, Metrics C, D & E should be further examined to see if one or more of them need to be excluded.
- o Step 3 – Run a Correlation Matrix of all Xs and the Y
  - In Minitab, go to *Stat* > *Basic Statistics* > *Correlation*; look for low P value and high R^2(adj) value.

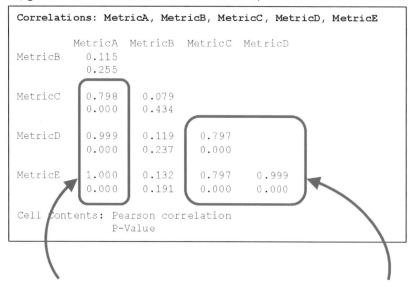

```
Correlations: MetricA, MetricB, MetricC, MetricD, MetricE

          MetricA  MetricB  MetricC  MetricD
MetricB    0.115
           0.255

MetricC    0.798    0.079
           0.000    0.434

MetricD    0.999    0.119    0.797
           0.000    0.237    0.000

MetricE    1.000    0.132    0.797    0.999
           0.000    0.191    0.000    0.000

Cell Contents: Pearson correlation
               P-Value
```

Despite the correlation of MetricA (Y) to Metrics C, D & E (Xs)…

There appears to be multicollinearity between Metrics C, D & E

- Again, based on the above Correlation example, Metrics C, D & E should be further examined to see if one or more of them need to be excluded.
- o Step 4 – Run a multiple regression generating Variance Inflation Factors (VIFs)
  - VIF calculates the degree of multicollinearity in at least one tested factor:
    - VIF > 10 = HIGH multicollinearity
    - VIF > 5 and < 10 = moderate degree of multicollinearity
    - VIF < 5 = little or no multicollinearity
  - In Minitab, go to *Stat* > *Regression*, then select "Variance Inflation Factors" in the Options box

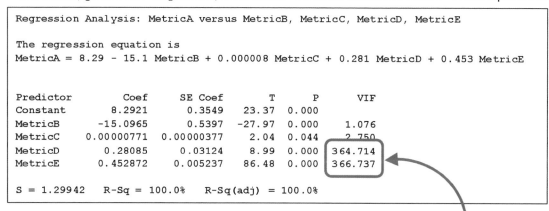

```
Regression Analysis: MetricA versus MetricB, MetricC, MetricD, MetricE

The regression equation is
MetricA = 8.29 - 15.1 MetricB + 0.000008 MetricC + 0.281 MetricD + 0.453 MetricE


Predictor        Coef      SE Coef       T       P       VIF
Constant       8.2921       0.3549    23.37   0.000
MetricB      -15.0965       0.5397   -27.97   0.000     1.076
MetricC    0.00000771   0.00000377     2.04   0.044     2.750
MetricD       0.28085      0.03124     8.99   0.000   364.714
MetricE      0.452872     0.005237    86.48   0.000   366.737

S = 1.29942   R-Sq = 100.0%   R-Sq(adj) = 100.0%
```

Very high VIF (anything > 10) indicates multicollinearity.

- Again, based on the above Regression example, Metrics C, D & E should be further examined to see if one or more of them need to be excluded.
  - Just because MetricC has a low VIF doesn't mean we keep it and exclude Metrics D & E. We already know from the other tests that MetricC may also need to be excluded. The team can validate this.

o Step 5 – Reduce the factors to the most critical (with no multicollinearity). 2 ways:
  • Method A – Manually
    ▪ If relationships exist between X factors from step 2 (Matrix Plot) and step 3 (Correlation), then re-run step 4 (Regression with VIF) and exclude one of these related factors. Repeat until the VIFs are < 5.
  • Method B – Stepwise
    ▪ In Minitab, go to *Stat* > *Regression* > *Stepwise*…
    ▪ This test attempts to automatically determine the critical X factors. As such, it is only as effective as the data you input to the test, so ensure the output results are logical and validated by the team.

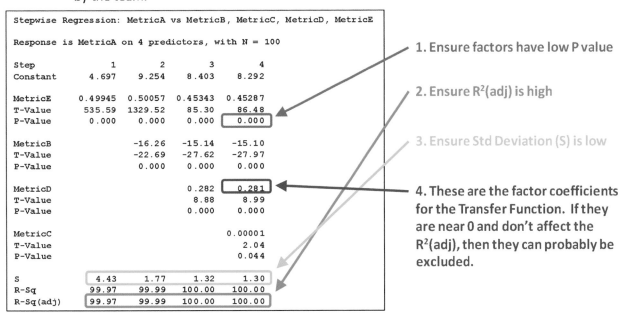

1. Ensure factors have low P value

2. Ensure R²(adj) is high

3. Ensure Std Deviation (S) is low

4. These are the factor coefficients for the Transfer Function. If they are near 0 and don't affect the R²(adj), then they can probably be excluded.

o Step 6 - Evaluate the quality of the final transfer function.
  • Build the transfer function and validate with team what factors to include/exclude.
    ▪ Ensure all VIFs are < 10 and preferably < 5.
    ▪ Ensure the residuals are independent and normally distributed.
    ▪ Ensure any outliers or unusual observations are validated by the team.
  • Use the Stepwise Regression to get the Constant & Coefficients for the Transfer Function.

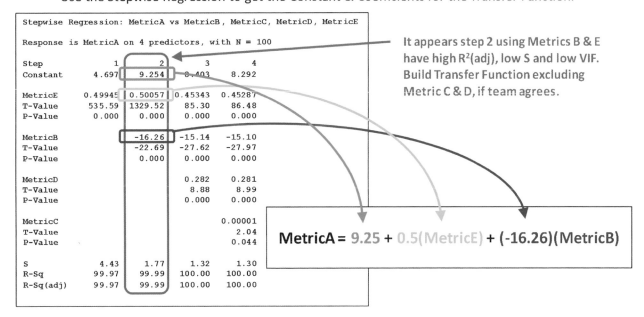

It appears step 2 using Metrics B & E have high R²(adj), low S and low VIF. Build Transfer Function excluding Metric C & D, if team agrees.

MetricA = 9.25 + 0.5(MetricE) + (-16.26)(MetricB)

SS: Improve

○ Step 7 – Assess predictive capability of the transfer function
  • Go to *Stat* > *Regression* > *Regression* > *Options*; add prediction intervals to test
    ▪ Helps answer the question "What would the output Y be when the input Xs have these values?"
    ▪ To do this, type in values for the X factors ("predictors")

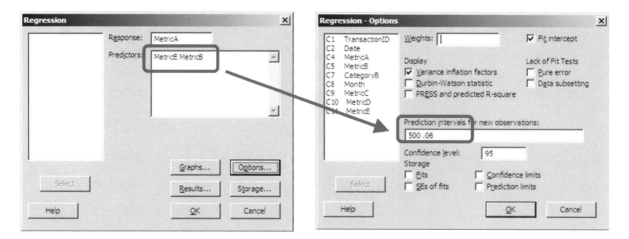

    ▪ Examine the PI (Predicted Interval) in the Predicted Values section to see the predictive capability

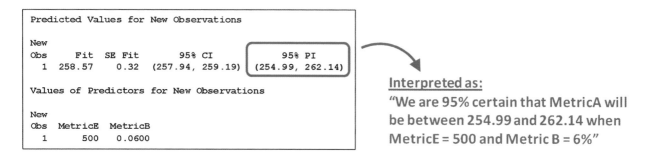

Interpreted as:
"We are 95% certain that MetricA will be between 254.99 and 262.14 when MetricE = 500 and Metric B = 6%"

Validate Results with the Team
○ Always validate your findings and interpreted results with your team.
  • The team (or any other supporting SME) is your BEST validation of practical significance.
  • It's helpful to keep the team updated regularly with findings to help steer your analysis.
    ▪ Example: setup recurring meetings to review the findings. I f they challenge a finding that you believe is significant, then explore other ways you can substantiate either your finding or their dispute.
    ▪ Your goal of analysis is not to be the mastermind who finds the silver bullet.
  • A silver bullet is only a paperweight unless you can shoot it at the right target.
  • You must work with your team to accurately find, aim at, and hit your target root cause.

Practical Application
○ Refer to the critical metric (output Y) and at least 5 factors (input X's) you identified in the Analyze phase for which you did hypothesis testing.
  • Run through the Multiple Regression Procedures to test for multicollinearity in your data.
    ▪ Does any multicollinearity exist? If so, how do you know it?
      – Is the multicollinearity logical? (That is, does it make sense? Did you know the interdependency existed before running this test?)
    ▪ How would you modify your transfer function to account for this multicollinearity?

Six Sigma-Improve – Lesson 4: Brainstorm & Prioritize Solutions with a Workout

A review of how we can run a workout to brainstorm and prioritize solutions that will fix the root cause.

Pre-Requisite Lessons:
- Six Sigma-Improve #03 – Testing for Multicollinearity

Identify potential root cause(s)
- Previously we learned about how to build a Transfer Function (example below).

$$\text{MetricA} = 9.25 + 0.5(\text{MetricE}) + (-16.26)(\text{MetricB})$$

- In the Transfer Function, find the factor having the largest coefficient.
  - The largest coefficient suggests the factor having the greatest weight or influence on the Y.
    - This doesn't necessarily mean it's the root cause, but it could be an ideal place to start.
  - MetricB has the largest coefficient of -16.26
  - Other metrics were excluded; had they been included, their coefficients would still be smaller.
- Run additional tests on MetricB to validate it as the root cause (if necessary).
  - At this point, your Team may have already confirmed MetricB as the root cause.
  - Additional tests may include the same type of VOP (voice of the process) tests done on the Y in the Measure phase (process capability).
    - The tests may help quantify how severely the root cause is affecting the Y.
    - A full process capability usually isn't required; by this time the team generally knows that severity.

Steps for a Brainstorming Workout
- Brainstorming is most effective when done as an extended meeting (e.g., workout).
  - Depending on the complexity of the solutions, the meeting should at least be 3 to 4 hours.
  - The meeting should include the entire Team and any other possible SMEs.
    - The Champion & Sponsor do not have to be included for the entire meeting.
    - It's ideal if the Champion and/or Sponsor kick-off the meeting and return at the end to review the results.
- Example agenda for Brainstorming Workout (with potential duration per step):
  1. Champion and/or Sponsor Kick-off (validate initial problem & necessity for solution) (15 min)
  2. Review Transfer Function; validate root cause (15 min)
  3. Notate ALL potential solutions that may fix the root cause (30 to 60 min)
  4. Build an Affinity Diagram of proposed solutions (15 to 30 min)
  5. Build an Impact Matrix (e.g., ePICK chart) mapping the proposed solutions (30 to 60 min)
  6. Select the proposed solutions and build a plan for any necessary research (30 min)
  7. Champion and/or Sponsor Review (acquire buy-in of selected solutions & next steps) (15 min)
- Items 3 to 6 are reviewed in separate lessons.

Wrapping Up the Workout
- By the end of the workout you should have the following:
  - A prioritized list of the primary improvements that should fix the root cause.
  - A prioritized list of the secondary improvements that may help fix the root cause.
  - Agreement by the team and Champion and/or Sponsor on these improvements.
  - A list of actions (with owners & due dates) of additional research for the improvements (if any).
- Why not build a Pilot Plan?
  - At this point, the improvements are still presumed to be unconfirmed.

SS: Improve

- If there are other stakeholders affected by these improvements, they _MUST_ be informed and bought-in.
- A risk assessment (FMEA) can help ensure there are no adverse repercussions by the improvements.
  - The team should have a break before diving into building a pilot plan.
    - The team may need time to digest the workout results and consider other issues that weren't addressed.
- When is it appropriate to begin the Pilot Plan?
  - Everyone may want to begin the pilot plan, but you should wait until you can answer these:
    - Do all stakeholders who are affected by the improvements agree with the improvements?
    - Are all potentially critical risks identified with a plan for mitigating those risks?
      - _The FMEA tool will help perform this risk assessment and will be addressed in a separate lesson._
  - If the improvements are not very complex and fall within the complete control of the Champion and/or Sponsor, then it may be appropriate to skip the risk assessment and build the pilot plan.

Practical Application

- Identify at least 2 other projects or initiatives you were part of in your organization and answer the following questions:
  - How were the solutions identified for those projects?
  - What method was used to identify and validate the root causes being resolved in each project?
  - How were the solutions tied to the root causes (to ensure they would actually resolve them)?
  - How involved was the team in the process for identifying and prioritizing potential solutions?
    - If neither the team nor other stakeholders were involved much, then how did the affect the outcome?
  - What could have been done differently in each project to improve the following:
    - The speed at which the solutions were implemented?
    - The buy-in from the team and other critical stakeholders?
    - The cost (time, equipment, people, resources, etc.) for implementation?
    - The final outcome of the implemented solutions?

Six Sigma-Improve – Lesson 5: Brainstorm Solutions with an Affinity Diagram

A review of how we can build an Affinity Diagram as part of a workout for brainstorming solutions that will fix a root cause.

Pre-Requisite Lessons:

- Six Sigma-Improve #04 – Brainstorm & Prioritize Solutions with a Workout

Review Steps for a Brainstorming Workout

- This topic reviewed here was originally covered on page 307.

Notate All Potential Solutions

- Notate ALL potential solutions that may fix the root cause (30 to 60 min).
  - Every proposed solution should be tied to fixing the root cause and the problem statement.
  - Write each idea on sticky notepaper and post to a wall for everyone to see.
  - Don't validate every proposed solution; the key for noting solutions is *quantity*, not quality.
    - Do not stifle the momentum of brainstorming ideas; do not belittle or challenge anyone's idea.
    - The validity or practicality of each idea will be considered later in the Impact Matrix.
  - Use the 6Ms to help stimulate other possible solutions.
    - The 6Ms were used as sources of variation in the Measure phase when exploring potential root causes.
    - The same format may be used here to encourage new ideas from different perspectives.

Manpower
Solutions related to people like turnover, poor training, etc.

Machine
Solutions related to equipment, hardware, software, fax machines, scanners, etc.

Method
Solutions related to policies, SOPs, regulations, etc.

Measurement
Solutions related to how things are measured like standards, performance, goals, etc.

Mother Nature
Solutions related to outside influences like the economy, customers, vendors, etc.

Materials
Solutions related to documentation, forms, backup, etc.

Affinity Diagram of Proposed Solutions

- Build an Affinity Diagram of proposed solutions (15 to 30 min).
  - An Affinity Diagram is merely the result from the process of logically grouping similar ideas.
  - The general steps for building an Affinity Diagram are:
    1. Each person quietly reviews (to his/her self) all the ideas noted on the sticky notes.
    2. At any time, any person can move a sticky note next to others that seem logically related to each other.
    3. If an idea applies to multiple groups, then re-write it on another sticky note and apply to both groups.

4. After everyone is satisfied, determine what logical groups were created and title each group.

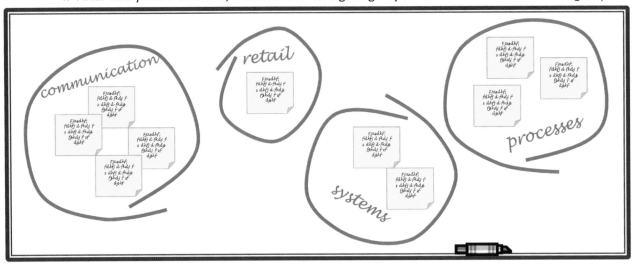

- Things to consider when doing this exercise:
  - Minimize talking while grouping ideas (prevent people from explaining why they're moving certain ideas).
  - Do not define the group titles *before* moving the ideas; only title them when all grouping is done.
  - It's OK if some ideas are by themselves and don't get grouped with others.

Practical Application
- As a fun, personal exercise, let's assume you're trying to reduce your personal expenses and you found a significant root cause is entertainment expenses.
  - First, consider all the types of entertainment expenses you may have.
    - For example, this may include non-essential items such as sports activities, dining out, movies, etc.
  - Use the 6Ms to brainstorm ways you can reduce the expenses associated with these entertainment activities.
  - Next, walk through the affinity diagram exercise by grouping the items you brainstormed.
    - How would you title the groups you created?
    - Which group seems to have the most ideas associated with it?

Six Sigma-Improve – Lesson 6: Prioritize Solutions with an Impact Matrix

A review of how we can build an Impact Matrix and PICK chart as part of a workout for prioritizing solutions that will fix a root cause.

Pre-Requisite Lessons:
- Six Sigma-Improve #05 – Brainstorm Solutions with an Affinity Diagram

Review Steps for a Brainstorming Workout
- This topic reviewed here was originally covered on page 307.

Building an Impact Matrix or PICK Chart
- Build an Impact Matrix mapping the proposed solutions (30 to 60 min)
  - An Impact Matrix (a.k.a. PICK chart) is designed to balance each idea between its potential impact/value vs. it's difficulty/complexity to implement.
    - Yes, NOW is when you can begin to challenge the validity of each idea.
  - The general steps for building an Impact Matrix are:
    1. Notate the titles from each group of ideas built in the Affinity Diagram.
    2. For each title, rank on a scale of 1 to 10 (1 = low; 10 = high) their impact/value and difficulty/complexity:
       - *For Impact/Value, consider the level of difference the idea(s) would make at fixing the root cause, potential savings, etc.*
       - *For Difficulty/Complexity, consider what change mgmt is required, costs, amount of time/coordination, etc.*
       - *It's OK if rankings are subjective. If available, use objective measurements to rank each item. For example, if savings can be measured for impact/value, then determine thresholds for the rankings (i.e., 1 = $0, 5 = $1M/yr, 10 = >$10M/yr).*
    3. Plot each idea's rankings as coordinates on a graph scaled as 1 to 10 for each X and Y axis.

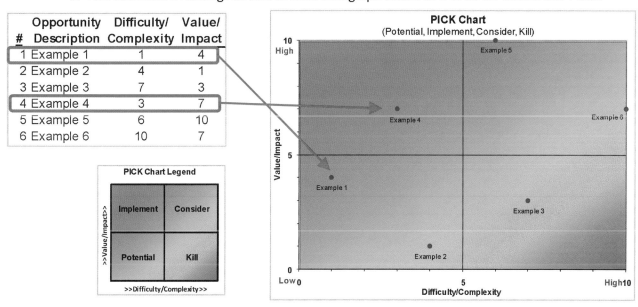

- Build an Impact Matrix mapping the proposed solutions (30 to 60 min)
  - The general steps for building an Impact Matrix (continued):
    4. Using the PICK chart legend, discuss the items in the "Implement" quadrant to ensure they make sense.

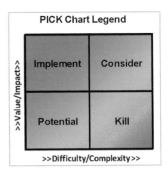

PICK Chart Legend

— *P = Potential = Low Value/Impact & Low Difficulty/Complexity; these have potential but are not the highest priority.*
— *I = Implement = High Value/Impact & Low Difficulty/Complexity; these should be given highest priority to implement.*
— *C = Consider = High Value/Impact & High Difficulty/Complexity; these are worth considering but are not highest priority.*
— *K = Kill = Low Value/Impact & High Difficulty/Complexity; do not implement these and remove them from future consideration.*

5. Compile the items from the "Implement" quadrant and prioritize them using team's best judgment.
6. Review the remaining items from the "Potential" and "Consider" quadrants
   — *These items should not be automatically included unless the team agrees; prioritize these after the "Implement" items.*
   — *"Potential" items may be easiest to bundle with the "Implement" items due to their lower difficulty/complexity.*

o Build a plan for any additionally required research
   • If an idea requires more research that may change its ranking, then identify the owner (the person responsible for leading that research) and due date to report back to team.
      ▪ Plan with the team how that idea will be handled if its ranking does change its final quadrant (priority).
o Use the PICK chart as a communication tool summarizing all potential improvements.

Practical Application

o Refer to the example from the prior lesson on the Affinity Diagram.
   • The example was as if you're trying to reduce your personal expenses and you found a significant root cause is entertainment expenses.
   • For each potential solution previously run through the affinity diagram, answer the following:
      ▪ On a scale of 1 (low) to 10 (high), how much does the solution impact or affect the value for reducing the entertainment expenses?
      ▪ On a scale of 1 (low) to 10 (high), how difficult or complex is the solution to implement?
   • For each potential solution, plot the values into the Impact Matrix or PICK chart.
      ▪ Which solutions fall into the "Implement" quadrant (high value, low difficulty)?
      ▪ Which solutions fall into the "Kill" quadrant (low value, high difficulty)?
      ▪ Do the plotted solutions fall into the areas you would've expected? If not, then why not?
   • How did this exercise help in objectively evaluating these relatively subjective solutions?

Six Sigma-Improve – Lesson 7: Risk Assessment with a FMEA Tool

A review of the importance of assessing risk and how to measure it using a FMEA tool.

Pre-Requisite Lessons:
- o Introduction #11 – ABC Model
- o Six Sigma-Overview #02 – Risk Analysis

Review: The Role of Risk in our Decisions
- o Remember the jelly bean example from the lesson on risk analysis?
  - • This topic reviewed here was originally covered on page 83.
- o Which method of counting the jelly beans is best?
  - • This topic reviewed here was originally covered on page 84.
- o Remember the ABC Model?
  - • This topic reviewed here was originally covered on page 40.

Why is risk so important?
- o This topic reviewed here was originally covered on page 83.
- o Six Sigma tools (like FMEA) help assess risk (and confidence) in business decisions.

FMEA Tool Defined
- o What is a FMEA tool?
  - • "FMEA" is a risk management tool that stands for "Failure Modes & Effects Analysis".
  - • It tracks all possible failures in a process, their potential impact and a plan to mitigate them.
  - • The FMEA scores and prioritizes all possible failure modes to help mitigate potential risks.
- o Below is the general layout of the FMEA tool and it's key components defined:

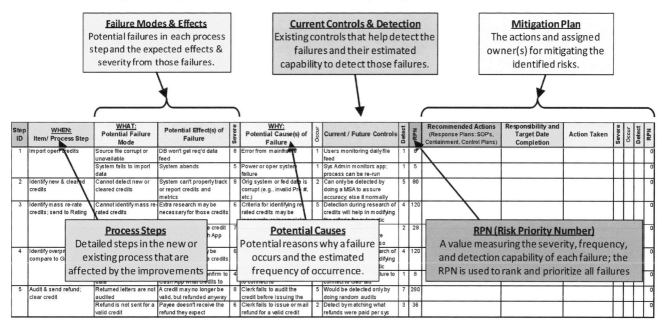

When and How to Build the FMEA
- o When is the FMEA tool used?
  - • It's generally used when there is a significant process change that requires a risk assessment.
    - ▪ It's most often used in the Improve phase of the DMAIC methodology to evaluate any potential risks from the proposed improvements.
    - ▪ It can also be closely tied to the Control Plan created in the Control phase of DMAIC, therefore it may be necessary to review or extend the FMEA *after* the improvements are implemented.

SS: Improve

- It's also used in the Design phase of the DMADV methodology before implementing a new process.
  - The FMEA is generally built by a team of SMEs during a meeting (2 to 4 hours).
    - The SMEs should include experts from any area affected by the improvements.
    - Below are the general steps for leading the meeting when building the FMEA:

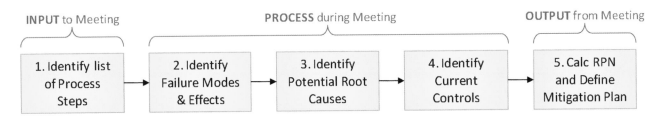

- o Is the FMEA tool required for every project?
  - No. Sometimes the Sponsor or customer is willing to assume inherent risks from the new improvements and won't require a risk assessment.
  - When risks are unknown or if there is any hint of doubt in the expected success of a proposed improvement, then the FMEA should be used to fully address and measure potential risks.

FMEA Process Steps 1 & 2
- o INPUT to Meeting
  - #1 – Identify List of Process Steps
    - These steps should be a part of the detailed process map that may have been created for mapping the improvements. Each process step should be noted with its own Step ID #.
    - It's OK to limit the process steps to only those deemed as critical or within control of your team.
- o PROCESS During Meeting
  - Meeting Kick-Off (~20 min)
    - The Sponsor/Champion should kick-off the meeting and return at the end to review the results.
    - The list of process steps should be agreed upon by the team; allow for some clarification as needed.
  - #2 – Identify Failure Modes & Effects (~30 – 40 min)
    - For each process step, brainstorm one or more potential ways a failure may occur for that respective step.
    - Rank the Severity on a scale of 1 (Lowest) to 10 (Highest) for each failure mode & effect.
      - *Below are suggestions for defining severity; these may be changed if the team agrees:*

Minor (Rank 1)	Low (Rank 2 - 3)	Moderate (Rank 4 - 6)	High (Rank 7 - 8)	Very High (Rank 9 - 10)
Unreasonable to expect that the minor nature of this failure will have any noticable effect on item or system performance or subsequent process or assembly operation. Customer will most likely not be able to detect the failure.	Due to the nature of this failure, the customer experiences only slight annoyance. Customer will probably notice slight deterioration of the item or system performance or a slight inconvenience with a subsequent process or assembly operation, i.e. minor rework.	Failure causes some customer dissatisfaction which may include discomfort or annoyance. Customer will notice item or system performance deterioration. This may result in unscheduled rework/repair and/or damage to equipment.	High degree of customer dissatisfaction due to the nature of the failure, such as inoperable item or system. Failure does not involve safety or government regulation. May result in serious disruption to subsequent processing or assembly operations and/or require major rework.	Failure affects safety or involves noncompliance to government regulations. May endanger machine or assembly operator (9 with warning, 10 without warning)

- #3 – Identify Potential Root Causes (~20 – 30 min)
  - Define what the potential root causes are for each failure mode & effect.
  - Rank the estimated occurrence on a scale of 1 (least frequent) to 10 (most frequent) for each root cause.
    - *Below are suggested ratios for defining these occurrences; these may be changed if the team agrees:*

Remote *(Rank 1)*	Very Low *(Rank 2)*	Low *(Rank 3 - 5)*	Moderate *(Rank 6 - 7)*	High *(Rank 8 - 9)*	Very High *(Rank 10)*
Failure unlikely. No failures ever assocaited with this process or almost identical processes (1=1:1.5M)	Only isolated failures associated with this process or almost identical processes (2=1:150K)	Isolated failures associated with similar processes (3= 1:30K; 4=1:4500; 5=1:800)	This process has occasional failures, but not in major proportions (6=1:150: 7=1:50)	This process or similar processes have often failed (8=1:9; 9=1:6)	Failure is almost inevitable (10=>1:3)

- #4 – Identify Current Controls (~20 – 30 min)
  - Define whatever controls are already in place that may detect each of those failure occurrences.
    - *The existing controls can include controls managed by other people or processes outside the team.*
  - Rank the estimated detection rate on a scale of 1 (always detected) to 10 (never detected) for each failure occurrence (i.e., the better the ability to detect the errors, the lower the score).
    - *Below are suggested rankings for defining the detection capability; these may be changed if the team agrees:*

Very High (Rank 1 - 2)	High (Rank 3 - 4)	Moderate (Rank 5 - 6)	Low (Rank 7 - 8)	Very low (Rank 9)	Absolutely No Detection (Rank 10)
Current controls almost certain to detect the failure mode. Reliable detection controls are known with similar processes. Process automatically prevents further processing.	Controls have a good chance of detecting failure mode, process automatically detects failure mode.	Controls may detect the existence of a failure mode.	Controls have a poor chance of detecting the existence of failure mode	Controls probably will not detect the existence of failure mode	Controls will not or can not detect the existence of a failure. No known controls available to detect failure mode.

- OUTPUT From Meeting
  - #5 – Calculate RPN and Define Mitigation Plan (~20 – 30 min)
    - The Risk Priority Number (RPN) is automatically calculated as a multiplier of the 3 rankings defined in step 2 (severity), step 3 (frequency), and step 4 (detection capability).
      - *The RPN can range from 0 to 1000; despite that wide range, any process step with RPN over 250 should be considered a potential high risk for failure.*
      - *Since the scoring is subjective, review the RPNs for all process steps to determine what is a reasonable threshold for what should be considered a high risk failure.*
    - Consider building a mitigation plan for the process steps having a high RPN.
      - *The mitigation plan isn't required, but for very high risk process steps, it can be very helpful to define them in advance.*
      - *As a team, define 1) the recommended actions in the event of a failure, and 2) the person responsible to perform the action and estimated turnaround time to complete it.*
      - *The remaining "Action Taken" and rankings are optional; for any process step having a very high risk of failure, it can help to apply a ranking and RPN for those mitigation actions to assess their inherent risks.*
- Now What?
  - The FMEA can help unify the team around their improvements to implement and it can build their confidence that all potential risks are identified with an appropriate mitigation plan.
  - The FMEA should be retained on hand for the entire team and distributed to any stakeholder that controls or is affected by the process improvements.

SS: Improve

- If any process steps are very high risk (high RPN), then they should be validated by any other stakeholder responsible for or knowledgeable of that respective process step.

Practical Application
- o Identify an existing high-level process map used in your organization.
  - Instead, you can build a process map for a simple routine process you follow such as driving to school or work, ordering a meal at a restaurant, mowing the lawn, etc.
    - Whatever process you use, ensure you only have 3 to 5 key process steps.
- o Build a FMEA using the process defined above.
  - Identify each critical process step.
  - For each process step, identify all potential failure modes.
  - For each failure mode, identify the potential effects from those failures and severity level.
  - For each failure effect, identify all potential causes and the occurrence frequency level.
  - For each failure cause, identify all controls that could detect the cause and its detection level.
  - Calculate the Risk Priority Number (RPN) based on the severity, frequency, and detection levels.
  - As needed, try filling out the remaining portion for building a mitigation plan.
- o Based on the FMEA that was built, try answering the following questions:
  - Which process steps had the most failure modes?
  - Which failure modes had the highest RPN?
  - Which process step had the highest combined RPN value based on all its failure modes?
  - How do these results compare with the level of risk you originally expected for this process?

Six Sigma-Improve – Lesson 8: Piloting Solutions: The Process

A review of the process for successfully building and executing a pilot, which is a method for testing potential improvements to implement.

Pre-Requisite Lessons:
  o None

The Pilot Process

  o Note: this pilot process can be followed in the same way for full implementation.
  o What is the process for planning and executing a pilot?
   • A well executed pilot will generally follow these steps:

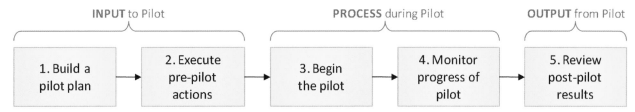

  o Can a pilot be successful without following these steps?
   • Of course! However, these steps will help you be most prepared for full implementation.
     ▪ They can help unify the vision and communication of the team and those affected by the pilot.
     ▪ They can help build confidence that the right actions and measurements are used for the pilot.
     ▪ They can help expedite the review of the post-pilot results and ultimately the full implementation actions.
  o The scope and targeted audience for the pilot must be pre-defined.
   • Does the team already know *what* to pilot and *where* to conduct the pilot?
     ▪ If NO, then before the team builds a pilot plan, they must identify them and consider these:
       – *What are all the improvements that are expected to significantly fix the root cause? (Ensure these are included in pilot.)*
       – *What subset process or location has similar characteristics of the destination where all the improvements will be implemented? (E.g., if deploying improvements across retail locations nationwide, which few stores represent the general performance, design, demographic, etc. as most of the other stores?)*
     ▪ If YES, then ensure all stakeholders are notified and bought-in *before* building a pilot plan.
       – *ALL stakeholders where the improvements will be piloted MUST be included or you could risk pilot delays or failure.*

The Pilot Process

  o INPUT to Pilot
   • #1 – Build a pilot plan
     ▪ A pilot plan is very critical to the pilot process.
     ▪ It can be built in a meeting with your team by following a separate 5 step process.
       – *Due to the complexity of building a pilot plan, it's covered in a separate lesson.*
   • #2 – Execute pre-pilot actions
     ▪ A pilot plan is only as good as the ability to follow the plan and keep all action owners accountable.
     ▪ The "Due Date" column on the plan can be colored red, yellow or green to track progress of the actions.

       Due Date Legend:
	= Complete
	= Due Soon
	= Needs Attention

       – *Below is an example of the legend used in the pilot plan to help track progress:*
     ▪ If the pilot plan has many actions with many different owners, then consider scheduling recurring meetings (weekly or bi-weekly) to review the progress as a team.

SS: Improve

- What if an action is late (reflected as red)?
  - *Try to contact that action owner before meeting as a team so they can try to complete the action or explain the delay.*
  - *For all red or TBD actions, continue to ask the team for new dates to update the pilot plan.*
  - *For any significant delays (especially if a delayed action is a pre-requisite to another action), discuss with the team the impact to the overall start date for the pilot and impact to any stakeholders.*
- PROCESS During Pilot
  - #3 – Begin the pilot
    - The date to officially begin the pilot should have been defined and agreed upon by the team.
      - *The start date should correspond with the due dates from the pilot plan to ensure all actions are complete.*
    - It's generally helpful to define in advance the tentative stopping point for the pilot.
      - *For example, the pilot is complete after a certain number of weeks, or process iterations, or improving a key metric.*
  - #4 – Monitor progress of pilot
    - There should be recurring team meetings (weekly) to help monitor the progress of the pilot.
      - *Communication across the team is very critical during the pilot in order to quickly catch & fix problems or errors.*
      - *It may be necessary to even have short daily meetings to monitor the progress and ensure the pilot is running smoothly.*
    - There should already be key metrics to analyze for measuring the pilot's progress and impact.
      - *It may be helpful to track these metrics at a daily level so that trends are more observable.*
- OUTPUT From Pilot
  - #5 – Review post-pilot results
    - The pilot results should clearly answer the following:
      - *Did the improvements resolve the root cause for the piloted area?*
      - *How much improvement was realized for the piloted area and can be expected for an extended rollout?*
      - *What unique or unexpected issues arose during the pilot that may risk the impact from an extended rollout?*
    - Based on this, the team should confidently know if, when, and how to do an extended rollout.
      - *If the team cannot answer this, then it may be necessary to continue the pilot until those questions can be answered.*
- Now what?
  - If the entire team agrees to an extended rollout, then begin to build an Implementation Plan.
    - Build it in the same way as the Pilot Plan, yet accounting for an extended rollout.
    - Continue implementing the improvements following the same process steps as used in the pilot.

Practical Application
- Identify at least 2 different projects or initiatives at your organization that involved the implementation of a significant process change and answer the following questions:
  - Were the process changes piloted?
    - If so, was a formal process followed for piloting the changes?
  - Was the piloted area representative of the full area where the changes would be implemented?
    - If not, then why not? How did that lack of representation affect the implementation results?
  - How successful was the pilot?
    - How helpful was the pilot in preparing for the implementation (e.g., finding unexpected risks)?
  - How successful was the full implementation?
    - If a pilot wasn't used before the implementation, then why not?
    - What problems (if any) could have been avoided if a pilot were done first?

Six Sigma-Improve – Lesson 9: Piloting Solutions: Build the Pilot Plan

A review of the process for successfully building a pilot plan, which is used for managing and communicating all potential improvements to pilot.

Pre-Requisite Lessons:
   o Six Sigma-Improve #08 – Piloting Solutions: The Process

The Pilot Plan Defined
   o Note: this pilot plan can be used in the same way as an implementation plan.
   o What is a pilot plan?
   • The pilot plan is a prioritized list of actions that comprise all improvements to be piloted.
      ▪ For each action in the pilot plan, the responsible owner and due date for those actions are identified.
      ▪ The pilot plan also includes a method for managing all actions by tracking each action's progress.
   • We know what we want to pilot; do we really need a pilot plan? Won't it slow us down?
      ▪ Many people begin a pilot without building a plan.
      ▪ Consider the old adage "He who fails to plan, plans to fail."
      ▪ Let's consider the risks/rewards vs. cost of a plan:

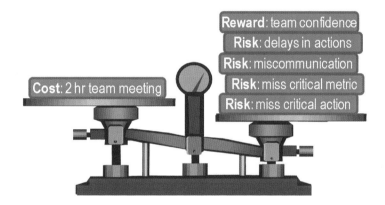

The Process for Building the Pilot Plan
   o What is the process for building a pilot plan?
   • The pilot plan can be built within about 2 hours with the team using the following steps:

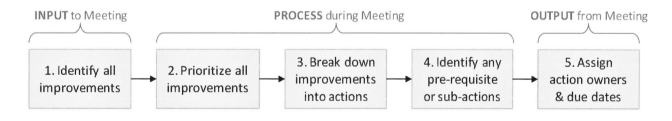

SS: Improve

o Below is an example of a pilot plan with the respective process steps:

#1 & #3 – Improvements noted as actions   #2 – Priority of Improvements/actions   #4 – Sub-actions & pre-requisite actions   #5 – Owners & Due Dates

Action Description	Prereq.	Priority	Owner	Due
Action 1: The first major action in the pilot or implementation				
1 A The first sub-action within this first major action.		Low	Hansen	1/5/12
1 B The second sub-action within this first major action.		Med	Smith	1/10/12
1 C The third sub-action within this first major action.	1A	High	Hansen	1/13/12
Action 2: The second major action in the pilot or implementation				
2 A The first sub-action within this second major action.	1A	High	Jones	1/9/12
2 B The second sub-action within this second major action.		Med	Hansen	1/14/12
2 C The third sub-action within this second major action.	1A, 2B	Med	Smith	1/17/12

Due Date Legend:
= Complete
= Due Soon
= Needs Attention

Building the Pilot Plan

o INPUT to Meeting
- #1 – Identify all improvements
  - At this point, this step should already be complete with possibly also a risk assessment (FMEA).
o PROCESS During Meeting
- Meeting Kick-Off (~15 min)
  - The Sponsor/Champion may want to kick-off the meeting and return at the end to review the results.
  - As necessary, review each of the improvements to ensure everyone agrees.
- #2 – Prioritize all improvements (~10 – 20 min)
  - If there are multiple improvements, everyone should agree on the level of priority for each.
    - *This is critical because some pilot actions may require pulling from the same resources. Defining the priority of the improvements up-front helps clarify for the action owners the priority each resource can provide to the sub-actions.*
  - It's OK if some improvements have equal priority as long as it doesn't create a delay or conflict among the resources required for the sub-actions.
  - Sort the list of improvements in order of priority and ensure the entire team agrees.
- #3 – Break down improvements into actions (~20 min)
  - Some improvements may require similar actions (e.g., coordination for IT changes, data extractions, etc.).
  - For very similar improvements, consider grouping them to share the actions (as long as it makes sense).
  - The action should be defined briefly; if longer explanations are required, notate them separately.
- #4 – Identify any pre-requisite or sub-actions (~30 – 40 min)
  - Begin by identifying all the steps and actions required to complete that one overall action/improvement.
    - *Sub-actions should represent logical steps possibly defined by different resources needed, approvals, system events, etc.*
    - *If the same action has different sub-actions that can be done simultaneously, then notate them as separate sub-actions.*
    - *It may help to start with the goal for the high-level action, then step backwards to find their respective sub-actions.*
  - If a sub-action is dependent on another sub-action, add the 1st action's # as a pre-requisite for the 2nd.

- Be patient, this part of the pilot plan get very detailed. Be sure all sub-actions are fully identified.
  - OUTPUT From Meeting
    - #5 – Assign action owners and due dates (~20 – 30 min)
      - This is extremely critical! Action owners & due dates must be identified for EACH sub-action.
        - *Without this, there is little accountability and the pilot is at risk for delays or failure.*
        - *It's OK if one person is designated as owner for one action and therefore all of its respective sub-actions.*
        - *This part of the meeting makes people uncomfortable; don't let that stop you from doing it!*
      - When is it OK to use TBD (To Be Determined)?
        - *"TBD" should <u>never</u> be identified as an action owner; every action MUST have an owner.*
        - *"TBD" can be used as the due date for some actions (especially lower priority ones) if that action's owner agrees.*
      - Be sure the due dates for a sub-action don't precede the due dates for its respective pre-requisite action.
      - Be sure the owners & due dates all seem reasonable.
        - *If an owner's name appears many times, then call them out to make sure they agree to that work and the due dates.*

Practical Application
  - Identify at least 2 different projects or initiatives at your organization that involved the implementation of a significant process change and answer the following questions:
    - Were the process changes piloted?
      - If not, then why not?
      - If a pilot was run, then was a formal pilot plan built before beginning the pilot?
        - *If not, then why not?*
        - *What problems during the pilot and implementation could have been avoided if a formal pilot plan were built?*
        - *What delays were encountered in the pilot (if any) that could've been avoided if a formal pilot plan were built and used to coordinate, communicate and manage all necessary actions?*

SS: Improve

Unit 8: Six Sigma Control Phase

The most common tools and concepts that pertain to the Control phase of the DMAIC methodology of Six Sigma which is intended to help us sustain the improvements that fixed the root cause of the problem we're trying to solve.

Six Sigma-Control – Lesson 1: Control Phase Roadmap (Level 3)

A deeper look into level 3 of the DMAIC roadmap that identifies critical steps and tools for navigating a project through the Control phase.

Pre-Requisite Lessons:
- Six Sigma Overview #05 – DMAIC Roadmap (Levels 1 & 2)

DMAIC Roadmap (Level 1)
- This topic reviewed here was originally covered on page 91.

DMAIC Roadmap (Level 2)
- This topic reviewed here was originally covered on page 91.

Improve Phase Roadmap (Level 3)
- The DMAIC roadmap can be drilled down even deeper to a 3rd level for each phase.
  - Level 3 questions can guide someone to the specific tool(s) for navigating a project or initiative.

	Question Levels 1 to 3	Tool/Resource
Control	**Did the improvements successfully and permanently resolve the original problem?**	
	Did you implement the improvements?	
	Did you assess the potential risks for full implementation of the key improvements?	Risk assessment (FMEA)
	Did you build an implementation plan for the key improvements?	Pilot/Implementation Plan
	Did you build a scorecard for the key improvements?	Scorecard
	Do you know if your scorecard data is accurate, and the method of collecting it (if manual) was repeatable and reproducible?	Measurement System Analysis (MSA)
	Did you get agreement from your team where the key improvements will be implemented?	Buy-in/Sponsorship (CAP model)
	Are the improvements successfully meeting expected results (sustained and in control)?	Control Charts
	Did you fully transfer control and responsibility of the improvements back to the process owner?	
	Did you define standard operating procedures (SOP) for the improvements (as needed)?	Standard Operating Procedures (SOP)
	Did you build a control plan to help sustain the improvements?	Control Plan
	Did the process owner accept responsibility for controlling the new improvements?	Control Plan
	Does the team (including the Sponsor & Champion) agree the project is complete?	
	Did you update the project storyboard to reflect the project's lifecycle and results?	Project Closure
	Did you get agreement from your team (and the leadership that owns the area where the improvements were implemented) that the project was successful and complete?	Buy-in/Sponsorship (CAP model)
	OUTPUTS: Updated final project storyboard, control plan, SOP, agreement from entire team that the project is complete	

Practical Application
- Identify at least 2 projects you led or worked on in the past.
  - For each project, review all the questions in the Control phase level 3 roadmap.
    - What questions and related tools/resources were not addressed in the project?
    - Why were they not addressed?
    - What different outcome or results could've been realized if they were addressed in the project?

Six Sigma-Control – Lesson 2: Building a Scorecard

A review of when and how to build a scorecard for key metrics such as the output Y for improvements that were piloted or implemented.

Pre-Requisite Lessons:
- Six Sigma-Improve #09 – Piloting Solutions: Build the Pilot Plan

Scorecards Defined

- What is a project scorecard?
  - A report that measures the critical metric(s) for piloted and/or implemented improvements.
    - It usually includes only one or two metrics – typically the output (Y) of the process being improved.
    - It often includes the targets (e.g., goals or LSL/USL) for what's being measured.
    - It generally tracks the metric over time (trending) to monitor its progress.
- How is a scorecard different from a dashboard?
  - A dashboard is generally a snapshot report of multiple metrics at a higher level of the business.
    - Below is a general comparison between a scorecard and dashboard:

Characteristic	Dashboard	Scorecard
# of Metrics Reported	4 or more	1 to 3
Method to Display Metric	Snapshot	Trending
Organizational Level	High (executive level)	Low (manager or process level)
Inclusion of targets?	Sometimes	Yes

Dashboard:

Scorecard:

A dashboard will snapshot multiple metrics such as speed...

...a scorecard may trend only one metric like average speed.

How to Build a Scorecard

- How do you build a scorecard?
  - The general process for building a scorecard can be defined as follows:

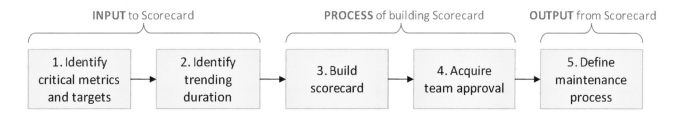

INPUT to Scorecard

PROCESS of building Scorecard

OUTPUT from Scorecard

1. Identify critical metrics and targets → 2. Identify trending duration → 3. Build scorecard → 4. Acquire team approval → 5. Define maintenance process

- Is a scorecard required when piloting/implementing improvements?
  - No, but there are some potential risks to consider when not using a scorecard:
    - **Inaccuracy** – a scorecard standardizes how the critical metrics are measured and reported. Without it, some team members may pull the wrong metrics and make wrong conclusions.
    - **Miscommunication** – a scorecard unifies the team's understanding of the progress and status of the improvements being measured and their relationship to the defined targets.

SS: Control

8

- **Duplicate Reporting** – a scorecard lets the team depend on one resource to create the scorecard rather than each person duplicating work by attempting to pull the critical metrics themselves.
  - If the above risks are low, then a scorecard may not be necessary
    - For example, if there is a small team and the critical metrics are already standardized and separately reported from a single, reliable source, then a scorecard may not be necessary.

Building a Scorecard

- o INPUT to Scorecard
  - #1 – Identify critical metrics and targets
    - The critical metrics should at least include the primary output (Y) that the improvements are targeting.
      - *Other critical metrics can be included, but there shouldn't be too many (aim for no more than 3 metrics).*
    - The metric targets are the business goals for the metrics.
      - *These will generally be reflected as a lower or upper specification limit (a.k.a., LSL or USL).*
      - *If the business has goals defined for the critical metrics, then be sure those are included. If the project has a different set of goals for these metrics, then it's OK to include both the business and project targets as long as they don't conflict.*
  - #2 – Identify trending duration
    - Basically, this answers how far back you want to track the metrics on the scorecard.
      - *A good rule of thumb is to include about 8 to 12 periods of metrics on the report.*
      - *The periods will depend on the frequency of the reported metrics. For example...*
        - ➤ *For metrics reported monthly, include about 12 months worth (i.e., one year's worth)*
        - ➤ *For metrics reported weekly, include about 12 weeks (i.e., about 3 months worth)*
      - *It's acceptable to include more than 12 periods if the type of metrics allows for reporting more than 12.*
        - ➤ *Just as with a dashboard, the goal is to limit the scorecard to one page.*
- o PROCESS of building Scorecard
  - #3 – Build scorecard
    - Believe it or not, this is the easy part. It's a matter of designing and formatting the metrics.
      - *Acquiring the data to include in a scorecard is generally the hardest part.*
    - The scorecard should at a minimum include a visual graphic
      - *This is typically a line graph reflecting the actual metric(s) and respective targets.*
      - *The detailed data can be included if space allows, but the scorecard will more often be driven by the embedded charts.*
    - Build a draft layout of the scorecard including dummy data for the team to approve the design.
    - Validate the data reflected in the scorecard as you build it.
      - *Since the scorecard is generally derived by referencing detail from another source, be sure it's pulling that data correctly.*
  - #4 – Acquire team approval
    - As noted previously, the team should approve the initial draft design of the scorecard.
    - In addition, the team must agree on the final scorecard design once real data is included.
    - Be certain the entire team agrees or you may find yourself doing a lot of re-designing.
- o OUTPUT from Scorecard
  - #5 – Define Maintenance Process
    - Now having a completed and approved scorecard, you need answer the following:
      - *How long will the scorecard need to be maintained?*
      - *Who will perform the on-going creation of the scorecard?*
      - *Who will be responsible for communicating the scorecard content and any future design changes?*
    - Typically, the customer is the one who will maintain the scorecard.

- *It's not common for the project leader (e.g., a Black Belt) to perform this work; it's usually the Process Owner or a SME.*
- Before handing-off the scorecard for someone else to create/manage, ensure it is fully documented.
  - *The process for creating the scorecard should be provided in simple, yet detailed steps.*
  - *This implies that the process should be simplified as much as possible (or risk being called on frequently for assistance).*
    - ➤ *Use simple formulas and references in the scorecard to the source data.*
    - ➤ *Use formatting that allows the user to easily import the new data and automatically update the scorecard.*
    - ➤ *Use macros and pivot tables/charts that can compile multiple or complex steps.*

Scorecard Example
- o Below is a fictitious scorecard used for tracking quality and efficiency in Billing:

Metric	Jan 2012	Feb 2012	Mar 2012	Apr 2012	May 2012	Jun 2012	Jul 2012	Aug 2012	Sep 2012	Oct 2012	Nov 2012	Dec 2012
Bills Processed	4,258,654	4,471,587	4,248,007	4,460,408	4,371,200	4,458,624	4,681,555	4,634,739	4,542,044	4,678,306	4,771,872	4,485,560
Effectiveness:												
Billing Errors	68915	74578	78855	70882	67116	69181	65828	73969	80969	73794	69132	64099
Billing Quality	98.38%	98.33%	98.14%	98.41%	98.46%	98.45%	98.59%	98.40%	98.22%	98.42%	98.55%	98.57%
Efficiency:												
Billing Delays	15645	29638	19546	18025	24794	17948	11264	16625	20615	12675	18649	11088
Billing Efficiency	99.63%	99.34%	99.54%	99.60%	99.43%	99.60%	99.76%	99.64%	99.55%	99.73%	99.61%	99.75%
Billing CT (days)	2.30	2.30	2.40	2.30	2.20	2.20	2.00	2.10	2.00	1.90	2.00	1.90

This scorecard has only a few key metrics that are trended over time.

Visually displaying the metrics is always ideal. Only plot critical metrics and use creativity (like coloring) to simplify it.

Practical Application
- o Identify at least 2 different projects or initiatives at your organization that involved the implementation of a significant process change and answer the following questions:
  - Was a scorecard used for tracking the critical metrics related to the process change?
    - If not, then why not?
      - *What problems (if any) were encountered that could have been avoided if a scorecard was used and closely monitored?*
      - *Were there any delays for finding any critical failures that would've been discovered in a scorecard?*
    - If a scorecard was used, then what problems were avoided or mitigated due to using a scorecard?
      - *In what ways (if any) did the scorecard not help avoid or mitigate any problems? What can be done differently next time?*

Six Sigma-Control – Lesson 3: Control Charts: Finding the Right Control Chart

A review of a method that can be used to easily find the right control chart for the situation at hand.
Pre-Requisite Lessons:
- Six Sigma-Measure #15 – Statistical Process Control (SPC)
- Six Sigma-Measure #16 – Testing for Special Cause Variation
- Six Sigma-Measure #21 – Defining the VOC & Defects

Reviewing Impact of Variation to the Process
- This topic reviewed here was originally covered on page 147.

Finding the Right Control Chart
- How do I know which control chart to use?
    - The four most common types of control charts include:
        - I-MR chart – Individuals-Moving Range control chart
        - Xbar-S (or R) chart – Mean and Standard Deviation (or Range) control chart
        - P chart – Proportions control chart
        - U chart – Unit proportions control chart
    - The type of chart to use depends on two main conditions:
        - Data type (Continuous or Discrete)
        - Sub-group size (for continuous data) or Defect/Defectives (for discrete data)
    - Use the drill down below to identify which control chart to use:

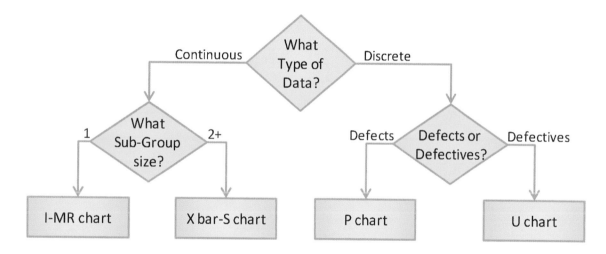

Practical Application
- Identify at least 3 different metrics used in your organization and answer the following for each metric:
    - Does your organization use a control chart for that metric?
        - If so, then what control chart is used?
        - If not, then why not?
    - Use the previous drilldown to find which control chart should be used for the metric.
        - How does this differ from what control chart (if any) is currently used for that metric?
            - *If they are different, then why are they different?*

SS: Control

Six Sigma-Control – Lesson 4: Control Charts: I-MR Chart

A review of when and how to use the I-MR control chart.

Pre-Requisite Lessons:
- Six Sigma-Control #03 – Control Charts: Finding the Right Control Chart

Review of Control Charts
- This topic reviewed here was originally covered on page 149.

I-MR Chart Defined
- What is it?
  - It is a combination of two charts used together:
    - The "I" in I-MR refers to plotting "individual" data points.
    - The "MR" in I-MR refers to plotting the "moving range" of those individual data points (i.e., the absolute distance between each successive data point).
      - *Just as in the individuals chart, the moving range chart will display the LCL/UCL and apply the same special cause tests.*
      - *Below is an example of how Minitab automatically calculates the moving range:*

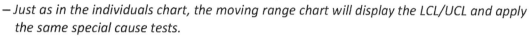

Data Point	Moving Range
2	
5	3
3	2
1	2
4	3
6	2

- What are the chart's requirements?
  - The plotted data must be continuous (i.e., numerical values).
  - There must not be rational sub-grouping in the data (i.e., no sub-groups exist).
- How do I access the chart in Minitab?
  - Go to *Stat > Control Charts > Variable Charts for Individuals > I-MR...*

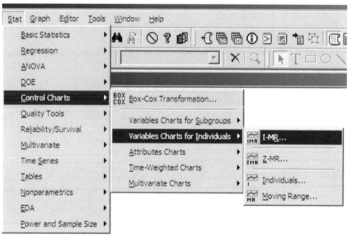

SS: Control

I-MR Chart Example

o Below is an example of the I-MR chart:

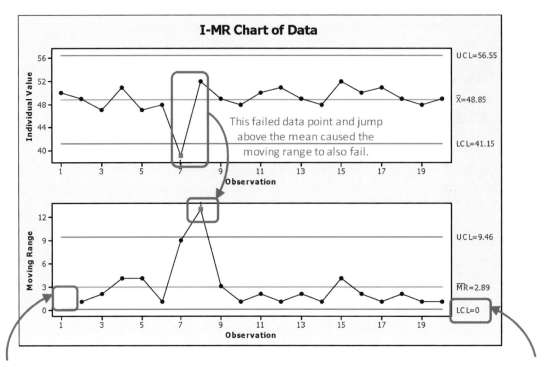

The 1st observation of the moving range will never have a data point to plot.

Since the moving range uses absolute values, the LCL will never be below zero.

Practical Application

o Identify at least 2 critical metrics used by your organization that are continuous values.

- Acquire some sorted, historical data for each metric that includes at least 20 data points and run them through the I-MR chart.
- Ask yourself the following for each metric:
  - For the individuals chart, was there any data point that failed the 1st test (falling outside the LCL or UCL)?
    - *If so, then can you explain what caused this failure? Does it appear to be a special or common cause variation?*
  - For the moving range chart, was there any data point failing the 1st test (falling outside the LCL or UCL)?
    - *If so, then can you explain what caused this failure? Does it appear to be a special or common cause variation?*
  - If any failures were noted, then what actions should be taken to help fix and/or prevent future failures?

Six Sigma-Control – Lesson 5: Control Charts: Xbar-S Chart

A review of when and how to use the Xbar-S control chart.
Pre-Requisite Lessons:
  o Six Sigma-Control #03 – Control Charts: Finding the Right Control Chart

Review of Control Charts
  o This topic reviewed here was originally covered on page 149.

Xbar-S Chart Defined
  o What is it?
  - It is a combination of two charts used together:
    ▪ "Xbar" refers to plotting the means of multiple data points.
      – *Xbar describes X which is a statistical notation for sample mean.*
    ▪ "S" refers to the "standard deviation" of the data points.
      – *The Xbar-R chart may also be used but it plots the moving range between the means instead of the standard deviation.*
      – *Below is an example of how the data may be setup in 2 ways: "in one column" (left) or "in one row of columns" (right):*

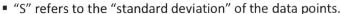
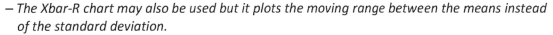

Data in "one column"

Group	Sample	Grp Size
A	76	Sample1
A	76	Sample2
A	75	Sample3
B	77	Sample1
B	76	Sample2
B	75	Sample3

In this setup, Minitab requires you to identify the column that defines the sub-group size.

Data in "one row of columns"

Group	Sample 1	Sample 2	Sample 3
A	76	76	75
B	77	76	75
C	75	77	76
D	74	75	76
E	75	77	76
F	76	74	75

In this setup, Minitab requires you to list all columns with the data.

  o What are the chart's requirements?
  - The plotted data must be continuous
  - There must be rational sub-grouping in the data (i.e., at least one sub-group).
  o How do I access the chart in Minitab?
  - Go to *Stat > Control Charts > Variable Charts for Subgroups > Xbar-S...*

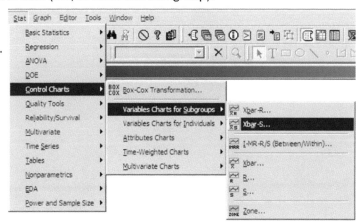

SS: Control

Xbar-S Chart Example

o Below is an example of the Xbar-S chart:

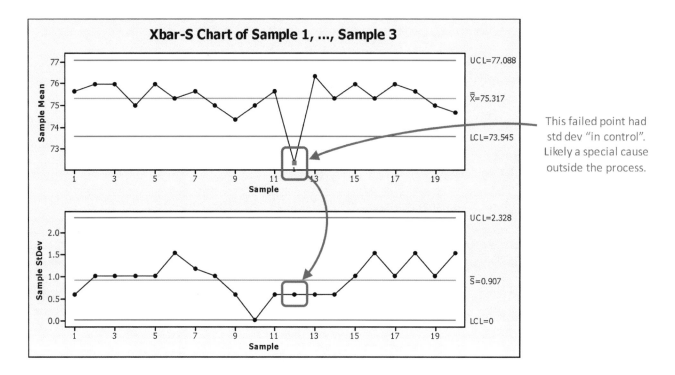

Practical Application

o Identify at least 2 critical metrics used by your organization that are continuous values.

- Acquire some sorted, historical data for each metric that includes at least 20 data points and run them through the Xbar-S chart.
- Ask yourself the following for each metric:
  - For the Xbar chart, was there any data point that failed the 1st test (falling outside the LCL or UCL)?
    - *If so, then can you explain what caused this failure? Does it appear to be a special or common cause variation?*
  - For the Standard Deviation chart, was there any data point failing the 1st test (falling outside the LCL or UCL)?
    - *If so, then can you explain what caused this failure? Does it appear to be a special or common cause variation?*
  - If any failures were noted, then what actions should be taken to help fix and/or prevent future failures?

Six Sigma-Control – Lesson 6: Control Charts: P Chart

A review of when and how to use the P control chart.
Pre-Requisite Lessons:
- o Six Sigma-Control #03 – Control Charts: Finding the Right Control Chart

Review of Control Charts
- o This topic reviewed here was originally covered on page 149.

P Chart Defined
- o What is it?
  - • It uses a binomial distribution to measure the proportion of defects in a sample.
  - • It's ideal when the volume of units (opportunities) vary within each stage (per day, shift, week, etc.).

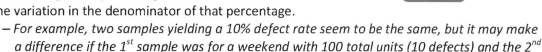

  - ▪ Unlike using a raw percentage, it accounts for the variation in the denominator of that percentage.
    - – *For example, two samples yielding a 10% defect rate seem to be the same, but it may make a difference if the 1st sample was for a weekend with 100 total units (10 defects) and the 2nd sample was for a weekday with 1000 units (100 defects).*
  - • Only the first 4 of 8 special cause tests are available to run on these charts.
- o What are the chart's requirements?
  - • The plotted data must be continuous, but represent discrete values (i.e., # of defects).
  - • Sub-grouping is expected (since it's discrete data); a column must identify the groups.
- o How do I access the chart in Minitab?
  - • Go to *Stat > Control Charts > Attribute Charts > P...*

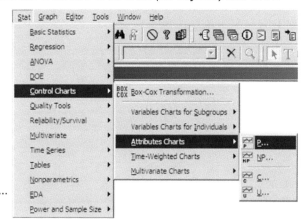

P Chart Example
- o Below is an example of the source data used and the resulting P chart (though the results look the same as the U Chart, the difference is in the control limits):

Period	Volume	Errors
1	550	50
2	520	49
3	530	47
4	580	51
5	520	47
6	520	48
7	480	39
8	550	52
9	570	49
10	590	48
11	550	50
12	520	51
13	600	70
14	570	48
15	550	52
16	560	50
17	580	51
18	530	49
19	520	48
20	540	49

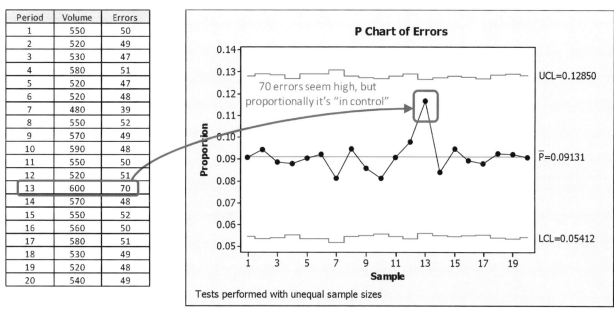

P Chart of Errors

70 errors seem high, but proportionally it's "in control"

UCL=0.12850
$\bar{P}$=0.09131
LCL=0.05412

Tests performed with unequal sample sizes

SS: Control

Practical Application

o Identify at least 2 critical metrics used by your organization that are discrete values.

- Acquire some sorted, historical data for each metric that includes at least 20 data points and run them through P chart.
- Ask yourself the following for each metric:
  - Was there any data point that failed the 1st test (falling outside the LCL or UCL)?
    - *If so, then can you explain what caused this failure? Does it appear to be a special or common cause?*
  - If any failures were noted, then what actions should be taken to help fix and/or prevent future failures?

Six Sigma-Control – Lesson 7: Control Charts: U Chart

A review of when and how to use the U control chart.
Pre-Requisite Lessons:
  o Six Sigma-Control #03 – Control Charts: Finding the Right Control Chart

Review of Control Charts
  o This topic reviewed here was originally covered on page 149.

U Chart Defined
  o What is it?
  - It uses a Poisson distribution to measure the proportion of defectives per unit in a sample.

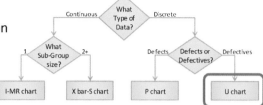

    ▪ A Poisson distribution measures the discrete probability of the # of events occurring in a fixed timeframe (based on a known average rate).
      – *For example, measuring the # of accidents at an intersection, the # of calls to a business, etc.*
  - It's ideal when the volume of units (opportunities) vary in each stage (per day, shift, week, etc.).
    ▪ Unlike using a raw percentage, it accounts for the variation in the denominator of that percentage.
      – *For example, two samples yielding a 10% defect rate seem to be the same, but it may make a difference if the 1ˢᵗ sample was for a weekend with 100 total units (10 defects) and the 2ⁿᵈ sample was for a weekday with 1000 units (100 defects).*
  - Only the first 4 of 8 special cause tests are available to run on these charts.

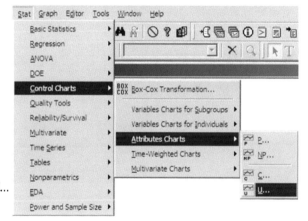

  o What are the chart's requirements?
  - The plotted data must be continuous, but represent discrete values (defective rate).
  - Sub-grouping is expected (since it's discrete data); a column must identify the groups.
  o How do I access the chart in Minitab?
  - Go to *Stat > Control Charts > Attribute Charts > U...*

U Chart Example
  o Below is an example of the source data used and the resulting U chart:
  - Though the results look the same as the P Chart, the difference is in the control limits.

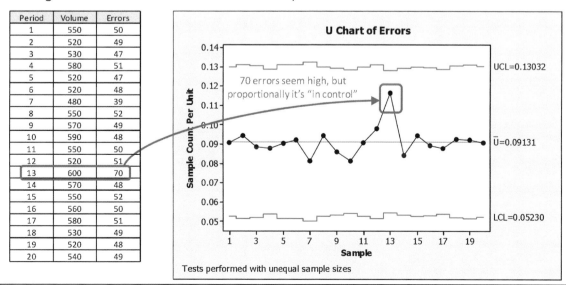

Period	Volume	Errors
1	550	50
2	520	49
3	530	47
4	580	51
5	520	47
6	520	48
7	480	39
8	550	52
9	570	49
10	590	48
11	550	50
12	520	51
13	600	70
14	570	48
15	550	52
16	560	50
17	580	51
18	530	49
19	520	48
20	540	49

U Chart of Errors

70 errors seem high, but proportionally it's "in control"

UCL=0.13032
Ū=0.09131
LCL=0.05230

Sample Count Per Unit

Sample

Tests performed with unequal sample sizes

Practical Application

o Identify at least 2 critical metrics used by your organization that are discrete values.

- Acquire some sorted, historical data for each metric that includes at least 20 data points and run them through U chart.
- Ask yourself the following for each metric:
  - Was there any data point that failed the 1st test (falling outside the LCL or UCL)?
    - *If so, then can you explain what caused this failure? Does it appear to be a special or common cause?*
  - If any failures were noted, then what actions should be taken to help fix and/or prevent future failures?

Six Sigma-Control – Lesson 8: Control Charts: Recalculating Control Limits

A review of how control limits within control charts can be recalculated to account for process changes such as implementing improvements.

Pre-Requisite Lessons:
- Six Sigma-Control #03 – Control Charts: Finding the Right Control Chart

Review of Control Charts
- This topic reviewed here was originally covered on page 149.

How to Recalculate Control Limits (Stages)
- Remember, control limits reflect the VOP which may conflict with the VOC.
  - A process considered "in control" may still not meet customer requirements.
  - The control charts are very effective at finding special cause variation that could affect the VOC.
- When is it appropriate to change control limits?
  - Control limits should only be changed (recalculated) when there is a change in the process.
  - In Minitab's control chart dialog box, go to "Chart Options...", then the "Stages" tab.
    - Add the column that defines when the observations reflect a different process. See example below:

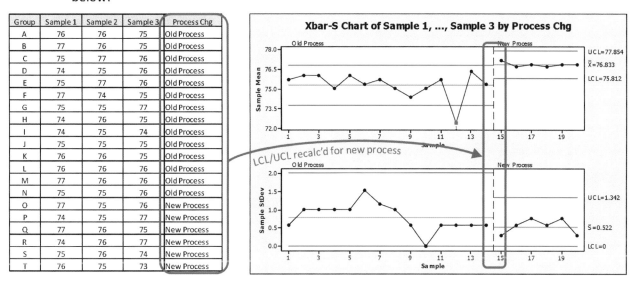

Practical Application
- Refer back to any 2 of the critical metrics used in the practical application for the prior control chart lessons (e.g., I-MR chart, Xbar-S Chart, P chart, or U chart).
  - In the sorted, historical data previously acquired for each metric, add an additional column that contains a discrete value per row which allows for grouping the data into 2 or more groups.
    - If there happen to be logical changes or trends in the data anyway, use that as a breakpoint for segregating the data points into 2 or more groups.
    - Re-run the same control charts previously run for the metric but select that new column in the "Stages" tab of the Options box for segregating the data.
  - Ask yourself the following for each metric:
    - After segregating the data across the grouped stages, was there any data point that failed the 1st test (falling outside the LCL or UCL)?
      - *If so, then were those failure points also failure points in the original control chart before you added the stages? If not, then why do you think those stages caused the difference?*

Six Sigma-Control – Lesson 9: Building a Control Plan

A review of how to build a control plan to help sustain the implemented improvements.

Pre-Requisite Lessons:
  o None

Control Plan Defined

  o What is a Control Plan?
    • In general, it's a defined plan that outlines all necessary steps in order to sustain improvements.
      ▪ In practice, it can be comprised of a one page document that defines all the controls necessary to sustain the improvements implemented in the new process.
      ▪ There are many different versions of control plans; the example herein is a direct and simplified version.
  o Who builds the Control Plan?
    • It should be a product of the team, however it doesn't need to be formally built by the team.
      ▪ The team must agree to the Control Plan, but it can first be built by one or more SMEs and later modified and validated by the team.
  o What resources are needed for building the Control Plan?
    • The following items can be referenced for helping to build the Control Plan:
      ▪ Metrics from Analysis (e.g., project Y and statistically significant X's)
      ▪ Project performance goals
      ▪ Voice of Customer – VOC (e.g., Lower/Upper Spec Limits, etc.)
      ▪ Voice of Process – VOP (e.g., Lower/Upper Control Limits, etc.)
      ▪ To-Be Process Map (or Value Stream Map)
      ▪ Kanban system measurements
      ▪ Training documentation (when implementing new process)
      ▪ Standard Operating Procedures (SOP) or Job-Aides

Control Plan Example

  o Below is an example of a Control Plan having 2 critical metrics:

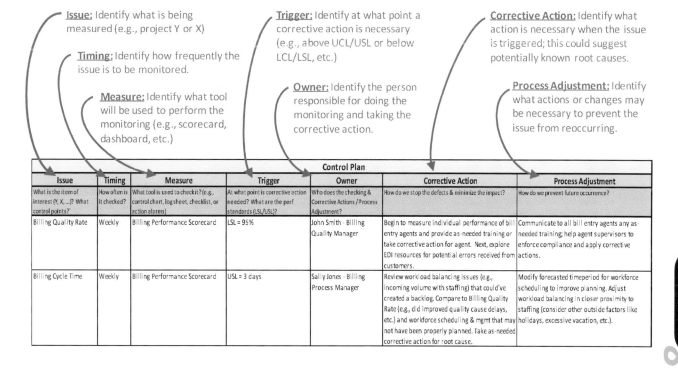

Issue: Identify what is being measured (e.g., project Y or X)

Timing: Identify how frequently the issue is to be monitored.

Measure: Identify what tool will be used to perform the monitoring (e.g., scorecard, dashboard, etc.)

Trigger: Identify at what point a corrective action is necessary (e.g., above UCL/USL or below LCL/LSL, etc.)

Owner: Identify the person responsible for doing the monitoring and taking the corrective action.

Corrective Action: Identify what action is necessary when the issue is triggered; this could suggest potentially known root causes.

Process Adjustment: Identify what actions or changes may be necessary to prevent the issue from reoccurring.

Control Plan						
Issue	Timing	Measure	Trigger	Owner	Corrective Action	Process Adjustment
What is the item of interest (Y, X, …)? What control points?	How often is it checked?	What tool is used to check it? (e.g., control chart, log sheet, checklist, or action alarms)	At what point is corrective action needed? What are the perf standards (LSL/USL)?	Who does the checking & Corrective Actions / Process Adjustment?	How do we stop the defects & minimize the impact?	How do we prevent future occurrence?
Billing Quality Rate	Weekly	Billing Performance Scorecard	LSL = 95%	John Smith - Billing Quality Manager	Begin to measure individual performance of bill entry agents and provide as-needed training or take corrective action for agent. Next, explore EDI resources for potential errors received from customers.	Communicate to all bill entry agents any as-needed training; help agent supervisors to enforce compliance and apply corrective actions.
Billing Cycle Time	Weekly	Billing Performance Scorecard	USL = 3 days	Sally Jones - Billing Process Manager	Review workload balancing issues (e.g., incoming volume with staffing) that could've created a backlog. Compare to Billing Quality Rate (e.g., did improved quality cause delays, etc.) and workforce scheduling & mgmt that may not have been properly planned. Take as-needed corrective action for root cause.	Modify forecasted timeperiod for workforce scheduling to improve planning. Adjust workload balancing in closer proximity to staffing (consider other outside factors like holidays, excessive vacation, etc.).

SS: Control

8

Practical Application

- o Identify at least 2 projects or initiatives you worked on in your organization.
  - • Ask yourself the following for each project:
    - ▪ Was a control plan created to help sustain the improvements?
      - – *If so, then how closely was the control plan followed? What problems occurred (if any) that were found and quickly resolved because of the control plan?*
      - – *If not, then why not? What are some of the critical elements you would've added in creating a control plan? What problems occurred (if any) that could've been avoided or resolved more quickly if a control plan was used?*

Six Sigma-Control – Lesson 10: Documenting a New Process with SOPs

A review of the necessity and how to build standard operating procedures (SOPs) when making changes to a process.

Pre-Requisite Lessons:
- Six Sigma-Define #06 – Building Process Maps

SOPs Defined
- What are Standard Operating Procedures (SOP)?
    - SOPs outline the process steps in detail in accordance with business policies.
        - SOPs are generally more detailed than job aides or desktop procedures.
        - They often include detailed steps for troubleshooting possible contingencies.
        - They often cite business policies and regulations.
        - They often describe how the procedures align to and affect other business areas and their SOPs.
        - They often assume no prerequisite knowledge by the user in order to successfully execute the procedures.
- Are SOPs required for closing a project?
    - Not necessarily. It depends on the amount and complexity of changes made by the project.
    - SOPs are the ideal form of documentation to ensure sustainability of the improvements.
- Who creates the SOPs?
    - The Process Owner and Process SMEs should help author the SOPs.
    - The entire team should validate the SOPs.
- How do you build the SOPs?
    - Start with any training documentation used during the pilot and/or implementation steps.
    - Ensure the format (layout) conforms to the business standards or any other existing SOPs.
    - The SOPs should be tested by allowing inexperienced employees to try to follow them.
    - The SOPs should document the authors, dates, and include version (revision) control.

Practical Application
- Identify at least 2 critical processes in your organization.
    - Are there SOPs defined for these processes?
        - If so, then...
            - *How closely are those SOPs followed and enforced?*
            - *Are the processes steps measured for tracking adherence to the SOPs?*
            - *How are the SOPs enforced? (e.g., what consequences exist for anyone who doesn't follow the SOPs?)*
        - If not, then...
            - *Why were SOPs not created?*
            - *What problems or failure points could be mitigated if SOPs were created and enforced? How could you measure the effects of those failure points (e.g., in lost revenue, reduced cost, etc.)?*
            - *Is the return of greater adherence to the process steps worth the investment of building SOPs? If not, then why not?*

Six Sigma-Control – Lesson 11: Closing a Project

A review of the actions that are essential for successfully closing a project.

Pre-Requisite Lessons:

- o Introduction #05 – Project Financial Savings
- o Introduction #10 – Project Storyboard
- o Lean #13 – Adapting Lean to DMAIC Flow
- o Six Sigma-Control #02 to #10 – All Prior Control Phase Lessons

Is the project ready to be closed?

- o How do you know when the project is done?
  - At a minimum, all of the actions below should be complete.
    - If these are not done, then go back to your team to learn why they aren't done and try to complete them.

☑ Improvement Actions

☑ Are all actions complete (and updated) on the Implementation Plan?
☑ If any implementation actions were cancelled, were the cancellations agreed upon by the team?
☑ Are methods defined and in-place for measuring the improvements?

☑ Post-Improvement Actions

☑ Have a reasonable # of measurement periods passed since improvements were implemented?
☑ Has the data collection method been validated by the team? (e.g., does it need a MSA or FMEA?)
☑ Have control charts been built and analyzed for measuring the improved process?
☑ Does the process appear to be in control? (i.e., no test failures and w/in control limits?)
☑ Does the process appear to meet the customer req'ts? (i.e., w/in customer spec limits?)

☑ Pre-Closure Actions

☑ Are Lean tools in-place & effective in the process? (e.g., 5S, kanban, poka-yoke, etc.)
☑ Has a Control Plan been built and approved by the team?
☑ Have Standard Operating Procedures (SOPs) been built and approved by the team?
☑ Has the type and amount of financial benefits been calculated & validated by Finance?

- o If all of the above actions are done, then there are a few final steps to close the project.
  - These final steps will help ensure all communication is properly done with the team, the project leadership (Sponsor & Champion), and any other potential stakeholders.

Why do we need formal project closure?

- o Is a formal project closure really necessary?
  - Yes! Though the team may act like the project is done, the formal closure is essential.
- o Why is the formal project closure so essential?
  - It assures that the gains from the project will be sustained after the Black Belt leaves.
  - It gives confidence to the team and leadership that the problem is fixed and won't reoccur.
  - It formally transfers management of the project improvements back to the right owners/SMEs.
    - The Process Owner benefits from the successful results of the project.
    - The Process Owner is more likely to provide support for future projects.
    - Counteracts the "project of the month" mentality among employees.
    - Other employees will see how the tools were applied toward achieving successful results.

Confirm Project Closure with Sponsor
- o The project isn't closed until it's confirmed by the Sponsor.
  - If the team agrees the project is done, then it should be reviewed with the project Sponsor.
  - If possible, invite the entire team to participate in the review with the Sponsor.
    - The team will greatly appreciate the opportunity to meet with the Sponsor and add to the discussion.
- o Tips for the final review with the Sponsor:
  - Keep the review meeting brief (no more than 30 minutes); allow time for discussion.
  - Use the project storyboard as your guide for discussion.
    - Don't review the entire storyboard. Stick to re-stating the problem, the improvements, and the results.
    - Don't review the Measure or Analyze phase elements unless the Sponsor asks about them or they're relevant to the improvements or results.
  - Always give credit to the team; include specific examples of their contributions, if possible.
  - Ensure you specifically ask the Sponsor: "Do you agree in closing the project?"
    - This may seem obvious, but it's always good to ask it to avoid any potential confusion later.
  - Ensure you specifically ask the Sponsor: "Do you agree with the benefits from the project?"
  - Ask the Sponsor if there are any other stakeholders that should view the project results.
- o What if the Sponsor can't or won't meet for the final review?
  - If the scale/scope of the project is relatively small, then notify the Sponsor in writing.
    - If the Champion (and rest of team) want to close the project, then inform the Sponsor of that and give them an opportunity to reply or keep the project open if they disagree.
    - Don't wait for a reply from the Sponsor before officially closing it.
  - For projects that are large or yield large benefits/results, continue pursuing a formal review.

More Actions After the Project is Closed
- o Though the project may be formally closed, there are still a few wrap-up actions:
  - Send a follow-up email to the Sponsor confirming project closure.
    - Include an electronic copy of the storyboard and any other referenced materials.
    - Re-state any follow-up actions the Sponsor requested including any other stakeholder reviews.
  - Hand-off any additional opportunities or findings from the project.
    - If there were any other findings that were discovered but not included in the improvements or results, then ensure they are reviewed with the pertinent stakeholders affected by the findings.
    - If these additional findings become new projects, then be ready to lead/support them as needed.
  - Compile & store all electronic project files in a shared location accessible by the team.
    - The team may need access to the source files used for future referencing.
    - Any raw data used for analysis should identify its source and how, when & where it was pulled.
  - Send the team a brief summary about the project.
    - It should summarize in 2 to 3 sentences the problem statement and project results.
    - It can be useful for each team member's performance evaluation or even on their resume.

Celebrate the Results with the Team!
- o Take time to celebrate the results with the team.
  - Schedule a team luncheon (off-site or pot-luck) or get a cake.
    - If the results are significant, then don't be afraid to ask the Sponsor if they'll pay for the luncheon/cake.
  - Ask the Sponsor if they'll support giving awards to the team.
    - If the project yielded big financial benefits, don't be afraid to ask the Sponsor for monetary awards.

- Non-monetary awards can include certificates with the brief project summary signed by the Sponsor.
  - "Say cheese!"
    - Don't forget to take pictures of the team during the celebration process.
- Why do we need to formally celebrate the project results?
  - Though it's not required, it could help in the following ways:
    - Success breeds success – share the success to help encourage more success.
    - People on a successful team are more willing to serve on future teams.
    - The team's work deserves recognition.
      - *Remember, they used advanced statistical tools to resolve a critical problem for the business that had no known solution.*
    - People generally appreciate this kind of formal closure and recognition.

Practical Application

- Identify at least 2 team projects or initiatives you worked on in your organization.
  - Ask yourself the following for each example:
    - Was there ever a formal closure done for the project?
      - *If not, then why not?*
      - *What negative effects could the lack of closure have caused the team members?*
      - *How did the lack of closure affect the ultimate results and buy-in from the project?*

Six Sigma-Control – Lesson 12: Getting Feedback with a Plus/Delta Tool

A review of how to acquire feedback from the team by using various tools including a Plus/Delta tool.

Pre-Requisite Lessons:
- None

Get Team Feedback

- After all is said and done, it's important to get the team's feedback on the project.
  - The team's responses can be very revealing about what did or didn't work well in the project.
  - Their hindsight view can be extremely helpful for future projects you lead or support.
- How do you get the team's feedback?
  - The best possible method is with anonymous surveys.
    - The surveys can be in handwritten format distributed during one of your last meetings.
    - Online surveys are ideal because it's easier for the team to fill out and can be easily compiled for you.
    - Surveys work best for answers that are short, yes/no or on a Likert scale (e.g., strongly agree, agree...).
    - Though open-ended questions soliciting essay-style answers should be avoided, you should request write-in answers to clarify any constructive criticism they provide.
  - The Plus/Delta tool can be useful for open discussion.
    - The tool can be used in a group meeting where two columns are drawn with a plus (+) at the top of one column and delta (Δ) at the top of the other column.
    - The team identifies things that worked well (noted on plus side) and things that didn't work well that should be changed (noted on delta side).
    - You may need to encourage discussion by reminding the team of different meetings or events or outcomes that occurred during the project.
    - Keep in mind that this is not anonymous, so some team members may be reluctant to provide direct, critical feedback.

Practical Application

- Identify at least 2 projects you worked on in your organization.
  - Create a plus-delta for each project by asking yourself the following:
    - What are the positive steps and results that worked well during the project?
    - What are the challenges that occurred during the project that didn't work well?
  - For each of the plus-delta items you identified, how can you apply the "plus" type of items and improve on the "delta" type of items for any future project or initiative that you will work?

Index

19318463R00199

Made in the USA
Charleston, SC
17 May 2013